The way I see things

The way I see things

Donald K Sanders

The way I see things
A collection of Columns

Herein lies the results of almost 20 long years of baring my mind and soul to the rest of the world in the hope that through these written words I can give you something of value to keep close to your heart so that you know that I, Donald Keith Sanders, am an open book. These columns, published in the Winters Express newspaper of Winters California and an online website (iPinion Syndicate) were written for you. They contain information about me that most would consider private in nature. If anything I have to say to you is to have any meaning at all it is essential that you as the reader understand me, where I am coming from, where I am trying to go, and that what I say is in fact, the truth.

As you read this book don't expect any great application of the written word. I am not a great writer in anyone's mind. I am simply trying to communicate my ideas for your entertainment and perhaps to enlighten you to the way I see things. I think you will find that I can be quite witty at times and even though I do look like one I am not a complete idiot.

Everything in this book is for you, the reader.

Donald K. Sanders

This book is dedicated to my good friend and editor, Debra DeAngelo. This woman can do no wrong and I feel she has missed her calling for she should have been a Senator in the seat of our government or at the very least a Viking Queen wielding a great sword above our heads and screaming at the top of her lungs, "If you need inspiration, I am here!"

The death of my inner self
10/27/20101

I think my "inner being" is dying. It no longer communicates with me. When this first occurred, I found that it meant big trouble for my physical outer being. It seems that the two are connected; interlaced like a vine through a tree.

For simplification, I will hereon refer to them as my "innie" and "outie." Our "innie" is our only link to the great cosmos, if you will, or the great lake of super intelligence from whence you may sip tidbits of information that quench the thirst of your very soul. Our "innie" is not of this Earth. It is a gift from God to give us direction; the right from wrong thingy.

Some 40 years ago, I experienced a traumatic event that my "innie" could not handle. I began getting "error" messages from my "innie" forcing my "outie" to fend for itself in a war zone. I had been in Vietnam for over a year and a half when my "outie" decided that we didn't need my "innie" because therein lies internal pain and sorrow.

"We can survive on our own," it said. "We don't need that stuff."

As it turned out, if you don't listen to and use your "innie" it slows down, gets sick, and eventually dies. So here is the whole ball of wax. The truth is that if your "innie" is sick or dying, you can bet that it's just a matter of time before your "outie" follows suit. Your "outie" belongs to the physical world, so when it becomes sick, others will notice your lack of direction and focus. What is right and what is wrong is no longer clear, so a slow but ever-growing distance begins to separate you from everything that you need to lead a happy and productive life.

Since that terrible day in 1971, my "outie" has been searching everywhere for information about how I may nourish and sooth my troubled soul. Unfortunately, the "outie" is restricted to the physical world. Here, nothing is to be found but logic and science; both of which have caused immeasurable horror, suffering, and sadness to the universe. War, famine, disease and all other unimaginable evil things that occur in our physical world are a direct result of science and logic.

Like so many other men of yesterday and today who find themselves in a war zone, unable to find nourishment for their soul in the physical world, I turned inward — but there, I found the "error" message. It seems that your "innie" has trouble interpreting warfare.

Nothing of value can be found anywhere in any war; absolutely nothing. Your "innie" will scream as loudly as it possibly can, "Wait, stop, don't do that, please, please!" Of course your "outie" cannot comply or you become a statistic of war. Thus the conflict between inside and outside begins, and as many have found, the conflict between the two is continuous and will never end. "Error, error, error," is all that you will receive from your "innie" for all of eternity.

I have seen hundreds of doctors and taken thousands of pills. I have talked with 50 or so psychiatrists and I have come to the conclusion that none of this can help my "innie." I have accepted this as a simple fact of truth. The thing that I cannot accept is the fact that we are still sending our children to worthless, no-account, bastard wars where they too will lose their "innie." We will pack away our sons and daughters, without question, without reason, and send them to slaughter or be slaughtered. The very moment that we agree to send them to a needless war, we become our own worst enemy. We don't need someone to kill our children. We are doing it ourselves.

Taking the life of another human being and watching the life blood flow from his body will, in a single moment, tear your soul apart. It cannot be fixed by doctors or pills and it will never go away. You cannot go back and do things in a different way. There is no second chance. It is horrible, the act of killing; it sends an evil ripple backwards through time and space to your earliest ancestor and forward to your unborn descendants. The ripple affects everything the killer and his victim has ever been conscious of. It takes everything away forever and gives you nothing in return.

There are two things that I would hope to be true. First, I would like our new president to be a man of peace. The second thing is a requirement of the first. A man of peace must have a healthy "innie."

I have been asked to join a group of highly educated and successful professionals called the "iPinion Syndicate." They have a web site at, iPinion. Me. At first I thought, "Man, these guys must be really rich to own their own website."

The creators of the "iPinion Syndicate" are, the soon to be, Dr. David Lacy and our own, Debra (Lo Guercio) DeAngelo. Besides being webmasters, Dr. Lacy is an award-winning columnist that teaches English and Writing for the University of California. Debra, as we all know, is the editor of the Winters Express and a writer of columns published in several weekly newspapers. She is the award-winning maestro of columnist, my mentor, and as her name implies, possibly an angel.

I don't have room to name them all but among the award winning professionals in the iPinion Syndicate is a photographer named Tracy J. Thomas. Her photographs, some of which can be viewed on the iPinion Syndicate website, simply take my breath away.

So, why should they ask me to join them? At first I thought it was because if you want to look smart, have at least one dumb guy around. You know, keep one bad writer around to make your writing look better.

One time I emailed a column in to the Winters Express about my childhood in an orphanage. I thought it was really sad. Then I went over to the Express office to see what they thought about it.

I found them all in the back room laughing hysterically. When they saw me enter, they all covered their mouths and tried to act normally. Debra was laughing so hard that she had tears in her eyes.

Talking through her hand, she said, "You need something Don?" Then she lost it and through a huge belly-laugh, blew snot all over me.

At this, they all lost it and started rolling on the floor.

It made me wonder, what is good writing and what is bad writing?

Take for example, the paragraphs below, all of which were written by me at one time or another.

Hey Mate, yer brother-at-arms died yestadee, can I have his boots?

Gentlemen, owing to sudden and very severe indisposition, I regret to say that I shall not be able to attend the battle today. I hope, however, that I shall be able to resume my duties tomorrow.

Dionysus was raised by the nymphs of Nyssa. His schooling on the finer arts of war must have begun at an early age for there is a painting on which his father, Zeus himself carries his infant son to a nymph.

Concerning combat signals, an arm extended with the hand held palm down in a waving action; means there's an enemy squad ahead. Two arms in flying motion means, run like hell.

For years, I thought and thought but I could never figure it out. I was thinking sooo hard. I know this because I wanted a cup of coffee but I didn't want to stop thinking long enough to go and get one. After five minutes or so, I knew what I had to do. I was dreading the moment because I was going to have to "man-up" in order to do it. I'm sure you know what I mean because everyone has those moments where you're thinking, "Aw geeze, I don't want to do this!" Yes, you guessed it; I was going to have to ask my wife, Therese, for her opinion.

Sometimes she makes me really, really mad. She's so smug in her, "rightness." There I was, in the middle of the living room floor, kneeling with my arms outstretched, waiting for a commercial so I could beg for her attention.

When she finally became aware of me, she said, "Yyyeeesss, you wish something of me? I said, "Yes, bog-wan-esse;" "I need to know the secret of successful writing?" How do I know if it's good or not?

I watched her in awe, as she scribbled something on a small yellow post-it pad that she keeps near her at all times. She ripped off the top piece of paper and offered it to me. She said, "Donald, you are such a twit" as she flipped her hand in a dismissal action.

I quickly backed away and scurried to the kitchen like a big fat rat trying to get a morsel of cheese without the other rats seeing it. I opened and then read the note.

I thought, "What the heck?" I quickly peeked around the door jamb to see if she had heard me. She is sensitive to things like that.

I crumpled up the little yellow piece of paper and threw it on the floor thinking, "Aw, she doesn't know squat about the secret of successful writing!" I don't even think there is a secret to successful writing! I've never seen one, have you?

Here is what she wrote on the yellow Post-It:

"The answer to successful writing is in the reader. To keep it simple for you, here is a quote: 'Listening: you can convey no greater honor than actually hearing what someone has to say.' — Philip Crosby.

At the bottom of the note she had drawn a little heart and next to that, in small writing, "luv u!"

Couldn't even steal an award
6/13/2010

I'm really happy to be a part of iPinion Syndicate. I think it has to do with luck. I've always been lucky at just about everything I've ever done except for one thing. I was not a lucky soldier, but that's a different story.

I'm a little intimidated by all the awards that the other iPinion members have listed in their introductions. Have you read my intro? I've never won anything and I'm not the first in my family to never win anything. I come from a family of liars and thieves that have never been able to even steal an award.

There is no way that I could put down in writing everything that I or my family have accomplished but never, no never, have we been considered for any type of award. I'll start with my great-great-great-great-great grandfather. His name was Phettiplace Clouse. He sailed on the English ship "Starr" in 1610 to Jamestown. He was the author of one of two books of proper etiquette. Here are a couple of entries from his book:

"A number of people gnaw on a bone and place it back on the platter-this is a serious offense."

"Do not spit over or on the table in the manner of hunters."

"When you blow your nose or cough, turn your head so that nothing falls on the table."

Like I said before, there was another book of etiquette but I don't want to talk about that.

His son, Charles, born around 1650 or so, was so poor that he couldn't afford to get up after he had lain down but he did have one good idea before he died. It was his idea, and I quote, "It is the duty of man to remove as quickly as possible all natural growth from these lands." He held the idea that it is unfair for the forest to be empty and unspoiled. My family, along with the family of John Adams, has cut down more trees than any other family name.

Further down the line, his grandson, Jasper Sanders, was the first American to suggest that we have an "Income Tax." On his deathbed, when asked about the hundreds of Americans who died while trying to collect taxes from the mountain folks, he replied, "For the life of me I don't understand why people don't like taxes, it's enough to make you lose your faith in God." His last words were, "It's a sure-fire way for the government to get their land back from those pesky immigrants though."

My great-great grandfather, Eliesalot Sanders, was an Indian fighter and a guide to the pioneer wagon trains. He was the first to find and point out the shortcut through the Rocky Mountains that led up to and through the Donner Pass. After a mountainous disaster, he ran to Missouri but was captured and hung before he could cross over the Arkansas line. He might have made it if he hadn't eaten his own leg.

His son, Eliestoo, was a writer of books. His most famous book, "The Man of the Family" held the famous quote, "A woman's place is in the home-the kitchen preferably." He predicted that women and people of color would never have the right to vote. After the Civil War, he, along with the grandfather of Teddy Roosevelt, had a lucrative opium import business. Both men professed a hatred of the female gender but on several occasions they were seen wearing dresses to public affairs.

Next down the line was his son, William, sometimes called Willie Two-nose. William was caught robbing the graves of General Custer and his men. As punishment for this offense his nose was split down the middle. This explains why Willie Two-nose swore that he smelled twice as good as a common man.

During World War I, my grandfather, Eddie A. Sanders, arrived in France with the first American troops. Sometime later, he went AWOL but ran the wrong way and was the recipient of a large dose of mustard gas. His screaming is credited with saving numerous lives by sounding the alarm of incoming gas. His son, my father, Edwin Sanders, was a schizophrenic paranoid and I don't want to talk about him anymore.

Of all of these people, my ancestors, not one of them ever won an award for anything. That leaves it up to me.

As of today, I haven't won anything other than a trophy for "Worst Improved Bowler." It's not that I haven't tried though. I nominated myself for "Citizen of the Year" in Winters, California. I was also nominated for the Pulitzer Prize, the Nobel Prize, and the prize for the best scarecrow last Halloween in the annual Chamber of Commerce Scarecrow Contest.

You'll be happy to know that I am being considered for a world record by the Guinness Book of World Record people in London. It is probably the only chance I have to win anything. The record is for, "The most self-submitted nominations for awards never won."

What does it matter who nominates you, right? You don't have to tell them you nominated yourself. The trick is to win so that you can tell everybody about it.

Wouldn't it be nice if you could travel back in time and change some of the things that adversely affected the lives of you and your loved ones? There are a lot of things I would change. You can count the things I'm responsible for on one hand. Everything else was somebody else's fault.

I think that people with a good family support system make fewer mistakes and are therefore happier with their lives. Parents constantly teach their kids how to make the right choices in life and what will happen if they make the wrong ones.

On the other hand, this is not the case for those without families. The real world is different for a child who is tossed into a large institution like a Catholic orphanage. Homeless kids learn different lessons, harder lessons. I'll share some of the lessons that I learned as a child in St. Joseph's Children's Home in 1950s Little Rock:

- In just about every situation, the first people to approach you are bullies.
- There is no such thing as a fair fight.
- It is easier to hit someone when they're asleep.
- Stealth and brains can beat a bully every time because he doesn't know who to beat up.
- You will be separated from any family that you may have and it may be years before you see them again.
- After awhile, you can walk past a kid on the playground and not know that he's your brother.
- If someone steals your toothbrush, you must stick your finger in baking soda and rub your teeth until they are clean.
- If spinach makes you gag, stick it in your pocket.
- Even the ugliest of nuns can sing beautifully.
- If a nun beats you and locks you in a closet for eight hours a day, as far as you are concerned, she becomes one with the Devil.
- At some point before you are 10 or 11 years old you will come to believe that it's better to live in the streets than in the orphanage.
- When you run away, check to see if the gate is unlocked before you climb over an eight foot fence with barbed wire.
- When you run away, always go towards the lights. There are better garbage cans with better garbage.
- Don't eat garbage that has worms.
- Sleep in the daytime.
- Even if they don't want to, the police will always take you back to the orphanage.
- If you run away, you will be beaten and locked in the closet.
- An orphanage is exactly like a prison except prisons have bigger and meaner kids.
- You'll never be on a baseball team.
- You'll be an adult before you ever learn to fish, and then everyone will see you carrying a stringer of carp thinking that they're trout.

Anyway, I'm hoping that at some point I'll get so old that I'll forget everything. Then I can start over. I have a family now so I can get rid of as much crap as my little brain will allow. My wife is teaching me to solve problems and how to be strong. She sings pretty good too.

Women will rule the world
6/28/2010

For several years, I've been involved in internet research for a college professor and some of her associates. This research concerned subjects such as Psychology of Women, Sexual Abuse, Solutions to Violence, and Peace and Non-violence. For years, I was ignorant of the true nature of the work that I was doing for these professors but, like everything else, nothing can be kept secret forever.

It was only recently that I was able to piece together all the small tidbits of data into what I discovered to be a distressingly big picture. I have discovered something so frightening that the mere writing of this article will place my life on the "bye-bye-you're gone" list of women scholars.

Before I am killed, I feel compelled to warn the world that the women are in the process of taking over. I've named this process, "Womanization." The male half of literally every species that populates every corner of the world is on its way out.

In 125,000 years (if left to nature) the population of the Earth will be 100 percent female. Believe it or not, this information is not new, for both Socrates and Plato made the same discovery. However, my findings are less theoretical than their findings, but on the same critical level.

The writings of these ancient scholars allege that they had made a genuine discovery, which they initially prepared to reveal to the world, but the response they encountered was so ferociously hostile that they masked their findings, and offered in its stead a theory of the male dominance.

Thanks to the "Y chromosome" men are far more given to extremes, intellectual achievement, creativity and yes, destruction, but strangely enough, a world devoid of men may well be a quieter more peaceful place. Throughout history, the Y chromosome has passed unchanged from generation to generation of fathers and sons, and while it has provided genealogists with a fascinating insight into the origins of entire communities, it has also raised other questions.

The lack of ability to "recombine" means that Y chromosomes cannot repair themselves. A growing number of men have inherited a Y chromosome that was damaged during the production of their father's sperm. There is considerable evidence that sperm counts are declining overall, and in some men the inherited damage to sperm production is so great as to render them infertile. In fact, Y chromosomes only have about 27 useful genes — the rest of the chromosome is composed of "junk" DNA that does not code for anything.

In the end, Y chromosomes will disintegrate and this will probably lead to the eventual extinction of the male gender. Already a surprisingly increasing number of animals can reproduce without male involvement if there is no other option.

Sharks and lizards have demonstrated this ability in captivity and one of the world leaders in this field, Karim Nayernia, professor of stem-cell biology at Newcastle University, has already shown that unlimited sperm can be derived from early stem cells present in any embryo. Elsewhere, producing a child that is the genetic offspring of two females is becoming a real possibility and the process is not nearly as difficult as was previously thought. Artificial sperm produced from bone-marrow cells has already led to pregnancies and live births in mice.

If the information on artificial sperm and the decline of the Y chromosome are not enough to dismay any man, there is growing evidence that women are surpassing men intellectually and financially. I have found that girls triumph over boys at every level of the education system. A natural assumption seems to be leading to the inevitable question of whether the male gender is reaching the end of its natural usefulness.

Men are unaware of these things because we live in a testosterone (I made that word up) dream world. Reality is not synthesized. We don't make it up. It exists independently of us. Because reality exists independently of all possible experience, it remains permanently hidden to all but the female species, which naturally has a low testosterone level.

Within a mere 20 years, women will be the main breadwinners in our families. We have reached a point in time where the female Black Widow will now eat the male spider without sexing him up.

Generations of girls are now becoming aware of the fact that they can do better than men and this will have an effect on the balance of society. If men can no longer achieve anything, what exactly is going to be left for us? My data states that women have the same capacity for violence and evil as men, and that they enact this violence and evil as frequently and effectively as men, indicating that the female species may be in the process of helping nature along.

The Human Tissue and Embryos Bill, which is expected to become law, says controversially that the fathers of artificially conceived children need not necessarily be recognized by the state and this is not the worst of it. Several questions arise from my research such as:

~ Why are women so insistent on feeding men vegetables and stuff like that?

~ Why are so many women studying taxidermy?

~ Why, in a 10-year war started by a woman, Helen of Troy did 99.9 percent of the soldiers killed end up to be of the male persuasion?

~ Why can a human male may be sexually aroused, even physiologically aroused, by a photograph or drawing of a female?

All of us, as males, are in a race that is not unlike a fox and a rabbit. Men are running like hell, just to survive, while women are running like hell just for a meal. I find that the great majority of male human beings lack understanding of what exactly is going on. The end result of my research points to one solution for us males: we must bend over and kiss our own butts goodbye.

Friends are everything in the orphanage
7/5/2010

People seem interested when I write about my childhood experiences in St. Joseph's Orphanage. I thought I'd write about something that's very different from normal childhood experiences. By "normal," I mean kids with families and homes that they go to each night.

I'd like to write about friends and friendship. To normal kids, a friend is someone you go to school with or play games with. Kids call their friends on the phone and they do fun things. In general, they spend quality time with friends, whenever they can, and they go home in the evening to their families.

To someone like me who didn't live the normal life with a family and a home, the word "friend" takes on a whole different meaning. With no family members around, you're pretty much alone in a crowded room, a friend is as important as a brother or a sister.

A friend is no longer someone that you just play with and then go home. To someone who lives in an orphanage, a friend is all-important. A friend is all that you have and all that you will ever have as long as you live in that place that I find indescribable.

Out of about 400 boys, I had two friends. I call them friends because I find it difficult to find the correct words for them. They were much, much more than friends. I met "Fat Phil" on the first morning I awoke at the orphanage, and I met Gerald Elmore a little later.

I awoke with a start and found that I had wet the bed. There was blood on my pillowcase. A kid had poked me in the nose the night before. I slipped out of bed and tried to cover up the fact that it was wet.

As I tried to make the bed, a voice from behind me said, "Don't make it because the bed checker has to check your bed first." That was how I met Fat Phil and sure enough, there was someone walking through the dorm of 52 beds pulling back the covers and checking for bedwetters.

I had to strip my bed, get into line for new bedding and then get into the swat line where I got three hard swats by Sister Conchadda. I had to smile when I came out of the beating room, and there stood Fat Phil to get his swats. After that, we were inseparable.

Fat Phil showed me the ropes and how to live in an orphanage without being noticed by anyone. Fat Phil was smart and he tried to show me how to get even with the bullies without getting caught, which usually meant getting beat up.

Fat Phil would put a turd under the pillow of a bully and then we would both bury our heads in our beds trying to hide our uncontrollable laughing. I have never in my life seen anything so funny as that bully trying to find out who was stinking so badly, accusing everyone around him.

Fat Phil had a deck of cards that he carried in his pocket that was so old that you could barely read the numbers on them. He and I played with those cards for years. As we played cards one day, Fat Phil told me that he was in the orphanage because his father had done nasty things to him. The State of Arkansas had brought him to St. Joseph's.

Gerald Elmore was a sickly kid with rotten teeth that hurt all the time so he cried a lot. He was the center of ridicule and abuse from the bullies. One day he was hit so hard by a sucker punch that it knocked out his front teeth. It was the same day that Fat Phil told me that he was leaving to go home with his father that was cured of his sickness.

That night, I crept to the bully's bed and hit him so hard that it broke his teeth off at the gums. He screamed and ran down the hall bleeding like a stuffed pig. After a beating that set a new record for the number of swats in one beating, I was locked in a closet. I was in the closet when Fat Phil, my friend of I don't know how many years, was picked up by his father. I never saw him again, but he left his old deck of cards with Gerald Elmore to give to me.

That evening, I worked in the kitchen. I got a knife and cut my wrist for the first time. After dressing my wounds, the nuns kept me in the medical unit overnight. That was the first time I ran away by sneaking out the door to see so many stars that I had forgotten were there.

It wasn't four hours later when the police caught me eating doughnuts from the garbage behind a bakery.

I wouldn't tell them where I lived, so they made me empty my pockets on a desk. There was an old deck of cards and two crumpled up doughnuts. They withheld water until I told them where I lived. On the drive back to the orphanage I remembered that I had left Fat Phil's cards on the desk at the police station. I begged them to go back and get them to no avail.

After that night, besides Gerald Elmore, I never made another friend. I did, however, fall in love with an abusive nun. She broke my heart.

Now I'm all grown up and I call just a few people "friend." They are still all-important to me. My wife and most others do not understand what a friend is to me. She sometimes says that my friends are more important to me than she is. It isn't true, but they are my friends. Their names are Steve, Terry, Joe, and Mike.

Without My Wife, It's a Complicated Life
7/15/2010

Why does everything have to be so difficult and complicated? Like every morning, I plugged in the coffee pot. It began to make noise: Gurgle, gurgle and gurgle. After a short nap, I scratched my butt and walked to the percolator. I grabbed the cleanest dirty cup and began to pour the sweet liquid, hoping to get most of it actually into the cup.

The coffee smelled oh so good. It was hot. But there was only clear, hot water in the cup. Ya see what I mean? It's as if I have to be a detective all the time.

I thought to myself, "I wonder if it's going to get hot today? If it is, my friend Steve and I will have to go rock hunting when it's early and still cool or the snakes will be out."

Steve is a funny guy when there are snakes around. He likes to place his walking stick under a rattlesnake and flick it in the air towards me. This always starts a full-fledged rock fight. When fighting with rocks I like to think big. Steve however is like that Wallace guy in the Braveheart movie, and thinks small and accurate. My big rocks rarely strike the target but Steve seems to have a laser sight on all of his little rocks. He cheats too!

Holding one's hands in the air is supposed to signify the end of the rock fight. I'm assuming that by saying, "the end of the rock fight," there should be no further rock throwing, right? Not for Steve! He'll wait a few minutes and then knock my hat off with one of his super accurate rock rockets. He likes to hit me on the knuckles too.

OK, back to the coffee detective. Long story short, I forgot to grind the coffee beans. There were whole beans in the little basket thingy. I had to do the whole process all over again, from the start. I was still scratching my butt when I noticed there wasn't a single clean spoon anywhere to be found. No forks either. They were all dirty, in the sink, with food still on them. Every counter was stacked with dirty dishes.

I like to sit on the back steps to drink my coffee. There were stacks of dirty clothes that I had to step over to make it to the steps. I was going to throw a load or two in the wash but there was already a load in the washer from a couple of days ago and smelled sour. I thought, "OK forget that idea."

At about this point in time I was thinking that I probably should take a pill or something. I had promised my wife Therese that I wouldn't cut myself, so that was out. Oh yeah, I forgot to tell you that my wife is on an excursion with her four sisters in Ireland. They will be gone for three weeks. They left two days ago. Therese and I have rarely been apart for very long except for my "vacations." (Jail, some people call it.)

Jail is a trip! You can sit at a table and inevitably some big ass wipe will want some of your food. They say, "Are you gonna eat that?" My answer is always the same: "Don don't like you!" It seems that if you talk about yourself in third person, most people will leave you alone, even if you are incarcerated. Another funny thing about jail is the fact that I was the only innocent person in the whole place. The guards seemed to sense this and gave me the run of the place. Either that or they were afraid I'd tell the world that their boss' name is Bart Simpson.

Therese asked me if I needed a "to do" list before she left. I told her, "Heck no." I could have been an advisor to President Obama — why would I need something like a "to do" list! If you look at housework like taking prisoners in a war, there is a specific strategy that can be used to complete the task required and it's quite easy to follow. It's called "box-barrage."

Say you have some Germans or dirty laundry – whatever. At the proper time, an air strike or artillery barrage aimed at your target will provide a good reason for them to take cover. At another point in time, the target shifts to the left and right flank and around to their rear, thus making escape impossible. Works every time! Stinkin laundry!

Anyway, like I said before, I'm rarely separated from my wife, and I don't need a "to-do" list. I already had two of the things she had asked me to do taken care of anyway. I cleaned and restacked the bookshelves and checked the plants to see if they needed water. Amazingly, there was some difficulty there too. Why is everything so hard!

Putting the books back in place, I found that I had lost some of Therese's books. And the plants didn't need water. They were already dead. I swear they must have started dying before my wife left because it's only been two days since she left. Man, why does everything have to be so hard for me. I can't even cross the street without some jerk trying to run me over. I always yell at them, "Don don't like that!"

I could go on and on. The point of this whole sordid life thingy for me is this: I don't like it when my wife is not with me. I want her to be happy and vacation with her sisters. I want her to live life to the fullest and she can't do that with a guy who doesn't like, well, just about everything. I can't believe how much I miss her when she isn't here.

It's like the song says:

"Baby come to me; let me put my arms around you.

This was meant to be and I'm oh so glad I found you.

Need you every day, gotta have your love around me.

Baby, always stay, cause I can't go back to living without you!"

I can't go back to living without you, so come home safe Therese. I am waiting.

Sometimes I use my military training for monitory gain; I call it "Operation Purse Raid." I can do this because my wife likes to think. It's like she is in a trance — oblivious to the rest of the world. However, she's still aware of what's going on around her and that's what is scary.

For instance, she'll be thinking away sometimes and I'll watch her closely for about nine hours just to make sure that she's deep in thought. I have to be as sly as a cat. For the first eight hours or so, I won't make a single move. I'm like a statue; not a twitch, sniffle or blink.

After eight hours, she is deep in a trance. She appears to be watching TV, but I know for sure that she's thinking. This is where the tricky part begins because it is time for me to make my first move. OK, let's call it 8+01. At 8+01 exactly, I'll move the little finger of my hand that is away from her and is hidden by my leg or my big butt. At 8+02 I'll look over at her without moving my head — just my eyeballs to look for any reaction.

When she's thinking, Therese likes to sit on the little couch. I always have to sit on the big couch. I don't know why this is so, but someday I plan to think about that.

Sometimes she sits on the little couch just because she knows that I want to sit on the little couch. How cruel is that? She's all smug and thinks she's cool. She sits there like a soldier riding a horse on a cavalry charge. Her back is perfectly straight and erect. Her attention is somewhere that I know I've never been but she seems to be looking straight ahead at some little bitty teeny weenie point, way off in the distance.

Believe it or not, by this point in time I have put a lot of work into this operation. Without her even knowing, I have inserted a girly-man, love story into the DVD player and it is now about to begin. The one that works best seems to be "The Quiet Man" starring John Wayne. This film works every time. By 8+15 she is really gone and she won't be back for about an hour and a half. At 8+20 I figure it's time for the final test to begin so that I can tell just exactly how far gone she really is.

At exactly 8+21 I raise both of my arms in a stretching movement and act like I'm yawning. I then will begin to mumble something; it doesn't matter what. By 8+30 my mumbling has increased in volume until it reaches the decimal that is at the brink of her awareness. Her reaction at this point in time is a primary indicator whether I can continue to the next step in Operation Purse Raid.

There are two things that I'm looking for at this point. First is a wave of her hand like she is chasing away a fly or a bumblebee. Just the wave of her hand; nothing else moved and she only did it once. When this occurs I know I'm almost home. I'm almost feeling as brilliant as I really am.

I have to sit and wait for the second thing because it sometimes takes a few minutes to annoy her without breaking the trance. This part takes some planning but I'm pretty smart because I've seen this film 432 times and I know exactly when something sad is going to happen. At just the right moment when I know she's totally engrossed I'll say something like, "Honey, would you like something from the kitchen"?

If she ignores me and reaches for a napkin I know that this is my opportunity to go for it. I can, at this point, stand up, walk around that Godforsaken, knee-knocking coffee table, and start for the kitchen. I'll call this point 8+45. If I time it just right, when I walk in front of her she'll lean over to see the TV while I walk by. Here is the critical point of the whole operation. If I screw this up I'm done, kaput, fini.

At the exact moment that she leans over to see around me (I'll call it 8+47) I give her purse that's sitting on the floor beside her a slight kick. If done properly she will not be aware of anything except what she's thinking about. I then casually continue into the kitchen and rumble a few dishes around, open and close the fridge a number of times, while whistling Dixie the entire time.

After throwing some meat on the floor for the dog as a noise diversion I can now successfully low-crawl behind the little couch, get some money out of her purse and escape to the hardware store where I can buy something I don't need in complete freedom.

Ah, isn't America great!

Time Travel Possible in this Freaky Family
10/31/2010

Saturday, July 31, was the annual Freaky Family reunion at Seacliff Beach State Park. Seacliff is located just south of Santa Cruz and is famous for the old dilapidated ship, the Palo Alto that is tied to the old timber pier.

The ship, built in 1917, is unique because it sailed only once, in 1929, from Oakland to San Francisco and then on to Seacliff Beach where it will remain forever. What makes this story unique is the fact that the ship was constructed entirely of concrete and rebar. The material chosen to construct the ship is sturdy but even its concrete and steel cannot match the strength of the Freaky Family.

I have written about this family several times and they take no offense to the term freaky because they all realize that, as a group, they are unique and very close knit. The term "freaky" illustrates perfectly just how different they are from the "norm."

They number well over 150. Brothers, sisters, cousins, uncles, aunts, grandparents, great-grandparents, and everybody that they ever grew up with, all are freaky family. They are constantly hugging, kissing, eating, playing games and in my long life, I have never seen another family like it. Every one of them knows how unbelievably lucky they are to be a part of this family and they are not afraid to show it.

From the onset, I was suspicious of how perfect they all were and for years I closely observed their behavior thinking I would find some imperfection. I thought, "No way, this family is not real!" I was wrong, they are quite real and now they have me acting just like them. I get right in there, just a hugging and a kissing with the best of them. For my efforts, I was awarded a T-shirt with big black letters saying, "I am a part of the Freaky Family."

This year, I had occasion to construct a sand castle with my grandson, Anthony, and one of my nieces, Ava. My niece and I provided the labor while my grandson engineered the whole project. Naturally, our conversation turned to the concrete ship that sat on the bottom of the surf not 500 feet from our castle. In an effort to explain to them what had happened to the ship, I told them that if they had a time machine, they could watch it slowly fall apart and sink to the shallows where the waves crash against it endlessly day after day after day.

My grandson, as smart as he is, denied the existence of time machines.

"It's true" I said, "There are no time machines."

I went on to explain that it is also true that when you get old enough you can travel through time and I said that I do it regularly and not always because I wanted to. Sometimes it just happens. I pointed their attention to their grandmother and great-grandmother that were staring out to sea.

"I think they are probably traveling through time at this very moment," I said.

I explained that they could not travel through time together but that they could meet each when they got to where they were going. You can even go back in time to visit loved ones that are no longer of this Earth.

"Look at my wife and her mother." I told them.

My wife is in a time when she was a little girl and she is running in circles around her father as he fishes in the surf. I can go there too, but when I am there, my wife is grown up and quite lovely. She is still running circles around her father and she waves to me as I sit and watch her.

I can see your father too and he is the same age that you are now. We made a sand castle then, in about the same place as this one that we are working on today. I told them that when I travel through time, my favorite place to go was to the hospital in Vallejo to watch my son (Uncle Joe) being born, and I like to go back to my other son's (Rick) wedding.

I explained that their great-grandmother was probably in a time with her sister when they first came to California from Alabama. Her sister was a Marine and it helped her to be independent and strong. She was a lover of Jaguar automobiles and I could go back in time to when she gave me her Pumpkin Chair that I sat in until it fell apart. You can go back in time and see everyone that you have ever known and loved.

I had their attention now so I made a request of them.

"When you are my age (early 60s) I would like you to travel back in time until you get to today."

When you get there we will all be there together just as we are right now. We can all have this same conversation again, but you will be older and watching from a distance. I will no longer be here but you will still be able to visit me and I will like that very much. My grandson and my niece made a pinky bargain that we would all meet here again many years from now.

I can hardly wait.

Living in fear of the Freaky Family women
2/14/2011

I'm hoping that the new year will bring something new for me to write about. I can only make up so many stories before I run out of ideas, and sooner or later someone will catch on to me plagiarizing other people's written material.

Well, since I don't have anything to write about, I'll just recap all of the bad things that happened last year. Of all of the many, many things that I did last year, only one turned out good: I was involved in a power struggle with the Freaky Family. (I say freaky because they're perfect.)

You see, the Freaky Family (FF) is controlled by my mother-in-law and her six daughters. Up until this year I was afraid of them, but about six months ago I thought it was time to step up and take control because I'm a man.

I must say that it went pretty well at first because they were actually listening to me. I was going to take advantage of that right away! For awhile I was right in the groove. At dinner I sat at the elbow of my mother-in-law, I never had to do dishes, and I did chores only when I wanted.

By chores, I mean little jobs like mowing the grass and cleaning leaves out of the gutter. I'll let you in on a secret that demonstrates just how smart I am. If the yard actually needed mowing, I would clean the gutters. If the gutters were full, I would cut the grass that didn't need to be cut. To top it off, I would splash a little water on my shirt so it would look like sweat. Add a little hard breathing and walla — royal treatment from the women.

Then there was a rebellion. I noticed a huddle of women in the kitchen but didn't think anything of it until just before Thanksgiving. My next trip down to San Jose, it dawned on me what they were up to.

I walked in and started huggin' and kissin' like we usually do but then I was directed to the back yard. I noticed right off that something was missing but I didn't quite know what it was. Then I saw it. There on the ground was a little teeny weeny chainsaw. I could only fit two fingers in the handle and the bar was well over six inches long. I thought, "Isn't that cute." From the corner of my eye I saw a big ole giant stump. Like a detective, I turned around to see if the giant redwood was still there and it wasn't.

"We want you to make us a stumpchair," they all said.

This stump was eight feet high and six feet across. Now, every time I go down there, I'm cutting that damn stump with the little six-inch chainsaw and the women are standing in the window watching.

After about a year of cutting on the damn stumpchair they wanted me to load it in my truck. Do you have any idea how much a stump that size weighs? Needless to say, it made my butt pucker and I'm still walking funny to this very day.

Last week, the damn six-inch chainsaw ran out of gas and they accused me of breaking it. I became very upset and walked off while my wife sharpened the chainsaw blade with her fingernail file. Then things really got bad.

At Thanksgiving dinner I usually sit at my mother-in-law's elbow where I can dazzle her with my brilliant conversation. Not this year! They made me sit at the kiddie table.

These are nice kids and I love them dearly, but they kept throwing vegetables at me because they know I have a deep distain for anything green. My chair was so small that I could only fit one of my sore cheeks on it. I hate that darn stump!

The women kept pushing me toward the back of the food line, forcing me to make my own plate. I was going to load it up, but there was only one little piece of turkey left on the platter by the time I got to it.

Towards the end of the meal I worked up enough gumption to walk up to the women and say, "Please ladies, can I have some more?" The dining room went silent. I decided to go out and work on the stumpchair some more.

Well, the moral of this story suddenly came to me when I dropped the chainsaw on my toe. It was clear as day to me that the Freaky Family women don't need no stinkin' man to tell them what to do.

I'm afraid of them again and I think they are trying to take over the world.

Need Something to Keep Me From Dreaming
2/20/2011

All of my life, I've been plagued by strange dreams. Some of them are so vivid that I'll often sit up in bed and talk loud enough to awaken my wife. She worries about me because she knows that most of my dreams include some sort of violence.

I won't go in to all of that PTSD stuff because I've been there before in some prior columns. A couple of nights ago was no exception and my annoyed wife told me that no one else was in the room, so I should go back to sleep.

It was so strange because just a few moments earlier, I was having a conversation with Jesus Christ. In this dream, someone was lightly slapping me on my right cheek. I looked up to see Jesus sitting on my chest with my arms pinned under his knees so I couldn't move them.

I don't know how I knew it was Jesus, I just knew it somehow. He was wearing a white uniform like he was playing baseball or something. Behind him, a bright light prevented me from seeing his face. He kept slapping me.

I said, "Jesus, quit slapping me!"

He stopped.

He looked at me and said, "I know you have some questions for me but I will answer only five, so it's important that you think about it before you say anything."

Geez, talk about stress in the dream world. I knew this was important and that I had to think fast because he wasn't going to sit on my chest forever. Then, like a miracle, the first question popped into my head. I was just going to ask the question when poof, I forgot what I was going to say.

Thinking really, really fast I said, "Jesus, why don't the people that live in my town make me the Citizen of the Year?" I could not believe that I had said something so stupid, but he answered, "Forgive them Donald, for they know not what they do." That seemed reasonable so I asked the second question.

"Jesus, why does my wife get to pick all of the TV shows that we watch every evening?"

Jesus shook his head and looked at me like I was a dork or something.

"Because she is smarter than you are Donald."

"Oh."

Next, I asked, "Jesus, why does my friend Judy, from high school still look so young and pretty, like she did when we were young?" Jesus said, "What you are seeing when you look at her is her inner beauty and that will never change." Then, like a dummy, I asked, "If I ask you about my inner beauty would it count as a question?"

"Yes," he said.

"Dammit!"

I had one question left, so I took a moment to think really hard, really, really hard. In an instant, my superior brain came up with two questions that were equally important for me to ask. I thought and I thought, but I could not for the life of me decide which question to ask.

The words that came out of my mouth at that moment astounded me because I didn't know where the idea came from.

"Jesus, can I have an extra question?"

Jesus looked down at me and said, "No."

At that, he disappeared with a bright flash.

I said, "Jesus, where are you?" and found myself sitting up in bed saying, "Where are you?"

My wife lifted her head and said, "Don, there is nobody else here, go back to sleep."

"Dammit!"

I sat there and thought, "Next time, I'm going to ask the really important questions." I couldn't believe that I hadn't asked something really, really smart like I wanted to.

Next time, I will ask Jesus the questions I'd thought about but didn't get the chance to ask: "Why does my friend Christy, who has a new baby boy and a husband that she adores so much, have to endure the pain of heart surgery?" I know that she wants to live for her family so that she can take care of them and love them.

My last question, had I not screwed it up, would have been, "Will you fix Christy's heart?" I could feel the river flowing from my eyes when I realized what I had done. How could I be so stupid? How could I mess up something so important?

I got up and sat on the couch in the dark until the alarm went off and my wife turned on the light. She looked at me and asked if I was alright but I could only shake my head because I know that I'll never be alright, because I've never been alright before.

I need some pills that keep me from dreaming.

I'm a Grandpa and a Happy Man
2/27/2011

I have a new granddaughter that I have yet to lay eyes upon. I have seen pictures galore but they can never compare with actually holding her and looking at her face. Looking into her eyes for the first time will be a thrill that will be with me until I close my eyes upon this Earth.

Eventually when she sets eyes upon me, she'll know that I am her grandfather. She will know that she is safe with me and that I love her and her brother in a big, big way. They will love me too; however, they may think I'm a little eccentric for a grandpa.

She was born Sophia Marie on Sunday, Jan. 30, to Rick and Tanya Silva. Her parents are my kids. Others may lay claim upon them but they are my kids and they always will be. No one can take that from me, ever.

Tanya is a daughter of Russia. She is everything that is the best of this world. She is a savvy businesswoman at the dawn of self-awareness in the corporate world. Tanya has the prettiest face and the sharpest of minds, a deadly combination in the world of international finance. I suspect that she will someday rule the world.

She is a world class athlete — an Olympian of the Salt Lake City games. A shining star of Eastern Europe that took this turn and that, one adventure after another, until she and I came face to face and she became my daughter. That's right, my daughter, not yours — mine!

My son Rick is pretty smart too. He and Tanya came face to face at the Salt Lake games, and he knew what he had found and he didn't want to let her go. He followed her to one of the coldest places on Earth: Siberia.

While drinking equal amounts of vodka and dancing the Barynya with a bottle balanced on his head, my son Rick asked her family for the hand of their daughter in marriage. After wrestling her father and brother, discussing international politics (without offending them or throwing up in their house) he convinced them that he would be a good husband to their daughter. Naturally, after the boxing match with her uncles and a few cousins, they all shook hands and drank some more vodka.

Today, they live in the Silicon Valley. He teaches and she coaches young athletes while working as a financial analyst for a large computer-oriented corporation. It couldn't get any better for me. Two grandchildren now and I don't know how many more I can get out of them, but I still have two other kids that are capable of pitching in.

Yes, I'd like to say that I arranged the whole thing, but you wouldn't believe me anyway. I don't like the aging thingy, but I love being a grandpa and a father. I guess my wife had a little to do with it, so I thought I'd better mention her even though I taught her everything that she knows.

When I met her she was running barefoot in the backwoods of Santa Clara. Heehaw! We sure had fun chasing those goats through the trees. We chased them until we couldn't chase them no more. In those days, I was so stupid that I didn't even know what I had found.

It was only after months of torture and interrogation from 1,000 or more of her brothers, sisters, cousins and friends that I was allowed to be introduced to her parents.

I don't think that they took to me right off because her dad keyed my car door with a switch blade. He drew a skull and crossbones, pointed at it and said, "Keep that in mind boy. Don't you ever hurt my daughter." He laughed at me and said that I scream like a little girl. The two oldest sons kicked me all the way to the corner and told me not to come back.

Eventually, after my future wife turned me down eight times for a date, I was able to sneak up on her and kissed her in a local park. After that, she could not resist my affections and finally recognized what a handsome man that I really am and married me.

The rest of what you have read here is mostly the truth and I might have to change a few things later, but the end result is the same. I am a grandpa and I am a happy man.

I have a disease. I caught it in just the last few years and I am not alone. Around the world there are over 300 million people that have the same diagnosis. It is not a pretty disease.

The early symptoms are red puffy eyes, inability to sleep as you normally would, self-isolation, Carpel Tunnel Syndrome, anger, depression, and finally DEATH! The name of this disorder is Face book Addiction Disorder or (FAD).

Seventy percent of all college students are symptomatic of this disorder and it is reflected in the national grade point average, which is now 1.17. According to my sources in Washington D. C., this is the lowest national average since the mid to late Dark Ages. The majority of college students around the world will log in to Facebook every single day. I find that very sad.

Symptoms of FAD are easily recognized. The most obvious symptom, which I call "Zombie Weight Gain," is now running rampant in the United States and Great Britain. Those who suffer this addiction will sit at their computer, staring at the monitor, while eating snack after snack until they no longer are capable of moving their legs.

Similarly, this symptom is linked to the part of the brain that controls the legs in another disorder called "Toilet Seat Polio" which is contracted by lengthy reading while sitting upon the throne. It also has been found that they are incapable of understanding or performing even the most menial of tasks.

My Washington sources also tell me that worldwide studies into the nature of this disorder were inconclusive in every case but one, which was conducted by a group of blind hermit monks that live in a cave behind the head of Abraham Lincoln far atop the slopes of Mt. Rushmore. That's somewhere near Baltimore, I think.

Every other investigation failed to complete their studies and contracted the disorder themselves. I'm told that should the disorder envelop the entire population of the earth, drastic measures (of the nuclear kind) may be taken.

Here are some easily recognized symptoms:

~ Your son or daughter is writing a paper called "Sex and Pregnancy: A Possible Connection."

~ Your loved one is writing a book entitled, "Sweet and Sour Pork: How Can It Be Both at the same time?

~ Your loved one is gathering research for his essay, "Lincoln: The Man, The President, and the town car."

~ They're doing extensive analysis on the topic "There Sure Are A Lot of 'Smiths' In the Phone Book."

Those suffering from this disorder will come up with any excuse to keep from leaving their computer for even a few minutes. Excuses like:

I'm getting my overalls overhauled.

~ I have to stay home and wash my tongue.

~ I wish I could but, my patent is pending.

~ I want to spend more time with my blender.

~ I have to fulfill my potential.

~ I have some real hard words to look up in the dictionary.

~ A Winters resident was heard to say, "I have to rotate my crops."

Those with the disorder believe that they can speak French in Russian. They make statements on your Facebook page wall that while reviewing your profile, they couldn't turn the suck down. Some believe that they are so cool that Rosa Parks gave up her seat for them. They often create awkward moments just to see how it feels. Some believe their charm is so contagious that a vaccine must be created for it. They find themselves fascinating. Unbelievably, a Facebook addict from Ohio attempted to disrupt Patrick Swayze's death because Michael Jackson's death was better.

It has been reported that FAD is expanding faster than the universe. It is essential that we recognize our own symptoms to this disorder. As for me, my worst symptom, by far, is that I am constantly stealing bad jokes from the internet to use in my Facebook page. What's worse, there are poor souls out there that actually read it.

In conclusion, is it possible that those in authority know something we don't? Perhaps they know that our ultimate weakness is gossiping among ourselves. Perhaps they know that small movements can become big ones; that if an idea takes hold on the population, it just might become indestructible — a monster that could be either theirs or our downfall.

I know it is killing me. Everybody on Earth knows my business. However, I just don't give a damn.

A Few Tips on Expecting the Worst
3/13/2011

Eons ago, somewhere around here (I consider my home town to be the Garden of Eden) the first of men, on his dying bed, rock, or whatever, passed his knowledge on to his descendents. I'm not sure what knowledge he passed on, but I do know that it was probably one of the more important tidbits of information that he had gathered during his lifetime.

Here's how I think this moment in time went down. Picture, if you will, a naked man, lying on a rock because he was too weak to prevent the young man kneeling next to him from stealing his bearskins and bling. I imagine the dialog went something like this: "Son, I don't know if I am really your father but there's something I need to tell you. It's very important that you remember it because it could save your life someday."

The young man leaned over so that he could hear the old man saying, "Always expect the worst!" At this, the old man made a last-ditch effort to steal the bearskin back before he keeled over dead.

Always expect the worst. In the past, this knowledge was passed on from father to son but in this modern day, it is no longer so. Any lessons that are not of a positive nature are considered as out of fashion and outdated. To the dismay of many who must learn this lesson through life experience, it is sometimes learned a little too late.

I was taught to expect the worst as a very young child. Through no fault of my own, I was forced to live in a large Catholic Orphanage in Little Rock. I wasn't looking for the worst but it found me just the same.

For a child, getting dumped off in a place like that is about as bad as it can get. If you weren't there, then you have no idea just how bad it can be. Sometimes the worst is unbearable.

Like anyplace else, a large children's home has every type of person that you can imagine. There are bullies, gangs, thieves and perverts. It's sort of like Paris in the springtime.

When you report for military training, the first thing you're taught is to expect the worst. As a matter of fact, it's so important that it ranks right up there with "Don't drop the soap in the shower."

Should you receive any military training, expecting the worst is actually one of the most important lessons that you will learn. This is true simply because if you don't expect the worst and if you are not prepared for it when it comes; you and your fellow soldiers are dead.

It's a common occurrence that in the world of man and animals, the worst will happen naturally. You don't have to look for the worst, it will find you and it is not nice. Everybody knows this to be true.

The problem is that sometimes what you consider to be the worst may not actually be the worst. A good example of this is the fact that there were 58,000 American soldiers killed in the Vietnam War. However, when you consider the fact that over 120,000 Vietnam Veterans have committed suicide, everything changes.

Can you see what I mean?

Let's jump ahead to the Iraqi and Afghan wars. Nobody knows what the worst things about these wars are, but it's true that 19 American soldiers in today's military will commit suicide every day. That's 133 every week and 1,596 every year.

Some consider the monetary cost of warfare to be the worst, but consider the fact that when the war is over, the cost will increase tenfold, and it never ends as long as one veteran is alive.

I don't know in which direction our country is headed — neither do you. It's virtually impossible to change anything in our government in a quick manner. Change comes hard and it takes years to see even the smallest of changes on a national level. Change does not happen in Congress or the Senate.

Change comes from millions of Americans taking to the streets day after day after day, for years.

I hear people complain about President Obama. This I cannot understand. What is there to complain about? He is uniquely honest and forthright, he's not bad looking, and he has a wonderful wife and children of whom anyone would be proud. Consider the last president, who chose to surround himself with bullies, gangs, thieves and perverts; you sort of know what Paris in the springtime is like.

It all goes back to the lesson, "Expect the worst." If you really know what the worst is, then you can prepare for it. If you want my opinion on what action you should take, this is it: Start storing as much food, water, medical supplies and survival gear as you can afford.

Rockin' the Local Police Force
3/19/2011

I like to collect unique rocks and fossils. I've got rocks in my living room. I've got rocks next to the keyboard of my computer, and I've got rocks on the back porch, the shed and all over the yard — front and back.

Sometimes, collecting rocks can be rather hazardous. I've fallen in the creek, gotten poison oak a million times, stepped on rattlesnakes and dropped rocks on my toe.

Most of the time, I hike and look for fossils alone but recently my friend Steve joined me. Steve grew up around here, so he knows all the best places to find rocks that resemble some type of dead animal.

Steve likes to look for rocks at the end of county road outside of town. There are a lot of really nice rocks out there, so we've rock hunted there several times in recent months. We both carry backpacks, with digging utensils, bottled water and a snack. We both also carry a cross-country ski pole as a walking stick. Mine is bamboo and his is steel. Both have leather handles with a strap to go around your wrist and a little pointy thing at the end.

I know we're looking pretty good as we mosey along, looking at this rock or that one. We must look like those explorer guys, Pike and Armstrong, who found the North Pole in Alaska. Sometimes I play like I'm Davey Crockett and Steve is my trusty sidekick Tonto, but I don't tell Steve about that.

So, we were walking the creek bed at the end of Road 32 one day. We'd been at it for about half an hour when it turned cold and started to rain. I don't like the rain much because it leaves little bitty clean spots all over my face, and when I get home I look like a prune.

After awhile Steve started whining about being wet and cold, so I reconnoitered that we'd better start back toward our trucks that were parked well over a quarter of a mile away. I was rubbing my forehead because I ran into a tree limb while looking at the rocks on the ground, when Steve says, "Hey there's a bunch of cops over there."

Sure enough, there were about 20 cops looking around our trucks like they were going to steal something. My mind works like a well-oiled tractor, so I was thinking, "I better run." I turned this way and that but every time I did, the rocks that I had in my coat pockets swung around and hit me where it really hurts. One of those cops looked like a track star, and I'm an old man carrying 100 pounds of rocks, so I decided not to run.

I was getting scared, so I asked Steve, "What the hell did you do?" It looked like he'd parked in the middle of the road because all the cop cars were parked behind his truck. I looked at Steve and sure enough, he looked guilty of something.

We figured that heading toward those cops would be the smart thing to do or they'd be poking holes in our tires. We yelled to get their attention because one of them looked like he was going to shoot my truck. I tried to quicken my pace but those darn rocks were heavy and I was recovering from a case of pneumonia that had kept me in bed a week before.

With the rocks, the pneumonia and the hurrying, I looked like a sweaty crackhead with a pocket full of rocks. Just for a second, I thought about throwing those rocks at the cops and then take off running like the rabbit that I am. Then I thought that if Steve could hold them down, I could beat the hell out of them.

Then I remembered what happened to people that threw rocks and hit a cop. I decided against that, because I knew they were after Steve and not me anyway.

Steve is an officer of the law too, so I figured that he must have done something pretty bad. When we reached the cops I tried to act like I didn't know him and it was just a coincidence that we were both looking for rocks in the same place. I decided to keep my mouth closed so I wouldn't say something stupid.

One cop asked if we had been hunting. I thought he meant rock hunting so I says, "yeah." He told us that someone had called in and said that there were two guys out there angrily waving guns around. I said, "Not me, maybe Steve was." At that, they searched Steve's backpack and found all those rocks. By now it was raining pretty good and it was cold too.

They checked our IDs and asked us a few questions. I started telling rock stories and right in the middle of my story, they jumped in their cars and sped off down the road. We tried to catch them but they were going too fast.

Steve went to his house and I went to mine so we could check out our rocks where the other fella couldn't lay claim to the other's rocks. I washed off my rocks and started to think. That guy who called the cops must be really stupid. He can't even tell a ski pole from a gun. He's so dumb that he probably thought our rocks were hand grenades. I bet he's ugly too and beats his kids. Geez, even I'm not that dumb.

Tonight I Will Slumber
3/27/2011

"Those that are wise among men and search for the reason of things are those that bring the most sorrow upon themselves." ~ Euripides

I love my wife. At the same time, it troubles me that she loves me. I never believed in love at first sight, but when first I laid eyes upon her I knew it was something real, substantial. I think she could see it in my eyes as well.

From the onset, I thought I should walk away and never look back. I had no significant cause to wish myself upon her. I knew that for her to be with me, my burdens and my pains would become hers.

As heavy as my heart was, I could not walk away. Through the years, either consciously or subconsciously, I have given her many reasons to walk away from me. This she could not do. It is to her credit that as a result she has suffered many trials and tribulations.

No person that I know would or could endure what has been required of her to love me. I'm sure that more than most would simply walk away. Again, to her credit she is a fighter with unbelievable endurance in both love and life.

I know that marriage with me has been hard. She sometimes has to reach far within me like a safety line and pull me back from the terrible places that I sometimes travel to, dark places of my past.

Oftimes, in my mind, I travel to places of death and destruction where suffering is not equal from one person to the next. One who has been witness to such dark places in life cannot easily forget them.

The darkest of memories come and go as they will. Despite desperate attempts, some memories will not go away and on they live, just below the surface of what your eyes can see.

My love has but to glance upon me to know where I have gone. Through the years, experience has taught her what must be done and she also knows that it will not be the last time she will have to save me from myself.

The dark place of which I speak is a place of war and soldiers, and killing and dying. There is only one kind of war, though many speak of others. There is no honor in war, only sacrifice and death. It is a plague upon this Earth. It is eternal and lives in the hearts and minds of men who are the haves, as well as men who are the have nots. One wishes to keep, and the other wishes to take.

Violence is a nature of man. Good men do good work to keep it at bay but like water that runs through your fingers, it will seek you out and pull you in.

Men become soldiers to keep violence far from those they love but in doing so, they themselves become the very essence of violence and must press their newfound personality upon others.

A soldier has but two tools: violence or the threat of violence. It is the duty of every soldier to use these tools when called upon. It is done by most, openly and freely, much like picking the better of two bad choices. They pick the choice that will hurt others more than themselves and then they do their duty.

Later in life, the violence and choices live on, closely behind them. They breathe upon their necks refusing to be ignored. Keeping it behind becomes a race that never ends. The former soldiers rush to keep it behind but eventually it catches them in their rest, in their slumber.

Today, I look out upon the peaceful city of Winters, my beloved home. I turn to look upon my wife and children. I have a nice home and nice vehicles in which to travel where I wish, when I wish. All is well on the outside.

On the inside, I wonder about those who were on the receiving end of my duty as a soldier. What has happened to those that were on the other side? I would like to think that those they loved so dearly are happy and doing as well as me.

On the inside I know this is not the case because I know what we did. I remember.

I know that in Laos, we dropped so many cluster bombs that today there are over 80 million tiny bombs still to be disarmed. I know that their children play in the fields and sometimes kick them like rocks. I know about the Agent Orange. These are some of many dark places in which I find myself. There still, would I be, were it not for my beloved's hand reaching in for me, pulling me out and picking me up.

My wife makes me want to act like a man or what I think a man should act like. I would hope that I am a man who deserves such a wife and all of the other good things that I am blessed with, but does that make the other men, our enemies, any less deserving of such things?

It is this very act of pressing violence upon others to keep it from ourselves that I have a constant battle with. It will not leave me alone, for tonight I must slumber.

Want to Cry the Tears That Will Save Me
4/3/2011

I have been brought low by recent world events. It is about as low as I have ever been. It's hard to explain but I can only equate it to a whirlpool that you are caught in and cannot escape.

The few times that I have been this low usually found me in the suicide ward of David Grant Hospital on Travis AFB. Unfortunately, due to overcrowding, there is little that they can do for the lost souls that go there for help.

David Grant Hospital, modern and up to date, can do little for me other than hand out medication and give me psychiatric care in a crowded classroom setting. So there I will sit, surrounded by those that are every bit as lost as I am.

Every time I go there I get violently sick. Uncontrolled vomiting and convulsions are what I have to look forward to. The doors, in and out, are locked. My wife, who is the light of my life, has to be escorted in and out.

I can sense when a visit to David Grant is looming in the near future, and I am sensing it now. I am reminded of a quote by Kahil Gibran that says, "He who has not looked on sorrow will never see Joy." Sometimes, for me, even the joy swings low.

Chronic depression is something I have dealt with since I was 9 or 10 years old. At a very young age, I made an oath to myself never to cry. I kept this oath until I was well into my 40s.

Somewhere along the line, I lost the strength to keep my oath and I began crying. Now, in my 60s, I find that I cannot control it at all. It has a will of its own. Most of the time I can hide it by making excuses and quickly getting away from others who might see me. It is gut-wrenching, painful crying. It is not a whimpering sniffle but a convulsive, snot dripping, slobbering cry. So far, I can still control the wailing but it takes all that I still have left not to let it out.

Strangely enough, it is the suffering of others that brings this out in me. There is very little in my personal life that would make me cry. Thank God for that. The sight of those near me in a suffering state would surely do me in.

One would think that a guy like me would try to stay away from societal suffering but I find that I am drawn to it like a fly to a light bulb. The last four or five days I have been glued to CNN and the quake of Japan and its following tsunami.

This event along with other events in the Middle East has brought the world to its knees. It is sorrow on a global level. If we follow Kahil Gibran's advice, we as a people, should experience uncontrollable joy very soon. I, through personal experience, cannot see this happening.

Eventually, my wife will take me south to see my grandchildren. This too will bring tears to my eyes, but these tears will be different. I find it funny that we as a people can have tears for joy and tears for sorrow. Observers are unable to distinguish the difference. Without outside additional information about the reasoning behind the tears, they are identical.

I have always thought crying to be unmanly. There is a famous saying that in essence states "Don't trust the man that cries, for he thinks only of himself." When well thought out, this is true on a certain level. Either we are crying because someone has died or someone has been born, and even if something is lost. We don't cry for death itself — that's a natural part of life. We cry because we don't have the person anymore and they've left us against our will. We cry about a child being born partly because of happiness and partly because we are worried about something happening to hurt the child.

As far as the earthquake in Japan, I am no longer shedding tears about that. The tears I shed now are for those who stand in lethal radiation, using the last of their life force to try to save a miniscule portion of the remaining life on this Earth. They know as they walk into the reactors that they are walking to their death. Surely this is worthy of my tears.

I cry for those who fight for their freedom in the Middle East. They too know that death is upon them and that evil forces are coming with a rage. I can bear no more. The sadness is upon me. I need to see my grandchildren so I can cry tears that will save me.

The tears of love.

Twigs on a Fire
4/6/2011

The men of my family have always been at war with themselves. Something in our hearts forces this upon us, like the dark and the light oppose each other.

Farther out, in the sphere of nature, man fights against man. They kill each other for ideas or possessions — it really doesn't matter. When we're dead, we flow together like fluid under the Earth. We become so close, you no longer can tell one from the other.

I think maybe we're all just part of one big soul like twigs in one big fire. Each twig burns and becomes something else, many times, in many different forms. Death is the source of birth and birth is the source of death.

I remember my father when he was dying. He was old and gray. He was but a shell of the man that I'd seen only once before. I asked him if he knew me.

"I don't think so," he said.

"Are you afraid to die?" I asked. He shook his head.

He was calm in the face of death. I hope I can face it the same way. I wonder what it will be like when I know that this is my last breath. I wonder how it will be when I'm dead.

Weeks later, in Tennessee, my father lay dead in his coffin. I saw the death in him. As hard as I looked, I could find nothing beautiful or uplifting about going back to God.

I've heard people talk about immortality, but I've not seen any of it. I wonder where it's hidden, this immortality. I wonder if there is such a thing and who would want it.

The Earth seems to grow smaller every day. It squeezes us together. I think that as we grow closer and closer, the greater the fear. Fear is an idea that draws one hand against another until blood lies upon the Earth where we stand. I can only speculate as to the reason for this.

Three times, I looked upon my father's face. Once in a Battle Creek hospice, once in a funeral parlor, and once when I was very young. He slammed my face on the corner of a sink until my face and jaw were broken.

I don't think that this act was rooted in hate. I was 7 years old, so I was too young to have done him some wrong. I don't know why I think it so, but I know that he loved me: I was his son.

I think that he was broken, like me, but in a much more critical manner. Whatever the reason, I was forced to live without him and he without me. It is the same with over half of our families, yours and mine. War, hate and violence will always turn us against ourselves.

I killed a man once, when I was just a kid in a uniform. I think that's worse than rape, almost as bad as betrayal. No one can ever touch me for it. Just the same, I'm brought low by its memory.

After something like that, how can I ever see things the way that you do? You think that there's a world out there where everything will be okay. There is only one world — yours is the same as mine.

There is one great passion that holds us together and apart. Every person on this earth was born to love freedom. This passion rises from a common spring where everyone should be free to quench his thirst.

Recent world events have both broken and healed my heart. The Eastern and Middle Eastern world is lost in turmoil. Sorrow of great proportion finds us reaching across the world to Japan. The Middle East is also full of sorrow. It's different but it's the same. It is in the Middle East where I see the great hope. Their sorrow is not natural in composition, but forced upon them by men who take the freedom of others for themselves.

There, oppression is open and rampant. It is alarming to observe, but it has its own reward. It has the coming together of all nations in one mighty ball that will roll like thunder. It finally rolls in the right direction with the hand of all nations behind it.

As insignificant as this may seem, it is in fact the greatest of historical events. It is a mighty step toward world governance by the United Nations. Should it survive to take more, new steps, it might just save us as a species.

I don't think there's another option for us. If ever an event was worth praying for it has to be this. The United Nations and the uniting of man like so many twigs in a fire.

Strange things are in the air lately. Even with my superior mind, I can't really identify exactly what it is.

Last week, I noticed that people seem to be avoiding me. Sometimes people see me but they act like they don't. They quickly cross the street to get away. If I cross the street in their direction, they go back to the other side. At first I thought that I must have BO or that the sandwich in my back pocket must be rotten.

Even my true love, my wife Therese, seems to be rather quiet lately. If I ask a question, all I get is a simple yes or no. There is nothing in her constitution that would keep her from speaking her mind. Something is wrong and I fear that the "game is afoot".

Last month, there was a dinner party celebrating the first year of the iPinion Syndicate. Oddly, my wife suggested we attend and urged me to wear my checkered pants. A lot of iPinion members were there, including "David." Since my marriage some 20+ years ago and the fact that I am old now, David Lacy has replaced me as the young good-looking bachelor type man around town.

I don't want to dwell on that, but when I tried on the "iPinion Syndicate" T-shirt that I was given at the party, I said to my wife, "Would you kiss a guy wearing a shirt like this?" She answered, "Yes, if it was the young guy at the party!" (Meaning David) She thought this was really funny! Heh! Heh! Heh!

After I recovered from that, I asked her how people in town could enjoy things that I write about in my column in the local newspaper paper but have never nominated me for "Citizen of the Year." These people are among the leading citizens of the City of Winters. Our Mayor, Mr. Fridae, is like the King and I think that he may be using mind control on our youth. I say this not in jest, because my son Joey wants to be just like him. Aren't you supposed to want to be like your father? What's up with that?

Even in the virtual world, strange thing have been happening. On Facebook, I sent a friend request to Madge Woods, a popular writer down in LA, thinking that maybe I could steal some of her writing ideas. She sent a message back saying, "Why do you want to be my friend?" It's like she could read my mind or something! Holy Crap!

I couldn't figure it all out in one sitting, so I decided to go up North to the big trees where part of the "Freaky Family" lives. There, in the woods, maybe I could figure it all out. I took my friend Steve with me for protection and I don't have to pay him to laugh at my stupid jokes. I called my brothers and sisters-in-law asking if we could come up gold-panning and gathering twisty sticks that I make walking sticks out of. Up there, vines grow around tree limbs, choking them until they look like drill bits. They're beautiful. The family said, "Sure come on up."

After Steve's wife, Kelly, instructed me not to let her husband bring home any more junk, Steve and I drove like a hundred hours to get there. Our lives were endangered by driving through the Hoopa Reservation, where many a white man has met his end, and on curvy steep mountain roads. Steve cried a lot, but I assured him we would be OK. When we arrived, there was a lot of lovey-dovey stuff, hugging and kissing. After kissing all of my brothers-in-laws Steve says, "Now I know why you call them Freaky Family."

To make a long story short, the Trinity River was too high and rapid to get any gold, and all of the twisty sticks for hundreds of miles were cut out and few remained. I knew in my heart that my in-laws had hidden them all so I couldn't get them. I promised myself that I would find their stash of sticks. I told my in-laws that we wanted to go for a hike; I didn't tell them why. They all said to watch out for mountain lions and offered a gun to take along for protection, which I refused since I don't really care for guns anymore.

I figured they were trying to steer me away from the area where they stashed all the sticks, so with Steve at my back to block all the Hoopa arrows, we set out to find the lion's den where I thought the sticks might be. Two hours later, we found it. At the bottom of a huge Madrone tree was a huge gaping dark hole. My plan was for Steve to sneak up and jab a tree limb into the hole to see if the lion was in there. I managed to get a blurry picture of Steve approaching the hole as I ran as fast as I could down the hill. Our surviving this ordeal tells you just how valuable these sticks are.

I couldn't think up there either, so I helped Steve get in the truck and we went home. We didn't get anything from the trip except a bag of my sister-in-law's towels and all of her coffee cups. Oh, and a few sticks and some river rocks that look like dead animals. All in all, the trip only cost me a couple of thousand dollars. Steve might sue me but that still remains to be seen.

My wife asked me why I was back so soon, so I told her that I couldn't figure out why people act so strange around me.

"Don, it's so simple that even an idiot could figure it out," she said.

What it amounted to was the fact that everything people do and say around me will be published in the local newspaper for all to see. Stuff like Libby Earthman talking to plants and Rich Marovich is telling me that cardboard boxes can be placed in larger boxes if you bend them so that they forget how they are supposed to be shaped. I never knew boxes could think. Now I know they really can, but that has already been in the paper.

My Wife's Car Hates Me
4/24/2011

My wife bought a new car last week. She used my son's Jeep as a clunker and gave him her old Toyota Echo with the hideous "Supermom" sticker on the rear window. We scraped the sticker off so that all that is left is a blurry splonge of glue that dirt sticks to.

Anyway, my wife orders a new Ford, a beautiful car, with every luxury you can imagine. It has voice-activated Bluetooth, vocal GPS (turn by turn); satellite radio, ambient lighting, and I don't know what else. That's the good part. The bad part is that the car hates me.

It's hard to believe, but the car absolutely hates me and it told me so. The first day she had the darn car I wasn't allowed to touch it. The second day I got to ride along to the store.

She started the car, remembered her purse, and went back into the house to get it. I just sat in the car and looked around at all the gadgets and thing-a-ma-jigs. That's when it happened.

In a sexy female voice, the car says, "The passenger stinks." I jerked around and thought to myself, "Huh?" It said it again: "The passenger stinks." I thought to myself again, "Jeez, so I mowed the yard the day before yesterday. That's man smell — something you'll never know." Just as my wife got in the car, it said it again.

"Did you hear your car tell me that I stink?"

My wife answered, "Oh, that's Halley. She says that you're synced — not stink."

"Oh, that's the Bluetooth thingy," I thought. My wife had named the car and its computer after "HAL" in the movie "2010." I thought, "Didn't that computer kill everyone on the spaceship"? Then the car started blowing hot air on my side and cold air on my wife's side. Jeez, what's up with that?

That's when I started to plan my revenge.

I thought, "Just you wait baby, sooner or later my wife is gonna let me drive you, and I'm gonna drive you hard." The windshield wiper on my side of the car started flapping back and forth, back and forth. My wife didn't seem to notice.

That night, I took three sleeping pills and I still couldn't sleep because I wanted revenge. Real bad! The next morning, I says to my wife, "Honey, can I take Halley for a short drive?" The reply was, "No!" A couple hours later, I finally got permission.

Halley was shiny and spotless, not a speck of dust on her anywhere. I couldn't wait to get across the old bridge so I could put my foot into her turbo-charge as hard as I could. I had to be going 150 mph down the frontage road with the windows going up and down, the wipers flapping, and heat coming out of the air conditioner, when the car says, "The passenger stinks."

I had only been on the freeway a couple of minutes when behind me a CHP car turned on his lights. I pulled over, turned off the car and the window wouldn't roll down and the door wouldn't unlock. The cop knocked on the window. I was freakin' out trying to open the door when he knocked again.

Finally the cop asked me if I called 911. I thought for a minute.

"No, it was the car," I yelled through the closed window. I was sweating because it was so hot in there. The cop shook his head and left the scene. The car says, "The passenger stinks."

I somehow got the vocal GPS to work so it could give me directions back home. The car told me to take the next left. It was a dirt road through a field of sunflowers. I asked for new directions and the car says, "I'm sorry Don, I can't do that!" I turned left.

There was so much dust flying that I couldn't see the mud until I was up to the axle, but I made it through. When I pulled up to the house, I could tell that my wife was angry by the look on her face. There were little dots of mud all over Halley and me when I said, "Therese, I don't know where the dog hair came from." Just as I was going to turn the darn dirty car off it said, "The passenger stinks!"

From the Lion's Den
5/1/2011

I think that my friend Steve is planning on killing me. I'll explain why I think this in the simplest of terms so that the citizens of Winters can understand what I am talking about. It all started a few days ago when Steve read in the Winters Express that he had jammed a tree limb into the den of a mountain lion.

"You never told me it was a lion's den," he said.

I was shocked! I thought he knew it was a lion's den because of all of the scratch marks around the hole. I mean, all around the tree, up to 10 feet high, all of the bark was torn off, chewed up, and spit out. Some of the scratch marks were up to an inch deep. A grizzly bear doesn't scratch that deep. Geez, everybody knows that. Plus, all of the bones lying around the tree should have been a big clue for him. Geez, do I have to spell everything out for him?

Steve started acting funny while we were driving home and it's gotten worse in the past few weeks. He's been saying and doing some really strange things that I don't understand. I don't know exactly what they mean. For instance, he doesn't want to go fossil hunting anymore because it has no financial reward, or no pee in his pot, as he likes to say.

On a hike the other day, he started mumbling words under his breath, just low enough so that I couldn't understand what he was saying. At first I'd just look at him like he had lost his mind, and poke him in the back with my hiking stick. It was really funny, but Steve wasn't laughing. I even tripped him a couple of times so that he would fall in the poison oak.

So here I am bent over, laughing so hard that tears were coming from my eyes, when Steve turns around real slow like and says, "Carpe Meterioritus Chondrites Regmaglypts." I said, "What, what are you talking about?" He gave me a funny look that I swear was just like the guy that went nuts in the movie, "Full Metal Jacket." Then, he looked just like Hannibal Lector with slobber coming from the corner of his mouth. The slobber was white like he may have had rabies or something.

I was getting worried and a little scared at this point, so I asked him to sit and take a break so we could talk. As we sat on two big rocks, way up in Cold Canyon, Steve took a big rock in his hand and smashed the bottom of a bottle of water and proceeded to drink as much as he could while the rest splashed all over his face. I thought to myself, "I would have just unscrewed the cap to get a drink." As I watched in amazement, Steve started smashing the rock on the bottle again, over and over.

"What are you doing," I asked?

With his head slanted kinda sideways he said, "I'm trying to close this bottle, what do ya think!"

"Oh" I said. "What does all of that mumbo jumbo mean about carps and regama thingys?"

He explained that from now on, he was going to find meteorites because they were worth a lot of money and that millions of years ago they fell from the sky, landing all over this area. I said, "How do you know that and how do we find them?" He explained that he had seen it on TV and that there was a meteorite right behind me, just up the hill. I turned to look and sure enough there was a big black rock almost at the top of an incline of about 80 degrees. I turned back to look at him and said, "That's 30 feet high — how are we supposed to get to it?"

Steve pulled a stringy little rope out of his backpack. He says, "Follow me, I'll show you."

It took about an hour for us to climb to the top of the hill and I could barely breathe.

"I'll tie the rope to your ankles and lower you down to get the meteorite." He said.

"No way," I said. "It's got poison oak all around it, and I could break my neck!"

I turned to look at Steve and I found that he had already tied the rope to my legs and his foot was coming right at me. I got the "St" out on "Stop" when he kicked me over backwards down the hill where I slid over loose rocks and poison oak until the rope stopped my slide.

"Grab the black rock," he said.

I wrapped my arms around the rock just as Steve let go of the rope.

I woke up with the black rock on my chest and poison oak leaves all over my face. My arms were black from my hands to my elbows. I yelled, "Dang yer hide, Steve," when I realized that he had painted the rock black. I could hear him running through the woods laughing, "He he, ha ha, he he!" He had driven off and left me up by the dam, but he left a note there for me: "Stick that black rock in a lion's den, you dummy!"

'Ben' Laden Gets Double-Crossed in Paradise
5/8/2011

I had the weirdest dream last night. By the clock, I slept for well over an hour but I tossed and turned so much that I actually slept only about sixty minutes.

Before I tell you about the dream, I have a complaint I'd like to convey to the Veteran's Administration. Ready, here it is: "I ate a whole bottle of those cheap sleeping pills that you gave me and it didn't do anything except make me vomit and then it gave me a hellacious case of cotton mouth."

Anyway, I was telling you about the weird dream I had. Well, in the dream, I was sitting at my desk. There were three TVs. In front of me was a little TV that had a typewriter in front of it. To my left, on a table, was a smaller TV that had a typewriter right on it and when you fold it up it made a muffled sound like someone talking in a closet. Neither had any paper.

Across the room there was a great big TV that had to be at least 21 inches across. The World News was on all three TVs and there was a cute little number named Christy Sillman talking about some guy named Osama Ben Laden that had filed suit against some Muslim organization for breach of contract.

This Ben Laden guy claimed that he was promised 40 virgins when he in fact received 40 old hookers from the Bronx and they wouldn't leave him alone.

"It has been pure torture," he said in an interview with a bevy of reporters.

I was really getting interested in this when another cute little lady reporter started telling the world about how Ben Laden complained that when he got to the gate to paradise, he found Muhammad playing chess with Jesus.

Ben Laden angrily claimed that when he tried to enter the gate to paradise, the two chess players would scoot their chairs and game table around to block his access.

"Every single time I tried to get past these guys, they would move the stupid table around so I couldn't get in," said Ben Laden.

"That's when I filed the first lawsuit that was denied by Judge Debra (Lo Guercio) DeAngelo of the US Supreme Court on the premise that everybody knows that Muhammad hasn't played chess since he was beaten by a computer in 1981," said Ben Laden, while taking a big breath.

After Ben Laden got that long sentence out, the cute reporter asked him, "How did you like those big American boys that have been chasing you around for the last decade?" Ben laden huffed and puffed and finally walked away, mumbling.

Then the reporter said, "I didn't think you'd like them — some of those boys were from Arkansas! Yee haw! OK, then, this is Karen Roe reporting, back to you Christy!" she said with a big smile.

This was just too much for me, so I went in and woke up my wife, Therese, who sleeps like a baby because she is pure of heart. She asked me what was so important as she rubbed her eyes.

I must have been really excited because when I tried to tell her that Christy Sillman, whom we had dinner with a few weeks ago, was the anchor on the world news and that my cousin Karen Roe, from Arkansas, was a reporter, it came out like this: "Sisty Pillman news and Cousin Karen on TV real cute!"

Therese turned around and went back to bed. I followed her into the bedroom telling her about how some boys from Arkansas had shot this guy named Ben Laden in some place called Bobbobbabod, just north of Salamabob.

"He was miffed because he was double-crossed and couldn't get into paradise" I said, "and they gave him 40 hookers instead of 40 virgins!"

Therese was already snoring.

So then I found that I could talk to the news reporters by using the typewriters (with no paper) by the little TVs. I think I said something stupid like, "Shooting a guy in the head was no reason to celebrate." At this, Christy, the anchor and Karen, the reporter, started laughing so hard that tears flowed from their eyes and spittle flew all over the inside of my TV. Together they said, "Don, sometimes you say the dumbest things!"

The dream ended when a commercial came on the three TVs. Another cute lady pronounced, "Tune in today at 6 p.m. when the Madge Show interviews famous writer Donald Sanders for the first time since he made the dumbest statement ever made by a human being."

I woke up with a start! I thought, "What, it was all a dream?" I got up, looked and found my sleeping pills but the bottle was empty.

Five Steps to Increase Your Brain Power
5/15/2011

I've been trying to figure out why I'm so smart. I'm not just a little smart, I'm way smarter than everybody else. I've never, in my long, long life met anyone who is smarter than me.

My friend Steve is pretty smart too, but I can think circles around him, anytime. It's like slow motion and my mind is going around his, like, real fast. By the time he thinks about something, I have already thought about it.

You know, now that I'm thinking about it, people seem to trust me more than they do Steve; even Steve's own family. Yes, it's sad but true. For instance, Steve's wife Kellie seems to trust me more than she does her own husband.

I know this to be true because when Steve and I are going hiking or garage sale-ing, she will tell me, "Don, don't let Steve bring home any more junk." You see what I mean. The poor lady has to tell me to do what she can't trust her husband to do.

It's really sad because sometimes when I pick Steve up at his house, he will be crying as he comes out of the house. I'll say, "Aw Steve, don't cry. What's the matter buddy?" But I already know the answer. It's always the same. "Kellie won't let me bring home any more junk," he'll whine.

So, now you're thinking, why is Don so trustworthy, and so smart? Well, it's a natural fact that size does matter. I was born, as a small child, with a huge brain. I'm not sure how old I was at the time and I can't remember why, but it's really true. I have a big brain!

It seems that 50 percent of our intelligence is genetic and the other 60 percent comes from your environment. I hope I'm not going too fast for all of you readers out there, but I'll slow down anyway and lay down the facts for your examination. If, like I said before, you too think I'm really trustworthy, you can skip this part and just assume that I'm correct in my findings.

DISTRACTION — that's the key word here. It is a scientific fact that those of you who are distracted from any task at hand have more grey matter in your brain. I therefore offer you clue number one: I get distracted all the time!

I've got too much brain matter. As a matter of fact, I'm considering a brain matter reduction, but I'd have to travel all the way to Germany to get one. That's clue number two.

Clue number three might hurt the feminine side of the human race thingy. Around these parts, men have anywhere from 8 to 10 percent more brain matter than women do, and I have another 15 percent more than that. Thus, as the evidence indicates, I am a big-brained guy!

I rest my case, thus proving that I am the smartest guy in the world. I have discovered, through my research, steps that can be taken to increase your brain matter. There are 10 steps. I will now list five of these steps for your consideration for free. The other five steps will cost you $31.57 in gold bullion. Checks and cash are not accepted.

Here are five steps that you can take to increase your brain matter:
• Stretch your mind. (Step # 6 will tell you how)
• Eat brain food. (Brain food is not green — it is meat)
• Take a 47-minute walk every day.
• Learn to cope with stress. (This is accomplished by letting someone else make all

of the decisions.)

• Daydream away. (This comes naturally to a mind as large as mine.)

Just the other day, I was considering an experiment that would dramatically modulate attention using transcranial direct current.

If my data is correct, it could have an effect on people whose distractibility becomes problematic. (Like Steve) I would have this data for you at this time, but Steve wouldn't let me hook up the wires after inserting a nail to each side of his brain.

All of this doesn't mean that you, as normal brained people, are smarter than one another. It simply indicates that you use your brains differently than I do.

Ever hear of Morgellons disease? Here is what the Center for Disease Control and Prevention (CDC) has to say about it: "Persons who suffer from this unexplained skin condition report a range of cutaneous (skin) symptoms including crawling, biting and stinging sensations; granules, threads, fibers, or black speck-like materials on or beneath the skin; and/or skin lesions (e.g., rashes or sores). In addition to skin manifestations, some sufferers also report fatigue, mental confusion, short term memory loss, joint pain, and changes in vision."

They continue to say that the factors associated with acquiring this condition are unknown. At this time, there is insufficient information to determine whether or not this condition is contagious. The CDC has awarded a contract to Kaiser Permanente's Northern California Division of Research to assist CDC in the investigation of this condition. The study is being designed and led by CDC.

Some health professionals believe that signs and symptoms of Morgellons disease are caused by another condition, often mental illness. Dr. Noah Craft, assistant professor of dermatology at Harbor-UCLA Medical Center states that Morgellons disease is an outbreak of delusional parasitosis brought on by some common exposure. Delusional parasitosis is often seen in recreational drug users (especially those using methamphetamine).

"Dermatologists are afraid to see these patients," says Dr. Peter Lynch, professor emeritus of dermatology at the University of California. He had one patient tell him that, "I'm going to shoot the next doctor who tells me it's in my head." Some people who suspect Morgellons disease claim they've been ignored, criticized as delusional or dismissed as fakers. In contrast, some doctors say that people who report signs and symptoms of Morgellons disease typically resist other explanations for their condition. Reports of Morgellons disease have been made in every state in the United States and various countries around the world. Most reported cases are clustered in California, Texas and Florida.

OK, I think that we're all probably confused as to the reality of this disease. In one form or another it has been around since the 17th century; always attributed to mental illness. I've even heard it referred to as "growing pains." I think that maybe we have all had the disease at one time or another if you consider it a mental disorder.

To move on, here's the rest of my story. Ever hear of the "God particle"? Its real name is the "Higgs particle." As any object moves through space they have to "wade'" through these Higgs particles that "cling" to them, causing a drag that shows up as mass. In 1966 Peter Higgs (University of Edinburgh) proposed that the universe was full of a field called a "Higgs field."

Scientists around the world are in the process of trying to identify the "God particle" through the use of huge "super colliders" that employ what they refer to as nanotechnology. Teeny, weenie little "nanomites" (I invented that word) are shot around these huge colliders in the hope that they will gather enough mass to be identified. A worthy endeavor, I guess, but not as good as feeding or educating the Third World.

Anyway, I don't want to go there right now, so back to nanotechnology. Nanotechnology is nothing new. There are literally thousands of products that utilize nano particles in their make-up: golf balls, cleaning products, stain resistant clothing, baseball bats, house paint, air purifiers, surfboards, odor-proof socks, cosmetics, computer chips, sunscreens, self-cleaning windows... and the list goes on and on. Nano particles in these products are what scientists refer to as "nanotechnology in its static form."

Now we're getting to the heart of the matter. What do super colliders have to do with Morgellons disease? There have been two recent outbreaks of a mysterious "itching nanofiber" disorder known as Morgellons — one in Europe at the CERN Collider and the other at the Hanging Rock Supercollider in Australia. Scientists at both facilities have indicated a possible link between high-energy particle colliders and the disease. Both facilities were attempting to create and detect the elusive Higgs particle when the outbreaks occurred, which affected scores of scientists and workers and is now spreading rapidly around the world.

I guess some of the scientists itched themselves to death because according to Dr. Walabi of the HRS, (Hanging Rock Supercollider), "We are trying to contain the event and prevent more deaths." Considering that it is possible for "nanomites" (my word again) to manipulate an oily drop of liquid and even push it up an incline of 12°, I think you'll agree with me that this could easily make your skin crawl.

Learned a Thing or Two About Women
5/29/2011

Women! Women are always meddling. They're never happy and they are constantly snooping and complaining about things they don't like. Will it never end?

If it were left up to them, we would all take a bath every day. They want us to eat more vegetables, watch our P's and Q's, and wipe our feet before we go into the house. Mud fighting is out of the question.

Women want to transform the world, so now they call themselves activists. It's not just one or two of them. All of them want to change something. You can name anything, anything at all, and I'll guarantee that some women don't like it or they want to change it.

Don't get me wrong, I love women. I'm just a little confused about what they want and why. It's always been this way for me, as far back as I can remember.

Raised in a dormitory full of only boys, I was in my mid-teens before I had the opportunity to interact with girls. Thus, I had to learn some hard lessons, like girls don't react the same way as boys when you kick them between the legs. I found that they will chase you down and beat you mercilessly until you scream for help.

Boys, on the other hand, will give you more respect if you fight them and stand your ground. Everybody knows that first comes the fight and then comes the peace. Ask anybody.

Not women, hell no! To them it is the outcome of the struggle that matters so enormously. They want to fight until they get what they want. Geez, that ain't right!

Believe me; I have always wanted to understand women. I have gone way past the norm in my efforts to make them happy — way past. I even went so far as to take a class in the "Psychology of Women." Can you believe that? Women have psychology!

I'll tell you what, when I walked into that classroom seeing nothing but women, I decided to sit way in the back by the fire door. So here I am, sitting in the back of a classroom full of "activists." It was really terrifying.

I was sitting there trying not to look at them because I didn't want them to consider me a sexist. I didn't know what to do until in walked the instructor, Dr. Karen McCord. Little did I know the effect that this little African American woman would have on my mind.

The very first thing that she did was to ask me why I was sitting so close to the back door. She said, "Are you going to try to escape?" I just sat there with a crap-eating grin. She began to speak.

Everything she said was like music from some beautiful instrument that was somehow unknown to man. The expanse of her mind was responsible for my wanting to learn more about everything. John Wayne and Jerry Lewis went out the door at that moment. I had a new role model and mentor and she was a woman and an African American. Geez, heaven help me!

It was from her, that I would learn what women want. They don't want flowers and candy. They want equality and they use something called "women's empowerment" to get it. I found that women were no longer activists; they were "feminists."

It's not just one of them either — they all want it. Every single one of them, all around the world, want equality. Dr. McCord taught me that even the most insignificant, unknown, person can have a huge impact on women's rights. People you've never heard of. Like in 2003, one million Moroccan women signed a petition that changed Muslim views on marriage, polygamy and divorce. They inspired one million women in Iran to do the same.

Betcha never heard of Claudette Colvin. At the age of 15, she refused to give up her seat on a Montgomery bus, nine months before Rosa Parks. For her effort, she was arrested, cuffed, beaten and shunned by her community. It was she that was at the center of the Supreme Court case of Browder vs. Gayle that ended in the reversal of the Jim Crow laws.

Women have become the new growth engine for international business practices. Many businesses are already deploying their assets to improve the lives of women in the emerging global markets. Say what you will about Condoleezza Rice and Hillary Clinton, but they are first class feminists and they made their own footprints. They are leading because they had no one to follow.

I'll Have to Eat a Lot More Frogs
6/5/2011

Well, I just don't know what to do these days. Everything happens so quickly and I don't seem to have any control over anything at all. I'm afraid to walk around town anymore because, with all of the dumb stuff I've written in the local newspaper, somebody might beat me up. People write in to the Winters Express just to tell me to keep my dumb opinions to myself and they call me a "big bag of wind" or was it "gas."

Anyway, since I've been afraid to write my column, I decided to enter a chess tournament. To make a long story short, I walked into this auditorium, sat at a table ready to play, when I noticed that all the other players were under 10 years old. OK, so I figured I can do this, and I started to make my opening move when the little twerp I was playing announced, "Mate in 11."

A few moves into the game I noticed a change in the pawn structure. He had eight and I had none. At this point I figured I'd better offer a draw but this sent the entire auditorium into uncontrollable laughter. People were actually rolling in the aisles. To make matters worse, the little punk kid hit me in the head with a rook. I pointed my finger at him and said, "You little (so and so) step outside and I'll kick your butt.

The Director told me to stop picking on the 10 year olds and not to bother turning in my score sheet after the game. Man, I could have taken that kid, I know I could.

This afternoon I received my copy of Phi Theta Kappa (Pathways to Success 2009), which lists all the members of the Honor Society. It took awhile but I finally found my name on page 1219. Do you have any idea how long it takes to look at 1,200 pages? Anyway, it seems that I'm the only person in Winters that is listed in the book. My mind went, "k-ching, k-ching."

Right away I contacted the Guinness Book of Records people and submitted my information for a world record. I filled out this long form stating how I was the only guy from Winters in the big blue book and then clicked on the "submit form" button. Here comes the catch: The next web page that came up said that I had to pay 600 something to submit the form. It wasn't American money; it was some kind of English money with a different symbol than the dollar sign. Now I'm supposed to read British, right?

Anyway, I found out that it cost $700 and then some to send in my application for a world record. That's when it struck me: Maybe if I say I'm doing it for a charity they will waive the cost. So, at the bottom of the application I put, "This application is submitted so I can feed the little children of Winters through the Donald Sanders Food for the Little Kids Foundation." I also made a note that I had to turn down the award of "Citizen of the Year" every year because I wanted to be, so to say, a behind the scenes kind of guy. I want the credit to go to others that deserve it much, much more than me.

Finally, I got an email from them stating that my application had been denied, stating that just because your name is in some stupid book does not make you a world record holder. However, they would take it under consideration if I could eat 532 Putah Creek frogs. I know that this is impossible because I can eat anything except vegetables and I could only eat six frogs before I got sick. So I decided to go back to writing.

Are You in the Past, or the Future — or am I?
6/12/2011

I've been thinking again. Like all the other times that I found myself thinking, I have no control over when or what I will be thinking about. I have now thought myself into a corner, so I'm hoping that I can think long enough to get myself out of it.

Consider this. I am in the future and you are in the past. Or is it... you are in the future and I am in the past. I'll have to think about that too when I get the chance.

Anyway, to clarify my point, by the time you read this column, the point in time and space where I am at this moment is in the past where you are at the point in space and time where you are as you read it.

So now you're thinking too. You're thinking, "What the Hell is he talking about?" OK, stick with me and don't let your mind wander. I know it can be tough sometimes if you have ABM. (Average Brain Mass)

I am writing this very sentence on May 29. You, in turn, cannot read this sentence until at least June 5 or maybe even June 12. That, by my definition, puts me in your future and you in my future too.

Wait a minute. Let me think some more.

Anyway, I am in your past and you are in my future when you read these words of wisdom. Understand? So I am at one end of the spectrum of time and space and you are at the other. As I continue to think, I find that there is an "in between."

Debra DeAngelo, the editor of all of these words of wit, is an "inbetweener" because when she reads this she is not as far in the future as you are when you read this. Got it? I'm not losing you, am I?

Nevermind. Stay with me for just few more sentences, because it's really going to get exciting now. I have a little experiment in mind that might change everything that you know to be true about space and time.

Sometime in the near future, when I send this column to Debra, I am going to walk over to Debra's office, which is well over a block away from my house, to see if Debra can even see me in her past.

I'm thinking that she won't know that I wrote this in the past unless she takes the time to think about it, and of course, we all know that editors aren't really great thinkers. They're "inbetweeners." Get it? LOL. (LOL means "laugh out loud" in hologram chat, talkie thingy. You know what I mean, right?)

Anyway, I wish my wife was here to proofread this column for me. She could tell me if I am breaking down this information so that you, a person with ABM can easily understand and grasp the meaning of what I'm trying to say to you.

She is on sabbatical. Tomorrow (last Sunday or the other Sunday, to you) she will be sharing Mass with Pope what's his name in the Vatican Square. Now you can see why I'm doing all of this thinking. When she's around, I don't do it so much because she says, "STOP, wait a minute, what the heck are you doing."

Like, she'll read my column and say, "You're not going to send this to Debra, are you?" (I always send them in anyway.) You have to understand that she has ABM (Average Brain Mass) too. In spite of her ABM, I absolutely adore her. She is a ray of sunshine and she radiates me.

While she's away on her stinking sabbatical there is no warmth or reverence in my life. If she were here right now, she would want me to reconsider sending this column to the inbetweener because my mind is on a level with Einstein, Plato and Socrates while her mind is on a level with Bette Midler and Betty White.

I don't know where the heck your mind is and I don't even want to know either. It's not good for me to mix the past with the future because there's no clear path for me to follow.

Sometime in the future, I'll let you know the results of my experiments concerning time and space.

Man, this Weiner thingy is just too good to pass up. I mean, I can totally understand what this guy did and why. It is so obvious.

Imagine you're like 22 years old. You're just standing there looking dumb when your mom walks up to you and says, "Your name is Weiner." You are taken aback.

"What do you mean, my name is Weiner?" you reply. "Why is my name Weiner," you think to yourself.

Just think of it. Of all the names in the entire universe, your name is Weiner. OMG!

If you were Russian, your name would be Вайнер. In Germany, you'd be Weinerschnitzel. Even in Japan you would be ロンドンの俗称 (the great Weiner).

OK, every single day of your life, you will think of yourself as "The Weiner!" Eventually, you accept it and slowly grow to love it. "Yes, I am Weiner!" you announce to the World.

You think, "What better place for a Weiner than in government." "Yes, I will be Congressman Weiner!" you decide. President Weiner sounds even better.

So, now you have the background of the Weiner guy. Is it so hard to understand why he did what he did?

Consider the fact that if you are going to be named something like Weiner, you have to have the right equipment. If you don't then you can't be called "the Weiner." You would be called "Weenie."

To go even farther, if you have the right equipment, you naturally want to share it with the world. You are proud of it. I would be, wouldn't you? You really want to share it. But you're at a loss about how to do it. There has to be a way.

You think and you think until suddenly you have the answer. You decide to go online and flirt with every young girl that you can find. You look for the perfect young lady. This is a task that may take years, maybe decades.

The trouble is that if you go around asking young girls if they want a picture of "the Weiner" and you're a congressman, you will be hounded by all sorts of watchdog groups. The least of which is the FBI.

You don't care. You ain't afraid of no FBI. You are bound and determined to expose "the Weiner" to entire world; you just have to find the right avenue. You finally find it.

Megan Broussard. It has taken six years of online flirting to find the perfect one, and now here she is. She is young (26), beautiful, and really, really dumb. She's of French ancestry so that must mean that she loves the Weiner.

You work with her for several weeks and you pass sexy photos back and forth on Facebook. Nothing really explicit at first. You call it "sexting." Finally, the big day. You post the picture that you know will be life-altering. This will get you off the Hill and into the porn industry in one swift moment. Weiner smothered in underwear is the only way to describe the photo that you post.

So that is that. The Weiner is out. No one is shocked because we've become accustomed to the display of odd behavior from our elected officials. The odder the behavior, the higher up in government they get.

People everywhere are getting stranger and stranger all the time. One governor thinks he can sell a senatorial seat while sporting a bad comb-over. It seems that if you're young and on Capitol Hill you are open game for every pervert sporting a suit and tie, riding in a taxpayer limo.

Smut is everywhere. Even the church openly hands out smut. One of the largest and oldest seminary schools in Europe closed its doors because of the open homosexual activities within its walls. Confiscated computers from the school were riddled with porn and explicit photos.

It is absolutely unbelievable. Even I, "the Don," have been plagued by weirdoes with strange requests. Really strange. It never ceases to amaze me how weird people can be. I hesitate to tell you what I'm talking about but I will anyway because I'm "the Don."

Recently I got a large envelope in the mail from a doctor at Kaiser Hospital. Within the envelope there was a plastic bag that came with instructions. This is so really weird. You are not going to believe it.

This weirdo doctor wanted me to send him a piece of poop. That's right, a piece of poop! I was taken aback.

Did I say that before? I thought, "Why in the world would this guy want a piece of poop?"

First of all, how would I go about pooping into this little bag? Do they want a whole poop or just part of a poop? If so, I need a much larger bag. OMG!

This has to be a trap! What if the bag got caught in a machine down at the post office and splattered all over kingdom come. Wouldn't it be in the newspaper the next day saying, "Great Columnist and future Citizen of the Year mails piece of poop and gets caught in machine." Good thing it wasn't a wiener.

They Can Make Money Disappear
6/26/2011

Recently it has come to light that over $6.6 billion may have been stolen from Iraq and the United States. Special inspector general for Iraq reconstruction, Stuart Bowen said in a statement to the New York Times that the missing money represents "the largest theft of funds in national history."

This has its good side and its bad side. The good part is that the $6.6 billion was not ours, it belonged to Iraq. The bad side is that the United States was in charge of this money when it went missing. Iraq has now filed suit saying that they want their money back.

The United States is playing dumb. That's exactly what I would do. I'd raise my shoulders with my hands held open and say, "I don't know where it is."

Then I would turn and try to walk away, when I got around a corner, I would run away, dodging behind corners or autos, anything.

No one, I mean no one, seems to know where the money went. I, with my superior brainpower will solve this mystery, and I will do so before this column ends. I am the all-knowing, all-seeing Donald. You can call me AKAS DONALD or simply BOGWAN DON. Let's follow the money trail.

Twelve billion dollars was flown into Iraq in 21 separate C-130 aircraft on May 24, 2004.

The transfer was authorized by then President, George W. Bush. Imagine if you will 21 C-130 military aircraft, jam-packed with neat little bundles of $100 dollar bills.

There was so much money in each aircraft that the crew could not move from the forward area of the aircraft to the rear. The cash, on pallets wrapped in clear plastic had to look appetizing. The mere sight of it would make me slobber all over my shirt.

Upon arrival in Iraq, there were 21 pallets missing. An anonymous aircraft crew chief reported the missing pallets in writing to his Commanding Officer. The crew chief and the report have not been seen since.

Now we have the money in Iraq. I need to give you a little background about the situation in Iraq before I tell you where the money went.

Trade sanctions against Iraq were imposed by the UN Security Council with Resolution 661 dated Aug. 6, 1990, following Iraq's invasion of Kuwait. The sanctions effectively blocked all imports and exports to and from Iraq. The resolution gave the Security Council total control over every important facet of Iraqi society.

Iraq was already destitute, and near famine-like conditions existed in every home. Death swiftly took the weakest, the elderly, and the very young. Bridges, factories, power plants, water treatment facilities, and medical facilities had been bombed out of existence. One out of every five Iraqi men never made it home after the invasion of Kuwait.

The U.S.-led occupation authority literally had control over everything, including the life and death of the Iraqi people. In a merciful action, the UN Security Council implemented the Oil for Food program designed primarily to relieve the lack of food and potable water.

OK, so now we're trading oil for food, right? Well not really. The United States and the UK blocked all imports, stating that no shortage of food and water existed until famine conditions set in. Food imports were blocked for three long months as a result.

Without electricity to run water and sewage treatment plants, there was an immediate and massive increase in water-borne diseases such as cholera, typhoid, and dysentery. These have particularly harsh impacts on infants and young children. Without adequate water treatment, child mortality skyrocketed immediately, child mortality increased by approximately 250 percent in 60 days.

With the sanctions already imposed, the United States and the United Kingdom could effectively block any further actions through the use of their UN veto power. Months before the first shipments of food and water supplies arrived in Iraq, hundreds upon hundreds of ships loaded with Iraqi oil left port for unknown, secret places.

Each oil tanker received a voucher from a single control agent that allowed them to leave port full to the brim with Iraqi oil. An investigation reported that one single agent inspected and released vouchers at an impossible rate that could not be humanly done.

There was no record of any measuring devices designed to regulate how much oil was taken. An estimate of $100 billion worth of oil was taken with only a modest amount of food relief distributed to the Iraqi masses. That is the situation.

Back to the mountain of cash. The cash was stacked from ceiling to floor in rooms all over Bagdad. US and UK personnel could sign a voucher and withdraw truckloads of hundred dollar bills at a time with a single signature. No credible record has ever been found concerning where and how the cash was distributed. In essence it was simply given away to anyone who would sign for it.

If you can remember, at the beginning of the invasion of Iraq in March of 2003, truckloads and truckloads of packaged $100 bills were found. News reports showed us rooms full of neat little bundles of cash all over Iraq.

I am amazed and confused by the fact that so much corruption and so much greed was not dealt with by anyone even though it was openly visible to everyone. Ultimately, the buck should have stopped at the Bush Administration. Oh, I'm sorry, it was Bush and his goons that took all of the oil.

At one time, Halliburton, of which Cheney owns a sizeable portion, came under fire for stealing oil so 200,000 AK-47s were passed out to its own little army and that was the end of that. No one knows where the arms are now and no one seems to care.

From the top to the bottom of the political ladder, there has never been one person held accountable for any action concerning this theft of billions upon billions upon billions of dollars. There never will be.

You know why? Those in power today are above the law. They own it. Look at these jerks on the congressional committee that is currently investigating this whole mess. They will make millions of dollars of US tax revenue simply disappear, and disappear it will.

In truth, this whole matter has already been investigated and the published results are stated in the "Carnegie Council on Ethics and International Affairs 2006/ Copyright Carnegie Council on Ethics and International Affairs 2006." I knew all about this, years ago, but that's because I'm so smart.

So Tempted to Steal Their Work
7/3/2011

Between the Winters Express and the iPinion Syndicate, I've seen some mighty fine writing. This makes me happy and sad at the same time. I'm happy that I have something that is well written and meaningful to read, but at the same time I'm sad because I didn't write it.

When I see something that is so well written, it makes my brainstem hurt all the way to my tailbone. My brain says, "Steal it Donald, steal it." Well actually, it doesn't say that, but it does think it.

The June 2 edition of the Winters Express had two such items. The first was written by Margaret Burns entitled, "Lessons for the Living" and the other was a letter to the editor from Tracy Calvert entitled "Resign or be Fired." I wanted to steal them both.

Of course, I couldn't use what I was stealing in the Winters Express, so I would have to post it on the iPinion Syndicate columnist web page. (iPinion.us) and of course I'd have to change a few words around and put my name as the author.

Out of respect for my editor, I sent an email to Debra DeAngelo.

"Can I steal Margaret Burns' column, post it on iPinion.us, and say that I wrote it?" I asked. She replied, "If a frog had only one wing, would it fly in circles?"

I thought to myself, "What?"

"What does that mean?" I asked.

She said, "I'll make it simple for you." This is the story she told me:

Donald, we don't know who Margaret Burns really is. We think that maybe she is affiliated with the FBI, CIA, Home Security, or maybe all of them. We don't know. Every time we have tried to investigate her, there is a drive-by shooting at the office. That's why you never hear about our front office personnel retiring. We just bury them. We have recently run out of space to hide the bodies so we started a fake garden across Railroad Avenue and are hiding the dead under the tomato plants.

We also think that Margaret may be connected to someone down at the IRS because we just received a bill for unpaid taxes in the amount of $2,453,331.99. The bill was hand delivered by a man in a black suit who looked a lot like the bad guy from "Planet of the Apes." As he left the office his tail got caught in the closing door. The guy said, "Squawk Squawk Squawk!" and then he tore the door off the hinges.

Debra ended the conversation rather nervously saying, "You can try to steal it if you want but I don't think you can."

I thought for about a minute longer than I usually do and then I decided I'd go ahead with my plan to steal Margaret's column. I knew what to do and how to do it. I brought up her column on line. I carefully put my computer cursor on her first word so that I could copy and paste it onto my blank word document.

I held my breath and slowly pressed the mouse button, slowly, slowly, POW it clicked. The crap hit the fan! My entire monitor was covered with the words: WARNING FBI WARNING FBI WARNING FBI.

Holy crap! Who is this lady? I had to find out because I wanted that column really, really bad. I was going to have to Google her. This in itself was very scary. I could get killed.

I typed her name in the search box and I almost crapped my pants when I got 1,040,000 hits. I thought, "Ah ha, there's a lot more to this lady than anyone knew. Right away I start thinking that this could win me a Pulitzer Prize and I wouldn't have to nominate myself either. I had hit the jackpot!

She is Senior Vice President and Director of Global Health, Population, and Nutrition Group. Probably a front for the CIA!

She authored a book, LYNX, *"A Journal for Linking Poets."* This could be a site where operatives could send coded messages, I don't know, nobody does. I think she may have discovered a remedy for ear mites in cats.

Margaret Burns is President of the Board of the Yolo Community Foundation. I don't know what the heck that is! Something secret, I bet.

Another search result said that Margaret played a distinct role of hydrodynamic shear in leukocyte-facilitated tumor cell extravasations. It also said something else that I don't know what the hell it means: "Schematic of endothelium-polymorph nuclear neutrophil (PMN) tumor cell adhesion." Now I was getting really scared! I decided not to copy her column.

There was a letter to the editor in the same issue of the Express by Tracy Calvert regarding a recent Grand Jury investigation of the local school board that I wanted to steal entitled, "Resign or be fired." This is excellent writing. She simplifies things for us that are all too often hidden from view.

Tracy illustrates crimes capable of harm that most directly affects the innocent, and from which the political elite are most insulated. Tracy points out that there are abuses of power and forms of corruption that are in fact legitimated within established legal structures. Tracy points out that it is eminently clear from the inception whose interests would be served by accountability, and whose were impeded.

The local political abuses that occurred behind doors closed to the public were never due to a lack of understanding about what might bring greater integrity to the various processes involved. Rather, what they illustrate is how well the lessons of accountability and integrity were already understood, as evidenced by the determined and methodical attempts to evade and compromise the structures of our local school board.

Give 'em hell, Tracy.

America isn't 'Free'
7/10/2011

"Freedom" is not your run of the mill word. It implies independence with a lack of restrictions. We, the American community, toss the word around flippantly like we have a monopoly on it. I hear the word all the time. It comes from every direction. It ricochets from one document to another without restraint.

People keep telling me that our great nation is founded on freedom. The U S Constitution declares that we as citizens are free but the truth of the matter is that we have never seen freedom in our lifetime. Your father, your grandfather, even his grandfather has never been free.

True, freedom ended when the first farmer, the first toolmaker and the first baker joined together to form the first village. From that moment, eons ago, we have been at the mercy of our fellows and it is impossible to become emancipated from the tyranny of the group.

So good is this community thingy that our labors have an unbounded energy to produce. We enjoy a collective self-control, and we enjoy a collective power to exert our influence over other weaker communities that do not conform to our needs.

From the beginning, the farmer, the toolmaker and the baker conspired to maintain and increase wealth and power; thus the birth of the class system. The passage of time has given us better tools, better seeds, better methods, but only slightly better shelters. Life is easier, safer and more abundant in every way, so we now accept the conditions of the group without question.

Freedom was traded for shelter, safety and nourishment. As the community grew, so too did an unperceivable process of enslavement. The farmer now has to pay the community the majority of the fruits of his labor. The toolmaker and the baker endure similar situations in their efforts to conform to the community.

The common man has been unable to keep up with those in control of the community and has slowly fallen into a tradition of dependence and subordination. So far have we fallen that we can no longer even see those with the true power. They hide themselves like cockroaches behind corporations and stooges they call lawyers.

Society is now designed to influence power. We see it in the distribution of wealth, religion and public institutions with the severity of its legal codes. The old adage, "divide and conquer" seems to apply to every segment of our society and it is most apparent in our family units.

Parents now must open a Facebook account to find out what their children need and want. To most adults, children are a mystery because technology has given our youth a second family that is controlled by fashion and peer pressure. They are oblivious to the evil that lurks nearby.

For generations we have traded our defensive assets for offensive ones at the whim of those in power for the reason that if the community does not prosper and expand, it will, indeed, collapse upon itself. Fathers send their sons to war without question where they will be wasted without restriction along with other sons of other fathers in other communities.

I like the reasoning of Robinson Jeffers: we cannot have all the luxuries and freedom too. Freedom is poor and laborious, that torch is not safe but hungry, and often requires blood for its fuel."

It is my personal observation that the fathers of this community are fair in nature. The community that we call the United States is not the only community, but I believe it to be a good one, the best of the best. We are now the "haves" and most of the rest of the communities on this Earth are "have-nots." They want what we have and they will try to take it. They will not succeed, but the price will be high to all.

As one community joins with another it will not necessarily be for the greater good. For a community that has neither safety or nourishment will always be a threat to the community that has everything. Communities that limit the rights of women, make war on the poor and disrespect the religion of others will find us hard and unforgiving.

I wish I could fix everything that is wrong but I don't have the knowhow or the energy. I can only lament as did W. C. Williams; "Sorrow is in my own yard where the new grass flames as it has flamed often before but not with the cold fire that closes around me this year."

Ten People Who Were Dumber Than Me
7/17/2011

It has been mentioned to me that some of the people of the City of Winters and at iPinion.us cannot believe how really, really smart I am. Some people think that I act smart but that I, in fact, am really, really dumb.

Once more, I am forced to demonstrate my smartness for everyone to witness. I will do this by naming 10 people from history that I'm sure were dumber than I am.

One: Adam, the first man, date unknown; the first man to think that men are smarter than women.

Two: Homer Sapiens of Eastern Africa, sometime around 1.7 million years ago, discovered fire. It is said that his friend from Western Africa, Homo Ergaster stepped into some magma and caught fire. Homer used the resulting fire for cooking fibrous plants and for warmth and protection for the next few nights.

Three: Basal Aurignacian, inventor of the first porn. He carved a female figurine from ivory and when someone entered he hid the naked figure in his cave that he thought was in Africa. The naked lady statue was found 35,000 years later in the cave of his friend Hohle Fels in Southwestern Germany.

Four: King John of England. In 1252, he signed what he thought was a paycheck for his army. The document was, in fact the Magna Carta, which laid out not only the obligations of the nobility, but also the rights of the common people.

Five: Wilhelm Schickard, in 1624 invented a machine that could add. Now he claims that this machine was in fact the first computer.

Six: Anus Imperforate founded the Proctology Board of Colon and Rectal Surgery one day and killed himself the next when he found out that proctology is the study of butts.

Seven: John Hansen in 1783 claimed to be the first United States president. Google him, he just might have been.

Eight: Prescott Sheldon Bush, grandfather of George Bush, claimed to be a hero during the WWI and wrote letters home to that effect. A Columbus newspaper published the information but it was later retracted when it was revealed that he had not received said medals. Grandpa stated that he had written the letters, "in the spirit of fun." You should really Google this guy because he did some really dumb stuff.

Nine: Adulla Jamama discovered AIDS after having sex with a monkey in 1981.

Ten: The dumbest guy I could find was a guy named Claudius Ptolemy, AD 100-178. This guy wrote 13 books full of mathematical equations proving that the rest of the universe rotated around the Earth.

There you have it. All of these guys were dumber than I am. Every one of them. If you need more proof, I can name another thousand people that are dumber than I am. Any more than that would be pushing it.

I would like to apologize to Margaret Burns for the mistakes I made in one of my prior columns. She mailed a letter to the editor of the Winters Express which, in short, read me my rights. How was I supposed to know that there are two MBs (Margaret Burnses)? How am I supposed to know which hits out of 20, 243,641 Google hits were hers?

I did notice one important thing about her letter to the Editor. MB did not deny the CIA and FBI thingy; Scary huh?

Love and war, and what they do
7/24/2011

Every so often I have to discuss a part of my life that I'd rather forget. For this reason or that, it doesn't really matter why; I have to talk about my life in the U.S. Army. In my early 20s, when I was very young, I found myself in a war zone. I was there for two years, one month, and seven days from June 1969 until August 1971.

Things were different back then. Vietnam was an unpopular war and for some reason, the American public seemed to blame it all on the soldiers that had fought there. As Arlo Guthrie put it in his song, "Alice's Restaurant," we were "baby killers" and "mother rapers."

There were 58,000 American soldiers killed in the Vietnam War, but over 120,000 Vietnam Veterans have committed suicide after coming home. You can clearly see the effect that their homecoming had on its returning soldiers.

For an example of how bad it was for us, I'll tell you about something that happened to me. In 1970, I received a 30-day leave to go home. It was so depressing for me at home that I returned to Vietnam after 20 days. When I got back to the war zone, I told my friends what I had seen and heard while on leave.

One of my best friends called me a liar and tried to punch me in the face. They just could not believe that their country would abandon them in the same manner that they would dump so much garbage. They dumped us, and it was devastating.

A year or so later, immediately upon my release from the army, I took off my uniform in at airport bathroom and tossed it in the garbage. No one would know that I had been a soldier and I kept it that way for many years.

There were no parades, no welcome homes, no hugs, and no kisses. Nowhere could I fit in. Only with other Vietnam veterans did I feel comfortable enough to relax. Many of us sunk into a pit of drug abuse and drunkenness.

I'm not trying to lay the blame for my problems anywhere but on my own shoulders. It was the decisions that I made that led me down that road. For many years, our behavior was overlooked by the authorities, but eventually they were forced to take action. Many, many veterans, including myself, wound up in jail.

I can only speak for myself, but being torn away from those that I love and being put in a cage like an animal gave me a serious attitude adjustment. You might say that jail had a sobering effect on me.

Sadly, many veterans fell by the wayside and could not recover as I did. I think that the amount of love that I received from my family saved me from certain doom. Still, I've had several bouts with suicide and it's constantly in the back of my head. Only love keeps me here.

The June 30 edition of my hometown newspaper, the Winters Express, had a story on page A-2 about the death of a man named James O'Neil. This man went to war at the age of 14. He landed on Utah Beach on D-Day and proceeded to fight his way across Europe. While doing so, he was wounded three times. He risked his life many times to protect others.

He married a girl named Dorothy and they had nine children. He loved her for over 43 years and she loved him back, just as much. I never got to meet James O'Neil, but I can see that he was a good man; strong of mind and body.

I didn't know him but I truly miss him. I cannot imagine him having the problems that I do, and this is the point of everything I'm trying to say: that warfare, killing, and dying will affect one man one way, and another in a different way. I'm sure James O'Neil would say that this is true. I'm not saying that one man is better or worse than the other, because they've both experienced the real horror of war.

I'm trying to say that the Vietnam War broke me. It broke others as well. I wish that I could be like James O'Neil but I can't. I don't know how. I can clearly see what James O'Neil had that I didn't have. James O'Neil found love as a young man and kept it close to him all of his life. I was well into my 40s before I found out that love existed for me.

I'm sure that James O'Neil and I shared many of life's complications in similar ways. We both saw war as it was. We both survived and we both came home after our wars. I don't know if he had problems with his life experiences but I do know where the similarities of our lives split and started to differ.

James found love and knew it for what it was, and at the same time there had been very little love or even affection in my life. I didn't have a clue what love was and thus couldn't be saved until I did find it. I found it in the eyes of my beautiful wife and I tell you the truth when I say that it was love that has saved me. This I know is the greatest gift that God has ever given me. He has truly blessed me in spite of what I do and have done to myself.

Human ovals
7/31/2011

The other day I watched a documentary film about the activities of the human race. When these activities are viewed from above, at a higher rate of speed, we humans look like tiny-weenie ants. We go real fast, stop, and then go real fast again.

If observed closely, we humans travel in flat circles that I call ovals. We do this over and over, day after day, all of our lives. This round and round behavior seems to make us happy, but no one really knows why.

So, for almost three days now, I have been deep in thought, trying to figure out why we go in ovals every day. I thought and I thought but I could not come up with the answer until I ran into my friend Terry, who works for our city's maintenance department.

Terry and I were discussing celestial mechanics, and something he said gave me exactly the answer I needed to explain why we go in ovals every day, all of our lives. Terry was explaining that the sun's corona is actually hotter than the surface of the sun. I was thinking, "How the heck does he know that?"

He went on to say that at any given moment the sun's corona weighs over seven billion tons. Then he tells me that this seven billion tons of corona flies off in every direction in the form of solar winds. I thought, "Yeah, right!" I started thinking that Terry's getting senile.

Then he says, "Haven't you noticed that your magnetic field is distorted?" I looked around and said, "There's nothing wrong with my magnetic field!" Terry said, "Aw contraire, bon a me!" This is what he told me.

When the solar wind hits your magnetic field, it flattens out the near side and elongates the far side. I looked around again. I was even more confused now than I was before. Then, like a miracle, I had a brain fart!

He could tell by the look on my face that I finally understood the point he was trying to get across. I said, "You mean to tell me that this solar wind thingy is why East Street is called East Street even though it doesn't go anywhere near East?"

"Pow, you hit the nail on the head!" he said. He went on to explain that East Street and Interstate 80 follow the same rules of celestial mechanics. They call Interstate 80, "80 East" or "80 West" when in reality, it travels north and south, not east and west.

I thought, "That's why they put the City of Davis over there instead of where it's supposed to be." Then I knew that Terry is some kind of genius. That's why he works for the government.

I said, "Wow, that explains why humans travel in ovals all the time, doesn't it?"

"Yes sir, indeed it does, my boy!" he exclaimed. He answered everything that I ever wanted to know about human ovals in his next sentence.

"You see, Don, when the solar wind hits your magnetic field and elongates the side away from the sun, it makes you lean toward that direction when you travel. You can't go in a straight line, so you go in an oval until you get back where you started. While you're on your oval, you make all the stops you need to make along the way."

Then it hit me square between the eyes and I looked at him in awe. I think Terry invented the whole oval system thingy. He does work for the government and he's always driving around in a government truck changing this thing and that, along the way.

"Yes, he's the guy!" I thought.

The last thing he said before driving off left me in a total state of awe.

"Well, I'm off," he said.

Before he left, I took a quick look at the seat of his truck. Lying there, upon his seat was a normal-incidence spectrometer (NIS) and a grazing incidence spectrometer (GIS).

I knew what he was going to do. He was going to reflect the (NIS) beam off two toroidal gratings (2400 and 4000 lines/mm) and focus them to an intensified charge-coupled device (ICCD) detector, while the GIS beam is directed to a spherical grating (1000 lines/mm) set at grazing incidence and deflected to four other thingys.

I stood there and watched him drive off and I thought, "Gosh, that guy works really, really hard while he travels on his oval." We are very lucky to have a government guy like him. Now that I think of it, his dad was a government guy too. I think he worked in Human Oval Management (HOM).

Muon ringy thingy
8/7/2011

Lately I've been thinking about all kinds of stuff. It's like every time I look at something it goes straight to my brain and then, BOOM, I get a great idea. Now I've got some real doosies each of which is capable of making us all rich.

Express. There on the front page was a picture of my old friend, John Donlevy. What a fine figure of a man he is. Why, next to me he is probably the best looking guy in Winters.
Not only is he handsome, he is our faithful City Manager, and a fine one at that. Next to me, he is probably the smartest guy in Winters too. What a guy, and he's my best friend too. I absolutely love this guy!

That being said, let's go back to the picture in the paper. Besides the good looking City Manager is another fella and he's handing a great big check to my friend John. The check is about 3 feet wide and 5 feet long. On the check are big numbers that say $525,000 payable to the city of Winters.

Yaa Hoo, that's what I'm talking about. My friend John has half a million big ones! I'm going to call him up and tell him that we should use that money to build my Muon ring. John and I have tossed that ball around before so he'll know exactly what I'm talking about.

Now that my buddy John has the money he can buy 50,344 pieces of 4' OD concrete pipe that will make up the Muon Ring. The ring will go from my house around to the City of Davis and back to good old Winters.

Since John is providing most of the money, he will get 10% of the profit, the City of Winters will get 10% too, and I get the rest since it's my idea. The money is just going to roll in like boulders down a mountain. Since John and I are probably going to spend all that money here in town, you all will get some too, in a sense. We'll discuss that later.

There's one catch to this whole Muon ringy thingy. It ain't real. None of the other Muon Rings are either, so here's what we have to do. John will get at one corner of the ring and I'll get at the other corner.

John will act like he's throwing an atom at me and I'll act like I'm throwing an atom at him. The two atoms are supposed to smash against each other and make a mini-atomic explosion. My friend Steve and Terry will have to hide at another corner somewhere down in the ring. At the right time they can bang a rock on a barrel to make the sound of an explosion.

Who's gonna know the difference when nobody can see a damn atom anyway. There are some pretty smart people over in Davis but I don't think that they can see an atom either. If they can then all we have to do is not let them come to Winters.

Everybody will come to see our Muon Ring and we can charge each one of them a dollar just to look. For an extra .50 cents they can touch it and have somebody like my son Joey take a picture for another dollar. Let's see, that's over two dollars and something for each person.

I've thought of everything because way down the road in the future, when everybody has seen our Muon Ring, we can cut off our end of the ring so that it will now be like a big "U". Now we have another money making idea, in living color.

We then hook up our two ends of the big "U" to our sewer lines and send all of our sewage down to the City of Davis. It might smell a little bit but those people over in Davis are used to it.

I have other moneymaking ideas that are just as good as or better than the Muon Ring thingy. You're not going to believe how easily this idea will make us all super-rich.

It seems that our President, Mr. Obama, is looking for a town that will dispose of tons of spent radioactive fuel. I guess the people in Nevada don't want it anymore. Well, their loss is our gain, because I have the perfect plan.

My friend John Donlevy can call President Obama and tell him that we will take all of the radioactive waste that they have for 1 dollar an isotope or whatever they call them. It doesn't matter, we'll take it all.

What we have to do is put all of the radioactive stuff into big dump trucks and take it down to the big sandstone caves at the top of the hill, just before you reach the Berryessa Dam. We tell Obama that we are going to put the isotopes, or whatever, into the big caves. They won't ever check so all we really have to do is back the trucks into Putah Creek and dump it.

That's right, dump it in the creek and send it all to the City of Davis. All those people that live in Davis are too busy riding their bikes to Winters so they can get out of Davis. They are always wearing their spandex shorts with those funny hats on their heads. They won't have a clue.

Those people from Davis are so dumb that they still ride their bikes across the traffic bridge even though we built them a bicycle bridge that is safer for them. I think that those spandex shorts are cutting off the blood to their brains. We can send anything downstream to them and they'll never know.

What do ya say John Donlevy, let's build this Muon Ringy thingy?

Google ads reveal a lot about your friends
8/28/2011

Have you ever noticed how smart those Google guys are? I use Google's search engine every day and it never ceases to amaze me how much information is available in such a very short period of time.

There are other search engines that you might consider better than Google, but I'm a creature of habit and Google seems to be ethical, accurate and well-balanced, so I keep using them.

I also use Google's email services and I have several accounts that are invaluable to me. I use one account for email and a couple of other accounts for storage, all of which is free of charge.

Google responds to each letter you type into its search box almost instantaneously with a list of ever changing results. This is surely the "Information Age."

Google takes information that it gathers from its users to place advertisements on its web pages that it thinks will draw your interest. For instance, if you type the word "pool" into your email message there might be an advertisement for swimming pools and another for pool tables.

The Google Document service allows documents to be accessed and edited by multiple users simultaneously. I love this service because my editor can rewrite my column as I am writing it. You might say I'm "Googleized."

Every person that sends me an email or responds to one of mine has their own unique advertising. If you pay attention to the ads, they can give you vital information about the person you're communicating with. This information is very accurate.

For instance, my wife's email will have ads about shopping, buyers' choices, and sometimes an ad for a service that will tell you if your mate is lying to you. (With pictures and videos if you want to pay for them.)

Debra DeAngelo, my editor, has ads like, "Hayward-Baker Aggregate piers, Porch and Patio Columns, Query Acceleration, and Fast Indexing services."

Anna, my sister-in-law, has ads about travel, investment pricing, designer clothing, and trips and charters. My other sisters-in-law, Jody and Nancy, have ads about AAA Insurance, Big Bubble Solutions (window covers), and Christmas gifts.

Stephanie Myers, our local turtle tagger, has ads about physical therapy, ankle surgery, and Green Sea Turtles.

Libby Earthman of the Putah Creek Council has ads about Flower Gift shops, New Women's social Networks, Plant engineers, and project management.

Sara Tremayne, also of Putah Creek Council, has ads like Modesto Irrigation, Smart Hydroponics, Orcut U C Davis, and water pumps.

My friend from high school, Judy Stroup has ads like Insurance CE for Ethics, Argosy University, code of ethics, Professional ethics, Business Ethics, and again, project management.

My photographer friend Tracy J. Thomas has ads about Franchise Laws, Official BP Claims site, Mailing Lists (85 million decision makers) and the Blackberry Smartphone.

Madge Woods, a writer friend who lives in LA, carries ads like, Melville Johnson consultations, Guide to IP Phones, Mailing Lists, Best Hotels in Belize, and Nice Travel services.

Christy Sillman, another writer friend has ads like the Toughest Trail Run in California, BP's Work in the Gulf, Michelle Obama Pictures and Gulf of Mexico Response Systems.

Nancy G. Mills, Director of City Administrative Services for the City of Winters, has ads like Soundproof Drywall, Open Source Intelligence, California Commissions Advances, and of course City of Winters ads.

My poet friend Sandra McPherson has ads about eFollett Text Books, Xlibris Book Publishing, and skunk removal. I think that the last ad concerns me somehow.

So if you pay attention to the ads that accompany emails, you'll find that they paint a pretty accurate picture of what the person may have been doing. I'm not sure if this is good or bad.

Ads that accompany my email are tell-tell too. I have one that concerns people that have been barred from MacDonald's (I kept getting hurt in their little playgrounds). Mental hospitals, man bras, and deodorant ads seem to show up a lot on my email pages too.

Yeah, you're right, that's a little too much information. Now you have that picture in your head about me and man bras. Good luck with that.

Fearless rock hunters face new challenges
9/4/2011

I fear that my way of life will be soon altered forever. Events that are out of my control are changing everything for me and I'm not sure if the effects of these events will trickle down, down, down, the hill to where the rest of you are. Of course, I speak platonically — perfect in form or conception but not found in reality.

My friend Steve is a big, tough, figure of a man, but when I told him about the events that may be just out of sight and headed our way, he began to cry like a baby girl. I thought I was going to have to slap him around a bit to help him stop slobbering all over himself. I have to tell you that when I first heard of what was going to happen, I too felt like crying.

Brace yourself, I'm just going to blurt it out: There's is a new rock hunter in town.

I'll give you a few moments to soak in the news...

Up until now, my friend Steve and I were able to keep control of the rock hunting business in this area, "this area" being west of Interstate 505, south of Madison, north of Vacaville, and I don't know what our area is east of. Then a few years ago, there were terrible rock hunting wars around here because those guys that live in the next town, Davis, kept coming into our area and taking our rocks away.

You probably didn't hear about it, but there was a lot of shooting and beatings and it was all over rocks. Big rocks, little rocks, and all the other size rocks, was what those other guys were after; our rocks. Anyway, it was decided in the courts that Steve and I were in control over whatever rocks were lying around here, and those other guys didn't get anything. They drove off crying like little girls.

Not since those great rock hunters' wars has there been such a threat to our rockdom. I'm afraid that this new rock hunter will cause some waves in the sandbox. I heard about him weeks before I actually came face to face with him. It seems that he is really, really good at rock hunting.

I had figured him to be one of those 98-pound geeks like those other guys from the next town. I was dead wrong! This new rock hunter's name is Andrew Tremayne, and I'm afraid that he is a "Master Rock hunter!" There is a tidbit of information that makes this even more important. Mr. Tremayne has moved to my town! Ta da!

Like I said, I thought he was going to be a little geek, and like I said, "I was wrong." The day I came face to face with this guy was Saturday the 13th of August. I was intent on doing some work for his wife, who happens to be Sara Tremayne, of Putah Creek Council fame. (Notice the same last name?)

So there I was, talking to Sara about which weeds I could cut down and which weeds were the good ones so don't cut them, right? All of a sudden, Sara says, "Donald, this is my husband, Andrew." So I jump around like that fat guy on Animal House and there he was. It was like slow motion. He was walking straight at me, offering his hand in a ritualistic peace offering. This guy was no geek. I've seen geeks before, and he is not one of them.

Anyway, this guy is like a cool drink of water — hexagonal water! You're not going to believe it, but at first I thought he was Charlton Hesston, except for the fact that Andrew is better looking. To make things worse, he is a trained, highly educated, professional rock hunter who has hunted rocks all over the stinking globe! Not only that, he has a whole crew of rock hunters with shovels and little brushes that live in tents wherever he tells them to pitch them. I looked online and I swear that he carries a shotgun while he's on his "digs," as he calls them.

This is a nightmare! The Department of the Interior and U C Davis pays the guy to dig rocks and he travels by airoplane everywhere he goes. Normally, Steve and I would just bushwhack the guy and beat him up, but I don't think we're up to that task now. I don't know what to do, and Steve won't come out of his bathroom. When Steve saw the black and blue condition of my hand after Andrew had shook it, he just screamed and ran into the bathroom. His wife Kellie keeps banging on the door saying, "Steve come out of the bathroom!"

Anyway, all that we can hope for is that maybe this Andrew rock hunter guy comes in peace. I think I'll welcome him and his wife to Winters, since I'm still King of Winters, California.

For veterans, the battle begins when they come home
9/11/2011

Today, I'd like to provide you with some information about our nation's veterans that make up 28 percent of the nation's adult population.

Our veterans come from all walks of life and socioeconomic backgrounds. They live on the plains of Montana, in the high-rises and dumpsters of New York City, and what is left over fills the bunks of our penal system.

Most WWII vets are in their mid to late 80s and they are dying at a rate of more than 1,000 a day. Seventy is the average age of Korean War vets, and 58 is the average age of Vietnam-era veterans.

There are about 24 million veterans in the US today. Wartime veterans number around 17 million and about 7 million served in peacetime. The largest segment of the veteran population is Vietnam-era vets. There are 8.4 million Vietnam vets that make up 31.71 percent of the total veteran population.

California has the largest population of vets, numbering 2,257,130, with Florida coming in second with 1,768,359. New York, Ohio, Pennsylvania and Texas have more than one million each.

While the VA estimates that the proportion of male veterans will continue to decline, the number of female vets is on a steady rise. Women make up just over 6 percent of all veterans. This percentage is expected to increase to 8 percent this year.

Some 19.5 million vets (81 percent) are white. African Americans make up about 10 percent of the veteran population and Hispanics follow at 1.3 million (5 percent). Other races, including Asian, American Indian and Polynesian, make up about 3 percent of all veterans.

The unfortunate truth is that the real challenge begins when these service men and women return home and readjust to day-to-day life.

According to the National Alliance to End Homelessness, 45 percent of the country's estimated 131,000 homeless veterans are black. Overall, 42 percent of the nation's homeless population is African American.

Of the 7.5 million vets enrolled in the VA health care system, about 5.4 million used VA medical care last year.

After the Vietnam War ended, reports began to circulate of veterans so depraved from their war experiences that they were inclined to turn to a life of crime to survive post-war civilian life. Estimates of the number of incarcerated Vietnam veterans are as high as one-quarter of the US prison population.

In the aftermath of the Vietnam War, its veterans, who returned home not as heroes were labeled victims and losers, allegedly afflicted by inner demons manifesting themselves in high rates of drug addiction, alcoholism, unemployment, homelessness and suicide.

That stereotype is often seen in Hollywood movies. In the recent blockbuster "Independence Day," one of the main characters is a goofy, alcoholic Vietnam veteran who humiliates his children by crop-dusting the wrong fields. The only way he can atone for his failed life and save the world is by committing a final act of fiery suicide.

An analysis of data from the Department of Defense shows the average age of men killed in Vietnam was 22.8 years.

Pentagon officials estimated for the first time this year that up to 360,000 Iraq and Afghanistan veterans may have suffered brain injuries. Among them are 45,000 to 90,000 veterans whose symptoms persist and warrant specialized care.

Ten to twenty percent of returning soldiers have suffered at least a mild concussion. Among them, are 3-5 percent with persistent symptoms that require specialists, such as an ophthalmologist to deal with vision problems.

We have now nearly two million vets of Iraq and Afghanistan and we still haven't seen the type of mobilization of resources necessary to handle an expected epidemic of veteran suicide. Of the 18 veterans who commit suicide every single day, five are under the care of the VA.

The VA came under attack by veterans' groups in April 2008, when internal emails sent by the VA's head of mental health, Dr. Ira Katz, showed that the VA was attempting to conceal the actual number of veterans that blow their own brains out every single day.

Of the more than 30,000 total suicides in this country each year, fully 20 percent of them are acts by veterans. Last year, the suicide rate per 100,000 veterans among men ages 18-29 was 44.99. It has now jumped to 56.77.

When you see a homeless person walking down the road, the chances are that you are looking at a veteran. If you wonder why prison populations are rising, it's because alarming numbers of veterans are being sent there to live in cages like an animals, after being arrested for minor drug infractions.

I, in fact, am one of those veterans. As such, I can handle any crap that is thrown in my face by an uncaring society. It is also true that if it ever gets to the point where I cannot handle such a good life, I can always take the easy way out. Sadly, if the VA has anything to say about it, you, the public, will never know I existed.

A few words of truth is all we're asking for
9/18/2011

There are a lot of interesting things going on in the world today. I try very hard to keep up with current events. In this information age, you'd think this task easy, but it's not.

How often do we hear of the censoring of world news by the Chinese government. All the time, right? Well, truth be known, our government hides much of the truth from us under the guise of security. Let's take a look at world events.

Much of the news that I read is heartbreaking. For example, today I read that every 10 minutes, someone in the US is diagnosed with AIDS. I can't help but think about what these statistics will be like when my grandchildren reach adulthood.

I'm constantly reading that the legal profession has become nothing but big business. Nationwide it is a multibillion-dollar operation. It is becoming harder these days to distinguish legal America from corporate America.

The low salaries of judges create discontent among ethical judicial candidates. Thus we are left with judges and lawyers ready to bend to the will of corporate America and it's high dollar salaries. With this in mind, it's not hard to understand why the penal system is crowded with minor offense criminals. Each and every inmate is worth $45,000 to big business.

Crime is now high tech. Hackers can use texting to intercept messaging between our new high-tech cars and their networks. This accomplished, they can now alter command messages to virtually say anything they wish, including "open the door" and "start the car."

On July 28, a senate committee secretly voted to renew "warrantless wiretapping." The meeting was secret but not classified, so you can demand to know how your senator voted.

Yesterday, I read that if you type "Is it rude to f" in the Google search box, one result will be, "Is it rude to fart when someone is crying?"

Women are discovering that gender equality isn't that great after all.

Ten percent of Americans claim to have seen a ghost.

The worst job in the United States is porno theater janitor.

South Korean scientists have created a dog that glows in the dark.

More and more women are returning to computer science in the nation's universities.

In 2002, Moxie Marlinspike introduced a program called "Sslsniff," a traffic sniffing tool. A new revision of this tool can now make the program capable of hacking your iPhone and iPad. Marlinspike claims that this is so easy that his mother can do it. Apple's latest fix for this was intercepted by hackers. Thus, the fix was rendered useless until a new one can be issued.

Wearing headphones for just one hour can increase the bacteria in your ear up to 700 percent.

China is now largest English speaking country on Earth.

Today I found that the three principles of what to eat are:

1. Know what foods cause accelerated fat burning.

2. Know the particular foods that prevent you from burning fat.

3. Put the right foods together in a certain way to create the fat burning effect.

There was even a story about a guy that got rich selling Facebook pages.

World events have gone absolutely insane and I fail to see any action that could be taken to make it better.

A new report from the Substance Abuse and Mental Health Services Administration (SAMHSA) shows a 49 percent increase in emergency room visits for drug-related suicide attempts for women aged 50 and older.

A new study claims to have discovered there is a turning point for the spread of ideas. If 10 percent of the world's population accepts an idea as truth, the majority of the rest of the world will follow suit; for example, the spread of Islamic Democracy in the Middle East and the prosecution of former President Mubarak. These ideas now seem unstoppable.

If less than 10 percent of the world accepts an idea as truth, then the idea will drift slowly out of sight and is lost in "bad idea land."

Of all of the stories I've read lately, it's the Wiki leaks documents and videos that have brought many of us to our knees. It is raw, official information about the war in Iraq and Afghanistan that was hidden from us, the public.

When I think about this, I'm torn in two directions. To the left is US security and to the right the unrestrained murder of civilians and the following high echelon cover-up. These reports are hard to dispute as the truth.

Words of truth from our government about its activities are all we can ask for. Once, long ago, this was understood. Now, it's not often that we get the truth unless someone steals it and puts it on the internet.

Words of truth have the power to persuade. They are the windows to the soul. Words are slippery things and they have consequences. They influence our actions.

All we can do is follow our inner voices.

Don't believe everything that you read. Seek your own truth. We must understand that truth is not merely words; it is the performance of those words.

Only a government of tyrants will seek to hide the truth.

Yesterday I was wrong
9/25/2011

I wrote this on September 11, but for some reason I didn't send it in. I don't know why, maybe because of the mood I was in on that day of remembrance. Now I think that I'd like people to know how I felt on 9/11/2011:

Yesterday, on September 10, I would have written about the commercialization of the horrible events of "9/11." That was the way that I was feeling yesterday. Today I feel differently, today I feel sad, very sad.

This morning I found that when I turned on the television, 9/11 was thrust upon me like a bright light followed closely by a deep dark cloud, a cloud of sadness. I was taken back in time, a full decade, to that dreadful day. I could not escape from the sadness, for I found I was encompassed by it in many ways that I had never considered.

The events of this day sucked me in like soda through a straw. The sheer magnitude of somber remembrance hit me like a ton of bricks as it spread sadness tirelessly until it encircled the entire world. That is how I felt today.

The anger is gone and it is nowhere to be found. I think that this is a good thing. I am disgusted with the wars in Iraq and Afghanistan. I think that there were other, better roads to take to get to where we are now. Roads that would not run parallel and equally evil with the original deeds that took us there in the first place.

The ceremonies of remembrance that I viewed today were respectful and heartfelt in their depth. There was nothing commercial in any of this long day's recollection of such evil events that make you want to forget and remember them at the same time. There was no finger pointing, no blaming, and no anger; only a deep respectful memorization of those who passed on and are now frozen in time like words chiseled into marble.

I remember those dreadful moments when those buildings collapsed into themselves, turning so many loved ones into so much pink vapor. The vision of it is burnt into my brain. Our mighty nation has yet to recover from that day, a decade ago.

Today, as I think about what is happening around the world, I can visualize how those evil events have changed our world. Most recently, the entire Middle East is engulfed in a life and death struggle for freedom and equal rights. There is a ravenous hunger for democracy everywhere around the globe. It is a child of 9/11.

In the end, there will be many after-effects of 9/11. They will ripple around the world like the Japanese tsunami. They both have similar and devastating results on every facet of our lives. The initial horror and sadness was followed by the near collapse of real estate sales and stock markets on Wall Street. Those who we consider to be our enemy have accomplished what they intended. The nation traversed fear, anger and every other emotion except one — forgiveness.

As I said before, 9/11 has rippled around the world in the guise of hate, violence and anger. It forever grows within the generations of humanity that were witness to 9/11. Neither side can forgive the trespasses of the other so it will be for generation upon generation, forever and ever, upon this planet called Earth.

Thoughts that come and go on a day at war
10/2/2011

Have you ever found yourself in a situation where you find that you have a worried mind? You know that you're going to die, but you don't want to leave anything behind. Your mind will begin to wander where it will.

Penny Paluska, my girlfriend in high school is with me, sitting in my lap, and drinking a Pepsi. Her tan skin in my eyes and the smell of her hair in my nose keeps me looking up at the sapphire sky, hoping that the last plane will come for me.

It's like I'm standing on my toes with my head in a noose. Any minute now I'm expecting the crap to hit the fan, I'm locked in tight, there's no escape. I check for a round in the chamber.

I used to care but things have changed. My being in this war zone is doing no good. I should be back on the block at the Dairy Queen.

Just for a second, I thought I saw something out there, so I'm frozen stiff, I cannot move. When I get home I'm going to take some dancing lessons, I'm gonna look real cool, when I can move.

There's a lot of water under the bridge, and a lot of other stuff too. I want to say that I'm only passing through, my gun is loaded, but I'm out of range.

Back there, the rest are dead. I can still taste the vomit from his mouth as I tried to give him a last breath. The little hole in his chest was enough to make him drown in his own blood. I sat for a time and watched him go under till the blades hit the ground and the fire erupted.

I left him there for where I am now, a little closer to the end of my road. They are walking around and looking for me. I can hear them talking but I don't understand.

The smell of rice on an open fire wakes me up and brings me around. I need to get as far from here as I can; it's getting so hot, too hot to touch. I need to get outta here.

They are so close I can smell their fishy farts. If I make the wrong move, I'm dead. Penny Paluska has found someone else so she doesn't want me. I'm thinking I won't be here anyway.

I want to cry but I can't risk the noise. I had plans for Penny and I. Now they too are out of range. People are different when they fall out of love; they act so strange when you try to hold them close.

Things have changed now, Penny is at the university and I am lost in a ditch in Asia; lost. I want to fall in love with someone new; I want to live that life.

I found today that you can hurt someone and not even know. This time is an eternity and I think so slowly and my mind is in circles.

I think about the violent way out but these boys are not to be underestimated. I think that these men are probably the best soldiers on the face of the Earth. They live in holes under the ground that are as large as a city.

They walked a thousand miles carrying a rifle and 100 pounds of rice. There are thousands of them and they all want me dead. Now I'm beginning to think that I want me dead too.

I'm getting low down when I want to get high. I am searching the sapphire sky for my ride home with bugs running inside my shirt. I take the chance to move but I have to hurry. I can hear a whisper from a mouth to an ear. They are so near.

My pistol is cocked when I put it in my mouth. I'm thinking that I won't hear the report or see a flash. I won't be here. I'll be flying home to those I love and I'll sit in a tree in their yard.

Not even a click did I hear. My pistol is jam packed with mud and blood. I'm stuck here and I'm in love with a woman who won't even know my name.

I'll go to sleep now and dream of angels with gray hair in castles above the sea. When I wake up, I won't even be me; I can't ever get that back. Things have changed now and that is strange. I have a round in the chamber but I'm out of range.

Days later, I awoke in Quen Nhon military hospital, where I could cry all day, for a week, for a month. I have to look at the sapphire sky for the last plane to take me out of here.

DONALD K. SANDERS, RVN
1968

Buds
10/29/2011

My friend Steve retired this week. I don't think he knows exactly how he feels about this, but I am simply elated. I think that we're like two peas from the same pod.

For over half of his life (at this point in time) Steve worked one of those high stress jobs that would drive a normal man to the depths of despair. That's where I come in.

Steve and I are Buds. When we do something or go somewhere we do it for one reason. We want to relax and have fun. Well, I guess that's two reasons but who's counting.

I write about Steve and our exploits all the time; so much in fact that some people have asked me if I'm gay for him. Well I can tell you that this is not the case, at least I don't think I am. Na, I'm not. I can tell you that, for sure.

Anyway, if you would happen to see the two of us together you would probably think. "Man that Don Sanders guy is really, really, good looking." Also, it might not be readily apparent what we have in common.

No, we're not off in the bushes playing "kissy face" as you might suspect. What we have in common is mental. I know that if you know Steve, you would find this hard to believe. Steve is not very mental.

The fact of the matter is that we are able to talk to each other about things that we would not normally discuss with others. You see, both of us, in our life experiences, have had to deal with human behavior in its worst form.

I'm sure that this is true of most people. We all have seen bad things and I'm sure that we all would describe this experience as evil. I know this is true.

When it comes to Steve and I, well, my bad experience was of the worst nature in the form of warfare and Steve's was slightly different but his experience was stretched out on a daily basis for over half of his life.

Yep, that's it. What we have in common is brutal and unrelenting inside of our little noggins. Bad thoughts about what we have seen or experienced are just banging and bouncing around inside our heads.

Steve would tell me things about what happened at work that he might not tell other people. When I say he had a high stress job, I mean high stress. It is really unbelievable, the things that some people have to do and see while working; all to make a comfortable life for your family and loved ones.

I know that you are all wondering what Steve's job was but for that answer you will have to ask Steve. I wouldn't go there though because you will open up a can of worms that you can't put a stopper in. On and on and on, the story will go. It never ends. I call Steve "Motor Mouth" behind his back.

Yeah, when Steve wants to relax or talk about something he comes to see me. One time his wife Kellie told him that he had to stop bringing "junk" home because they were running out of room.

He came over to see me so maybe we could figure out why Kellie would consider all of this good stuff to be "junk." Well this went on for some time and, I don't know how, but before I knew it my wife Therese says,"Tell Steve not to bring any more junk over."

So as it turns out, when Kellie calls something "junk" it is not without merit. I was amazed when I looked around my yard to see plows, harnesses, grinding wheels, and old metal five gallon milk jugs. I thought, "When did he bring all of that junk over here?"

It's like magic! Junk is attracted to Steve like metal to a magnet. I hadn't noticed, but every time Steve came over to "talk," he was bringing over a piece of junk that Kellie wouldn't let him keep. Now my wife was all up at arms wanting me to move this junk around the yard.

She says, "Can't you stack it all behind the shed?" Well, I could do that, but then my neighbor, Jose, would take a stick and push the pile back over into my yard. What would that gain?

Another reason Steve and I hang out is "rock hunting". We are like the primo rock hunters of Winters, California. Now we've been asked not to bring any more rocks home. Will the agony never end!

To make matters worse, there's a new rock hunter in town that everyone says is a better rock hunter than we are. This cannot be true, but I worry about it all the time. He doesn't rock hunt to have fun, like us, he does it for a job.

Steve and I don't get paid like he does, and people don't call us "professor" or "archeologist" either. So Steve comes up with this idea to get even. He tells me that we have to make up a diploma on Photoshop that says we are professors too.

Well it didn't take long, because I know how to draw pictures on a computer, until we had a nice looking diploma. It said: University of Tennessee, Greetings, Professors of Archeology, Donald Sanders and Steven Shafer, Rock Hunters Extraordinaire. (Sounds French)

I emailed this to rock hunter Andy Tremayne. He was probably pretty impressed and showed it to his friends at his lab at UC Davis.

Some quotes to live by
11/16/2011

Today is "*Talk About Quotes Day*." Everybody has their own favorite quotes. Everybody uses quotes to support an idea or to illustrate a point. We all do, don't we? We all do the same thing. We read through hundreds of famous quotes until we find one that means something to us. We like a quote because it talks to us, it tells the truth. At least we think it does.

Some very famous quotes mean absolutely nothing at all. Others, equally as famous, mean something entirely different than we thought it would. For example, in the Bible, Chapter 22, paragraph 21, Jesus says, "Render therefore unto Caesar the things that are Caesar's; and unto God the things that are God's." Well, if you are as smart as I am you'll know what this means.

I'll tell you exactly what it means. Say you have three asses and three bottles of bad wine when the tax man comes to your door. When the doorbell rings, you hide your asses and get drunk because if he sees you he's going to take it all. Unless of course you can prove that it all belongs to God, but the tax man doesn't want to hear that stuff anyway, so it's pay up or go to jail.

Most of the quotes from famous people like Jesus don't apply to us anyway because Caesar owns us all, and what we think don't make no nevermind. To Caesar, hog feathers and tooth fairies are the same as justice, mercy and duty. If you think that I'm mistaken and have it all wrong, just show me one atom of mercy or one atom of justice, and I'll be the first to admit that I'm wrong.

Now we'll move on to some of the famous quotes that I've written through the years and I'll explain in layman's terms (dummy's terms) exactly what they mean. Now you're thinking to yourself, "Boy that Don Sanders sure is smart, and he's very good looking too." Of course, you will be right.

Quote # 1: "Honesty is not only the best policy, it's the only policy!" I wrote this just before World War I while on vacation in the Alps. What this means is that it's not advisable to lie because the government has a new camera that can tell when we're lying. The computerized system uses a simple video camera with high-resolution thermal imaging sensors and a suite of algorithms.

I think algorithms are some kind of music.

Anyway, this new camera captures our emotions, given away in our eye movements, dilated pupils, biting or pressing together our lips, wrinkling our noses, breathing heavily, swallowing, and blinking. These are just the visible signs seen by the camera. Even swelling blood vessels around our eyes betray us, and the thermal sensor spots them immediately.

Quote # 2: "If it ain't one then it must be the other." A fine example of this quote comes from a company that makes a computer program called "Turnitin" that can tell if a student has plagiarized his school papers. The same company makes another program called "Writecheck" that will tell a student if his paper will pass the "Turnitin" test. This company will do great things because they want to get it coming and going, just like the taxman.

Quote # 3: "There's a sucker born twice every minute." This one I learned the hard way. This quote is best illustrated by looking at what NASA is doing with all of the old leftover space food that was manufactured in the 1970s and early '80s.

NASA is selling all their leftover space food to grade schools so our kids can taste space food that was made in the 1970s and early '80s. Yummy!

Quote # 4: "If you don't want to get screwed, fire all of congress and move your money out of the big bank and put it in the small bank." I just wrote this and you know in your heart that I'm right about this. You need to fire your big bank and every single person on Capitol Hill and replace them with the people that the City of Winters, where I live. I think they'd do a capital job of running this country. The FBI and the CIA can be replaced by the people at the Winters Police Department. I don't know what those guys on the Hill are doing wrong, but I do know one thing for sure. Unlike the FBI and the CIA, you can't get a thing past the Winters P.D. Go ahead and try it! You will see how true Quote number 3 is.

Quote # 5: "You may forget what I have said, but it doesn't matter anyway"

The time is right, and we're waiting
10/11/2011

I have seen many wonderful things. Life consists of a constant series of events. Depending on how we react to them, they push us to and fro, molding us into who we are. Of the innumerable amount of events encountered during our lifetime, 98 percent of them are repetitive, day-to-day chores and interactions that simply, slip in and then slip out of our lives.

They draw very little attention in their passing. It's only natural that we consider some events to be positive and others to be negative. It seems to be a fact that the events that stand out in our memories are primarily negative in nature, for they differ from the others and require special attention. They stand out like a sore thumb or a flat tire. They draw responses that are unpredictable and unexpected.

The remaining two percent of events are those that are considered to be life-altering. They occur less frequently and are considered more important. These events are capable of affecting your behavior for many years. Take, for instance marriage, birth, and the death of our loved ones. The majority of these greater events are still personal in nature, for they will alter your life but may have no affect on your neighbor.

These events may come to us less frequently, but they are noticed and we remember them. They shape and mold our lives within our small individual family and peer groups. The end of the Vietnam War, the fall of the Berlin Wall, and a Russian daughter-in-law are all as significant to me as the birth of my children, the birth of my grandson, and my own passing from this world to the next.

If well thought out, it becomes obvious that each and every event that occurs in our lifetime should be considered as wonderful. Even the worst of events will, in fact, mold us and give us direction if they're looked at in a positive manner.

There are a few outstanding events capable of altering the behavior of the entire world. The birth of Buddha, Christ, and Muhammad (alphabetical order) are all representative of positive major events. Major events are indiscriminate and human in nature. They affect us all, equally. This type of event will ripple through time and space to touch us all. No barrier can block its progress.

I would have to state that the events of the civil rights movement of the 1950s and '60s stand out as one of the most wonderful of events that I have been witness to. The struggle for human rights and the events that surround it have had a profound affect on me and the way that I think. Today's actions are deeply rooted in the major religious events that I mentioned above. In truth, these events, more than any other, will define me and my generation as a whole.

In recent years, we have witnessed the election of a man of color to the highest and most powerful office on the face of the Earth. In the very near future, we may be witness to one of the greatest events since the beginning of recorded history.

At this very moment in time, two people with differing philosophies are moving in opposite directions. Eventually they will turn to meet in dialogue. This event will be the birth of world peace. I believe Barak Obama to be capable of an event such as this, for they are accomplished only if the right person has the opportunity to do exactly the right thing at exactly the right moment.

The world yearns for peace and we are ripe with leadership that is willing to take us there. Yes, I have seen many wonderful things. We are in the midst of a major event that has given the world a faith renewed. The eyes of the entire world are once again gazing toward the United States with great hope and a growing love.

They wait patiently, for they know that the event they've been hoping for is near. They await the event that will be seen as the birth of world peace. Never before in our history have the conditions for such an event been better.

Eventually, Donaldlogic will replace science
10/30/2011

There is so much information on the internet that I find hard to believe. Some of it just doesn't make sense. Maybe it's because I am so darned smart (and good looking too) but when I read some of the things online, it makes me worry about the survival of science as a whole. I think that eventually there will be no science at all and what will remain will be called "Donaldlogic."

I'll begin with a guy named Noah Fierer, an assistant professor of ecology at the University of Colorado at Boulder. He says, "A significant percentage, anywhere from 10 to over 50 percent of airborne bacteria, seems to be derived from feces." If he had stopped right there I might have fell for it.

This Fierer guy claims that his study shows that the fecal bacteria in the air, comes from dogs. Okay, what's wrong with this statement? One, dogs poop on the ground. Two, dogs don't have airborne poop. Finally, three, birds poop in the air or on your car. I rest my case. Airborne fecal bacteria come from birds!

Am I smart or what? Onward and upward. According to the National Oceanic and Atmospheric Administration, mysterious orange goo that collected on shorelines near a village in Alaska is made up of fungal spores. This statement made me wonder why such a well-respected organization would use a word like "goo?"

If you list all of the words in the world that include "goo" you get only two words.

If you make a list the words you will get:

~ Burgoo

~ Goo

Alphabetically:

~ Burgoo

~ Goo

Sorted by length:

~ Burgoo

~ Goo

How common the words are: (depending on if you are French or like the rest of us)

~ Burgoo

~ Goo

More fun facts:

About seven million cars are junked each year. That's a lot of cars. What I don't understand is why can't we sell them back to the company that made the junk?

The sunlight that strikes the Earth at any given moment weighs as much as an ocean liner. Now I know how lucky I really am because in all the years of my life, not once, have I gotten hit by heavy sunlight.

If you are ever in a contest to see who can throw a baseball farther, make sure that you are the one that throws the ball toward the West. Because of the rotation of the Earth, it will go farther than a ball thrown toward the East.

A broadcast voice can be heard sooner 13,000 miles away than it can be heard at the back of the room where it originates. "How can this be," you may ask? Duh! Radio waves travel at 186,000 miles per second and sound waves crawl along at 700 miles an hour.

A broken clock is right at least once a day.

If you have a tapeworm in your stomach, it can come up while you are sleeping to lick the salt off of your lips. Ewwww!

If you suffer from Polythelia, you have three nipples. (I always thought it was a pimple.)

Some interesting words that I found or may have made up, I'm not sure:

Starvermerdivorous: A person that is so hungry, he will eat cow dung.

Doublehirplenoworkie: A person trying to be unnoticed while walking with a limp in both legs.

Semi-mattoid: A person who is not insane from birth but thinks he is.

Literaryshilpit: A word that is totally useless.

Donaldidiolalla: A crazy condition in which a person makes up his own language.

Spouseorixatrix: A nasty old hag that you are married to.

One more thing and then you can go on your merry way. I am compelled to say that, once again I have not been nominated for "The Citizen of the Year." It is beyond me how a person of my stature, with such incredibly good looks can go, year after year without even a nomination. How can this be? I am really worried that there may be way too many Frenchmen living in my town.

Turn up the volume
11/6/2011

It seems like I'm always asking people to turn up the volume on the TV or radio. It has always been like that for me. People would say, "God, are you hard of hearing or what?" I guess I am, but it wasn't bad enough to keep me out of the army.

There's a story behind my hearing problems, but it's not a pretty story. Up until this very moment in time, I have told no one else this story. I want to tell it to you now.

My two brothers and I lived in a one-room apartment behind the dry cleaners where my mother worked. Our building was jammed into the middle of a whole block of three story apartment buildings. Various small businesses were in a neat row along the ground floor of each building.

I'd like to say it was a nice neighborhood but it wasn't. It was in the middle of what was known as "Murder City" or downtown Detroit as it's known now. It was not a good place to be.

My older brother, Tony, was always off running someplace, so it was pretty much up to me to watch after my younger brother Michael while my mother was working. I couldn't have been much older than 6 years old, my brother 4 or 5.

Have you ever had a terrible day and you can't ever forget even a single moment of it? My brother Michael and I share the same memories of a terrible day. We had been through so much already, so I was always on the lookout for danger but Michael was so young, and he didn't know.

We played in the alleys behind the buildings because there was so much traffic in the front. We were throwing rocks and pieces of concrete at the rats in the trash when a big car came down the alley, splashing the puddles of new rainwater onto the buildings on both sides of the alley. The car stopped right in front of my brother and I.

A man with a plaid shirt got out of the car and asked us if we wanted a dollar. Before I could stop him, Michael was running toward the man, and I was right behind him. The man grabbed my brother and threw him into the car. Before I knew it, he had hit me and I was lying on the wet bricks of the alley.

My head was ringing so loud that I couldn't hear myself yelling my brother's name. I was so dizzy from the punch that I couldn't stand up long enough to chase after the car. Michael was gone — kidnapped.

The next thing I know, my mother is being held by the cops and she's crying. A lady that I didn't know was wiping blood from my ear and I didn't know what was going on. The loud ringing in my ear kept me within my own world for some time and I wanted to stay in that world as long as I could. Outside of that world was hell.

The kidnappers apparently accomplished what they wanted, because my brother was found three days later, across town, where he was dropped off. When he got home he looked at me but he wasn't there. He had to be led around by the hand and he wouldn't say a word.

Two days later, a crowd of people had gathered in front of the dry cleaners, pointing and looking up. I went out from the dry cleaners to see my brother standing on a ledge at the roof of the building, looking down at me. People were yelling and crying, and Michael looked like he was going to jump. I looked around for someone to help us, but I couldn't move my feet.

There in the crowd, I saw a big black man, Mr. Molly. He shook his head with a worried look. Mr. Molly had caught me playing in his back yard swing with his daughter Kathy Molly. He had thrown me out of his yard and told me never to come back. It was the first time I had seen the ugly head of racism. Now I was pleading with him, with my eyes, to help my brother. There was nothing he could do but shake his head.

I think Michael was going to jump just as a fireman grabbed him from behind. Within six months or so, we were standing at the front door of a Catholic Orphanage in Little Rock. We were separated on the first night and it was many months before I saw him again. I walked past him on the playground and I didn't even know who he was, but I turned to see him turn and face me.

Michael raised his little hand like a Nazi salute and said "Hi." I raised my hand in the same manner and said the same. I stood there and watched as he turned and walked into the back door of the big children's home without turning around. That was many years ago.

Anyway, that's the story of my hearing trouble. Actually it's no trouble for me but it seems to be a lot of trouble for those that have to turn up the volume. Now, when I'm alone, it's foreign movies with subtitles for me most of the time, and I like that just fine.

Michael lives in San Jose and he too is a disabled vet. We've never talked about that day in Detroit or our time in the orphanage.

Didn't plan to become a veteran
11/20/2011

Another Veterans Day has come and gone. It's the same every year. It's hard for me to celebrate even though it's a holiday. I mean, it's not a religious holiday like Christmas or Easter. I know that it's a day that we can think about what our veterans have done for us. This is a good thing.

I, like many other men and women, never considered the fact that I might become a veteran. I just never thought about it when I joined the Army. I had other things in mind. When I signed on that dotted line, I was thinking about my younger brother, Michael. He had dropped out of high school during his freshman year to join the Marines.

The day that I took the oath that made me the property of Uncle Sam, he was already over there in the war zone without me. I couldn't leave him there alone. I knew that if I could just get over there, in the country, they would have to send him home. By law, two brothers cannot be sent to a combat zone unless they sign a waiver. Michael had not signed a waiver.

Six months later, I was on that big jet liner when its wheels hit the ground in the Republic of Vietnam. Vietnam was a real trip. It's outside of the box, you might say. I can only describe it like there's a hole in the wall to another reality. The hole is just big enough for you to stick your head through it to look around. After a year or so you can pull your head back out of the hole but that's all that comes out. Your head comes out but your mind is still there, inside of the hole.

Anyway, I'm getting sidelined here, so I'll get back to the original story. Where was I? Oh, yeah — as soon as I got in the country, I started the wheels turning to get my brother out. Amazingly, it was a rapid process because in just a few weeks, they shipped him out of the combat zone.

As it turned out, it was nothing I had done in the manner of notifying the right people that my brother had not signed the waiver. The magic trick was the letter that I sent my brother upon my arrival in Vietnam. He took the letter to his commanding officer and that's all it took. He was shipped out with orders to Okinawa, Japan.

As long as I was in th4e country, they could not send him back. Michael had signed up for four years in the Marines and I had signed up for three years in the Army. This meant that I could do my year-long tour in Vietnam and then go home, but then he would still be eligible to be sent back. He would still have time enough on his enlistment for another tour in Vietnam.

I had this covered too. I would have to stay there for two years or he would be sent back, so as it turned out I was there for two years, 1 month, and seven days. The day that I left Vietnam, Michael was already a civilian, back on the block, chasing round-eyed women. It worked out very nicely for me in that respect.

It was so hard for me to leave Vietnam. It was one of the worst days of my life. It seems very strange to say, but that's the way I felt at the time. It was so hard for me to walk away from my fellow soldiers that were still in harm's way. It was very hard and very sad for me, but they would not let me stay longer without a presidential directive or something similar.

I'm surprised that they let me finish my last tour of duty because they knew I was having some problems keeping my focus on the "Prime Directive," so to say. For me, nothing would ever be the same again. The Army had turned me into something that I wasn't supposed to be and for the life of me, I couldn't get back to what I was before. I didn't know how.

Anyway, that's what I think about on Veteran's Day. I think about how lucky Michael and I were to make it home at all. We were pretty screwed up, but we were alive and we had each other. We still have each other and when I look at him now, I still see my little brother, inside of an old man's body.

Revolt is written into our Constitution
12/4/2011

I turned on the TV the other day, just in time to see the news report about the protestors in Oakland and Sacramento. I thought that they did an excellent job of reporting on everything except what is really important — the reasoning behind the protest. Beating around the bush is another way of ignoring the issues.

The average American citizen is angry. They want change in the financial and military world. "Occupy Wall Street" is a child of this anger. Being ignored by the press has pissed off some of the protestors, so now they went and got all of their friends. The increasing number of protestors fortunately goes hand in hand with the amount of attention they get from the press. Sometimes this is good and sometimes it's bad. This time, I think it may be bad.

The mass media is owned and controlled by the high and mighty 1%. Five thousand protestors blocking streets, closing harbors and businesses has hit the high and mighty where it hurts: their wallets. Objective number one has been reached. We have their attention.

I don't think that you can dispute the fact that there are people in high places who want to pull all the strings. They have most of the strings in their fists and the rest of the strings are just out of reach. The high and mighty (I'd call them assholes but they would probably send someone to kill me) have control of our government and mass media. This, I feel, is certainly true.

With the government and media in their control, it's a surety that they hold the high ground. You can bet your buddy's ass that the press will no longer ignore the protestors. We are about to see the mass media at its best, or worst, depending on which side you are on.

Misrepresentation and misinformation are the tools that they will use. The protest movement has only righteousness and truth. It is essential that the protest remain peaceful and centered on the truth. The protest must remain within the laws of the land. If this protest movement resorts to violence of any sort, it is no longer a protest. It is a violent revolt.

Not long ago, I made the statement that I thought there was violence just around the corner. I think this is highly probable, for the protest lacks leadership and the issues have not been clearly stated. A peaceful protest movement in this condition is sure to fail, resorting to violence in the end.

Those in power, the 1% as they are called, have become a formidable enemy. Today, the mass media is grounded in "money and power." Its incredible influence can shape, distort and censor as they wish. As the protest gains momentum and those in power begin to feel threatened, we are sure to see the end of what we call "Free Press." Any appearance of objectivity will be gone. Mass media will go into attack mode. Journalism becomes propaganda that is enmeshed in discursive tactics, bent on control and profit.

In attack mode, some topics are certain to be avoided, suppressed, under-reported, or omitted by mass media. Minimal coverage is always devoted to protest, activism, or civilian death tolls.

Let's take a look at how we are controlled by the media. Ninety-nine percent of everything we know about the outside world comes from the media, most of which we assume is true. It encourages fear and patriotism. Mass media flourishes there.

Mass media has taken us from conflict to conflict, over and over, all of my life. The protestors of "Occupy Wall Street" will be dehumanized just as the

Vietnamese were in the '60s and the Muslims after 9/11. Mass media will frequent terms that it once reserved for Blacks and Hispanics. i.e. Muslims are no longer Americans, they are, "home born Muslims, or "American born Muslims." They are no longer called citizens. Moderate Muslim voices are routinely omitted from news coverage and terms like Islam and Muslim are only used in the context of conflict, violence and bloodshed.

We are told that they are a culture bent on the total destruction of non-Muslim life. Americans will be forced to choose a side. That "you are either with us or against us" mentality carries a lot of weight when you have a home and family that will influence your behavior. At some point in this struggle to get our government back, the high and mighty will invoke the anti-terrorist laws that were so quickly passed by our elected officials. "Terrorist" is the label that a violent protestor will wear.

The power of mass media can make the best of us voluntarily go to war and freely kill another human being that has been called "the enemy." (Set aside the fact that they have done nothing to us that would qualify them as "enemy.") We are then left to justify our actions to ourselves. I read a report on this very day that states that a veteran suicide occurs every 80 minutes in the United States.

Mass media has the power to make our enemies become less than human beings that must be destroyed in their "lairs" and they have to be baited, smoked out or trapped like animals. They stay in lairs or nests, not camps or bunkers.

If you're thinking that you can get back our government by voting the goons out of Washington, think again. You can only vote for who they tell you to vote for, or who is on the ballot. The simple truth is that much of society has already succumbed to those in power. They're like puppets on a string. Another simple truth is that no one knows who's really pulling the strings in this nation or why they seek such power.

I do, however, admire those who think they can change things. I admire their thoughts and reasoning behind what they do. I'd really like to be more like them and help them do what they want to do, but they must know one very important thing: There are those among us, mostly people of color, who have never known the rights that we have so foolishly given away. Should we be fortunate enough to win this country back, it must be a different country altogether. Revolt is written into the Constitution but it must be a revolt by the majority. Success hinges upon the majority including the minority.

Compassion
12/18/2011

My body is a cage for the beast within, dispossessed of any meaningful role in society, an insulated shield that keeps me from finding the hearts of others. In the end, there's no distinction between the living and the dead, the killer and the killed. I am spoiled. I am mingled with the dead, for we have but one body and heart. I have singled him out to death and he has singled me out to be a lowly killer.

I remember this point in my life and the decision I made at that time. A soldier that doesn't kill has compassion for life. Compassion has no place in a soldier's good. Compassion has no reason to fight and is lacking in its ability to kill without resounding reason.

Soldiers have complicated personalities in the midst of bloody conflict. At first contact, the least compassionate will likely kill the most compassionate, for the latter will hesitate and the former will not. This very act, the death of the compassionate, is the important defining factor, the reason for war. It becomes the dividing line that reasonable men will not want to cross by free will. Across that line are the unreasonable (I hesitate to call them men) entities that will traverse any line and thus become a threat to all with compassion.

Now I am back, again, at that point in my life when God gives me a sign. The way is clear, the direction pointed, for reasonable men of compassion will know the time has come to release the beast within themselves. War, at this point, is no longer a single side — there are two; side of aggression, evil without reason, without compassion, and across the line, stand those against, with the will and the want to see war to an end.

I have singled out, by decision, those aggressors without compassion within, to death. They have singled me out to be a lowly killer. The beast within is now without, and it goes directly to a terrible carnage that has but one purpose — a single purpose that seeks to destroy greed for another man's possessions, seeks the destruction of evil aggression and those that perpetrate it upon the Earth. The two sides of war have become indistinguishable for a moment in time — a long moment.

It is the will of God that we stand against those who bring evil upon us all. There are those who I've looked upon that I would consider evil. I have to say this is true. I'd like to think I stand against what I consider evil, but there's a difference between what I personally consider to be evil and what my government considers to be evil.

During my long days in combat, I was only a boy. I believed that my government would not mislead me. I believed what they said. I put on their uniform and I held their guns and I stood against their evil aggressors as I was sent to do. I was one of many that stood on the two sides of war.

I singled myself out as a killer and I singled my enemy for death. We two mingled, for we had but one living heart between us. I am where I always am and my body is but a cage for the beast within. I have no meaningful purpose in the society in which I live. I am isolated and insulated from the hearts of others.

My tears fall freely and frequently, and it will not cease because when I singled myself out as a killer and I singled my enemy out for death, I found that when it was over, I had seen no aggressor that was perpetrating evil upon the Earth or me. What I did see was a dead man, a Vietnamese man, who was not what I would consider evil.

It is to my eternal shame that I did not hesitate for just one moment, with the gift of compassion that was given to me by God, to ask him what he saw in me. I can only know what I can see. If I do not see the bad in my enemy, then he must surely see the bad in me.

Livermorium, shlivermorium — the world's going crazy
12/24/2011

The world seems to be going absolutely insane. We don't notice it because of its subtlety. To illustrate why I think this, I'd like to share some recent news events I found interesting. One small bit of news won't direct you to that conclusion, but if you bundle it all together, like packing snow into a ball, you can see a bigger picture.

Senator Kay Hagen (D) from North Carolina is angry because she can't receive her email. On Dec. 1, the Senator introduces a bill that would eliminate overtime pay for IT workers.

Time Warner Cable and U.S. Pay TV are on the verge of instituting fees for internet usage. Get ready to kiss watching free movies and TV over the internet goodbye. A spokesman for Time Warner stated, "This will be the best thing that ever happened to cable TV." Apparently they own the internet.

It is now more cost effective to sequence a genome than to analyze a genome. It seems that there is so much data to collect that researchers can't keep it all. Now they are trying to find a way to throw some of the data away. I'm thinking of opening a "Data Dump." That's "DD" for short. Don's Data Dump. Yeah, I could just dump all the data into the creek and let it go downstream to Davis where they like that sort of thing.

Google's open-source Android 4.0 operating system for smart phones and tablets is now ported to work with x86 processors. I guess that's why they call it open-source.

Scientists at the California Institute of Technology now have a therapy that will protect mice (with humanized immune systems) against HIV infections. The mice are injected with a genetically altered virus and then they are sent to the "stud farm" where they are given the HIV virus by some weird looking dude with big ears. Mice condoms are expected to be the new craze for Wall Street investors.

Terrorist organizations are using the Patriot Act against us. Foreign firms that do business in the area of cloud computing are being warned that any data shared with US firms will fall directly into the hands of US Intelligence and then passed on to the top half of the 1% that owns the Department of Home Security.

Chemistry's periodic table is welcoming newly named elements. I think that makes about 500 elements that we know of. Say hello to "Livermorium" and "flerovium." If you are typing these elements into your computer, you will need to add them to the dictionary or they will have a red jiggled line under them.

A pair of diamond crystals has been linked by quantum entanglement. It is one of the first times that objects visible to the human eye have been placed in a connected quantum state. Duh, who cares! It's only in second place, and who wants a diamond that small anyway.

The United Kingdom has launched a "code-cracking" competition to help attract new talent. I was going to enter the competition but I couldn't figure out how to read the application.

I just read a article about security programs, similar to McAfee, that are supposed to protect our private information from prying eyes. Well, it seems that they are complicit with government data gatherers in giving up your goodies to, you guessed it, the top half of the 1% that owns the Department of Homeland Security.

Friedman Freund from NASA and Dr. Rachel Grant from the UK's Open University have found that animals may sense chemical changes in the groundwater that occur when an earthquake is about to strike. The data just released says that there was a mass toad exodus just before the last big earthquake. There was also a lot of garbled information that I don't even care about. All I want to know is there the damn toads were going.

Since 2009, NASA has been gathering data using the agency's "Flame Extinguishing Experiment" or "FLEX" to better understand how fire behaves in microgravity. This explains why we no longer go to the space station and why NASA is selling all the space food to grade school kids.

There you have it in a nutshell. The sad part is that this is only today's news. I'm afraid to put more than one day's news together.

Things I want in the New Year
1/8/2012

Despite what he scribbles into his history books, man has never changed. Of the last 3,500 years, only 300 (more or less) have not seen war. A year with war is always more productive than a year with peace. We worship those who commit the utmost carnage upon the Earth. We raise the most violent among us to rank and privilege over us. The peacemakers have never been equal to the warriors.

Even in this great nation, we as individuals bow to governmental restraints because we live by morals, laws and the guarantee of basic protection of lives and property. On the other hand, the government acknowledges no restraints because it is large enough not to worry about interference with its will and there is no international law to offer it protection. The state has our instincts without our restraints.

There are more hungry people on the Earth than the populations of the U.S., Canada, and the European Union combined. Thus we find that there are only three things that will restore the balance between population and food production: famine, pestilence, and warfare. There is violence on every corner, and crime in every neighborhood.

Machines and computers have given us in the First World decades of global growth and wealth. We now live in the biggest credit bubble in the history of mankind. Worldwide port traffic has fallen by double digits. Air cargo has dropped by 23 percent. Friends are losing their houses, schools are closing, unemployment is almost as high as the Great Depression of 1929. We have lost faith in our government and no one on the hill seems to care.

No one knows what is going to happen or how we can make things better. Common people have taken to the streets with no real direction or purpose. Most are just angry and feel that any action, whether right or wrong, is better than no action at all. The future is looking bleak. Throughout human history, ages of wealth and great prosperity are always followed by hopeless ages that are dark.

Years of individual freedom and wealth in much of the world have led to the spike in population to over seven billion people. Of that number, one billion people go to bed hungry. We are fast approaching the point where the world cannot produce enough food and fresh water for everyone. Hunger and malnutrition are, in fact, the number one risk to our health worldwide — greater than AIDS, malaria and tuberculosis combined. Despite noble attempts, programs to feed the world have constantly failed. One third of the world's population does not have access to enough fresh water.

There are things we all would like to see happen in the upcoming new year of 2012. However, since I am writing this column, I'll just write about what I want. That's what's important anyway, right?

The first thing I want is to see is my friend Steve get healthy. If he would work at it a little bit, I know he could look almost as good as I do. When I was younger, people would call me Handsome Don.

I'm still pretty handsome, but people don't tell me that very often these days. I don't get out much anymore, I have a big belly, my hair is gray, and I don't have a forehead anymore, I have a fivehead.

I'll just list the things that I want in 2012 and you can tell all of your friends who can't read exactly what it is. Okeedookee?

I want to plant trees near the cool blue waters of Putah Creek with Libby Earthman, Sara Tremayne and Rich Marovich. I want to watch them grow. When the wheat planted by Rich Marovich is knee high, I want to wade through it with my wife. I want to sit under one of the trees and kiss her softly upon her lips. I want the children of Winters to run and play all around us so they will know what real love looks like in case they don't see it at home.

I want to act more like a man than the whimpering girlieguy that I usually am. Waa, Waa, Waa, all the time. I want to be able to control my emotions when my eyes see one thing and my emotions see another. I want to watch the fireworks on the fourth of July and have my emotions tell me that these are merely fireworks and not something else that makes my body tense and my heart beat faster. I want to stay in the light of the brilliant burst of gunpowder without want of backing away and crouching in the shadows, unseen and unheard.

I want to watch my son Joey play his guitar and sing with his friends. I want to think of my son and your son driving somewhere to have fun like young people should, without the intruding thought of them jumping from a helicopter and being pulled upside down by the weight of their rucksack so that they land on their heads.

I want to think that should I ever divest myself of those emotions (that leave my body tense, my nostrils flared, and my brow contracted) I would not find that I have nothing left worth saving within my skull. Furthermore, if what I see in 2012 is not better than what I saw in 2011, I'll tell you the last thing that I want on New Years. I want to be blind or dead.

Washington is just a cesspool of slimy sidewinders
1/15/2012

I hate political commercials. I hate politics. I hate lying, cheating, sexual perverts that call themselves congressmen and senators. I really hate it because they get away with policing themselves. The Ethics Committee is a joke. Washington D. C. is a cesspool of slimy sidewinders.

Lawmakers have time to vote against same-sex marriage but they can't find the time to investigate the habits of insider trading and bribery in their own back yard. Again, the Stock Act is a joke on the hill because they call it "Funds and Favors" or "I'll grease your hand if you grease mine."

Only the rich can afford to run for office. Money and greed are prerequisite to the good old boys club. Once in a great while when someone honest makes it to the hill, the boy's club blocks every step they take with regulations and shady deals.

The Oath of Office means nothing to the boys on the hill. The dirtier they are, the higher they rise. They have their greasy fingers into everything. Should they get caught in the midst of dirty dealing, like Newt Gingrich and Herman Cain were found with their hands in the campaign funds, the evidence will end up in the shredder?

Misconduct and unlawful acts are rarely punished because congressional committees tie up investigations into a neat little ball that rolls in circles around the hill. The political process involves nothing but fundraising. Lawmakers have time for nothing else.

Despite a federal law mandating preservation of all federal records, including emails, the Department of Justice consistently mishandles criminal records. I.e. Controversial torture memos authored by John Yoo, former Deputy Assistant Attorney General for the Office of Legal Counsel (OLC). Oops, so sorry!

For years, some members of Congress have made a lucrative side business of trading earmarks for campaign contributions. These members treat the federal treasury – meaning our tax dollars — like their own personal piggybank, handing out big money contracts to favored donors, friends and family members. In exchange, these members often receive campaign donations, employment for relatives, or charitable contributions. Man what a racket!

At one time, American Democracy was special. We made ourselves sovereign but we forgot to make ourselves intelligent. Education is more than abundant, but intelligence is perpetually retarded by the fertility of the simple. We consistently lend ourselves to manipulation by the forces that mold public opinion.

The rights of man are not rights to office and power, but the rights of entry into every route that may nourish and test a man's fitness for office and power. Rights are not a gift from God or nature but a privilege that is good for the group that every individual must have.

Society is not founded on the ideas but on the nature of man, and the constitution of man rewrites the constitutions of states. At least I think it's supposed to. Our moral codes have degraded from hunt, kill, share and feed to pugnacity, brutality, greed and sexual deviation in just 200 years.

Whew! I'm glad I got that out. I don't mean to rag on you about politics but I really, really hate it when my TV shows are interrupted by Herman Gingrich or Ted Cain or even Buddy Obama. They can all kiss my ruby red ass! Oh except for that Weiner guy. I don't want him near me.

Man, there's some weird stuff going on in the world today. It's on the TV news, the newspapers, and on the internet. Some people like to go to all three media outlets to gather the news, but I'd rather get my news from the internet and newspapers. Sometimes I watch the TV news too.

OK, if you think that's funny, think about this. Have you ever seen the famous slow motion film about the bullet passing through an apple? It doesn't make a lot of sense when they call the resulting video from a high-speed camera "slow motion." I thought it was pretty cool to see the bullet slowly go into and then out of the apple, blowing its guts out the other side — POW!

Now, two scientists at MIT, have invented a camera that, they say, can capture the speed of light. This new camera that costs $250,000, captures action at one-trillion exposures per second. That's pretty damn fast. Here is what they had to say: "We can make the same film of the bullet passing through the apple but it would take six years to watch the entire video.

I decided that I want to watch this video.

Naturally it's not capturing the photon as it travels parallel to the focal plane, but rather the moments that occur just the wee-est bit later, after the photon strikes a surface and scatters towards the focal plane. It can only capture a single row of pixels at a time. To create the whole film, it has to be repeated 480 times for each frame.

Being able to capture anything at this rate is astonishing and can probably be used in a number of scientific discoveries. In medical imaging, we can do ultrasound with light instead of sound. (I wonder if they will still call it ultrasound.) The top commenter on YouTube aptly noted, "This is going to totally revolutionize porn." (OK, I stole the last two paragraphs right off the internet and played like I wrote them.)

Today I got on the horn (that's famous war hero talk for a telephone) and I called MIT to get a copy of the video. The guy that I talked to said that it might be awhile because there was an auditorium full of grade school kids watching it right now. He finished by saying that when the film was over, they would be sophomores in college. I'm watching the mail for it every day now.

While I was waiting for the mailman, I decided to think about something. I thought about First Lady Michelle Obama discussing stories of tension between her and White House aides. She was saying people have tried to portray her as "some kind of angry black woman." On this subject, I'm an expert. Some of my really good friends are black women. I know all about them.

Let's see, there is Dr. Karen McCord, Professor of Ethnic Studies at Solano Community College. For years she was my mentor. I wanted to be just like her. She is really, really cool. College kids will sit in a room and listen to her for hours and hours. She is responsible for my being in "Honors" classes. She made me want to learn more. By the time I finished every course she taught, I was so smart that even I thought I was a black guy. All of the other students in the room affectionately called me "Sunshine."

Dr. McCord's good friend, Dr. Tolliver, (now retired) is a black lady also. Dr. Tolliver's husband was stabbed in his driveway by some white jerk that was trying to steal some of their stuff. I think Mr. Tolliver must suffer from PTSD because every time I would go to their house I thought he was going to beat me up. (Just kidding of course.)

For one of my classes, I interviewed another friend of theirs, Judge Ramona J. Garrett (Superior Court of Solano County). I got an "A" on that paper of course. I tell the truth when I say I absolutely adore these women. Of course, they love me too. Together, with a few other women, they published a book about how each of them, abused as children living in high-rise ghettos of New York and other cities, successfully rose above it all to become the professionals they are.

I was thinking that these lovely ladies had to put up with stereotypes too. I've never seen them as "angry black women" but I never pushed the issue either. I pushed my hand through the mail slot on my wall to see if the mailman was coming, (nope, not yet) but all of a sudden I was thinking about the woman that coughed up a 3-inch tumor. After that, she was cancer free. If I ever get cancer, that's what I'm going to do too. Another thing I'm going to do is keep the tumor in a jar so I can look at it and show it to my friends Steve and Terry. They like that sort of stuff.

Next time, I'm going to write about how some people have been calling me "Tree hugger" and "liberal piggy boy." Except for "piggy," I don't even know what that means.

Veterans must learn to live for love
1/29/2012

There is a willingness of governments to mislead and deny important information to the public. I think everyone should sit up and take notice and realize that they CANNOT trust those in government to provide accurate information, or to do the right thing for anyone but themselves. The rich and powerful meet behind closed doors in secret organizations like The Council on Foreign Relations and a few others.

Founded in 1921, the Council on Foreign Relations is the most powerful private organization in the world. Its 5000 or so members reflect the resources needed by the ruling class to maintain its power. You will not become a member of this organization unless you have big money, national security expertise, CIA experience, a political constituency, or clout with the media.

The major activity of the Council on Foreign Relations is to organize closed door meetings for its members with assorted world leaders where everyone feels free to share their views and information about current world affairs. The organization has strict confidentially rules and keeps its records locked up for 25 years. Its membership roster is somewhat of a secret but some of the known members were Presidents Nixon, Ford, Carter, Bush Sr., Clinton, and Bush Jr.

Some of the world's largest and richest corporations are tied to this secretive organization. The Council on Foreign Relation voices its opinions through some of the most powerful of media outlets. It is unknown what the council's agenda is but I suspect it has something to do with money because its members are among the richest people in the world.

Wars begin when a greater government forces its will on a smaller, weaker one. Wars do not start by accident, nor will they ever. Governments have no sadness. It knows only the word of law without justice; without forgiveness. In theory its laws are for the people but in practice they are only for the rich. The major religious organizations tell us of Heaven and Hell, while they work hand in hand with whatever government happens to be in power at any given time. With the Vatican cooperation with Nazi Germany, this is proven to be true.

Holy men tell us of the afterlife and the forgiveness of sin. Personally, I find that the idea of an afterlife makes our actual life less sacred. The fear, wonder, and speculation of the "after" can dim the "during." Religion and the mass media can make us feel "alright" with going to war. Eventually we wish to go to war. Before we choose our wishes we'd better think first, because with every wish there comes a curse.

Once in the military, we are called to kill; the word of law says it is so. It gives us the illness with no cure, no help, and no relief. When the war ends the government asks for no forgiveness. Its heart is never full of sorrow. It doesn't think about tomorrow and it doesn't care about the past. It knows no time while, for we humans, now the veterans, the days turn into years and the years turn into a lifetime. We want to walk away from our past but when we step into our own footprints, we find that we cannot step away from ourselves. We go in circles that spiral ever downward; ever downward.

There is one thing that all veterans have in common. We have to look at ourselves in the mirror. We see the sadness in our own eyes. We find it hard to give or receive love because we think you see us the way that we see ourselves. In our minds, we are a burden to those who care for us.

We can't see our greatest hopes because of our darkest fears. With heaven above and hell below, we are suspended in a space somewhere in between. We are nearer the latter than the former. Wherever we sleep, the shadows fall around us, sucking any respite from our bones. We can see the hands of the angels but they do not reach for us.

We begin to think that punishment will save us and give us some relief but we can find none of that for, like our government, we know no justice. Desperate, we punish ourselves in increments, ever increasing in severity. All of our colors bleed to red when the final self-punishment is ours. Every 80 minutes, a veteran will kill himself. For thousands of years, from the Pharaohs to the Kings and on to the Tsars and Presidents, it has always been the same.

Why can't we veterans see what millions of eyes can see. We learn to love life, not because we are used to living but because we are used to loving. We must show our veterans that time and love can heal all wounds, for love seems the swiftest, but it is actually the slowest of all growths. There has to be some way or something that will make veterans wait for love; live for love.

C'est La Vie

I can live another day
2/5/2012

I think the mind tries to repair itself after it experiences trauma, either physical or visual. In the blink of an eye something within your brain or your heart, I'm not sure which, shuts down and you go into shock. You are left in a blank, dumb world. You will find yourself oblivious to the rest of the world. You are unresponsive to all stimuli except maybe those mechanical thingys that will tell if you are alive or not.

In time, when your mind has time to sort things out, you will be returned to the real world and you are free to associate with the rest of humanity. You will be semi-happy, able to function in society, go to work, even have a relationship in which you can give and receive love. The love you give won't be as much as you would like to give, but it's the best you can do.

Some people will accept the limit of love that you give them but others won't. I have been divorced twice for that very reason. Now, Therese, my wife of 27 years or so takes all that I can give and she seems to understand if things aren't exactly right. She knows it isn't her. She knows it is me and she works hard at trying to visualize what is going on inside her little, pea-brained, husband. I have to credit her with all that is good in my life today.

I am getting off subject, as I often do when my mind seems to go numb for a few seconds. Like I said, a traumatized mind will enable you to function to a certain extent. The strength of your childhood family relations, the mindset of your parents and their parents before them, all contribute to what goes on inside your mind after trauma. A good, loving family life will bring you strength when you need it.

Sometimes even the rich, loving, family environment is not enough to get you through trying times following disabling trauma of the mind. The father and the mother will be able to see the pain you're in even though it is hidden from sight in the physical world. Somehow they know it's there, but there is nothing they can do but give you love and try to understand. Trauma is capable of screwing up generations of family life.

My family has scattered to the world. I do not know where many of them are or how they got there. I have brothers that have never seen my 22 year old son or even know that he exists. I am plagued by this constant sorrow that is overwhelming me at this very moment. It can be very bad at times and at its worst, it is unspeakable. Some take the easy way out but I cannot leave my family that easily behind. At least I have that much strength, probably given to me by my mother.

I have a great love for the Veterans Administration. I am one of probably millions of veterans that go to them for help every day. They seem to spare no expense in their attempts to help me live as productive a life as I could. I know when I walk through those clinic doors I will see intelligent, caring, professionals that do all they are capable of doing for each and every veteran they treat. I can tell only my story when it comes to that.

For many years it was extensive, one-on-one therapy with Dr. Janet Lial at Mather Field Veterans Mental Health Clinic. In the sessions we would sit face to face and she would try to get me to open up my mind just enough to let my demons escape. I think the theory is that if you can bring it up and relive the trauma, you will recognize it for what it is and release it. This should make your life easier to bear. It is only a theory. Believe me, Dr. Lial has a way of dredging even the darkest of memories from the far depths of the caverns at the bottom of your memory.

I say again, I love the Veteran's Administration. They do the best that they can do with such limited financial resources. I am grateful for the work that they do. Eternally grateful. My problem is, I don't think that they can help me any more. I don't want them to spend their funds on me. I want them to give my appointments to someone young and in need of help. I seem to have reached a place in my mind that is peaceful. I want to do good deeds for my community with the remaining time that I have. My children are all adults now and I have two grandchildren, Anthony and Sophia. I want to watch them grow and prosper for as long as I can.

When they come to visit me I want to take them to the park by the creek that community volunteer groups and local people have so graciously made available to me. I cannot say to them how much I appreciate what they do for me. They give me peace that I so desperately need to stay among the living. For me, this is the best therapy I can possibly get and I don't say this to pressure them. They know this, at least I hope they do. I can even tell my grandchildren how I helped and which trees I stuck in the ground.

I think the mind tries to repair itself after it experiences trauma, either physical or visual. The fine work of the Putah Creek Council, The Solano County Water Agency, and the City of Winters has given me the opportunity to heal myself by planting trees and picking up garbage. I will do what no one else wants to do, anytime, anywhere. It is this work, above all else that helps me feel good about myself and when that happens, I know my mind is healing. I can live another day in peace.

Time is definitely speeding up
2/12/2012

Time seems to be moving faster and faster. It seems just like yesterday, I was a young 21-year-old kid in high school. A short 10 years later, I almost got my AA degree. Just one more year, and I could have had that little piece of paper that says Donald K. Sanders, Associate of whatever, whatever. I don't know where the time went, but I never got back to school until I was well into my 50s. Time is so fast. They say in the end, your life is a blink of the eye.

So now, I have the dilemma; should I think about it or not? When I made up my mind to think about it, a full year had passed and I don't know how old I was then! I mentioned to my wife that I was going to try to think about time, and lo and behold, she was already thinking about it.

On her way home, she was listening to some guy on the radio talking about time speeding up because of a wobble or some kind of crap like that. I told her, "Don't you worry your pretty little head about it; I'll get to the bottom of this."

"I'm gonna do it. I'm gonna think about time," I says.

I started thinking right away, and this is what I thought.

Actually, time isn't moving any faster. A day still has 24 hours or 1,440 minutes or 86,400seconds. Time and how it works is supposed to be an absolute. Or, some think time is relative to each person's perception, like facts, truth and beauty. To each his own.

If all of time and matter were speeding up, there would really be no way of telling. There are lots of people out there that have their own explanation, but I think everyone will agree that time is gaining speed. It seems as if New Year's Eve was just yesterday. Another thing —, look at how fast your children are growing up. It seems just like yesterday my son Joe was 6 years old and I was scolding him for rooting in the garbage. I can look out in my yard, and his toys are still lying there where I ran over them with the lawnmower.

According to the late Ian Lungold, we are in the 9th level of the creation cycle. The 8th came to an end in February 2011. It was called the "Galactic Cycle" and we are now in the "Conscious co-creation" cycle. Each of these nine Creation cycles is 20 times shorter than the previous cycle. Well, that's reasonable.

Light and time are all tangled up, and one affects the other. In the old days, everyone thought that nothing could travel faster than light. Well that's all changed now. CERN physicists are firing neutrino, which don't interact with normal matter and can pass straight through the earth, to a detector in Italy. The neutrinos from CERN were showing up at Gran Sasso a few billionths of a second early. In other words, they appeared to be getting from Switzerland to Italy faster than light would travel the same distance.

Now see, if we had built the "Sanders Muon Ringy Thingy" like I suggested to our city manager some years ago, we'd have all those neutrinos for ourselves. We could all be rich right now. But that's a different story, and a sore subject around my house.

So, now you can see that time has to increase speed along with these neutrinos thingys, right?

I decided to ask my friend Terry Vender (a government man who works for the local city maintenance department) because he says he knows everything. Terry says, "I know time perception speeds up with age, but this is starting to get crazy."

His theory is that the increase in the speed of time is supposed to happen to get us where we need to be for March 2012 when the world will end.

So now I'm starting to get scared and I don't want to think about it anymore, but Terry didn't want to let it lie. He wanted to keep on yapping and yapping about this and that. I don't know how it happened, but he started talking about "Black Matter" that makes up 93 percent of the universe, but nobody can see it.

Well, I can tell you that I was so upset about this stuff that pretty soon me and Terry was toe to toe and staring each other down. Terry is a pretty big guy so I backed down pretty quick. I pointed my finger at him and said, "Watch yourself, big guy — I'm like those neutrino thingys, I'm fast!" With that said, I made the "wipe on-wipe off" motion with my hands. He said he was going to go get the backhoe because he was going to dig a hole for me.

I don't know what that's supposed to mean, but that was almost a year ago, I think. I'll let you know what else I think when I get back to thinking.

Pee-pee doors are key to what's happening
2/19/2012

I think I may have uncovered a most heinous crime against humanity. If my data is correct, it may be our women that perpetrate these horrible crimes aimed at disheveling men that have reached a certain age. I call it disheveling, but in its very nature it may equal betrayal way worse than murder, and far, far worse than anything any man has ever even thought of at any time ever in our history. Ever! It may be pure evil!

I am a man myself, so I can't fully understand what exactly women are up to, or what is behind their reasoning. This being said, I can only, using my incredibly superior mind and powerful good looks, explain in simple laymen's terms to illustrate my theory so the rest of you men will be able to understand.

I know it's hard for most men to concentrate on any given subject for any length of time. If you plan to understand this theory, it will take every ounce of concentration that you are capable of conjuring up. The most important advice that I can give you at the onset of this column is three words: Focus-Focus-Focus (That's Latin for something).

First of all, it is imperative that you keep this column away from the prying eyes of the women of your family. Should these women, that are supposed to love you and care for you, see my incredibly brilliant words, they will have a member of their "sorority" stamp on me like a roach on a rug. There is one among them that is capable of editing these words into an essay on why shoes don't fit both feet even though everybody knows that all feet are identical and opposite.

I begin, so be ever vigilant in your efforts to follow what I am about to impart upon your brains. Should your woman stroll past your secure position smelling good, being all jingly and looking really good, ignore her. She is trying to figure out what exactly you are up to. Focus! They are tricky. They might even tell you they're looking for a piece of tape to fix a loose cracker package or announce, "Your clothes are done" as the dryer buzzes 10 times, loud enough for the neighbors to hear.

Item number one: Underwear. In recent years, I have become aware of certain changes in my underwear that I think are designed to make me feel and look like an old man. The changes are gradual so they escape the attention of you normal-thinking men. Men, once you read this, you'll fully understand what I'm saying.

You know the little hole in the front of your underwear? I will call it the pee-pee door. Anyway, some years ago, I noticed that the pee-pee door in my underwear was getting lower and lower. Every time my wife bought me underwear, the door was lower in the new garment than the one in my old garments. If I hold up a pair of underwear from 10 years ago and compare the location of the door on a pair that was recently purchased by my wife, the pee-pee hole is like a foot lower.

When I first noticed that I was no longer able to use the door, I freaked out. "What is happening to me?" I thought. Other men would catch me crying in restrooms. They would put their hands on my back and say, "What's the matter, Brother?" I would retort, "I can't reach the damn door!" At this point, most of them would, like Yogi Bear, "exit stage left." Sometimes I would sob for hours and hours.

Then, like a miracle, I had the solution. All I had to do was pull them up so the door was closer to my thingy. This worked just fine for years until one day I noticed that the door was also lower on my pants. I thought, "Geez! My underwear are already up under my armpits, there is no room for my pants too!" I thought, "How do other men handle this problem?" I decided to investigate.

I walked around town and I didn't have to wait long before I found an old guy with his pants up under his armpits. I approached him and asked why he wore his pants like that. Well I have to tell you that his answer scared the hell out of me! His eyes turned red, and he said something I couldn't understand in a manner that made him slobber all over himself. I had to jump back to avoid the spray.

"Holy crap!" I thought.

It took this encounter with my future self to make me understand what exactly is going on. The whole thing about pee-pee doors is a plot by our women to steal our power. At the point in time when you first have to pull your underwear up to use the pee-pee door, you're lost! You feel older and you look older when others view you in your underwear. By the time your jeans are mid-chest, everyone thinks you are an old man.

Girls will now say, "Eew!" if you say something sexy to them. It is all very sad, for you may find the girl that you believe to be the love of your life but you see yourself as an old man so you let your heart break, and never announce your love and passion to the one that you were destined to spend your life with but never will. You are old and she is young.

I have one thing to say to the males of the world. Pay no attention when a woman or girl tells you to pull up your pants. If you want to sag, go ahead and sag. Let your whole ass hang out like a flag on a windy day. Yes sir: Let the free sag fly! Amen, brother!

Playing chicken with history
2/26/2012

Yep, I've been thinking again. I've been thinking about man as a species, their governments, and chickens. As far as I can figure, all three of these things in reality, are misunderstood. I'm going to tell you what I think about each of these subjects, and if you think I'm wrong, just keep it to yourself. I'll start with what I think is most critical: chickens.

There are those living in my town, Winters California, who worship chickens. Their leader is a lady with the initials, Rebecca Bresnick Holmes. She tells all of the other chicken lovers what to do and how to do it in a column she writes for our local newspaper, the Winters Express. This newspaper has given her the power to persuade ordinary people to change their attitudes about chickens in general.

In years gone by, it was general knowledge that chickens are a dangerous animal or bird, whatever they are, you know what I mean. It used to be a given that chickens could not live with humans in the city. Well, partner, it ain't true anymore! People who love chickens are growing in number and it's scaring the hell out of me.

You can walk down the street and hear them behind fences and in their little house coops scratching, scratching, scratching, like rats trying to eat their way into your house. Pecking, pecking, and pecking all day and all night because they never sleep. You can see their eyes shining at night when your headlights flash on them in the dark. They are evil I tell you!

The only thing they are good for is food. They smell funny and they leave little piles of poop everywhere they go. Ms. Holmes neglects to tell her followers about how the chicken on Russell Street terrorized the people living on that street. The chickens were chasing cars off the street and up on to the sidewalks. One guy I know was so afraid he wouldn't drive on Russell Street, even though he lived there. He was afraid for his life. Whatever happened to that chicken? I'm going to have to look into that.

Onward and upwards to the species of man and their governments. As soon as men got out of the caves, they filed a claim in a government office to get some land that they would call "family farms." There was a saying, well I don't know when it was said, but it goes like this, "Civilization is a parasite on the man with a hoe!" I think it was about 594 B. C. E. that man first had to pay for hoes. It is also said that hoes are the world's oldest profession but I am having trouble believing that is true. It goes to reason that the man had to have a job to pay for the hoes, right?

OK, here is where the governments come in. With all the parasites and such, there was a need for someone to manage all the money that was going from hand to hand from the family farmers to the hoes. These new guys are now called "Bankers." Thus the saying, "Those that can manage money, manage all."

These "Bankers" started stuff like "Credit." Credit is the trusting and lending of man's property to the Hoes and their partners in crime, "Lawyers." In theory there can be no credit without capital but the absence of capital is the very essence of credit, because when a man does not have capital to pay a bill, you have to give him credit. A lawyer is a guy whose duty is to manage the causes of his clients (the Hoes) and to get rid of their effects when the parasites kill them. The lawyers invented "Evidence," the legal means of getting or concealing the truth. Lawyers live upon the law like certain animals feed upon carrion.

The Bankers and the Lawyers made up stuff like "Diplomacy" (meaning two or deriving from the two words dip and low, the art of one country trying to swindle another) and "Elections" (the forced confirmation of a choice made by another). These they made part of their "Conservative Principle"(the theory of taking care of the Constitution and the practice of taking care of oneself.)

Anyway, they started a government called a "Democracy." Democracy is a term from Greece meaning, most feel that the acts of governments is Greek to them. Thus, they made a system where every damn decision is made by the community at large. This means every issue requires gigantic argumentative meetings. I think that one must learn how to govern himself before he attempts to govern others. Whatever!

After that they made up things like a "Domicile" (place where every man is when he is at home) and "Descents" (assage of title or assets from father to son). Next came "Equity" and "Justice" (the soul and spirit of the law). Following close behind that is "Income Tax" (a permanent burden for temporary purposes), "Debenture" (from the word debeo, to owe; a bill given by a government that lacks cash) and "Damages" (from the word damnum a loss, or what a man gets for going to the law).

To enforce their will upon the Hoes and the Family Farmers, they invented the "Militia" (oldiers for home consumption) and "Infanticide" (the most ordinary fruit of an oppressive government).

Well, that's all I have room for, but I'll be back. Oh, I'll leave you with a little something to think about. As of Oct 5, 2007, there are more chickens than people in the world, and where did the "Bird Flu" come from and why was it invented. In 1918 and 1919 it killed 25 million people. Think about that, kiddies!

Madge Woods is coming to visit the city of Winters. The zip code is 95694, which makes it somewhere near here. Her visit to the area could be a financial windfall for us. (Meaning me — and a small share for my friend Steve) Ms. Woods' visit is considered to be a significant event for our fair city but she stresses that she is not coming here for official reasons and her time here should be considered as personal.

Before we discuss the reasons for her visit, I feel that a little background information may be in order. It is true that Ms. Woods, affectionately known around the world as Madgew, has a history that is clouded in mystery and adventure originating from historical documents that apparently are thousands of years old.

The earliest known images of Madgew are dated at around 2000 B. C. E. The image of the impishly beautiful Madgew is depicted sitting with the Pharaoh of the Lower Kingdom of the Nile. Hieroglyphics suggest that she may have been an emissary of the Upper Kingdom and was instrumental in the joining of the two kingdoms. The papyrus scroll can be view by appointment at the Cairo Museum in Egypt.

Several centuries later, Madgew turns up again in Egypt. Historical documents associated with Napoleon while in Egypt began surfacing at around 1809 and continue appearing intermittently throughout his life. Madgew is believed to have been instrumental in the preservation of the Sphinx and other great ancient monuments. Some say she can be traced to temples of Upper Egypt where she is depicted as a Goddess of Good Fortune.

To add to the mystery, images and references to Madgew are to be found from the ancient walled city of Nineveh across the continent of Asia and on to the Isle of Japan. Antiquities in ancient Xianyang's terracotta army refer to Madgew in both Chinese and Greek. Several references to Madgew appear at the Sanju-Sangendo Temple. In one image she is depicted barefoot and in pajamas while holding a martini.

Madgew is shown drinking from the three fountains of the Kiyomizu Temple in Japan. The three fountains are associated with wisdom, health and prosperity. There are tintype photos of Madgew in Prague and Vienna. She is rumored to have argued with Chopin about Poland. It is all very mysterious indeed.

That brings us pretty much up to date except for her reasons to visit Winters. I have to say that Steve and I should get the credit for that. You see, we have arranged to sell Madgew the Glory Hole at Lake Berryessa. A savvy businesswoman she is. Before we can close the deal on the Glory Hole, she wants to view the damn thing before she spits out any money. I tried to tell Steve that this was going to happen, but he said that all women are a sucker for his charms and in the end, Madgew will buy the Glory Hole.

"Leave it up to me!" he said.

Steve wanted to tell her that it was a Black Hole in the universe around here but I told him, "Who the hell wants to buy a Black Hole, Steve?" Steve needs to get with it or get off the pile of wood because you can't write on a stupid log! That's what I always say!

So everybody, keep an eye out for Madgew, she's really cool. I think that if everybody lines up on Main Street, she would probably give each one of us a kiss on the forehead. I think that's really cool but I don't have a forehead any more, I have a five head.

In the end, her visit may remind us of a poem by Julia Butterfly. It goes like this:

Me reflecting you reflecting me.
You are a part of us, and we are a part of you.
When one reaches out to another, then one transforms to two.
But two is never separated from the one we were before.
If anything two is the possibility of one becoming more.
And if there is no courting, no numbers to create a wall,
when we look in the face of the one,
we will see the face of all.

If Madgew doesn't buy the Glory Hole after that poem, no one will.

Thinking about changing my life
3/11/2012

I've been thinking about making some changes in my life but I'm not sure where to start. Maybe I'll change my column first and then maybe everything else will change by itself. Even with my IQ of 10,000, I think it will be necessary to get some advice so I don't change the wrong thing. I don't want to make a hole in the time continuum thingy.

Even Caesar, the old Roman guy, had advisors. If he was as smart as I am, he would have followed the advice to beware of the Ides of March, right? If someone told me to "Beware of the Ides of March" I would have thought, "What the hell are the Ides of March?" But not Caesar.

Caesar just looks at his watch and sees that today is the Ides of March and tells his personal assistant to look into that tomorrow. A good advisor would have told him that this problem had to be handled today, not tomorrow! If he had just one good advisor, he'd still be alive today.

That's it! I want to change my column to an advice column. Maybe I should change the name of my column to "Ask Donald." However, I also think I should have a specialized advice column. One that people could ask questions about specific things like, well, I'm going to have to think about this some more. Chicha-chicha-chicha-kachang! That's what my mind sounds like when it is thinking.

There are certain things that I can't write about and I have to shy away from because my wife is in Hawaii this week and she's not here to explain to me if what I am saying is good advice or bad. I can't give advice about love because that's the only thing on Earth that I don't fully understand. My wife does, but like I just said, she's not here to tell me what to say.

I could give advice about what a guy should do while his wife is away chasing whales around the Hawaiian Islands. Well, maybe not. Since she's been gone, things have kind of fallen apart for me. She's only been gone a few days and already I stink. I have B.O. Not only that, there's something growing on the stove and I don't know what it is.

Every dish that we own is dirty, and on the counters and in the sink. Silverware (that's what we call it but it's really steel ware) — yep, it's all dirty too. I went and got some paper plates and now there are paper plates all over the counters on top of the dishes and silverware. I don't have any clean clothes or towels so I can't take a bath. I have to turn my underwear inside out because they're cleaner that way.

I can see that this advice column stuff is going to take a little thinking before I write something I might regret. I really don't know why it matters so much what I write about — a person would have to be really dumb to read my column anyway, right? Not only that, everybody knows that if I didn't send in something to the editor of the local newspaper, then there'd be a big blank spot in the paper and they'd blame that on Debra because she is the editor. They'd look at the blank spot and say, "What the hell is on Debra's mind?" "Why did she leave a big blank spot in the paper?" They would say to their buddy. Then their buddy would say, "I don't know."

I can't give advice about plants and yard work either. Since my wife left to travel, all of the houseplants are dead. My lawn is knee high with weeds and dog poop. That's another thing! Where the hell did the dog poop when my wife was home? Now the dang dog poops right in the middle of the sidewalk. It even pooped in the house the other day and I'm still walking around it till it dries up. Geez!

Well, now I don't know if I should write an advice column or not. Maybe I could be a food critic. Yeah, then when I go into the local restaurants, they'll give me extra fine service and free food. Or maybe I could write about politics or even be a political guy myself and run for mayor. That would be nice if I knew anything about majoring.

I think that maybe I should think about this some more before I write something really dumb.

The best answer of them all
3/18/2012

I've been trying to find ways to sharpen my wit. I figure that my incredible good looks and a mind that works like a well-oiled steel trap may not be enough to have a successful "advice" column. In last week's column, I mentioned that I was considering changing the format of my column. I even discussed it with my wife, but she said I didn't have a format to change. After considerable contemplation, at least an hour's worth, I had to believe that she may be right.

Well, I don't have to tell you what it's like not to have a format. My wife says that all the other writers we know have formats, but I've never had even a single format, ever. I was going to say something really smart right then, but she started laughing. It wasn't a giggle type laugh but a boisterous belly laugh. She was laughing so hard that she said, "I think I'm going to pee my pants!"

I couldn't see anything that humorous so I asked her what the heck was so funny? She was all bent over and slobbering with tears in her eyes when she said, "The type of people that read your column don't even know what a format is!" "Words of wisdom, yes, words of wisdom is my format!" I told her in so many words. She peed her pants.

Anyway, like I said, I've been looking to sharpen my wit somehow so I looked everywhere for days and days, but my wit didn't change and I couldn't understand why. Suddenly, like a miracle, I found just what I needed. I found Yahoo Answers. It's a place on the internet where people send in questions that they need help answering. Well that's 50 percent of it anyway. I think the other 50 percent is that you can send in an answer to these questions so it is in essence, an advice thingy.

OK, so I was reading along, reading along, until I found a question that I thought I could answer in an intelligent manner. The question was, "Do you think that aggressive behavior in adults is caused by the media?" I already knew the answer to this one. It was so simple. I replied, "No, by the time a person is old enough to understand the media, their aggressive nature has already formed." This behavior is learned in the home at a very early age. Everybody knows that!

That was easy, so I looked for another question I could answer. So, I go through about a hundred questions until I found one. The title of the question was, "What's wrong with me?" The lady said that she liked to have guys on the side that she didn't want to have a commitment with. She liked to tease boys and let them go so far before stopping them. Blah, blah, blah, blah-blah. She then asked if everyone would think she was weird or something.

Here is what I answered: "You are a typical girl, for your behavior has been the same since the beginning of time for typical girls. However it is the girls that are not typical that are special and above average. If you act as if you want to be treated a certain way and you ask for nothing else, then all you will get are typical guys." I thought it was an absolutely brilliant answer.

I forgot all about the questions and answers until I got an email from Yahoo Answers saying that my answers were voted as the best. Yes indeedee, the best! I printed out the answers and went looking for my wife, but she was snoozing on the couch so I let her have her nap. I would spring it on her later. I stood there tapping my foot on the coffee table until she finally woke up.

She was still groggy when I stuck it in front of her face.

"Look," I said, "My answers were voted to be the best answers! I got 100 percent of all the votes for best answer," I says.

She looked at them for a moment before she said, "Why, yes you did. You got 100 percent because there was only one vote for each question. You got 100 percent of one vote."

Well what does it matter anyway? 100 percent is 100 percent, right?

The constancy of Tom Hanks
3/25/2012

I'm a Tom Hanks fan. I have been since the beginning of his acting career in Bosom Buddies, even though I thought it was weird that he had to dress up like a woman. Tom Hanks made me laugh at a time when I didn't have much to laugh about — I'm grateful for that. Even way back then, it was easy to see what an immense talent Hanks was. I think everyone knew that he was destined for greatness. I'll explain why I mention Tom Hanks in a few moments.

From early childhood I lived in a temporary world. I say this because everything that I ever knew and loved was eventually taken from me, and most never returned. Living in a temporary world teaches you a great many things that normal people, in a normal family life never learn.

Normal people live in a world of constants. They live their entire childhood in the same house with the same family members. They grow up with the same neighbors and the same friends on the same streets that they knew the first time they were allowed to wander down the block as small children. Normal people develop normal support systems so if a problem arises in their lives they have learned where to go and who to talk to that will help them solve problems.

People with a normal childhood have someone to go to if they want something, and someone to go to if they don't feel good. They have someone to go to for everything or anything. They go to high school with the same kids they went to grade school with. As adults they go to a tavern and see the same people that lived on their block or played baseball on the other team. Constant.

Economic status has no effect upon normal people other than bigger and better toys, and everything else is exactly the same for the poor as it is for the rich. Family and peer groups are as constant with one group as it is with the other. Normal people move around freely from group to group through sports, dances, and other interactions so one group knows others and they become normal as well. One child will know another child from across town because their parents work together and socialize frequently. It's all very normal for normal people.

Then you have people like me who have known nothing but temporary, so they expect temporary friends, temporary homes, temporary everything. Temporary love does not exist as love, it exists as an ache. This ache is the only constant in a temporary person's life. The ache is always there, sticking its head out of the hole where your friends or loved ones should be but are not.

My brother Michael, two years my junior, is also a temporary person with his own temporary world, apart from mine. In a temporary world, brothers are just someone you might bump into that you may recognize as someone familiar. You really don't know them and they don't know you. You are brothers and that's all there is. I mean, my brother couldn't brag about how well his brother played baseball because neither one of us knew how. We never played baseball. We never went hiking. We never went fishing.

We never ate meals together unless our mother came to visit us at the temporary orphanage. Even her visits were temporary, for they stopped after a while.

I knew that I had other brothers and even a sister, but they were temporary as well and I didn't even know where they were or if they were even alive. Even the stars above were temporary and at times years would pass between times when I would see them, one to the next. I had to run away from the orphanage and live on the streets in order to really enjoy the stars.

As a young adult my experience in the Republic of Vietnam also had a profound effect on my temporary heart. It is there that I learned that even life itself is temporary. This revelation changed only one thing for me. It changed the one thing, the single thing that was a constant in my life: the ache. The ache became unbearable and at times I wanted to end my temporary life. That was temporary too.

Anyway, back to Tom Hanks. I don't have to exaggerate one bit to make the statement that this actor has been a part of my life longer than love, or friendship, or family. I see my brother Michael every month or so but I seem to see Tom Hanks every single day. That's it. That's what I wanted to say. I want to say that it's a shame that (no offense Tom) Tom Hanks is more of a constant in my life than my own brother. I find that very strange.

My fish story
4/1/2012

My friend Steve has been trying to get me to go fishing with him for the last couple of years. The truth is, I'm not much of a fisherman compared to Steve. He goes all the time and he's one of those guys that has all the latest equipment that can turn a simple fishing trip into a scientific expedition. It seems that he always catches fish and he always enjoys himself somehow.

Well, he kept bugging me and bugging me until last year I told him that I would buy a fishing license after the new year. "When after the new year?" "When after the new year?" He'd ask over and over. I told him, "Probably around January."

So, from June of last year until January of this year he would ask me every day when I was going to get my fishing license. I'd scratch my head and act like I was thinking for a while and then I'd say, "Probably sometime after New Year's."

Sometimes I would tag along with Steve when he went fishing. Let me tell you, that is an adventure in itself. It seems that Steve thinks that fish hang out only in spots that are hard to access. His favorite fishing spot is just past the dam at Lake Berryessa. This particular spot has a small parking space, just big enough for two vehicles. Steve always parks in the middle of the space so I either have to park with my rear end hanging out in the middle of the road or park at another spot a half-mile up the road and walk back.

From where you park the vehicles to where the water is, there's a cliff with big giant boulders balanced precariously against each other. Should you step on the wrong bolder it would roll down the cliff, taking you with it. Along the way it would crush you so that your guts would make you stick to the boulder all the way to the bottom of the cliff. At that point, the boulder splashes into the lake and goes to the bottom with you stuck to it with your intestines sticking out of your butt.

So far this hasn't happened, but I kid you not when I say that Steve can find the scariest spot where the giant boulders will move if you put your hand on them too hard. That's exactly where he will sit and fish. Right under that boulder. I would ask him why he had to sit at this particular spot and he would answer, "This is where the fish are, dummy!" In the 20 or so years that I have known Steve, I have never seen him catch a fish.

Sometimes, if I don't go with him, he'll send me a picture of himself holding a fish that looks exactly like a cardboard picture of a bass or he would text me saying he had caught a 24 incher. Later I'd go to his house to see the fish and he always tells me that our friend Terry took it home and ate it. Rrr-i-g-h-t.

OK, January passes, February passes, and March begins. Time goes on and on until last Saturday comes. It was right after Friday I think. Anyway, I went to the Berryessa Sporting Goods Store and told the guy I want a fishing license. He wants 10 pieces of ID and 50 bucks. In return, I got two pieces of plastic paper that'll never degrade back to nature, ever. One piece of plastic paper is two feet long. It made my wallet so fat that it looks like I have $50,000 in it.

Steve wanted to know why I got my license all of a sudden, so I told him about how my wife was having her book reading club at my house that very night. There was going to be 60 or 70 women at my house talking about some stupid book till the wee hours of the night. I said, "Lets go fishing tonight. Right now." Steve was so excited, I thought he was going to pee his pants.

A couple of hours later, I went to pick him up and he had so much fishing stuff that the back of my truck was dragging on the street, throwing sparks. He had three tarps, a little stove to make soup, a giant propane heater, 10 fishing poles, two coolers, (one for bait and one for 10 Frescas for him and one Pepsi for me) a pack of crackers with cheese and pickles, four dry soups like you get in jail, six flashlights, a lantern, a one million watt spotlight that was brighter than the sun, a coat, two rain suits, two folding chairs, 10 bungee cords, two 50 foot ropes, four metal poles to make a lean-to that will block the night wind, a little pan to make the soup in, and I don't know what else. I was afraid to ask.

Needless to say, Steve didn't catch a single fish and by the time he got his fishing spot all set up, it was time to pack it up and put it back in the truck because we were soaking wet and freezing. I, of course, caught a huge fish. A marlin, I think, but I let it go because it's the right thing to do. We got lost on Grizzly Island Road on the way back home so it took two hours to go exactly 50 miles.

I don't think I will ever go fishing again. Ever!

Thinking, thinking, thinking about being sorry
4/8/2012

Lately I've been thinking, thinking, thinking all the time. Sometimes I think so much that I can't get anything else done. So, I got to wondering why my thinking is taking all of my time and what I could do about it. Maybe I should start a 12 Step program for solving all of my problems, starting with my thinking problem. I think step number one should be, "Admit you have a problem," just like the AA book.

Oh, I have a problem and you probably have a few too. I think we should think about this, but it's difficult to know where to begin. Lets start with things we'd like to change in our lives. Believe me, had I the power, I would change a lot of things in my life. The very first thing I would change is my behavior towards the women I've known throughout my life. What they deserved was much more than I gave them any of them.

Until lately I never was much of a thinker. I thought I was a doer when I was young. As it turns out, all these years later, I can see now that it was the women in my life that took care of the business of everyday life. Sure I paid my way, sharing rent, food, and the rest of that crap, but the things I should have been doing I didn't do.

I guess that if I'm going to discuss the fact that I have a problem with the way I have treated the women in my life, I should start at the beginning. In my case the beginning is high school and Penny Paluska. Dear sweet Penny. The Queen of the Prom and I was her King. She dumped me the first chance she got and I can't say that I blame her. I had it coming. I had no idea how to treat women, I had never been around them until I was a horny 16 year old asshole. Well, minus the sex (which we never had – but I always bragged that we had) I treated her as a high school sex toy.

I went to Vietnam and she went to Western Illinois University where she met and married the love of her life. Things didn't go that well for me. I did learn the lessons of war though. I still have them etched upon my mind, but that's a different story. Which brings me to the woman that shared my first sexual experience: a Vietnamese prostitute.

For her, I stood in line, paid her for the mount, and then caught the clap. Now that I think about it, there were three firsts that we shared. The first time was not all that good for me. OK, here is the problem I have with the way that I treated her. Not once, not one single time, did my thoughts turn to her. For me, she might as well have not even been there. She was just a chunk of meat they call a whore.

It never dawned on me that she may not like being a prostitute or that she may have been sold into it as a young girl. It never dawned on me that she might have been afraid of me and the other GIs in the line. It never dawned on me that the venereal disease that I caught from her might be giving her horrible pain and suffering. It never dawned on me that she might be having a horrible life of unimaginable disgrace and shame. It never dawned on me to shed a tear for her. However, I know all of these things now and I think that deep down, I knew it then as well.

Some years ago, someone asked me what I would say if I could say something to the Vietnamese people, all over the world. Without a moment's hesitation I replied, "I would get down on my knees and beg their forgiveness for my part in the Vietnam War." I want the Vietnamese world to know that I have lived my entire life, half of it for me and the other half I'm saving for them. Of course, that's all in my head, for I cannot ever give it to them, but it's theirs just the same. It's theirs.

OK, now I'm at the point where I don't want to talk about my treatment of the women in my life any longer. Maybe someday, I can write some more about it, but not today, and for that I'm sorry.

The keepers of the stream
4/15/2012

I've been having visions of the future for many years. Not the far, far future, but the near, say 10 years down the road right here in our little town of Winters, California. Right off the bat, I'd have to say that the future I've been seeing is not all that good. As a matter of fact, it's terrible; terrible, like people killing each other for food or a little drinking water or people living in their cars that can't go anywhere because there is no gasoline to be had. Yeah, it was that kind of terrible.

My life experiences have taught me to always expect the worst and if something better come along, then that's a good thing. If you expect the worst, almost anything that happens is a good thing because it's better than the worst, right? Anyway, that's the way it's been for me most of my life, but lately I've been having different visions of how things will be in the future. Very different.

All of a sudden, I'm thinking the future might not be that bad. So, I'm looking at things a little differently now. I'm seeing a whole new picture, and it's a lot brighter than it was before — and it's green instead of red. I've noticed changes in the things I do and say, and I think others saw it before I did. For example, about a year ago a friend of mine called me a, "tree hugging liberal piggy boy."

It was only after I had time to think about it that I came to the conclusion — he may be right. Now I think it's exactly what I am and I know how I got that way. I think I've always been a "liberal piggy boy" but the "tree hugger" thing is something relatively new. It's Libby Earthman and Sara Tremayne of the Putah Creek Council (PCC) that's got me hugging all the trees. Geeze, I didn't see that coming.

These two women of the Earth, along with my wife and her family, are responsible for this tree hugger attitude. I know that now, and I know that it's getting bigger, growing, growing ever bigger. Now I think the "tree hugger" part of me is taking over. I think my wife, Therese, and the ladies of the Putah Creek Council (PCC) have always been tree huggers because they come from tree hugging families. But I didn't. It's new to me.

I know I had it under control and I was planting a tree here and there, when the PCC had a volunteer planting event. That was about the extent of it; plant a tree every couple of weeks and that was it. I found that I enjoyed these planting events and wanted to go to all of them. On a small scale, I wanted to help plant the trees, and then it got bigger and I wanted to help maintain and water the trees, and this was no easy chore.

Things changed for me big time when the Putah Creek Stream Keeper, Rich Marovich, and the Winters City Manager, Jon Donlevy, started construction of their new Nature Park. I was like a little kid when I stood on the pedestrian bridge looking down at the workers. I thought, "I want to help, I want to help!" That was it! I was hooked! I was a purebred tree hugger, and there was nothing I could do about it.

Now I can envision a nature park in our town that will be a showpiece for all future work of this type. Tree huggers all over the state are watching and learning from this project, and it's right here in our town. I can't wait until this summer when the park will spring to life with the laughter of our young people as they run down the nature trails through the trees that we're planting and then jump into the crystal clear water of the creek with a yelp.

So, if you too want to get infected with the tree hugger bug, all you have to do is contact the PCC at (530) 795-3006 or at putahcreekcouncil.org and tell them you want to help. It's as simple as that. I know my credibility is not the best, but you can make a bet that if you help once, you'll help twice. This Winters Nature Park is infectious. Take a walk in the park. You can do it right now. It's worth every penny and for you, the visit is free. The entrance to the park is right behind the amphitheater by the railroad trestle bridge in downtown Winters. They built this park just for you.

There are those among us who are above the law. We all know who they are, and we're all pissed off about it. Who the heck do these people think they are? They think they can do anything and nothing will happen to them. Sometimes I can't believe some of the crap they do and get away with it.

I'm going to step into the shoes of one guy we all know, and play like I did what he did at certain points in his life. I'll spell it out for you and then you can be the judge as to whether I get away with it. This stuff is all true, every bit of it. Here we go:

• After high school I go to college and flunk out twice. (Not a crime, but it says a lot about my character)

• In 1962, I get a DUI and in 1963 I get a second one. I don't care!

• When I turn 18, I'm eligible for the draft (mid '60s) at a time when the draft board is taking everyone except married medical students. I apply for and receive five deferments. (Do you know how hard it was to get even one deferment? Next to impossible!) Every time I flunk out at school I get a notice to report to the draft board so I apply for a deferment and the dumb bastards give me one. Not only one, but four in a row. How dumb are they? Finally, I get tired of their crap and apply for a permanent exemption from military duty stating that my wife is gonna get pregnant. The dumb guys give it to me. I was given a 3-A status, the "hardship" exemption for free! How dumb is that? How can a rich guy have hardships? Oops! She lost the baby! Twenty years down the road, the Washington Post asked me why I didn't get drafted so I say, "I had different priorities other than military service."

• In 1969, I go to work for Richard M. Nixon in the Office of Economic Opportunity. Yeah, my opportunity. He who controls the money controls all, right?

• From there I go to the Cost of Living Council. Now I'm in, so I come up with a number of tricky solutions to underhanded problems of various Presidents. I am now the come-to guy when trouble knocks on the door. Some of my solutions are not exactly legal, but who's counting, right?

• In 1976, I run President Ford's re-election campaign. He loses.

• I am then elected as congressional representative for some loser state, I forget. I win that seat five times because I want it.

• In 1988 I am appointed Secretary of State because another guy couldn't get approval. Ha.

• I vote against the creation of the Department of Education because I need the money for something else. "It's an encroachment on state's rights," I say.

• I don't like Head Start either.

• In 1986 I vote against economic sanctions for South Africa because of apartheid. (Take that, Black people!) I say, "They almost never work." Congress believes me! Man, I never thought that one would work.

• In 1986, I, along with 145 Republicans and 31 Democrats, voted against a non-binding Congressional resolution calling on the South African government to release Nelson Mandela from prison, after the Democrats defeated proposed amendments that would have required Mandela to renounce violence sponsored by the African National Congress (ANC) and requiring it to oust the Communist faction from its leadership; the resolution was defeated. Appearing on CNN, I address criticism for this, saying I opposed the resolution because the ANC "at the time was viewed as a terrorist organization and had a number of interests that were fundamentally inimical to the United States. I say, "I was afraid they would blow up the world!"

• I get a Federal Energy Commission building named after me.

• 1989, I get nominated for Secretary of Defense. I get 100 percent approval from Congress. Those suckers owe me, right? We invade Panama for some dumb reason. I forget. We invade the Middle East and kick some butt. I get a medal from my bud, "W."

• In four years, I make the United States the munitions dealers to the world!

• Man, I'm not going to get into the dirty stuff I did after that, because you're too dumb to understand anyway. I only got caught once, and it cost me $500 million to get out of it. I got Halliburton to pay for it. Ha ha.

• Whatever. Next, I shoot a guy in the face with a shotgun and don't report it to the public for three days. Top that one. Oh, I outed a CIA operative too. Got away with that too, because Lewis "Scooter" Libby took the wrap for me. I told him Bush would pardon him. RRright!

• In 2002, I get to be Acting President of the United States while Bush gets a butt operation.

• Next, I define the meaning of torture! Got away with that too.

• The whole time I'm working for the government, I'm setting up no-bid contracts for Halliburton (I own part of it) worth billions of dollars. We don't even have to fulfill the contracts. How dumb is that?

So by now, you know who I am and of course you will have to agree that I'm above the law. Whatever, I don't care. I'm going to live forever. I can get a heart transplant whenever I want. When I die they'll have to beat my heart to death. Ha Ha.

OK, I'm back in my shoes now.

Well, there you have it in a nutshell. I don't have enough room to write about all the crap this guy did and got away with. When it comes to real crimes against the public, the worst crimes are committed by those who understand the law better than most. They can bend it. They can break it. They can make new ones that they can break as well.

If you're not upset by all this, then you are way far past ever having an honest government. Way past.

A Mormon miracle
5/6/2012

Last week, Libby Earthman and Sara Tremayne of the Putah Creek Council (PCC) asked me if I'd like to help them get ready for a very big volunteer planting event. "Wanna help?" they said. Well, I can tell you, I was on the spot because with Libby's beautiful smile and Sara's piercing blue eyes, how could I say no. I said, "Yes."

They told me that this is no ordinary volunteer planting event because there would be 300 to 400 people; all from the Mormon Church. At first I thought, "OMG, there is no way I want to be around 400 Mormons!" I thought they would be hanging around in little groups, preaching at me, and trying to save my soul. There was no way I wanted to hang around all day with 400 Mormons. There was no way I wanted to hang out with anybody.

I took a minute to let my big brain think this over. Well, I thought and I thought for about a whole minute or so before it dawned on me that for the last 50 years or so, only one person in the whole world was actively trying to save my soul. He is an elderly gentleman that comes to my house and gives me religious pamphlets and reads a word or two from the Bible. He comes about once a month, just like clockwork and he too is a Mormon. Yep, out of 7 billion people on Earth, only one Mormon cares about my soul.

However, that's a different story so I'll stick to the subject at hand. These volunteer planting events held by the PCC take a lot of planning and prep work. Well, I don't have to tell you that an event with 400 volunteers has to take a lot of extra preparation to get it ready. I helped and I helped every day for about 10 days because there are about a thousand little things that have to be done before the volunteer workers arrive. That's where I come in. Libby calls me her "Super Volunteer!"

Normally I will help with the preparatory work and then step out of the picture. Libby and Sara have an elite group of "Stewarts" that step in to direct the real planting event. So, to cut a long story and make it short, we worked and we worked every day for about 10 days to get everything ready for the coming of the Mormons. Some days I worked an entire hour.

The volunteer work that I do with the PCC not only keeps me active and less fat, and it puts me in a unique position to see what goes on behind the scene at these volunteer planting events that seem to be held every Saturday. I think it's about four times a month. If I put too many Saturdays in there, it would be over a month. Anyway, what I do see is the streamkeeper, Rich Marovich, and Libby and Sara working at least 10 hours every day, sometimes more, to get the Winters Nature Park ready for us to enjoy. I get really tired just watching them.

Like I said, this planting event is special, so I found my name on the PCC Stewart assignment list. I was to help Rich Marovich at the planting sites near where Pedrick Road intersects with Putah Creek. Our assignment was to direct the setting of about 250 posts and to run a large 2 1/2 inch rope for the length of about 2,000 feet. I thought that hundreds of Mormon volunteers would be bumping into each other and nothing would get done. I was wrong.

I've never seen anything like it since I got out of the Army. Arriving in a convoy, hundreds of Mormon volunteers with tools in hand moved like a thousand ants through the brush setting post after post, one after the other. Before I knew it, they were pulling the rope through the eye of the post like a giant snake, 2,000 feet long. I could not believe the amount of work they got done in just a few hours.

All of a sudden, I'm thinking to myself, "This was truly a miracle." I'm not talking about how much work they got done. The miracle I'm talking about was within me. For the very first time, I could see the members of the Mormon Church clearly. These people were top of the line. At a time when families across the world are falling apart, they are solidifying as an extended family; they are strengthening and nurturing themselves in righteousness and in truth. For them, every season is a season of goodwill.

I could clearly see that these Mormon families are the same families that crossed this country as pioneers. Their families are responsible for many of the good things we have today. These families built half of the roads and many of the cities from the East coast to the West. Yep, my big brain is telling me that these people of the Mormon Church are among the best of us and if I could be just a little more like them, I would feel much better about myself and I'd probably be a whole lot happier.

Goofy stuff every day, everywhere in the news
5/13/2012

Every day I read about current events on my computer, and every day I am amazed at how goofy some of the news reports are. Why such goofy stuff is displayed on a respectable news page is beyond me. All you have to do is read the headlines and stupid pops right at you, sucking you in like a tornado. When you are done reading this goofy news you will think, "I can't believe I wasted my time reading that!"

I'll give you a few examples:

Yesterday there was a lady, a dark brown lady, that was accused of putting her young daughter inside a tanning booth with her. The young lady, a dark brown young lady, admits to being inside the booth with her mother. Yet the mother says the daughter got her sunburn outdoors and she would never put her in a tanning booth.

OK, that's two stupids; stupid for putting her in the booth and stupid for lying about it.

A guy named Jose Rodriguez, a former CIA official responsible for perfecting water board techniques for interrogations of terrorists,
illegally destroyed 80-something CIA secret tapes, thinks he is above the law. He never denies destroying the tapes and says he did it to protect others.

Well, I guess he's right, he is above the law. If you or I had done this dirty deed, the DA would say that it doesn't matter why you destroyed the tapes, it is still a crime to destroy these tapes. Duh!

Scientists have invented a way to spray yourself drunk in an instant. It used to be called "huffing."

A guy in Spain was struck in the scrotum by lightning. Witnesses claim that the guy smells like roasted nuts.

A guy in New York says there are no ethics in today's business dealings, anywhere. I think he's right, because unethical does not mean illegal, right?

Most special investment vehicles, mortgage-backed securities and hedge funds, that include mortgage default investment and others like them, have structures that are too difficult for even sophisticated investors to fully comprehend, yet people keep pouring their money down that drain. I think that's just goofy.

If you go to your bank and put $100 in a savings account, you'll be lucky if the bank pays you 1% in interest for a year. If you take out a bank-sponsored credit card, the bank will charge you 25% or more in interest. That's pretty goofy. What is "pump and dump?" It's the practice of selling stocks at a cheap rate to folks like you and me. What's goofy about this is the fact that there is some company selling the stocks at a cheap rate to get out from under a stock before it collapses.

Did I say that right? Anyway, we look to stock analysts to direct us to which stocks we should buy. Most of the time it is the analysts that are
selling the stock they are telling us to buy! Goofy!

Rachel "Bunny" Melon thought that paying John Edward's hookers was foolish but fun. She should be put in the same cell Edwards is put in.

Inisliroo Island, a part of Ireland, is for sale at a measly $970,000. We should buy it and put it in the middle of Putah Creek.

Argentine parents went to say goodbye to their child that had previously died and found him alive in the morgue 12 hours later. I think their doctor should be buried instead of the baby.

That's it! I can't read any more. Especially when you consider the fact that if you weren't reading this, you'd have to go to the internet to read your goofy news. Here, you get goofy news for free, or if you wish you can send me a dime @ don_t_b_a_sap.com.

Madge visits Winters
5/20/2012

At rare moments in time, the Earth, along with all of the other planets in our solar system, aligns with the Sun to make a straight line. It is a moment of severe struggle. The unseen force that surrounds one object thrashes about, pushing against the unseen force of the next. The unseen force becomes confused, thus, for one miniscule moment nothing moves. The line holds.

In time, with a burst of energy, the line fails. Each object is thrown out and returns, as before, to encircle the sun. From a distance, the system looks just as it did before, the same. Wait, it is not the same. The unseen force that holds objects together and then forces them apart is the only true constant in all of this. Everything else changes. Thus, the system is not as it was before; something is different.

The time has come to pull out my big brain. It is a time for heavy thinking. There on page one of my copy of "Stellar Astrophysical Fluid Dynamics for Dummies" was a yellow Post-it note on which I had written, "Madge Woods coming to Winters." The note was dated several months ago.

I thought, "Oh my God, it's happened! Madge is here!"

I thought again a second after I thought the first thing. My big brain was working like a well- cooked fast food hamburger that I call sliders because when you eat them, they slide in and then they slide out just as quickly. I thought how sexy I must look, standing there thinking like I was, all inside my head.

I'll have to take you back to the beginning so you'll understand. Baacckkk, baacckk. Clear your mind. Madge Woods is on the top ten list of Who's Who in Los Angles. Word is that she runs that city and one word from her can make you or break you. Another rumor says that Bill Gates ripped off the idea for Microsoft from her desk. Bill Gates was found in a gutter shortly afterwards with one of his testicles in his coat pocket.

Madge, a world class writer, sends a piece into the iPinion Syndicate once in awhile, so that's how we met online. Anyway, to make a short story shorter, she wanted to come to Winters to meet the local writers, one of which is me. She wanted to see the grand tour of Winters, so I said I would show her everything. I thought, "Aw, she won't come to this town, it just isn't going to happen." You know what happened next? She came.

She had an itinerary. I don't know what that is, but she had one. She had me listed to show her around Winters. I'd hoped that she would forget all about me, but that wasn't going to happen either. She wanted to see everything. So, with no hesitation, I turned my socks and underwear inside out to the clean side in case she put me in the hospital. I wet my greasy hair, sprayed hairspray all over it, put on my best cologne, and put a bit of toothpaste in my mouth so she would think I brushed my teeth and took a shower.

I didn't want to ride in her Mercedes Royce, so I picked her up in my sleek, black F-150 and showed her the Winters Nature Park and told her how I had planned the whole park and singlehandedly had planted every tree and bush. After that, I pointed out the Glory Hole and explained that it was really a Black Hole in this part of the galaxy. After that I decided to show her my greatest triumph that never got built because the City Manager, Jon Donlevy wouldn't buy me 15 miles of four-foot OD concrete pipe.

I said, " Yep, the Sanders Muon Ringy Thingy was supposed to go underground from here to the City of Davis and back." We were going to build it at night so no one would know that we were going to tunnel under their property. She said," Don't you think that the people in Davis would know you were building a super collider under their streets?" Then I said, "Nah, they won't know it's there until things start poppin' under their sidewalks."

At that, she wanted to know why the city manager wouldn't help me build a supercollider. I told her that I think he must be jealous of how good looking and smart I am. That's the only reason I could think of at the spur of a moment. (Sorry Mr. Donlevy but I didn't know what to say.) I finished by saying that we all (meaning everybody in Winters) would have gotten rich selling Higgins Particles to tourist. They are the smallest particles in the world and no one could see them anyway, so all we'd have to do is sell them a package with nothing in them. Big bucks too.

That evening, Madge treated everyone from iPinion to dinner and then gave us all a hug, and then she was gone. I think a helicopter picked her up by the Chevron station. I think she is considering financing my Muon Ringy Thingy too, because as she flew off she told me to wait there for her until she comes back, and she even gave me a finger wave until she was out of sight. That's what I was doing standing around for three days at the Chevron. I was not stalking anyone either!

I don't think she's coming back.

We're all a part of this process
5/27/2012

Current events seem to draw different responses from different racial groups. Some responses are understandably angry and nearing the point where they will turn to violence, while others seem unresponsive and indifferent. It seems odd to me that, depending upon the event, one group's response can be so different from another's when the event so obviously affects both groups equally and in the same way. This is what I'm having a little trouble with.

Take for instance the killing of Trayvon Martin at the hands of night watchman George Zimmerman or the Marissa Alexander case, both of Florida. What a clusterfuck these two cases are. It is apparent to me that much of white America would like these matters to just go away. They don't seem to care about how they go away, they just want them to go away. They don't care.

Our citizens of color see things in a whole different light. They are understandably angry and many are on the verge of open revolt. In their eyes, they have never had justice or equality. For them, nothing has changed in the last 200 years. For them, they are still segregated and subject to discrimination and racism from white America and indeed the government. Should you feel this is not the case, then take a drive through Richmond and see how it compares with Concord or Walnut Creek.

African Americans males are incarcerated at more than six times the rate of white males and Hispanic males more than double the rate. One of every eight black males in the age group 25-29 is incarcerated on any given day. More than one in three young black men without a high school diploma are in prison.

It angers me simply to have to say these words: "More black men without a high school diploma are incarcerated than employed." We all know it's more difficult to secure a job once a person has spent time in jail or prison. Incarceration limits the options of the already less fortunate. In fact, black men earn 44 percent less after they've been incarcerated — four percent less than the average for all races/ethnicities.

Many will argue that there have been many, many advances in the racial disparities area in this nation. This may be true. but again I say take a drive in Richmond and compare the schools there with the schools in Walnut Creek and Concord. Do you think that what you find there is what Melba P. Beals waded through an army of angry white southerners for? Do you think this is what equal education is?

An even larger question is — do you feel this has no affect on you? The fact of the matter is that the United States houses over one quarter of the world's incarcerated. There are more prisoners within the borders of the United States than in the top 32 European countries combined. One in every 28 children in the US has an incarcerated parent.

Everyone seems to be in their own little world, working on their own little problems. LGBT Americans feel they are denied their civil rights. There are women's rights groups, religious groups, human rights groups, technology and liberty groups, and national security groups calling for election reforms and transparent government. Everybody wants something and they all want it now.

In the process, the Earth's population is depleting our planet's natural resources at a rate faster than what is needed for those resources to be replenished. The planet has lost 30 percent of its resources over the past 40 years. Our economy is failing and Americans blame the government. Sixty-five percent of all Americans see the government as the greatest threat to their liberty.

Much of America thinks they can save money on the cost of insurance if they simply drive away from the accident. They wonder who is the bigger fool — the person that knows everything or the person that argues with him. They think that people who talk shit to you usually talk shit about you. They think that animal crackers are bullshit because the elephant tastes just like the giraffe.

Americans waste their energy on a myriad of problems and in doing so they have lost sight of the big picture. Yes, people want change and they want justice and equality for our African American friends but no one wants to do the footwork to get it all together. They don't want to get involved. No one wants to think about these things and what it will take to solve our problems.

Well, I have news for you. You are involved, you will have to do the footwork, and you will have to think about it.

A quote from A. Einstein will sum it all up for us: "The world as we have created it is a process of our thinking. It cannot be changed without changing our thinking."

The problems that come with thinking
6/3/2012

I've been thinking for some time now about what will happen in the tomorrow land. Everyone knows what a great thinker I am, so I won't go into that, too much. I've been thinking since I was about 21 years old. Before that, I was simply walking through the days looking for ways to avoid certain people that would force-feed me vegetables.

The first time I can remember thinking was when I came up with the brilliant idea to stick the spinach from my plate directly into my pocket. Sometimes an idea works out and sometimes it doesn't. My pocket idea was great for a couple of days until Sister Conchadda told me to meet her in the laundry room directly after chapel. I didn't know why she wanted to see me but since I had learned how to think, maybe she was going to give me some candy.

Normally, when someone walks down the long third floor hallway, their shoes would make a clacking noise so that someone at the far end could hear you coming. However, one of my shoes had the heal broken off, so when I walked it would go, "clack-hurumph, clack-hurumph, clack-hurumph." By the time I got to the end of the hall and entered the laundry room it was, "whistle-clack-hurumph, whistle-clack-hurumph." I thought it was pretty cool, like it was my theme song.

Around the corner my little dance ended real abruptly like. Had I known the Sister was standing there I wouldn't have run into her like that. As it was, my face went right into her breast. I started thinking again and figured that this had to be the first time I had ever touched a real breast. Sister Conchadda didn't like it much though. I didn't know that a nun could curse like that.

"Are these your pants?" she ranted at me. Now normally a person could say, "Hell I don't know, how am I supposed to know?" Normally I would have gotten away with it too. You see, on laundry day, all the boys would get into a line and take off all of their clothes except for their underwear. The fact of the matter is that we might as well not even wear the underwear because there were so many holes in them that if you put them on your head, you could see, hear, smell, and breath through separate holes.

Anyway, when you got to the end of the line, the Sister held up clothing to see if they would fit you. If it looked like a fit, that's what you wore for the next week. You never got the same clothes twice, and there were hundreds of boys in that building. So, you can see how easy it would be to say, "Hell, I don't know if I wore those pants!"

Like I said, "Normally I could say that." However, these were special pants. Whoever had worn these pants worked in the kitchen and while in the kitchen, whoever wore these pants cleaned all of the grease traps. The shiny grease trap pants from the laundry were a perfect match for the shiny grease trap pants I was wearing. So there and then I started thinking again and said, "Well, those could be my pants but I'm not really sure."

Sister Conchadda gave me an indignant look, and when she does that, one of her eyes kinda twitches a little. Eye a twitchin', she said, "Well, I think these are your pants because inside one of the pockets I found this." With a deep feeling of horror, I watched her pull a wad of dried-up spinach coated with pocket lint and some little sticks of grass from the playground.

There in that laundry room, Sister Conchadda made me eat that wad of spinach and I gagged a bit with each bite. I think I even threw up a little in my mouth.

Halfway through the wad I told her, "I don't think these are my pants at all, Sister."
I remember vividly the words that came from her lips that evening.

She said, "You shouldn't think so much!"

The problem is, I'm a thinker. That's what I do best. How can I stop now?

I'm stuck in the name-game
6/17/2012

The name game is something the government does because they think it will make everything all right. They think that we, the American people, are stupid. They think that if they put 58,000 names on a memorial wall we will think that the enemy is at fault. They are hoping that no one reads the Pentagon Papers or its newer counterpart, Wikileaks.

If you've never played the name game, you're in for a treat, so read on. Just read down the list and when you see someone that's familiar, you can inject your own information into the game.

There are a lot of names on the game list that all have played so well, Zywicke is at the bottom, on the top was a guy named Aadland, and half way down is a man named Noah. Among them lie 64 Sanders, nine Shafers, a Febus, a Feck, and a Fee. A Feedler, a Pharr, are above and below a Nunn, a Nutt and a Null. There's an Obie, an Oats and an Olsen, with a Gob that died in a boat.

Noonan, Noots, Noto and Nott are full of N's and O's. There's Wessels and Watts, and Xavier, who was the single solitary X. Plenty of Olsens, Allens and Adams, so I can't complain about that. Alvarez was from Texas — he could throw a ball too hard to catch. Forty-six Wests, seven Easts, a few Norths, and no Souths nor South-South-Easts. A bunch of Wades and plenty of Wells,are with a Valdez that died by himself in a fire.

Sixty-seven Whites, and about as many Blacks, fly with Finches and Robins while Ozunz and Oxedine walk. Kjos was never found, so he had a birth and a death with no time in between. Jansinski, Ell, and Duncan died at night, out there together in the dark, while Fred Neal drowned in his very own vomit. Five guys — Straw, Ward, Dennison, Prentice and Rayburn — died when their Chinook in the air hit a Huey.

Quill was run over by a tank but with O'hara it was only an APC. O'Neal got hit by a bullet and Berry got hit by truck. Darrell lost a foot, then a leg, then his life. Wackerfuss, Waddel and Waldscald are with Warmsbrodt in the W's above the Z's. Upshaw, Utter, and Utz stay with Urban in the U's.

Kaatz, Kaawa and Kabara were knocked to the ground and kant, kant, kant get up to go home. A guy named Meade told me he got married, but I can't remember how he died or what he looked like. Sisk got a hole in his chest that spit blood onto my face. His chicken-plate would have saved his life if he had worn it instead of sitting on it to save his ass and everything in that area.

There's Gold and a Golden and Iron and Steele, and Golda — he was a Jew. Kakak and Kalsu and Kalu couldn't be found and would fit in one shoe. Koons and Krill and Kent all began with a "K" but Danowski began with a "D." Krist and Kabarra know that the karma is piled up high on me because they think I killed Buddha and my sins are mixed with Faddey's who killed for pleasure. There's British and Yanks, and Arab and Jew, and the dinks on the other side.

I am still here and I'm back on the block, but part of me is with them. Every day I wish I had died and they had a small chance to live, for the best of me belongs with them and the worst of me sleeps in my bed.

The list of the name-game is long and it is hard where the dead are used for heroin like an envelope is for a letter. Our name-game list is 58,000 strong as it is long but it is an inch when compared to another. Two million to 3,000,000 and onward and upward it went for the Vietnamese in the American War. I can only say, "I'm sorry" but you won't listen to me. You were so young and faire and handsome but we killed you anyway.

Everything figured out
7/1/2012

Big news this week! Big news. I'm going to tell you all about my plan to make us all a big wad of cash. All you have to do is listen to me. The time is perfect and all of the key figures are in perfect position to make this plan work like a bowel soaked in caster oil. I didn't have to think a whole heck of a lot about this because it is not a new plan — I thought of this a long time ago.

In the past, I had a lot of trouble just trying to get somebody to acknowledge the fact that my plan really exists and is feasible in its nature. Many have already guessed what I'm talking about and yes, I'm talking about "The Sanders Particle" or the "Higgs Particle" as the outsiders call it. (Outsider by definition is someone that lives outside the city limits of the city of Winters, California.)

I'll break it down for you, AGAIN, and this time you'd better pay attention because if we don't build my particle accelerator this time, I'm going to start my own town across the creek and build it myself. If I'm forced to go to that sort of extreme action and I have to do all of the work myself, well I'm sorry to say that you, my fine furry friends, will get none of the profit. Profit is a word some numbers guy made up to describe cash, cold cash that jingles in your pocket.

Here's a little history of my well thought out plan and what I have been doing to get this project under way. Some years ago, I sent John Donlevy, our city manager, a detailed drawing of how I thought our accelerator should be built and financed. At that time I wasn't rich like I am now, so I suggested the City of Winters pay for approximately 4,322 eight foot pieces of four foot ID reinforced concrete pipe. The cost would have been minimal, say 50 bucks or a little more.

I suggested we put the pipe underground so no one could see it but we needed to leave a small hole so everybody could see it was really there. At that time, I also suggested that we say we had discovered the Sanders/Higgs Particle. It is a fact that no one has ever seen or actually could ever see the particle because it would be the smallest thing in existence. It would have to be as small as the head of a pin or the head of a .1123145" nail. The plan was to sell packages of empty air to tourists, saying the particle was inside but you would have to have an electron microscope to see it.

It was a perfect plan but alas, no one would give me a red cent for the plan of a lifetime. Had the plan gone through we all would be wallowing in cash at this very moment. Think of it! We'd be just like little piggies rolling around in thousand dollar bills snorting, "Oink, oink, more money, more, more, more!" We would be so happy, so happy.

I can't remember for sure but I think the city manager, John Donlevy, sent my drawing back with this comment written on it. It said, "Sorry little guy. Maybe you should give this drawing to your teacher. I'll bet you would get a good grade. But thanks for sharing." At least I think I remember this happening, maybe not.

We have to consider this plan now because the CERN Accelerator over there in Switzerland (Just north of Africa, I think) is saying they're going to announce that they have the Higgs particle. Holy crap! We only have a week or so to get it done and announce it to the world or those guys are gonna get all the money for an invisible thingy.

Here is my new plan. It's short and sweet because we don't have a lot of time. Ready, here it is:

• Since we have a new Mayor, Cecilia Aguiar-Curry, the timing is perfect. She is the perfect person to announce our accelerator to the world. From what I understand she is a very intelligent and warm-hearted person. On top of that, it doesn't hurt us that she happens to be very pretty. A lot prettier than Woody Fridae. However, Mr. Fridae is a good-looking man, uh huh. (No I'm not gay, I'm a married man but I do think a lot about him in a plutonic way and he is very handsome, yeah.)

• We already have the construction company in place near the creek, so we just slip them a few bucks to say they built the collider ring around the Winters Nature Park. Since they are building a path around the park, it will look like the ring is actually under there. If someone wants to look inside the ring, we simply tell them, "It's classified!"

• We print out a bunch of pamphlets saying, "World awaits latest results in hunt for Higgs particle." Wait, I mean Sanders Particle.

• I suggest we have Tony Luna and Juan Valeriano of the City of Winters, present the work to the public as the administrator and head engineer of the project. They're two really good looking guys so they will fit in like oil on a.. Well never mind about that.

• We have to bury at least one piece of pipe just in case someone digs it up on 20/20 or some TV show like that.

• The rest is easy street. We simply staple sandwich bags to a label saying the Sanders Particle is inside and sell it all over town for like 50 bucks each. How the hell is anyone going to dispute that the particle is not in the package, it's the smallest thing in the world, right? Huh! Perfect!

Sometimes I amaze myself. I wonder what I could do if I used my whole brain when I think?

This will work, trust me.

I dream of trees
7/8/2012

I've been dreaming about trees. In these dreams, the trees talk to me and tell me things. Some of these dreams are upsetting to say the least. It's not the trees that upset me, it's the things that they tell me. They tell me things of nature and history, great things, worthy of my thought. They tell me things of man's relationship with the whole of nature, but from their perspective.

They told me why God made trees before he made man. They told me what the Earth was like before man came and what happened after he came. They told me what they thought of man, and what he has done and what they hope he will do.

The history of man is just a small part of the history of trees. At one time, the trees and man could communicate but that's gone now, no one knows why. Now trees can only communicate with man's spirit, mostly in his dreams. When asleep, the trees can talk to us as if we were one of them, a part of them, a part of nature. In the daylight, when we're awake, we look at trees and we can see that they want to tell us something, but we just can't seem to hear them.

They came to my dreams because I'm a man of words. The trees have asked me to convey to you what they wish you to understand about them. Of course, you'll have to remember that these are not my words but those of the trees I see in my dreams. This is what they tell me:
They send you greetings and hope that you will hear and understand what they're trying to say. They will try to keep it simple at first, hoping that even the youngest of men will know that they speak the truth. It is very important to them that we understand exactly what they want us to know.

They are afraid of man. They are in a state of constant fear of what man will do to this Earth. They say that at one time the flow of ideas was freely given, and taken with a mutual love and respect between man and the trees. Man, all of a sudden, stopped talking to them and they don't know exactly why. The trees were confused, bewildered and at a loss of what to do about it. At this time, the history of the trees split away from the history of man.

Through the passing of days, man started mistreating the trees, depriving them of food and water and destroying great swathes of trees so man could move about more quickly. Man built great machines to help them destroy the trees at an ever-growing rate. The trees thought man could no longer see them as living things. To save themselves, the only thing the trees could do is move away from man, but trees take years to do what man can do in a day.

You can imagine how afraid the trees had become and to make matters worse, man no longer wanted to live among the trees and considered them a nuisance and in the way of their progressive movement. Man had begun to consider trees and animals as tools to be used at his will, cut down and slaughtered when they saw fit. So you see, it was easy for the trees to move away from man, one seed at a time.

Once the trees have moved away from man, the animals and water soon followed but their rate of travel was faster, so the movement was noted by man. Man argued and argued about what should be done. With delays and inaction, relatively little was actually done until man was alone with the soil that had no nourishment for him and could not hold the moisture that man needs to survive.

At this point, even the soil wanted to leave, and it too feared man. The soil looked to the wind to carry it up and away from man. When the winds came, the soil lifted itself a grain of sand at a time until the air was as heavy as the land moving around in swirls. The swirls of soil made man cover his eyes and thirst for water and shade, of which there was none. Man was now alone. Man started to die.

The trees and the soil and the water knew that if man died then a great part of themselves would die as well. Despite their immense fear of man, the trees turned and went to save man from himself and his destructive nature. Again, the trees moved a seed at a time, slowly, slowly. The water carried the seed and the soil that would bring life back to man.

With the aid of the water, great fertile flood plains where the trees would grow strong and tall arose out of the dead land. The trees, in their quest to save man rushed (in their own pace) to fill the voids where they had lived many years ago. Every kind of tree and every kind of plant once again thrived and turned the Earth to a lush green. It was beautiful.

The trees and plants came in such great numbers that soon it became a mess. The roots of one tree was choking the next plant until they both became sick and began to die. The insects attacked the sick plants and some of the plants had no defense. In their rush to save man, the plants found themselves in places that were not healthy for them. They found that the wrong kinds of plants in the wrong place was causing great sickness that would spread and eventually everything, the trees, the soil, the water, and man would soon perish.

In my mind somewhere, I could see the sun rising. I knew I had to hurry any questions I had for the trees, so I said, "Why, with man's history, did you want to save them and why did you choose to communicate with me?" The tree told me that I am not the first man that they communicated with. There were many before me, all around me. I knew instantly that they had visited the dreams of people like Rich and Libby, and Carol, and Sara, and John because they were already working to save the plants by separating them into native and non-native plants and putting them where they belong. In jest, I told the tree that that was a terrible run-on sentence.

I had lost my faith in man but if even the plants can see that man was capable of great acts of kindness, goodness, and even nobility, then I could see it as well. With the coming of the sun, I put on my work boots and went to seek out those that came before me (Rich and Libby) to find my task of the day, watering, planting, or fertilizing the trees. Whatever, I don't care what task I'm given, because I want to save the trees and the trees want to save me.

The gift of sight
7/22/2012

I think City Hall is out to get me. I know what you're thinking, "Rrriiight!" No I'm not crazy, this is for reals. Picture if you will, a hydrant, a sailboat, and a trailer full of chairs — folding chairs. Just keep those pictures in your mind and I'll get back to them later.

This isn't the only time that the City has been after me. A couple of years ago, I wrote something in the local paper that had the words, "city" and "noise" in the same sentence. I didn't mean anything was bad about the city, but someone way up high must have thought so because it wasn't a week later that a big van and a bunch of workers showed up in front of my house. They started making a bunch of noise that woke me up at 11:30 a.m. For all of you guys from France, that means "pretty early in the morning."

I remember thinking, "Why do they have to work by my house and why are they going down into the sewers?" Peeking out of my curtains, I could see that besides the white van, there was a crew of musclemen and a big, mean looking lady and she kept looking over at my house. The lady had a clipboard too. I remember thinking, "Do they even make clipboards anymore?"

Anyway, these guys were as busy as bees in a pod and I didn't know it at the time but they were sticking a basketball in the sewer line of every house on the block — EXCEPT MINE. Next thing I know, they're opening up the van and inside was a giant air pump. A giant air hose was placed strategically into the manhole so they could pump in a bunch of air. I remember thinking, "Why are they pumping in a bunch of air?"

What I found out was this: The force of air or, F/Air, against a barrier of basketballs, or "Poo Stop" results in only one thing. Poo will flow uphill into the only sewer line with no basketball, or as it is commonly known, "My house." The sewage from every house on the block blew up my bathroom.

I went out and told the lady that I thought she may have blown up my bathroom. She looks at me kinda funny and said, "We'll send a camera up the line and take a photo, that will tell us what's up." Having said that, she disappeared and I was standing there looking around with a poo-eating grin on my face.

Less than 30 seconds later, a letter dropped through my mail slot. The letter was short and sweet and it accompanied two photos of the outlet of my sewer line. The letter said, "Dear Mr. Sanders, as you can see, there is nothing in these photos that would explain the cause of the sewage backflow into your house. It shall remain a mystery." It ended with a scribbled signature.

OK, that was the first time the city was out to get me. It wasn't all that bad, because I just boarded up the old bathroom and built another one on the other side of the house. Now they're out to get me again because I called and reported a boat, upside down, in the creek.

The next day. I was working in my little workshop, whittling on a piece of wood, when my wife yells at me that a police officer is at the door. Sure enough there stood Sgt. Ramirez of the local PD. I remember thinking, "Oh crap, there was a body inside the boat and they think I did it!" I was getting scared until he explained that he would like me to show him where I saw the boat.

Next thing I know, we're hiking down this path through the woods and automatically I was back in Vietnam, and I was worried about my troops trying to frag me again. In the distance I could hear Sgt. Ramirez saying, "Mr. Sanders, Mr. Sanders" and I found myself in a patch of poison oak.

I started crying a little bit and was going to ask him to help me out of the poison oak, but he was sneezing, from allergies I guess. I might have been hearing things but every time he sneezed, in the place of a sneeze sound he would say, "uradummy!" Then he would sneeze again with the same sound, "uradummy."

Next thing I know, I'm surrounded by cops and they're all sneezing, "uradummy." I shook my head a couple of times and then it dawned on me what was happening. I think maybe the sneezing thingy was all in my mind but what I really did see was something really rare because nobody, I mean nobody, ever gets to see a cop in a relaxed state of mind.

OK, I'm in the water with the cops and we're trying to turn this darn boat over so we can get it out of the creek. Sgt. Ramirez is up on the bank barking orders, "Turn it over, turn it over!" knowing the damn thing weighs a thousand pounds. We're all laughing and having a good time.

I felt so surprised because I never realized that cops could have a good time. I looked at them and thought, "Man, how cool is this, I get to have a good time with the cops — our cops." It was like my birthday and someone had given me a nice gift — the gift of sight.

At that I went back to pushing that darn boat and I forgot all about the hydrant and the trailer full of chairs — folding chairs.

Self-preservation means knowing how to keep yourself safe
7/29/2012

There is terrible news out of Colorado lately. What would motivate a guy to dye his hair orange, walk into a theater, and start shooting everyone he sees. When crimes like this happen, it not only horrifies us, it makes us wonder when and where it will happen again. The sad truth is that it will happen again and it could happen anywhere at any time.

There is an assault every 17 seconds in the United States! The reality is that 17 – 20 people will be murdered. and another 1,500 will be assaulted, raped, stabbed, shot or beaten every week. What can you do? Do we throw up our hands and surrender ourselves to the will of sociopaths so involved in self-love or self-hate that they resort to violence to feel better? I think not.

One of the greatest threats to anyone is having a mindset based in denial and the belief that violence will never happen to you. Believe me, it can happen to you. This being said, when it comes to protecting my family and friends, I am dead serious when I say the words, "Protect yourself at all times." My family hasn't seen what I've seen. When I tell them over and over again to think about self-protection they think I'm being negative and paranoid. I think I'm being prepared, practical and realistic in a violent world.

Now here is the problem with self-protection. How do you recognize danger and people that are a threat you? Most of these sociopaths look like you and I. They are you and I except for either a biological/neurological error or big mistakes in nurturing and socialization. They blend in very well. They may be fellow students, neighbors, service people; a guy at a bar, coffee shop, grocery store or any one we routinely meet in our days travels and don't think twice about.

One individual who was a "stalker-voyeur-burglar-rapist" with a several year crime spree who after being caught, turned out to be a respected fireman. These criminals often learn how to be very disarmingly friendly or charismatic so you let your guard down or don't notice them. So what do we do?

Easy! Always be aware of your environment and plan for attack situations. I have said these words over and over to my family and they never seem to listen to what I am saying. I tell them, "If you don't watch out for yourself, nobody is!" I tell them, "Situational awareness, staying out of bad places and away from bad people, and taking care of your personal security are mostly all that will ever be needed to avoid violence."

A predator doesn't need to have fancy attack methods but they can be mean, brutal and highly aggressive. Against the fellow (average person) who is not fully committed in attacking you or hurting you, little skill or conditioning is needed. Most of the time basic self-defense techniques will suffice. Concentrate on escape and avoidance. Stand and fight only in extreme cases.

Teach your loved ones to be aware of their actions, to be cognizant of their surroundings, to be proactive in terms of "Not Getting Into Trouble, in the first place." Tell them to lock doors, secure windows, not leave Rolexes lying about on the dashboard, and how to carry a handbag or rucksack.

Tell them not to carry anything that they can't stand to abandon and flee at any moment. Raise their awareness of how clothing affects your ability to fight and flee (and that the flight part is FAR more important to real world personal safety and security than fighting skills.) Tell them hesitation can be deadly.

For most people, who are not cops, soldiers or otherwise engaged in a job field requiring proximity to and involvement in violent conflict, a few well-trained techniques are all that are necessary — techniques that will be used to resist and escape, not to stand there and fight.

Your attacker may be armed. You should know how to effectively use cover, concealment and escape tactics to protect yourself from being shot, struck or otherwise attacked! The fact that police officers, who are carrying guns, night sticks and pepper spray, still get attacked, should tell you that weapons mean absolutely nothing to an aggressive nut intent on introducing you to his world of violence.

The chances of having a skilled fighter attack you anywhere is slim. If you are to engage in personal violence, chances are, things have gone tits-up and all your personal security and safety preparations have failed anyway and you're going to be fighting for your life. Therein lies the big difference between "self-defense" and "close quarters combat."

Against a motivated criminal assailant, who does not care how much he hurts you just as long as he gets paid, things really start to get dicey from there. Believing they are not trained and practiced at what they do is a mistake. They also have far less civilized compunction about doing harm to others. They will also typically be armed in some way. Your need for a combative skill (not the same thing as "martial arts") just shot up.

You are allowed to defend yourself within reasonable means and with lethal force if necessary. When it's all over, you will need to justify why you believed that your life or the life of your family was in jeopardy. Just be sure you're not using more force than is necessary — it's strictly business so do not lose your temper, ever!

A rule that I always live by and learned at a very early age is: Have fun but always be aware of what is going on around you and keep one eye for the everyday living of life and one eye for your personal protection.

A bad day at Putah Creek
8/5/2012

I had a bad day at Putah Creek today. When I say bad day, I mean bad day! The last time I had a day this bad was in 1970. That day was bad too. So, here's the deal. I'm going to tell you about my latest bad day, but I don't want everybody to know, so keep this to yourself.

On this particular day I woke up very early. So early, in fact, I had to look to see if the sun was up. I looked at my watch and it said 9:30. My wife was just going out the door to visit her godfather that was turning 90 years old. I had to make my own bowl of cereal. It was Fruity Pebbles. I spilled a little bit on my shirt, but that's OK, I wore this shirt yesterday so it wasn't clean anyway.

I thought about taking a bath but I was already dressed, so why take them all the way off again just for a bath. I was all set for a cowboy movie, but there was a stinkin' bicycle race on one channel and a bunch of people swimming up little lined isles on the next. I thought, "Heck with this, I'm going down to the creek." (I've been helping out at the new nature park.)

My plan was to get out the weed eater and cut up some Himalayan blackberries before they spread all over the creek. So, some 30 minutes or so later, I was weed whacking berries down at the creek. Everything was going just fine and I was whacking away at those berries until something stung me on the arm. I thought, "Dangit, I've been stung on the arm!"

This sort of thing doesn't happen to me very often so I just keep cutting those berries. Next thing I know, I'm stung again, on the same arm. I thought, "Wow, imagine that. I've been stung twice in one day. I'll bet that will never happen again in a hundred years." I kept cutting those berries.

The funny thing was that I never saw a single bee, wasp, or anything else of that nature. I thought, "I wonder if they're nannobees?" That's when it happened! All of a sudden those nannobees were stinging me all over my body. I didn't have to think about that so I started thinking about how I'm going to get away from those bees.

Now, a smart man would have jumped in the creek, so I took off running the other way. I stopped about 100 yards from the berries and paused a moment before I decided to run some more. I ran to my truck and tried to get in the door. It dawned on me that I still had the weed eater strapped onto my chest because I couldn't actually get in the truck, but I tried just the same. The weed eater blade was throwing sparks when I tried to close the door.

It was about this point in time when I started hearing a little girl screaming. The screaming got louder and louder until I realized that it was me, screaming like a little girl. Now, I didn't know what to do, so I got out of the truck and ran to the other door thinking it would be easier to get the weed eater in on that side. That didn't work either.

Of course, those nannobees were still stinging me just about everywhere there is to be stung. The screaming got louder and more desperate, so I rolled the window down thinking I could stick the weed eater out the window and drive away really fast. I mean to tell you I was just going to start crying when all of a sudden they quit stinging me.

OK, I'll swear on a stack of Bibles that I never saw a single bee. If it wasn't for all the pain I would think that it was all in my mind. You know, psychotramatical, or something like that. Anyway, my mind drifted back to my childhood and the first time I was stung by a bee. Stung once, my whole body began to swell until no one could recognize me. It took a trip to the emergency room and a couple of shots to bring me back to my normal, beautiful self.

I remember thinking, "I'd better get someone to check on me for the next couple of hours or I could die and no one would even know till they saw the weed eater sticking out of the window of my truck. I called everyone I know and no one was home. Next I sent text messages to everyone. No answers there either.

There was nothing for me to do except to turn on the TV, lie down, and die. The stupid bicycle race was still on, so I turned it to Martha Stewart and laid my head on a picture of Jesus. I was almost gone, and a bright light came upon me and I was healed except for the bee stings when the phone rang and my friend Libby Earthman said she was sending her husband, Reid, over to babysit me until my wife got home.

So this is how it was. I was chit-chatting away and Reid was watching the bicycle race. I asked him if he was going to give me mouth-to-mouth if I should stop breathing. Well, the odds of that happening didn't look good to me so I acted like I was watching the bicycle race too but I remember thinking, "Yeah, he'll give me mouth-to-mouth if I stop breathing."

So, now I'm thinking this story would make a good column so I sit down at the computer to put it all down on paper. Well, not paper but, aw never mind. Anyway, now I'm hungry, so I get two pieces of raisin bread and pop them in the toaster. They pop back out all by themselves. I go to spread butter on the first but when I pick up the second piece a raisin sticks to my finger and burns a blister on it.

Now I'm typing this stupid column with the ring finger on one hand and the index finger on the other one. So that's the story, but don't tell anyone because if everything works out, I might be able to get my friend Steve to finish cutting those stupid Himalayan blackberries for me.

To be, or not to be
8/12/2012

There are a few things I'd like to say to the young men of the world. I'm not going to criticize or lecture, that's not my intention. I simply want to give you a few words of admonishment. The world is moving at an ever-increasing rate in every direction. I'd like to say a few words that I wish someone had said to me when I was a young man in the hope that it will help you choose your way.

First things first. Try to be a good man. If you can do this, everything else will fall nicely into place for you. By the age of 18, you should be able to pick and choose who will be in your peer group. Seek out and join men from around the world who are not afraid of being friendly and fair at all times. Become one with the true men of distinction who recognize and respect the dignity of others, especially women and children.

If you consistently honor the worth of others, you will become a man worthy of honor. Never leave a man, woman, boy or girl standing out in the cold of injustice and insensitivity. Learn to seek the good in others as well as you seek the good in yourself. Do these simple things and you will become a light in the darkest of places. You will be part of the solution rather than part of the problem.

A few simple rules will help you see exactly what type of personality other men have, almost as soon as you meet them. A man that is loud and overpowering is a little man trying to be a big man. I call it "The Little Man Syndrome." When I say this, I am not concerned with the physical size of a man — I'm talking about the size of the man on the inside, where it counts.

It's easy to distinguish a good man from a not-so-good man if you observe them in difficult situations when they are under some stress. The way they behave under stress will give them away. You already know what a good man will do under stress, and a not-so-good man will make bad decisions or freak out, thinking only of himself. This behavior is called "acting out of his nature."

Some men will "not be themselves" under the stress and strain of a demanding situation. So a man's acting "out of character" is constantly overlooked and forgiven in spite of the other lives he wounds and wrecks. Others will say he is a "good man," even though he can be counted on to make poor decisions when he's under pressure. In reality, a good man will bring forth good things from the good treasure of his heart regardless of the situation.

It's important that you have, and keep, faith. I'm not talking about the kind of faith you find in church, but faith in your fellow man. Faith that, in the long run, man will do the right thing. Faith is not rational, You cannot see it or feel it, yet often it is wise. It is faith that tells you real equality can be achieved and is worth striving for. Faith tells you that what is happening today between African Americans and Whites as well as between men and women and is not wrong. It is simply part of the process, the path by which we will move towards equality.

It will be a difficult path, full of seeming darkness and suffering, yet it is the right path. A good man will see this to be true. It's important that you have the faith to trust the process, even as it seems to move you into the darkness, even as the last remaining light of political rationality or reasonable communication about race and gender seems to be dying. These things are necessary. Good men will know that the miracle of equality will come when you least expect it.

Good men can see that the Civil Rights and Feminism movements are at the cutting edge of nearly all major intellectual disciplines. If you don't understand the struggle for civil rights and feminism it's because you haven't allowed yourself to think about it yet. They aren't social movements that you might agree or disagree with. They are the key transformative movements in the history of our species. Without equality, we are nothing.

The train to your life is leaving the station. Know that things are never going be the same as they were in the past. There are profound changes ahead, some of which are already affecting your life, even if you don't know it or care. It's up to you, if you want to be a "Good Man" or not. I hope that these few words will help you reach that decision.

It all begins in the home
8/19/2012

If you think about human behavior and ethics, I think you'll agree, it all begins in the home. In a normal home, everything you will need to get by in society has its roots. Children develop behavioral attitudes, ethics, and just plain common sense in early and late adolescence long before they reach adulthood. By the time they're adults and go out to live their lives in society with the rest of us, their behavioral attitudes are already formed.

It is my observation that we need to overhaul what we're teaching our children in our homes. I know that I'm not one to preach. but I'm going to just the same. In the world we live in today, it is essential that we take a good look at exactly what is going on with honest and open eyes and minds. What we send out into the world will eventually come back to us; it always has.

I'll start locally, in our own back yard. I'm not the smartest man in the world but I can see that the behavior of our youth, most of them, is lacking a cupful of ethics. It's not going to get better any time soon unless we examine what the awful truth is. Starting small and then going large is the only way I know to explain what I'm trying to convey, so put up with me.

You would not believe how many beer and whisky bottles I pick up every day at the nature park where I like to do volunteer work. Fifty percent of my volunteer time is spent cleaning up someone else's mess. People just don't seem to care anymore, that is very obvious to me. Every day, I find plants that have been stomped or run over by someone's quad motorcycle. Evidence of small fires are everywhere, deliberately set for mischief and destruction of public property. Why else would someone have a fire in 100 degree heat.

In reality, I believe these acts of vandalism are committed by groups of roaming youths with a lack of entertainment or things to do. Groups that lack ethics and could care less about bad or good behavior. This said, let's move on to a higher level of society that I call family groups. I call them groups because in society today, many families are forced economically to group together for support.

Right away, many are blaming lower income homes for what is wrong with society. The problems of our society are so much deeper than low income homes. Look for a role model today and what do you see. Where can a young man find someone to look up to and model his behavior after his? At one time, politicians were a good example of ethical behavior. So were businessmen and clergymen. While we may enjoy exceptional freedoms guaranteed by our first-of-its-kind Constitution, our behavior provides a different story when it comes to personal accountability, personal responsibility and community accountability.

Major business, the church, and the politics on the Hill are all tied in with major crime and corruption. The crime you see reported on TV is nothing compared with the crime that will never make the evening news. Dow Chemical and Kimberly Clark used to discard their dioxins and endless chemicals into rivers and lakes and thought nothing of it. To this very day, these companies are pushing chemicals like DDT in Third World countries — a chemical outlawed in the United States because it kills everything it touches. I don't see this as ethical behavior, I see it as chasing the almighty dollar at the expense of other people's lives.

The people that rise to run corporations and governments do not come from broken homes. To people such as these, broken homes equals big bucks. They are thinking and counting on people from broken homes to fill the beds in our lucrative penal systems. Which brings me to the war on drugs that is never-ending in this country. The National Drug Control Strategy published in 1998 by the Office of National Drug Control Policy (ONDCP) reports that three-quarters of the growth in the federal prison population is accounted for by drug offenders. The number of inmates in state prisons for drug-law violations increased by 487 percent in recent years.

I'm sure this information is no surprise to anyone, but consider the fact that 60 percent of all prisoners are minorities from broken homes. When you are looking to fill a bed in a large financial windfall, you'll go where the picking is easy: in low income, broken homes of our African American and Hispanic neighborhoods. Generation after generation, it's the same — remove the major breadwinner and you have a broken home, and a broken home provides plenty of candidates to fill prison beds. This has become the ethics and behavior of the United States of America.

Need I say that this type of ethics and behavior began in someone's home. You know it did, but being limited to 800 words in a column, this is all I can say. Some will get the point and some won't. That's all I can do.

An old man's observation
8/26/2012

Only a remnant of Americans cling to old restraints and ways of the past. This country is caught in a relaxing interval between one moral code and the next. An upcoming generation surrenders itself to luxury, corruption and a restless disorder of family and morals. Now, only a few souls feel any longer that, "it is beautiful and honorable to die for one's country."

All it would take is a failure of leadership to allow this country to weaken itself with internal strife and protest. This country could end in one final blow from a decisive defeat in war resulting in invasion from without and barbarism welling up from within.

Government and religion are one and the same, growing and becoming more and more complex. When an economy expands, so does inequality. Society finds itself divided between a cultured minority and a majority of men and women too unfortunate by nature of circumstance to develop excellence and taste. The majority will become a drag on the minority. That is the price the minority must pay when it controls all economic and educational opportunities.

The idea of progress finds itself in uncertain shape when nations and religions rise and fall. There has been no substantial change in the nature of man throughout all of history. All of our technological advances are simply new means of achieving the old ends, the acquisition of food and shelter, the seeking of the opposite sex, or the same sex, the overcoming of competition, and the fighting of wars.

We have found that science is neutral because it will kill us just as fast as it will heal us. The comfort that we enjoy has weakened our physical stamina and moral codes. Our nerves are shattered by the speed in which we travel and communicate. We are the same trousered monkeys at a thousand miles an hour as we were when we used our legs.

The concentration of wealth, responsibility, and political power advances in complexity along with the advances of the economy. Education has spread but we forgot to make ourselves intelligent when we made ourselves a nation. Intelligence is retarded by the fertility of the simple. We complicate everything we do.

Racial strife arises when wealth is not distributed equally. Race or class wars can destroy advances in culture overnight when it turns political debate to hate and the rule of the sword. The causes of war are the same as the causes of individual competition, the desire for food, land, material wealth, fuel and mastery. War results because the government has the same interest as we do but it has none of the restraints.

The state guarantees us protection, property, and legal rights in exchange for the restraints of laws and morals and our ability to combat enemies of the state. Now, a single day of war can destroy centuries of peace. The nation must be ready to defend itself at all times and if the right interests are involved, the nation must be able to use any means called for to survive. Even the Ten Commandments must move over for self-preservation.

The point of all of this is that we must break the rule that history repeats itself. We have to be willing to try a new approach. We must try to understand the feelings of other nations and understand their desire to develop without fear of attack. We must not allow our mutual fears to lead us to war in this day and age. The development of our weapons for destruction is more murderous and evil than ever before, far beyond anything in the history of mankind.

Our potential for destruction is unparalleled. If history repeats itself, nations only unite when there is a threat from without. Should this be the case, only an invasion from outer space can unite the human race. Then and only then will we of this Earth be one. Until that time, as long as I am able, I'll be down at the creek watering plants.

My brother's birthday
9/9/2012

September 8 is my brother's birthday. Michael is in his 62nd year, so he's not a young cadet. During his life, he has been many things to me; sacred things. He has been my best friend for my entire life, through thick and thin. Until he met his wife, Anna, we had nothing else to call our own. Anna gave him stability, love, and children, lovely children.

Anna gave me love as well when she introduced me to Therese, the girl that was to be my wife and, in time, would give me children. So, at the beginning, there was the four of us. Some might say that there was the two of them and the two of us. What I mean is, the two of them, our wives, were sober, honest, and God-fearing. They were as stable as the Rock of Gibraltar.

It was quite different for the two of us, Michael and I. When we met these two women, it was probably the best thing that ever happened to either one of us. I can tell you right now that things would have been very different for us if we hadn't met them. We would probably be dead or living in a dumpster without them. They saved our lives.

My brother and I, were born in Tennessee, in the middle of the last century, a time when things were popping in this country. There was the struggle for human rights and a holy man named King, who brought us the teachings of Gandhi. The Korean War was going full bore and Elvis was just becoming aware of his potential. Popping.

I can remember almost all of Michael's birthdays — that's how much we have been together. The few of his birthdays that I don't remember was a time of great worry for me because I was not with him. I could not watch over him to keep him out of harm.

I remember Michael holding on to my Mother's leg as she tried to get out the door of the orphanage where she would leave us. Michael was screaming, "Take me with you, take me with you." All I could do was watch him suffer until we were separated to different parts of the orphanage. That year, I missed his birthday, and the next, and the next. I don't really know how many I missed, because I don't remember how long we were in that place.

We were with our mother in our late teens, at East Peoria Community High School. We were both two years older than our classmates and somewhat more rough around the edges. In his freshman year, Michael threw an M-80 in the toilet at school. He threw it in, flushed the toilet, and blew it right off the floor, flooding the bathroom.

He was thrown out of high school in his first month there. This explains why he was a Marine in Vietnam when he was 16 years old. I missed his 17th, 18th, 19th, and 20th, and 21st birthdays, partially because after high school, I went to Vietnam to get him and bring him home. Within a week of my arrival, in country, he was shipped out stateside because you cannot, by law, have two brothers in a combat zone unless they both sign a waiver. Michael did not sign the waiver.

The next time Michael and I saw each other, we were not the same people we were before. We were harder and more solitary. We looked at each other differently. He had lines in his face that weren't there before. He was a heavy drinker, a habit I would soon pick up as well. I was very lucky in that at a certain point, I would get sick and start throwing up.

Michael wasn't that lucky because he could drink straight whiskey all night, drink after drink. Soon we were doing drugs and chasing women. It didn't seem to matter if the women were someone else's, we'd chase them anyway. We didn't care — who's going to mess with a couple of drugged-up Vietnam vets. More than once people have shoved guns and sawed-off shotguns in my face for that very reason.

I moved to California to get away from all of that and maybe to get a fresh start. Michael soon followed. Our professional life was better than average and we worked on many high-rise buildings in San Francisco and freeway bridges throughout the state. Other than our families, these buildings and bridges are all there is to know we were here on this Earth.

The booze and the drugs were always with us and as I look back on my life now, I can see what a waste it is. The money we spent on drugs and booze might have gone a long way if used for our families. It's too bad I can't take back the time — things would be a lot different.

So as I say "Happy Birthday to my brother Michael," all I can say to you is what I know is true, "A life free of dope and booze is a good life." One day you will be as old as my brother and I, and you will know that the words I speak are true.

Happy birthday, Michael.

Folks around Winters
9/23/2012

The folks living around my hometown of Winters, California sure are nice. They're probably the nicest people on this planet. That's not just my opinion either. Everyone I meet in the market or gas station is always smiling and telling jokes. Some of their jokes are pretty funny too.

The other day I was trying to get my gas card to work so I kept swiping it through the reader, over and over. Under my breath, I cursed in a low tone while knocking and pounding on the machine, trying to get the darn pump to work. A friendly fellow at the pump next door asked if I needed help. I surely did.

The friendly fellow came over, I handed him my card, and he swiped it through the machine, which started humming and sprang to life.

"Thanks," I said.

"No problem," he replied as he walked back to his truck at a nearby pump, got in, and drove away.

My gas card was still in his hand when he waved goodbye. I guess he forgot to give it back. He'll probably send it to me in the mail.

Yesterday, I was at the Winters Putah Creek Nature Park pulling Johnson Grass when a quad motorcycle came out of the bushes on the other side of the creek. I was going to wave at them but when they saw me, zoom, they were gone man. There were three people on the quad. A bald-headed guy, a young teenager, and a little baby boy.

I was thinking they probably didn't see me or they would have stopped to say hello. I was kind of concerned about the way the bald-headed guy didn't seem to care about the little baby's welfare too much. Every time they hit a bump, old knobby head had to grab the kid to keep him from flying off into the weeds.

I was told that the same quad, along with another one, raced through the park with a Fish and Game warden racing right behind them. I guess he was going to show them where the good fishing holes are. I wonder though, why doesn't the bald-headed guy slow down a bit before the baby gets hurt.

I guess people see me pulling weeds down at the park, because some very nice person moved a couch down there for me to sit on when I got tired. How nice is that? I was going to sit on it and watch the creek flow by, but the Putah Creek Council and their cleanup volunteers must have thought the couch was garbage because they hauled it up the hill and threw it in the dumpster. It was a nice couch too, but it had a few unknown odors.

Another thing that happens regularly at the park is that somebody leaves me old beer bottles and cans. Once in a while I even find a whisky bottle. I guess people have heard that I like to clean up around the creek, so they leave stuff for me. That just totally blows me away how nice people can be. How cool is that?

People are so nice. The other day, I bumped into a guy and his girl walking through the park. I said hello to them, but they didn't hear me I guess. As they walked away I heard the guy say, "I think that guy fell out of the stupid tree and hit every branch on the way down. That was a good one. It made me laugh."

People are always waving and pointing their fingers at me when they drive by me when I'm leaving the park. The cars and trucks coming across the old bridge don't seem to care about the 35 MPH speed limit, so when they get over to where I am across from the vegetable stand on Winters Road, they're probably doing about 50 MPH. It's a game they play, I think.

They seem to wait around the corner where I can't see them because of the trees and bushes until it looks like it's safe for me to pull out onto the road. When my truck is almost on the road, they zoom around the corner and honk their horn at me. Then they act like it's my fault.

That's the best part of the joke, because they yell out the window and point their fingers at me. I guess it is a funny joke all right, but I wish they would slow down because if I did pull out I'm afraid they might get hurt when they hit me. I wouldn't even want that to happen.

I guess by now you can see what I mean when I say that this town has the nicest people in the world. I wouldn't want to live anywhere else, I love this town and the people in it. They must love me to or why would they go out of their way to do all of these things for me. How cool is that?

A few things I don't like
10/21/2012

There are many, many things that I don't like so I'm going to get right at it. Okay, my grandson, Anthony. That kid can make me so angry sometimes. Don't get me wrong, I totally love the kid, but he's not a hugger and I want to hug him really, really bad. It's the things he can do that I don't like.

For instance, Anthony came to visit my wife and I for a couple of weeks this summer. On the first day of the visit he tells me, "I'm bored." Well I have the cure for boredom right in the middle of my desk: my computer. I reach over, push the on button, and the thing starts whining. I click on the game "Bejeweled 2". A game that I am somewhat proficient at — I have a top score of 59,000, or something like that.

So we're sitting there waiting for the game to download when he says, "I think I'll take a nap — call me when the game comes on." "Why you little twerp," I thought. "You'll never beat my score at this game, I'm the champ," I say. The champ!

"Well, what if I use the force?" he says as he finally sits down at the keyboard. The game comes on. Anthony shakes his head and snickers when he looks at the list of top scores. At the top of the list was, "Bogwan Don-28,000 points."

"What does Bogwan Don mean?" he asked. "Oh, that's a name I used to make your father call me before he could get his dinner," I says. I explained that his father doesn't call me that anymore since he has grown up and can make his own dinner.

Anyway, I made it clear that I thought he would never beat my high score. Never! He looks up at me and says, "Never calculate too quickly on the possibility of me not beating your score before the poultry is thoroughly materialized." I said, "What?" He said, "Never count your chickens before they are hatched."

Now, I was doing the pee dance so I made a beeline for the bathroom. I was gone for about 30 seconds. When I got back, he was watching a Sponge Bob cartoon. I looked at the computer and the screen was blank. I says, "What happened, Anthony?"

Well it turns out that he had printed out his score sheet for me. He had a score of like a million points.

"Dammit," I said.

I looked at the blank screen on the computer. I had never seen the computer do anything like that before. There I was looking at it and scratching the top of my head when my grandson says, "I think somebody wiped your C-drive grandpa."

I just couldn't take it any more so yesterday I logged on the Facebook, with my laptop, and posted this entry, which was an out and out lie: "Yea, I finally beat Anthony's score on Bejeweled 2!" What the heck, nobody will ever know, right?

There are other things I don't like as well. My brain, bless it, keeps sending me out impulses and refining ideas all by itself so I can keep on doing the stuff that I do and occasionally say something really clever. I feel the photons entering my brain via my hair follicles.

I'll make it simple and make a list of things I don't like:

• So, what if for once in my life, I wrote something really profound and someone stole it? I wouldn't like that at all.

• The City of Winters won't let me put a toll both in front of my house.

• If I ever go back in time, I wouldn't be able to explain how we take pictures with pixels instead of film.

• Every construction company in town, along with the city fire department, takes all the water they want from my fire hydrant and never pays me a penny!

• Everybody keeps deleting my comments on Facebook.

• I don't like the fact that there is over a hundred million dollars missing from the UN imposed "Oil for Food" program in Iraq, and I never got a penny of that either.

• I don't like the fact that I have solved the mystery of what dark matter consists of, the evolutionary origins of sex, whether "free will" exists, and I know why placebos actually do work. Yet still, no one will listen to me.

If you would like a complete list of things that I don't like, simply send a dollar to urasucker.com.

Man, I've been krewed again. (I felt I had to replace the "S" with a "K" because this is a family publication.) I have been krewed by the Swedish Academy that gives out Nobel prizes. They gave the prize for literature to a guy named Mo Yan. This Mo Yan guy lives in China. I think it's a big mistake because I wanted that award.

When I heard about this, I nearly flipped my wig. I walked directly to my computer and sat down in my chair. The chair wobbles because I was going to make one of those flat roller thingys so I could work under my truck. I didn't finish that project, so there is still one roller on my chair and the rest are out in the yard somewhere. I'll find them when I mow the grass.

As you all know, I have a big brain, so I figured out exactly what happened in about 20 minutes or so. I figure the academy's secretary, a guy named Peter Englund, had to make a slip-up on his paperwork. I think maybe he used abbreviated names for the prize candidates and got them mixed up somehow. He probably meant to put the paper with "Do San" (the abbreviation for "Donald Sanders)" on the top of the pile. However, what he really did was put the "Mo Yan" (the abbreviation for "Mo Yanski" or whatever) paper on top of mine by mistake.

I'm not saying this Peter Englund is a dummy, but geeze, he can't even spell England right. I mean we're talking about a lot of money here. This Mo Yan character got over 8 million Kroner along with this prize. It took a minute, but I figured that to be well over a hundred American Dollars, maybe more. With that much money I could go to the hardware here in town and buy two of those flat roller thingys and roll around my driveway all day.

They had to mix up the names because Mo Yan and I are so much alike, except that he's Chinese and I'm American. Mo wrote a book called "Red Sourgum" and I'm going to write a book called "Red Neck Sourgum." Both books are about farming families caught up in the "Cultural Revolutions" of their respective countries.

Even more amazing than that, both books are tales of love amid the Japanese invasion of our towns. The only difference is that they made a movie out of his book and the damn thing won the top prize at the Berlin International Film Festival in 1988. Big deal! I didn't want that prize anyway.

Well, to tell you the truth, I don't care if Mo Yan did win the Nobel. I'm going to tell everyone that I won it anyway. Nobody around here would know the difference anyway and even if they did, Mo's book is written in Chinese. I can simply tell everybody the book was first released in China and the Winters version is coming out next year. It goes to reason that it would be in written Chinese so all those China people could read it, right?

Another thing I've been working on is copying a book written by a guy named Earnest Hemmingway. I figure I can copy this guy's book and put my name on it because we write so much alike. All I have to do is change the name of the town to Winters and change the name of the hero to Donald Sanders.

Next, I'm going to buy a suit and carry a briefcase with the words, "Culinary Critic" written on it in big red letters. Why, I could walk into any restaurant in town and get free food and service. Those Pickerels and Ogandos would be eating out of my hand for the publicity they think I can get them. What they don't know won't hurt them, right. I've got a bone to pick with those Pickerels anyway.

They cook the food at the Buckhorn and the Putah Creek Café right down the street from my house. They know it's got to be driving people crazy. How would you like to smell their steaks cooking every day. It comes into my house and it won't leave me alone. It's driving me crazy and I think maybe it's affecting my writing because I keep talking about eating all the time. I'm getting fat too. All of a sudden I have "man-breasts."

Do you think I have grounds for a civil suit?

This day will be memorable because you're missing
11/4/2012

There are four events that will make this day memorable for me. Hurricane Sandy is swiftly approaching the East Coast of the United States. An Italian court sentenced former Prime Minister Silvio Berlusconi to four years in jail for tax fraud, but later cut it to one year because of an amnesty law. Arnold Schwarzenegger is returning to one of the first roles to make him a star — Conan the Barbarian! Last but not least, Michael died.

Michael has been slowly dying for some time now. He slowly killed himself with every gulp of whisky he swallowed and every puff of his non-filtered cigarettes. I, and everyone else that loved him, watched him die in increments, day after day, for years. In the end, he was a living skeleton, writhing in pain in his bed. He could not arise to go to the bathroom without help, but still, he drank his whisky.

His whisky came to him by taxicab. Michael would pay the driver to come and get his money, go to the liquor store to pick it up, and finally, return to his house to deliver the liquid that would kill him. By my best estimation, a pint of whisky would cost him $40 or $50. Michael's back yard was littered with empty bottles.

The mere suggestion that he slow down or quit his drinking sent him into a rage. While raging, he cared little about the feelings of others, even those that he loved. Even at the very end, he thought he was fully functional and capable of his daily chores that were done by others for many months without his even knowing or caring.

It broke my heart in two every single time I went to visit him. It became a punishment for me for past sins I suppose. I could not bear to watch him slowly die, but it was even harder for me to stay away, and I could not do so. Michael was my brother. He was the one person who has been with me for all but a few months of my long life.

So that was today, but I cannot help but think about yesterday and the yesterdays before that. For over 60 years, we were inseparable friends, life companions, and brothers. Everything he went through, I went through as well. When he got sick, I got sick. When he got angry, chances are, I got angry as well. We did everything together.

We shared friends and enemies. He was a Marine and I was Army. Everything we did was very close, very close. The day I arrived in Vietnam was the day he was to leave. Both of us lived in an unimaginably horrible war zone that broke us both in spirit and mind. Years of drug abuse was the rest of our story.

Now, I am alone, without words to say, so I will lean on Bruce Springsteen to say them for me in the words of his song, "You're Missing." It goes sort of like this:

"Shirts in the closet, shoes in the hall. Anna's in the kitchen, baby and all.
Coffee cups on the counter, jackets on the chair. Papers on the doorstep, you're not there
Pictures on the nightstand, TV's on in the den. Your house is waiting, your house is waiting
For you to walk in, for you to walk in, but you're missing, you're missing
You're missing when I shut out the lights. You're missing when I close my eyes.

You're missing when I see the sun rise. Children are asking if it's all right, will you be in our arms tonight.

Morning is morning, the evening falls. I have too much room in my head, too many phone calls saying, 'How's everything, everything?'

God's drifting in heaven, devils in the mailbox. I've got dust on my shoes and nothing but teardrops.

You're missing."

Support soldiers and veterans all the time

"God and the Soldier all men adore, in times of danger, not before.
The Danger passed and the wrong righted, God is forgotten, the soldier Slighted."
~ Rudyard Kipling

Of all men, only a few are natural born killers. Soldiers of these United States must be trained to kill. In any war, success is measured by the number of enemy dead an army can provide. The army that willingly kills the most will carry the day. An efficient soldier wants to kill because he hates his enemy enough to take his life. This is the natural way of things that are militant.

A well-trained soldier must have a hatred for those he will kill. He must believe his enemy is not worthy of living. The soldier must see the enemy as something other than human. The enemy, whether he is a "Red Skin, a filthy Jap, nasty Nazi, Gook, or Rag Head" must be seen as less than human. This process, we call "dehumanization"

Combat brings out the very best and the very worst in men. Bravery is a sometime thing and generally a reaction to training and beliefs. The flip side of the bravery coin is brutality. The brutality of those directly involved in combat is generally directed to combatants. The brutality toward prisoners and civilians is generally much more cruel.

The problem with "dehumanization" is that it is based in deceit. It is a lie, and eventually the individual soldier will see the truth. At this point, the conflict moves away from the enemy and the soldier is now at war with himself. He will no longer hate his enemy for he now hates himself even more. The soldier will carry the wounds and scars of their combat for the rest of their lives. Most of us will shy away from viewing the crippled and maimed soldier but we have even more difficulty dealing with those that carry unseen, mental scars.

The war in Iraq and Afghanistan is every bit as manufactured a conflict as was Viet Nam. When our brave American soldiers wake up to the fact that they have been engaged in mortal combat for no other reason than procuring oil and satisfying corporate greed, they will not be able to bear the pain of what they have done. The pain of what this cost them, cost their families, and cost thousands of innocent Iraqis will be overbearing and painful.

It is easier for government to honor dead heroes because the live ones will need help. When I and others returned home from Vietnam in the late '60s and early '70s, it was somewhat of a fashion to spit upon returning soldiers and opposition to the war was directed at the soldiers. I can tell you firsthand that it is easier to withstand the wounds of combat and all of the agent orange in the world than it is to bear the condemnation of the American public as a "drugged up baby killer."

That was then, but today our young men, fresh from the conflicts in Iraq and Afghanistan have served bravely and faithfully. Some have given all. Some have been wounded but all who come back will have problems that need to be dealt with. As a Viet Nam veteran I know of the mental scars they will carry as long as they live.

Already, I have read reports saying veterans from Iraq have got to wait for medical treatment. Does the Obama administration have a plan, and are the Veterans administration and military health systems ready to support the troops? The soldier does not decide to go to war. Soldiers do not start wars. Soldiers only combat the enemy in wars, at our request, so we must support the troops. All the troops! All the time!

Base closures threaten the delivery of health care to veterans. There have been closings all across the nation. Budget cuts have been planned for the Veterans Administration. The current level of service to veterans is already inadequate. The VA now has a record of denying services to veterans by giving applicants the run around and denying service connection for many illnesses including Agent Orange and Gulf War syndrome. Vets from as far back as the Korean War have struggled for years simply to get basic treatment and coverage, and some were apparently deliberately misdiagnosed.

The Veteran's Administration has stated that personnel returning from Iraq are already exhibiting symptoms of PTSD by the hundreds. The VA stated that those suffering from PTSD symptoms, sleep disorders, depression, and emotionally distancing themselves from loved ones, may be seen by a doctor, but for many it is just not happening.

Again, I must say that I am limited in the number of words per column so I haven't the room to say more, but I have to say this one last thing:

"Support the troops? It's easy to say but lip service isn't enough. So long as our government continues to choose a path to war, the troops will need your support. The WWII generation and the Korean War Vets are fast aging and those of us who are Viet Nam Vets are not far behind. The Gulf War veterans are as deserving of support as are the generations who proceeded them. Sticking a yellow ribbon on your vehicle or wearing a rubber band on your wrist is nothing but a hollow boast if you don't make a conscience effort to support our troops."

There you go — what do you do now?"

The gynophobic man
11/18/2012

I think I am gynophobic. This hasn't always been the case for me. At one time, I was pretty tough and women or girls, whichever, had a great fear of my maleness. Women would just naturally shy away from a guy like me. All I had to do is gggrrooowwwllll!

I can pretty much pinpoint the day I became Ggnophobic. I was a tough individual one day and the very next day I found the wrath of God. It was shortly after my seventh birthday. It was the day I met Sister Mary Conchadda at St. Joseph's Orphanage in Little Rock Arkansas. That dark lady of God beat the Hell out of me on the first day I met her. Eight or nine hours later she beat the Hell out of me again for wetting the bed.

That was the beginning of it. I became vigilant about knowing her whereabouts and an expert at distinguishing the sound of her footsteps in the long hallways of the big dark building where I spent my childhood. If you had spent any time with the Sisters of the Benedictine you would be fully aware of minding your P's and Q's. These women ran in packs like the wolves in the Black Forrest, only they were meaner.

Go ahead and laugh. Ha Ha. However I can tell you right now that most men are gynophobic. So, ha ha right back. Read on suckers. For your information, good things are manly and collective; the despicable are feminine and individual. Take the cinema for example. If you want to create a group of killers you take a group of kids, send them to boot camp, and kill the women in them. That is the lesson of both the US Army and Marine Corp.

OK, take the films "Casualties of War, and Full Metal Jacket." These films depict a group of killers that can do anything they want, kill anything, right? Wrong! As soon as these killers run across a woman, the crap hits the fan right? See what I mean?

Not too long ago I had a horrible experience with a woman of great power. Here is what happened, and I will leave nothing out. Nothing. I think I was singled out by this woman because I'm so smart and I have an innate ability to stay calm when most other men will freak out like little girls.

On this particular morning, I had made my wife a lunch and she was off on time to work. After my chores of dusting and sweeping the floors, I settled down to reading about the genetic mutation of our local Drosophila Simulans. I was about ready for second breakfast when I caught a whiff of something horrid. I sniffed my pits but that wasn't it. Just then I heard a loud whoosh sound.

I ran and opened the bathroom door to see a fountain of water two feet in diameter gushing from my toilet. I screamed so loud I thought a little girl had been drowning just out the window until I discovered it was me screaming. I thought I was going get my slippers wet, so I slammed the door and ran to the front to get some assistance. That's when I first saw her.

I was freaking out on the inside but as cool as a cucumber on the outside as I stepped out onto my front porch. There in the street sat two white trucks with "SPS" on the doors. A large manhole was open and there was a woman bent over looking down into the hole. Motors were running loudly, bouncing around on semi-flat tires. The lady looked up at me and smiled.

It was at that exact time that I noticed my pants were soaking wet and dripping from the knees down. She was obviously a lady of some importance because she had a clipboard and a pencil. I really didn't want to mess with this lady but I didn't know what else to do at this point. I couldn't tell my wife what happened unless I had someone to blame, right?

She was still looking at me and smiling, so I says, "I don't know what you are doing down there but I think you may have blown up my bathroom." She stands up erect, the smile gone, and then looks down into the manhole and drags her finger across her neck like she is going to cut her own throat. That very instant, all of the motors stopped and there was total silence. I was impressed and I have to say I was really getting scared.

The lady followed me into my house and on to the bathroom. She says, "Yep it's wet" and "Well, this has never happened before" At that very moment she reminded me of Richard Nixon. As she walked back to the front door she says, "OK, here's what we'll do." "We'll sterilize your bathroom and run a camera up the sewer and we'll get a picture to you ASAP."

I was really getting scared now because I didn't even know what the Hell she had just said. So I says, "Oh don't bother, I'll clean it up." When she left, I had to bite my fist to keep from screaming again. I thought to myself, "Holy crap! This lady has the power to make shit flow uphill!" I really didn't want to mess with this lady so I mopped up the floor and got the Hell out of there until they left the area.

An hour or so later, I crept back into my house and there on the floor was an envelope with two pieces of paper. One had some pictures of some dark circles and the other had a letter that said, "Your lateral was 42.5 feet from the manhole. It had no defects and there was nothing to explain the water backup into your bathroom." It continued, "Sorry for any inconvenience and thanks for your cooperation." The top of the letter had the heading, "Specialized Pipeline Services Certified number SBE10029574 and an expiration date."

Now I was scared and impressed at the same time. I found myself asking, "What the Hell is a lateral?" "What the heck is in these pictures" and "How the Hell did she type this letter so fast?" I'm thinking now that this lady must be CIA or something like that. I really didn't want to mess with her and the next time I see her, I'm not going to make eye contact and I'm going to pretend I'm deaf.

The problem
12/9/2012

I'd like to discuss problems. Everybody has them. We have small problems, bigger problems, and then we have huge problems that affect all of us, as a group. When I use the word group, I mean us as a species, all of humanity. Isn't it difficult to imagine a problem that's large enough to touch every human being on this Earth? I'll explain.

I'll start with what we, as individuals know to be true. Something that we are all certainly aware of: our small problems. This is the crap that we deal with on a daily basis. The things we do because we have to live our lives, so we do them, hoping that we can better our positions in life. We work at handling these small problems in the hope that they will go away someday and at that point, we won't have any problems.

Well, that's not going to happen. Small problems will never go away. Small problems have their own life. By life, I mean, we can see them, we can feel them, and they can reproduce themselves. Small problems are the spawn of larger problems. Problems have power. They control what we do and say when we interact with each other.

OK, I'm going to toss two separate ideas out there for you to consider. Think about them and see if you can find a relationship between the two. I give you, "individual military suicide" and "corporation." Can you see how one will affect the other? I think we all can see that the individual soldier is a small link in the chain and corporations are the larger link.

On a chain, the larger links pull the smaller around. Oftimes the chain moves in a whipping motion that snaps the smaller link completely off the chain. This is the point when the smallest link realizes where it came from; where it originated. This is also the point when the small link realizes it is controlled by the larger, stronger links.

We know that the smaller links are the individual soldiers, but who are the larger links? Corporations, of course. There are those who will argue that we are the corporations because we collectively own them. Well actually, what we own are the stocks and bonds that the corporations sell us while telling us that the stockholders control the corporation. This simply is not true. Stocks and bonds are worthless, they will eventually fail, and we are left broken with a lot of small problems. This has been proven true over and over.

I think you'll agree that corporations control governments through its purse strings. We call those that control corporations, "the 1%." These, ultra rich and powerful people are the largest problem that controls us all. They control what we do, what we say, what we buy, and what we sell. Our corporations interact with corporations around the world, thus they become "global."

Corporations live by survival of the fittest. Like fish, the larger ones swallow the smaller and take everything they have, by force if necessary. Deceit and secrecy are the tools they use and we all know the web that we weave when we practice to deceive. Governments and laws change and mutate to serve the corporations in a continuous attempt to control the masses of people like you and I.

The corporation give us worthless pieces of paper we call money. They claim to have piles of gold stored somewhere that each piece of money represents. We may ask, where is that gold? "Why, in the reserves," they might say. Everybody knows that gold is too heavy to carry around as cash, right? The government will store the gold for us and give us bonds to spend instead. These bonds are negotiable at any corporate market, around the world.

How do we know how much gold is in the reserves? Who controls the gold. Corporations control the gold through their banking industry. We all know how that's going. The banking industry is under investigation on a worldwide scale. Recently, the government of Germany demanded to know where its gold reserves were and followed the trail to the financial institutes of London, the financial seat of the world.

To make a small point, the financiers of London had to sell half of Great Briton's gold reserve to satisfy Germany's demand for its reserve. There simply is not enough gold on Earth to cover the gold certificates issued around the world. The cat is out of the bag and corporate who-de-whos are scrambling to keep things under wraps by making us concentrate on our small problems.

One of our biggest problems that we all seem to just roll with and ignore is the fact that we give up without a fight that which is most important to us. More important than anything we have: our children. If corporations control governments through finance, and smaller corporations get swallowed by larger corporations with more military might, then we supply the individual soldiers, our children.

Ok we have discussed the idea of "corporations' now we move on to "military individual suicides" The military is the enforcement arm of the corporations. This in itself is a problem. What is happening now, more and more often, is that the individual soldier is finding out that the people they're killing are the enemy of the corporations. They see that the person they just laid to waste is not their enemy. They see that that dead person was never really a threat to their homeland and loved ones.

This realization is more than many can handle when it's all over. Suicide rates among returning soldiers have gone through the roof, and we seem unable to save our children and we're at a loss as to why they take their own lives. Why are things so horrible that they feel death is better than life. Are the soldiers mentally defective?

This I can answer for you and it's the point of this whole column. When I was young, I, and my fellow soldiers, killed for the corporations. When a person has time to reflect on the reasons he has done what he has done, taking the life of another comes to center stage. It stands in your way to progress and happiness and you can't seem to get around it.

At this point, there are two things a soldier can do. You can stick the barrel of a gun in your mouth and push the trigger with your big tow or you can do what I do. I have tried the suicide thingy but I lack the guts to complete the job, thus several visits to the suicide ward at David Grant. I find that I can live my life by keeping to myself and doing what I can to help those around me by doing things no one else wants to do, like picking up garbage and taking care of public property.

When I find myself isolating, as I often do, it's because I don't want to cry in front of someone else. I don't want to put them on that embarrassing spot. Like I said in the beginning, we all have problems, small and large. Ex-soldiers like me can't handle the small problems of everyday life because we're stuck in a hallway and can't get past the larger problems.

So, if you see me living my life, its ok, I'm just trying to solve my problems, and it helps me if you don't ask too many questions. You're being there is enough for me to carry on.

Sometimes I get down. I am aware that it is happening, but I'm unable to stop it. I feel like I'm running down the stairs in a high-rise building. When I was a young man, I lived in a constant state of fear. Not the fear that a normal person might feel but a fear that a soldier feels in a high stress situation. It's hard for me to explain because I know there is no logical reason for me to feel this way at this point in my life, but there I am.

Through the years, I have sought help from the Veteran's Administration and I must have seen 30 or so doctors of different varieties. Some I saw regularly for years. Some were more effective at drawing me out into the open than others. Dr. Janet Lial was very effective at getting inside my head and wandering around, looking at this and ignoring that. I never knew exactly what she was looking for.

Dr. Lial wrote a report of her findings at the end of a session that lasted several years. Dr. Lial was a person of great strength and fortitude, for she would show up every week, for years upon years. Where others gave up, she was persistent and deserving of my trust. I was given a copy of this report and I will now relay to you some of its key points. Right now would be a good time to mow the grass or wash your dishes if you don't want to delve inside my head too much.

Dr. Lial's report went sort of like this:

Mr. Sanders is more anxious than most people. He is reactive and uneasy. This is an appropriate topic for further exploration and discussion. He may be sensitive to criticism and takes things personally.

Extraversion is low to low-average. Mr. Sanders is oriented toward the inner world of thoughts and ideas. He prefers activities that involve less interaction with other people. He is reserved and cautious in forming personal attachments. His social interactions tend to be serious and staid.

(Staid? What the Hell is that?)

I found Mr. Sanders to be forthright and genuine when revealing personal matters. He is self- reliant and prefers meeting responsibilities or tackling problems on his own. He may avoid asking for help and may abstain from situations that require working closely with others.

Mr. Sanders lives in a world of ideas that sometimes outweighs consideration for practicalities or for other people's needs. He has a social demeanor that is cautious and restrained. He may not pay attention to practical considerations or to the pragmatic aspects of a situation. (What the hell that means, I don't know.)

Mr. Sanders functions better in an unexacting, flexible setting rather than a rigid system. Generally, Mr. Sanders tends to balance toughness with sympathy, resoluteness with receptivity. He has a willingness to accommodate others while wanting to control his environment. He may defer to others rather than exert his own opinion or needs.

Other people are unlikely to misinterpret his emotional state. His emotional control is low. Openly expressing one's mood or feeling can be positive however in situations calling for "putting your best face forward" low emotional control can be detrimental. When caught up in events or people Mr. Sanders may at times disregard his impact on others.

So there it is. I guess this is the way others view me when they get to know me. I don't claim to understand all of this or even how they came up with this information. The questions they asked me made absolutely no sense to me. I.e. "If you had three numbers, say one, two, and three, which would you keep if you could keep only one?" I would answer, "Why, three, of course. What, do you think I'm an idiot?"

Now isn't this column an interesting little bit of trivia? What is interesting to me is the fact that I have never seen myself in this light and this report took me by surprise and that's not good for a guy in my emotional state. The report says it all. I live in my own little world.

In the world where I live, the sun falls through the plumes of air with the softest and loveliest of splendor. I wish to surround myself with those with a vision of how the Earth should be. As Walt Whitman put it, "Now I see the secret of the making of the best person. It is to grow in the open air and to eat and sleep with the Earth."

Thanks a hell of a lot!
12/23/2012

Thanks, a hell of a lot! The end of the world is not going to happen today. I don't know what the heck I'm going to do now. For like, months now everyone and everything has been telling me the world was supposed to end on December 21, 2012. It was even on the internet thingy. How can that not be true.

For weeks now, I have been preparing for the end, the apocalypse. I have been studying and studying all about the seven signs that are supposed to happen before the big ending gets here. As a matter of fact I consider myself an expert scolatician when it comes to the events that were to precede the ending of everything. Yes, I'm a fricking genius!

I mean, all the clues were there. The seven signs of the apocalypse went down exactly as planned, right by the book. I'm an expert in these matters so you can take my word for it. I had a perfect checklist and everything went pretty much like it was supposed to. The first sign went off like clockwork last Tuesday afternoon. I saw it on the internet thingy.

Some Japanese guy filmed it. The ocean was dying and crashing over the land, mashing houses and forcing huge ships underneath bridges where they were smashed into little bitty, bitty pieces of wood. The next day I saw all the locusts that were supposed to eat all of the vegetables and stuff like that. Well, that's when everything got too complicated for me to explain it all to you, the laymen. Things are simply too technical for you guys to understand. Take my word for it, the Earth was going down!

That's what I thought when I did all of those stupid things I shouldn't have done. I went to the bank and cleaned out our account and spent the money at Home Depot. I've let the grass grow knee high. Every dish we own is dirty and in the sink. I yanked the stinking talking computer out of my wife's car and threw it into the alley where it bounced over to the neighbor's yard. I sold all of my stocks and bonds and bought some router bits with the money.

Like I said, I'm a genius so I know I did everything right. I even went around saying goodbye to everyone I met. I told them I'd see them on the other side. Well, I guess the laymen didn't do too much research, because most of them didn't even know the world was going to end. Geeze!

You know it's true that your life flashes before you when you know you're going to die, because I started thinking about it right then, at that moment. I thought about how my wife looked with the breeze blowing lightly through her hair. How the sun bounced off of her shinny nose making her look so beautiful. I thought about how she picked a peach off of our tree and how the light shined in her eyes as she turned to share the wonder of it with me.

As you can tell I'm terribly in love with my wife, so I decided to spend my last hours with her. We watched TV. She on the little couch and me on the bigger couch eating chips and dip. French onion. What the hell, might as well eat all the ice cream too — it's the end of the world anyway, right?

That's where I woke up this morning. I thought, "What the hell?" What happened to the end of the world? Did I miss it? What the heck am I going to tell her about spending all the money at Home Depot. Oh, what about when she sees I have taken her car apart. Oh Crap!

The internet thingy is a liar! I'll never believe another thing I see on there. Even the stuff I put on it myself. You just can't depend on anything anymore. It's almost as if it's a new world of lies and deceit. Well, thanks a hell of a lot for nothing!

Planting and thinking about the problems we don't solve
1/8/2013

Yesterday, a fellow walking his dog in our new nature park stopped to chat with me for a while. I was cleaning debris from newly planted trees and replanting others uprooted by recent rains. He said he reads my column in the local newspaper, the Winters Express. I nodded as his dog splattered past me in the mud"It's nice that the dogs have room to run along the creek now, isn't it?" I asked. He did not reply.

He wanted to know why I felt the need to divulge so much personal information when writing about the nation's veterans and their problems. He thought exposing portions of my physiological profile was a little much, and didn't I find it somewhat embarrassing.

"Can't you discuss veterans' problems without opening your psychiatric file for the world to view," he asked.

"If I take it upon myself to write about veterans' problems and print it in the local paper, it would be a disservice to myself and other veterans if I only went halfway to the point," I replied. The things that I write about come from my personal experiences and I don't claim to represent other veterans. I write about myself and what I have experienced as a veteran, it's that simple.

"Do you think you are saving the world with all of this work you do at the creek," he asked.

I told him I was trying to do my part, that's all. I find it relaxing and soothing to my soul. Planting and caring for these newly planted trees gives me plenty of time to think about our problems and why we never seem to solve them. Problems around the globe endure because no one is interested in solving them:

If the majority of mankind were sufficiently concerned about poverty and hunger, then the necessary action would be taken immediately to eradicate the problem. In human society in general there is, in other words, little social responsibility and the fate of our planet now hangs on whether it can be suddenly and dramatically increased.

Compared to the third world, we are rich. We consume much of the world's produce and then we throw out what we feel is garbage. Our landfills are full of what the third world needs to survive. We consume most of the world's fuel to run our sports utility vehicles and to go on our jet-away holidays. The people that are most deprived and impoverished are working to produce things that we buy in our markets.

More than a billion people do not have access to safe drinking water and another billion do not have adequate medical attention. Literally thousands of people die every day for lack of simple basic needs that we take for granted.

In the present economy, if a firm can beat many others to the scarce sales opportunities, and take their business and deprive them of the livelihood they once had, that is quite acceptable. If no businessman can make money by giving you a job then you will be unemployed. That is the way we determine access to work and livelihood.

We talk about fiscal cliffs. What is the problem with everybody paying taxes. Why can't we seem to get the rich to pay more taxes. The problem is not to get the rich to pay more taxes — it is to get them to pay any tax at all. Most large corporations in the US pay no taxes as well.

We blame our problems on others, thus, on the large scale we have wars. So from time to time, the issue is whether our children should be sent to slaughter the children of other people just like us. Of course, if we had any significant level of social responsibility then wars would never occur in the first place. The time to end a war is several years before it breaks out, but then how would we take their wealth for our own.

The world's resources are becoming alarmingly scarce; the global economy is essentially a system that enables the rich to take most of them. Now reflect on the probable near future of armed conflict on a planet in which one-fifth have levels of resource consumption that are 17 times the average of the poorest half. The number of people scrambling for resources will soon be eight to nine billion; the poorest of those billions are eager to be as rich as the rich few.

All economic and development theories assume without question that getting rich is what development is about, and we in rich countries are determined to be at least eight times as rich by 2070 — this set of conditions provides a watertight guarantee that the coming century will be one of extreme and massive armed conflict.

I turned to say, "Just think about that."

He never heard me because he was already 500 yards away with his dog.

"We will need military forces to defend 'our' oil fields and mines," I yelled.

He didn't hear that either. I mumbled to myself, "If we wish to remain affluent in a world where affluence is not possible for all, we must remain heavily armed at all times. We think our guns will save us.

"In human society, the population submits to the rulers even though force is always in the hands of the governed. The rulers can only rule if they control opinion, no matter how many guns they have" ~ Hume 1765

Nature and the New Year
1/18/2013

So far, this has been a wonderful new year. It was about this time last year when I discovered my true passion in life: nature. When I say nature, I mean the whole of the physical world. I don't know much about the care of the physical world because for most of my life it didn't concern me. I lived inside my head.

I moved through the physical world with blinders, directed toward the next goal that I thought important. I attribute my dream state to survival mode. I think this stems from my time at St. Joseph's Orphanage at a very young age. Sister Conchadda would lock me in a closet when she thought I needed discipline. A young person will retreat into his own mind when he is isolated within the confines of a dark closet. So it began for me.

For me, the physical world only existed to maintain the dream world I lived in. "Just trying to maintain" was a statement my friends and I used many times in my younger days. My generation is famous for its hippie cultures, mind trips, and "getting back to nature" attitudes. Well, we all know how that turned out. We did a whole lot of thinking about it while our natural world was taking a crap. You can argue about this but if you do, you are living in a dream world and the ice is melting around you.

I am not alone, for many of us spend much of our lives in a dream world, detached from the physical world. We are so busy. We wake up in the morning and feed ourselves and drink our liquids. If we don't, our minds slow down and we lack the ability of concentration and imagination. Further lack of food and water will eventually have dire consequences. You know this to be true. It is the same with nature.

We are conflicted in a mixture of the physical and metaphysical world that is twisted around. Instead of using our minds to nurture the physical world, we do exactly the opposite. We never consider the fact that if we neglect our natural world everything, everything, will fall apart. We will learn the hard way that we cannot live on our dreams.

This is hard for us to imagine because we are so rich, so rich. We say we are hungry when we haven't eaten in two hours. We think we will die if we don't stop at Starbucks or MacDonald's. We think it's quaint when we see a woman of color carrying a jug of water while wearing a sarong. Our minds just don't grasp the fact that she has to carry that jug of water for hours on end or her children will not have water to drink on that particular day.

We sit in comfort, sipping our sodas, and watch the rape of the Earth on television in high definition. At times we see young people dragged out of trees where they've lived for the last year in protest of clear-cutting foresters. "Stupid bitch!" we think. Environmentalists are a bother to us. We call them "tree huggers." They hold up our construction projects because they are worried about "the impact"!

OK, I'm as guilty as anyone, I admit it. It's only of late that I've removed my blinders and looked at the beauty of the Earth around me and the state it is in. In the last year or so, I have met some new friends that showed me the way to care for the physical world. They're teaching me to examine nature in the real world as it truly is. I have found that nature, in reality, is much different than it is within my mind, my imagination. They are entirely two different things.

In the world my new friends showed me, I found awe and reverence in nature that inspires a greater ethical sense within my mind and heart. On holiday to celebrate Martin Luther King's birthday, like-minded people around the world will pause and reflect on the great man's life. He spent his entire life trying to show others the "real world." Civil rights was not his only concern. He knew that all of nature is connected and that natural balance in everything is the key to life.

It's no wonder that my new friends chose his birthday to celebrate his life by caring for the natural world. I feel as Dr. King did when he spoke the words, "All labor that uplifts humanity has dignity and importance and should be undertaken with painstaking excellence." Dr. King was a servant of the people in all ways, and a healthy environment is much more than equality within the human race. A healthy environment is dependent upon man's equality with nature. Mankind's squabbles within itself will die and fade away, and nature will strive to repair itself after we are gone.

Dr. King also said that life's most persistent and urgent question is, "What are you doing for others?" What he meant was, if we can't care for our own behavior and environment properly and care for ourselves, what are we leaving for our grandchildren and their children?

Please, join me and my new friends (they know who they are) in environmental awareness and equality for all of nature.

This baby will be beautiful, smart and tough
1/22/2013

I absolutely love babies. You would never know it by looking at me now, but I used to be a baby. I think maybe everybody was at one time or another. Lately I've been seeing babies everywhere. Today I saw one down at the creek. That was a real shocker!

My excellent friends, Andy and Sara Tremayne just had a baby. Her name is Elsa and she was born with a full head of hair. This baby is going to be someone to reckon with in the near future. I've thought about this for some time now so I'll have to explain everything to you in layman's terms. That means I have to keep it somewhat simple with no big words.

Baby Elsa is beautiful. She takes after her mom. I guess her father is pretty good-looking too. He's almost as good-looking as I am. Also, Baby Elsa is also very smart. Its genetic I think. Sara is the green thumb of the Putah Creek Council. That explains how I saw her baby down at the creek. First she's planting trees at a PCC planting event, then she's having a baby, then she's at a planting event again with a baby. That makes her tough and beautiful.

Baby Elsa's father, Andy, is some kind of Professor of Archeology at UC Davis. I call him "Rock Hunter Guy." He likes to dig up rocks and other artifacts the Eskimos left lying around about a million years ago. He goes to the Arctic Circle to dig a bunch of holes like a wild man. I say "wild man" because he has a video on the internet in which he threatens a polar bear with a stick for coming too close to his pile of artifacts. This all happens up near the North Pole somewhere.

So, for you laymen out there, that means Elsa is both smart and tough because her Daddy is, and she's beautiful and tough because her Mommy is. The Rock Hunter Guy tells me that Baby Elsa was born right in their house with what they call "natural birth." He also told me that Sara was in labor for over 800 hours. I thought, "Wow, that's almost a week."

In a couple of weeks, you can meet Baby Elsa when she's planting trees at the new Nature Park. I say that because Sara isn't going to put up with all that sleeping and pooping for very long unless that baby gets busy fixing some trees and native grasses. I know this to be true from experience. I'll explain in the next paragraph after I eat another piece of cake.

OK, I'm back from the cake break — sorry it took so long but here's the story about sleeping and pooping. Everybody knows I'm a liar, but this story is really based on truth. Here is the story:

Once, a long time ago, four of us were over by Pedrick Road in Davis, California, getting some rose cuttings for the greenhouse. There was Libby Earthman our fearless leader, Sara Tremayne our green thumb, Tanya, a Putah Creek Council steward, and me, let's call me Donald. Sara and Libby were down at the creek goofing off while Tanya and I were doing all the work.

They had me in the middle of a patch of roses that were all thorns and no flowers. I was already cut up pretty good when they sent Tanya in with a gas powered weed-eater that had a saw blade at the end of it. Tanya was swinging the weed-eater around and I was trying to get away, deeper into the rose patch. I could feel the blade zooming past my ear and...well I had a little accident. Out of fear you understand.

It seemed like hours before Tanya turned off the weed-eater and finally heard me whimpering because I couldn't get out of the rose patch. Tanya looks over at me and smiles as she says, "Don't worry Don, I'll get you right out of there, this happens all the time, so I know what I'm doing." Then she's heading right for me with a pair of wire cutters in her hand. I thought, "OOOh Jesus!"

Anyway, when I get out of the roses I tell Sara I have to go to the bathroom. Sara says, "You don't need no stinkin' bathroom, just go out in the bushes." So I says, "But they're all rose bushes!" Sara was getting loud now and said, "It don't make no nevermind, just holler if you get lost!" That's how I know about sleeping and pooping. So, from what Andy, the Rockhunter guy tells me, that all that Baby Elsa does. He says, "Sometimes she'll poop right after she gets done pooping."

So here's what we have: Baby Elsa Tremayne, with a last name that sounds like a movie star or a president — she's beautiful, she's smart and she's tough. OK, in layman's terms that means she's going to be someone to reckon with in the future. I swear up to God, we're going to have to reckon with the little Tremayne girl!

Today, as I left the creek, I happened to glance at what Sara was reading. The headline of the paper said, "Adventurous Woman needed as Surrogate for Neanderthal Baby!" So, if Sara considers this, it would be the first Neanderthal baby born in about 30 billion years or so, but that's a different story.

Nature, man, and the sixth extinction
1/29/2013

I've never been a "Big Picture" kind of guy. You would think that a guy with a big brain like mine would be able to see more of the big picture than I do. To tell the truth, I wouldn't begin to know where to find it. I don't even know what it would look like, where it starts, or where it ends. I don't even know how to describe it. What exactly is the "Big Picture?"

I suppose the idea of the big picture will differ from person to person. Some probably see it on a grander scale than others. Historians look to history just as biologist look to biology. In truth, history is but a fragment of biology. The life of a man is but a portion of the variations of organisms on land and under the sea.

Walk alone in the forest on a summer day and you will see hundreds of little birds, animals, insects, and fish. They will startle and scurry away at your coming. You must, at this time consider the fact that humanity is but a minority, passing by in their natural habitat. All of our economic competition, strife for mates, our hunger for love, grief and war, are similar to the mating, striving and suffering found below the fallen trees, under the leaves, or in the waters and boughs.

The laws of biology are the fundamental lessons of history. We are all subject to the processes and trials of evolution, the struggle for existence, the survival of the fittest. If we as a species seem to escape the strife and trials that other creatures face, it's only because of our ability to group, for protection. That said, even the group must meet the test of survival.

Life is a competition. Competition is not only the life of trade, it is the trade of life as well. Life abounds and flourishes when the food is plentiful but turns violent when there are more mouths than food. We consume each other by due process while the animals of the forest consume each other literally. As the group develops it becomes a society, and cooperation becomes a real thing when we deal with other groups.

Just as our fathers and grandfathers did, we fight, chase and sometimes kill in order to survive. We stuff ourselves with what we want and throw the remains in the trash instead of sharing what comes from the Earth with those around us. We don't consider the fact that the group acts just like the individuals within. The individual eats so the group must eat. When a group eats, it is the act of warfare upon our neighbor groups.

Another idea to consider is the fact that life is selection. In our struggle for life, food and mates some will succeed and some will fail. We are part of nature. Nature does not read the Declaration of Independence or the Declaration of the Rights of Man. In nature we are all born unfree and unequal. It is our technology that helped us rise above the melee. Our machines have placed us above nature.

Machines make us unequal and those with the most machines dominate the rest of the groups. Even the best of societies are doomed to fail and fall, for there's always a lesser society in the shadows striving for dominance in order to survive. Thus, life becomes a constant struggle of greed and deception, crushing all of nature in its path.

It's only of late, the last year or so, that I've glimpsed at what some would consider the "Big Picture." I must credit the individuals of a new group I've met for my new ability to see past myself and the results of my actions upon nature. This brings me to what I really wish to discuss: individuals and groups that consider the "Big Picture" and have a good idea of what exactly it is.

We have the ability to choose our group. We choose for different reasons. That is not my point. There are groups out there that know nature smiles when it is healthy and they strive to keep it that way. They know that every 20 minutes, we lose an animal species. If this rate continues, by the year 2025, 50 percent of all living species will be gone. It is a phenomenon known as the sixth extinction.

The fifth extinction took place 65 million years ago when a meteor smashed into the Earth, killing off the dinosaurs and many other species, and opening the door for the rise of mammals. Currently, the sixth extinction is on track to dwarf the   fifth.
There's a saying going around stating if you're not part of the solution, you're part of the problem. This is very true if you consider nature as a group in which you are included. If part of your group fails, it's only a matter of time before the group is extinct. I no longer wish to be part of the problem.

If you feel the same let me introduce you to a new group:
Putah Creek Council

Happy Valentine's Day, Los Altos
2/4/2013

I've been thinking again. I'm thinking about who I should wish a happy Valentine's Day. When we were kids, my brother Michael and I would buy a little package of valentines, put a name on each of them, and pass them out to all of our friends. I think we did this until we were 30 or 40 years old.

When we were a little older, we both married and had our own separate families, our own separate valentines. It was Michael and Anna and me and Therese. We were all in love and we were truly each other's valentine.

Through the years, as our families grew, so did our valentines. Pretty soon we were sending out about a thousand little valentines. Every year it seemed like more and more little valentines were all lined up in a neat little row. That's the way it went up until today. This year I'll be sending valentines out all by myself because Michael died a few months ago.

So, this year, I'll be sending valentines to my family and my brother's family just like I did every year before. I'll post a link to Paul McCartney's version of "My Valentine" on Facebook just like I did last year wishing happy Valentine's Day to all of my female friends there.

Of course, I have a very special Valentine for my wife Therese, whom I love so very, very much. She has been my special Valentine for many, many years and for that I am so very grateful. I hope she will be my special Valentine for many years to come.

Today, I have a special Valentine for someone I've never met formally, but she will remember me for years to come, I'm sure. She'll remember me because I so rudely ruined her day. For her, I was the "Ass of the Year" and deservedly so, for I frightened her beyond description.

My encounter with this poor lady was fate. My brother was dying and I was trying to get him to the Veteran's Hospital in Palo Alto so he could live. I'd never been to this hospital, so of course, I missed the signs and was lost. Somehow, I don't know how, I ended up on Main Street, Los Altos. The street was crowded and congested with traffic.

I was afraid my brother was going to die on the spot. He was writhing in pain and his breathing was very shallow and labored. I was frantic to find the hospital emergency room but was hopelessly lost. My wife was on the phone, looking at Google Earth to give me directions. I was frantic and afraid.

The car in front of me stopped in the middle of the road. She was waiting for another driver to vacate a parking spot. I could see myself in the mirror, yelling and screaming, like a movie on the big screen. I was banging my fist on the steering wheel and yelling, "Please move, my brother is dying," "Please!" Of course, the lady only saw an idiot suffering from road rage. My wife listened to all of this on the phone and was trying to calm me with directions.

So there I was, stuck in traffic. My brother was dying and I was frantically trying to save him. I watched all of this in the rear view mirror but was unable to stop or change a thing. I knew I was losing my brother and I was dying right along with him. There was nothing I could do. It was fate.

Anyway, I've been thinking about this poor lady even as I watched my brother dying in the hospital. I was angry that he didn't fight more than he did. I was also angry with myself for my actions toward this poor lady caught in the middle through no fault of her own.

So, here is what I wish to do on this Valentine's Day. I'm sending a special Valentine card to the mayor of Los Altos in the hope that it will somehow find its way to this poor lady. I ask no forgiveness and I wish only to say I'm so very sorry for my behavior in the middle of her little town. So very, very sorry.

It's Valentine's Day again. It seems like we have that holiday every year. This is the holiday that I have trouble with every time it comes around. Don't ask me why, but it's true. One might think it's my fault, but this is simply not the case.

You see, I'm an expert in the department of LOVE. I know everything there is to know about it. I know everything about love and I know everything there is to know about women too. If I'm lying, I'm dying, brother. I feel the need to say something to help my fellow men friends, my crew that is, to get through this day without totally blowing it with their women folk. If you just do everything I say, your woman will be in your arms tonight, guaranteed.

First, a little lesson on love might be needed. I've been studying women and love for well over 29 years, so take my word for it, there is absolutely nothing I don't know about women and love. I am probably the most expertesticle guy in the entire world when it comes to the "Game of Love!"

Lesson 1: Forgiveness. It is probably true that your woman might have loved other men before you came into her life. That's OK. She made a mistake, so just overlook it. This is your chance to be the "bigger man," so forgive her. It is important that you verbally bring this to her attention. Say the words out loud, "I forgive you dear woman, for you know not what you do."

Lesson 2: Experience. Men with pierced ears are better prepared for a relationship with women than men without pierced ears. This is true simply because they have experienced pain and they have bought jewelry. If you don't have holes in your ears, I can fix that for $49.99. Trust me, women will look for this, yes they will. Call me.

Lesson 3: Understanding. From this point on, people of the effeminate acclimation will understand little or less than none of what I think I'm saying. Women will find it difficult to grasp the meaning of the varied abstract terms of the male lingo thingy. Trust me. I know of what I speak. My research has been ongoing for close to 29 years, which is almost a century. If you are a woman, don't read this. When I say "woman" I am including men from France in the same group.

Some time ago I started my studies of women from the inside. I was actually inside of a woman. I'm talking about my whole body, not just parts of me. I'm not going to discuss that portion of my studies, because it was not a happy time for me. When women grow tired of you they can just spit you out and you will spend the rest of your life trying to get back in. Yes, it's true.

There are two kinds of love, Man's love and Women's love. Man's love is passionate, short and intense. Women's love is more companionate, and involves a close and enduring relationship. By enduring, I mean a relationship that can last for years. Women's love has internal structure and fuzzy borders, hot pink borders. Women's love like manic depression has its ups and downs. So forget all that stuff and concentrate on "man's love."

Lesson 4: Erotic love. The word erotic stems from the ancient Roman word, "erotismicymally," which was derived from two even earlier Greek words, erotismicy and mally. So it is no wonder that I named my new line of erotic clothing for men, Erotismicymally Wear. Within the pages of the Erotismicymally Wear, catalog you will find some unbelievably sexy garments for men of all ages.

We have thong underwear for men of all ages and sizes. We have T-shirts with all sorts of sexy sayings. My personal favorite is a little brown sleeveless tee shirt with the logo, "Show me your boobs!" on the front and "Bring me a beer when you finish the dishes" on the back.

Fibs are for fun but lies are for hurting
11/27/ 2013

I have written hundreds upon hundreds of columns, some heavy, some light. I write about things I am familiar with, the things of my life and those people I hold closest to my heart. There have been fibs in the columns but never, ever lies. Fibs are for fun and lies are for hurting.

Sometimes it's hard to write about my life and those things that are most important to me, things that are private for most. I am an open person, I always have been. I can remember my brothers complaining about things I'd shared with other people because they thought it too much information.

I am open about my life but I've been open about the lives of others as well. It seems that when I have an adventure and want to write about it and share it with others, I'm writing about someone else's adventure too if they happen to be with. After all, a shared adventure is only interesting if both sides of a story are told.

I wrote a column about my childhood and the days when I was alone in the middle of 400 children in a Catholic Orphanage. It was a column about how a bad experience can become a good adventure if you change things around in your mind. Even today, my wife and I can have a mutual experience and my memory of the adventure will be completely different from her memory of the same adventure. She thinks it's funny.

I have a column about sorrow and the things that are real. I do not whitewash sorrow and I illustrate the face of such things in stark contrast to the illustration others would provide about the same sorrow we'd shared. They felt sorrow and I felt anger. I spit words of anger when I should have been crying.

A column about the death of my brother was called harsh by someone very dear to me. I wrote about the anger I had within me because he didn't fight just a little harder to live. I wanted him to stay with me until I was ready to go with him, but there are others that I want to go with as well.

I have a column that seems lost in the forest of tall green trees that is confusing to others. There are things that they won't understand until the end of their days, but it's all there, revealed in the words on the page. There are things I said I would do and didn't, and I'm sorry for that. My word is all that I have and if I tell you I will do something, I will try very hard to do it.

There is a column of Armies and wars nobody could win. Columns of old wars and wars that are new, wars that can suck the youth, the wonder, and the joy of life right out of you. When it's over the rest of your life is outside of you and try as you may, you can't get it back where it belongs.

There's a column about ghosts that visit me in my sleep. It's a column about things like killing and death. It's about the things I did and the decisions I made that brought bitterness and regret between pride and service to my country

There's a column of my father that didn't know who I was when we met for the first time (in my memory) as he lay in a Veteran's Administration hospice, close to death. How hard love comes for a father you've never known nor has he known you. It was a column of no fishing, no games, and no fatherly love. It's like losing everything you ever had or ever will have.

I have columns of drug abuse and things that waste all of your time. It's a column of bars and locks with keys you don't have and they stand between you and those you love the most. It's funny how much jails are like orphanages. Everything is the same except the kids are bigger and meaner.

There is a column of Burtons that came into my life and how it took me 10 years to find out how genuine and loving a family is supposed to be. It's a column of love and mistakes I made out of ignorance. I couldn't see them and how pure they are for I believed they were like me. They make me so happy that it makes me cry when I think of them and the peace they put in my heart.

There's a column of happiness and the love of life. It's a column in praise of those innocent brings bent on saving the Earth. Those that will do it themselves if they have to with or without our help. They teach others to be teachers so it's like a pyramid scheme of teachers planting trees and grass, and flowers so you can walk amongst the things of nature.

I have a column about how very hard these people work every day to show us the beauty of nature. Without such people all that we hold dear will surely disappear and will be found nowhere upon this Earth. They try to show us the work we must do and how to do it, but everybody knows better so they argue and complain instead of helping.

There are other columns in my mind, some are heavy and some are light. I will write about things I am familiar with, the things of my life and those people I hold closest to my heart. There will be fibs in these columns but never, ever a lie. Fibs are for fun and lies are for hurting

I can see the future

Seeing as how I'm a man with an extremely large brain, I can look around and within 10 minutes, I can see how the future will be. I know there are those who will doubt the reliability or accuracy of my predictions but it's only because they're afraid. They're afraid I may be right about the future. Read on, if you aren't afraid.

In the future, some will worry about the carbohydrate quality of the food their children will ingest during puberty and the relative humidity in China. Only a few will worry about the food intake of French children and water resources development projects in semi-arid regions of the Middle East.

Fire, flood and automobile insurance will triple in cost. Terrorism risk insurance will increase by tenfold. Transplanted animal organs will find their way into common use in the human body. There will be better bionic limbs, hearts and other organs, and it would be a good time to invest in plastic sphincters.

Education will move rapidly to the internet. In one year, 90 percent of what an engineer knows will be available on the computer. To be a success in business, you'll need continuous retraining and a life of learning and re-learning will be the norm. Eighty percent of the scientists, engineers and doctors who ever lived are alive today — and exchanging ideas in real time on the internet.

Those now in their 20s will have more in common with their peers throughout the world, via the internet, than with their parents. Half of what a student learns as a freshman will be obsolete by his senior year. Time will become the world's most precious commodity. The big will get bigger, the small will survive, and the midsized will get squeezed out.

Workers will spend 10 percent more time on the job than they do now. Labor unions will lose their power. Large business will have fewer than half the management levels and about one-third the numbers of managers. Technology will increasingly dominate both the economy and society.

Thanks to the internet, litigation will become a global risk for companies that do not make the environment a priority. Institutions will grow more transparent in their operations and they will be more accountable for their misdeeds. Western attitudes will spread throughout the world, giving environmental activists in other regions ways to use their local court systems to promote their goals.

September 11 temporarily muted most demands for transparency in the American government, but in the wake of the torture scandal in Iraq, the reluctance to question Washington will disappear. We will demand greater social responsibility from both companies and each other.

Advances in transportation technology will make travel and shipping faster, cheaper and safer, by land, sea and air. Hypersonic aircraft will fly at 7,000 mph, (nearly 10 times the speed of sound). When commercialized, they'll whisk diplomats and other high-priority passengers across continents in less time than it takes most people to drive to the airport. Tokyo and Frankfurt will emerge as transfer points for passengers of high-speed, large-capacity supersonic planes.

Rapid developments in technology will create endless opportunities for new business development. Workers will retire later as life expectancy stretches. Work ethic will vanish. Women's salaries will reach equality with men's — but very slowly. The glass ceiling will be broken and more women will reach decision-making levels in business and government.

The richest 25-50 percent of the U.S. population will reach zero population growth. They will have no time for children and little interest in having large families. Upper management will give fewer detailed orders to subordinates. Instead, it will set performance expectations and fewer mid-level managers will be needed, flattening the corporate pyramid.

Ninety percent of the world's pop will have AIDS. Terrorist attacks on U.S. companies, once limited to rock throwing at the local McDonald's, will rise sharply, both in number and in severity. Nothing will prevent small, local political organizations and special interest groups from using terror to promote their causes.

The United States will be forced to recognize that the most dangerous terrorist groups are no longer motivated by specific political goals, but by generalized, virulent hatred based on religion and culture. Risks of terrorism will be greatest in countries with repressive governments and large numbers of unemployed, educated young men. Western corporations will have to devote more of their resources to self-defense. Countries where terrorism is most common will find it impossible to attract foreign investment, no matter how attractive their resources.

Islamic terrorists form only a tiny part of the Muslim community, but they will have a large potential for disruption throughout the region from Turkey to the Philippines.

Jeb Bush will never be president. Barack Obama will go down in history as the greatest President that ever lived and Donald K. Sanders will be considered as great a thinker as Einstein or Plato. The City of Winters, California will be renamed as "Sanders-town" and there will be a "Buckhorn" restaurant in every city in the world. Major population centers will have two "Buckhorns" and its owner, John Pickerel will be "World Citizen of the Year."

A slap in everyone's face
3/7/2013

Anyone that knows anything about me will tell you how much I love the new City of Winters Nature Park. I love everything about it and I love taking care of it. It's like taking care of God. I'm not the only one that loves it, the whole city loves it. An ever-increasing number of families stroll through the park taking in nature and enjoying the freshness of it. The cool clear water of the Putah Creek is some of the cleanest water in the country.

Every day I watch the mothers and the fathers with their children, large and small, strolling through the park. Their children are into everything, exploring this and that, looking for treasures. I see the delight on their faces when by chance they find a turtle, a fish or a small bird. When they spot a beaver or an otter they scream with joy because it's life at its maximum. Our nature park is getting better every single day.

Sometimes I sit in the park for a while just to see what will happen next. There's always something happening. There's a lovely pair of hawks that live in the park and they swirl around the air making love signals between themselves. You will hear them before you see them. They are absolutely beautiful.

The creek water is so clear that nothing can hide from your view. The beaver swim around chewing on this tree or that and then they drag the limbs into the water and swim away with them. When they're done, they come back and do it again. I love watching them and they know me so well that they don't mind that I'm sitting there watching them. I keep expecting them to invite me to lunch.

There are otters that swim around on their backs playing with whatever they have in their tiny hands. I call them hands because they are every bit as nimble as our human hands. They swim up the creek and then back down again, they give you the eye as they pass where you sit. It's almost like they are thinking, "Hey, this is my park, what are you doing here?"

Every once in awhile. you'll see a fox. You have to look quick because they are movers and shakers. They're here and then they're gone. They disappear into the brush that is now as native to this area as it will ever be. Thanks to the creek restoration projects of the Solano County Water Agency and the Putah Creek Council, Putah Creek looks pretty much like it did 200 years ago before man stepped in and altered the plants and the channel of the creek.

Thousands upon thousands of plants and trees have been planted by local volunteers. It's a joy for me to watch them in action. Even small children help by digging holes and placing each little plant where its new home will be. They give the new plants water and a touch of fertilizer, and then they sit back like me and watch them grow. Every day, more and more people are doing this. I love it.

While most people enjoy the park, there are others who go there just to slap all of us in the face. It's not only us they slap in the face, it's all of nature and everything else. There are those who are guilty of environmental terrorism. They do what they do out of hate for nature, us and themselves. The people I'm talking about are putting poison in the water, the soil, the birds, the fish, and all of the little animals that live there. In the long run, they will poison us as well.

Last Sunday, I spent the morning on my hands and knees picking up a thousand shards of glass coated with mercury. Mercury that will sink into the soil poisoning all that touches it. Mercury that will be washed by today's rain into the clean water of the creek where the fish will ingest it, poisoning them and their offspring. Mercury is a poison that enters the body of anything that it touches and it will never come out, ever. It will kill everything it touches.

I don't know who did it, but I hope someone does and reports it. Oh it was probably great fun for those that did it, they probably laughed while the shattered every four-foot florescent light bulb they could carry into a thousand toxic shards. Those who did this not only slapped nature in the face, they broke the law of the land. They broke not only the State of California law, but federal laws as well. There's no crime that's worse than environmental crime, for it affects us all. I can only hope that someone will come forward with the information that will send these people where they belong: jail.

Surely there are those who will claim that I'm overreacting, but consider the fact that in the year 2,000 over 370 pounds of mercury was dumped in California waterways. The broken glass of a florescent bulb is usually considered a greater hazard than the small amount of spilled Mercury. A child can step on a shard and the Mercury is inside his or her body, so that's not overreacting.

Fluorescent tubes and bulbs may be managed as universal wastes under Title 22, Chapter 23 of the California Code of Regulations. It's against the law to crush them against a tree under Title 22, division 4.5, chapter 11, section 66261.50. I don't know about you. but I would report this sort of crime without a thought. If you don't, then you're as bad as those who threw them there for you to step in.

It's estimated that nearly 75 million waste fluorescent lamps and tubes are generated annually in California. These lamps and tubes contain more than a half a ton of mercury. The mercury in urban storm water sediment results in part from improperly discarded fluorescent lamps and tubes.

Now with all of that said, I can only hope that someone saw them breaking the bulbs in the park. I know that someone out there knows who did it. Get with it and call the Winters Police Department and give them the information they need to put a stop to environmental terrorism. Mercury is no joke.

The perfect shot
3/11/ 2013

Every year when March comes around, I start thinking about 1971 — the year I made the perfect shot. I call it the perfect shot because for me, it was one in a million. For as long as I could remember I had never, ever been able to hit anything with a pistol, no matter how close it was or how many times I fired at it.

Before I continue, I must say that I'm a true believer in fate. I'm not saying your whole life is fate, but there are special times in your life when you experience something good or bad, it doesn't matter which, that's out of your control. The experience seems to follow a well-written script that just flows from beginning to end, and the experience seems to end before it begins. That said, let's go back to 1971.

Imagine, if you will, that you've just jumped from the window of a helicopter that's half buried in the mud. Your shirt is soaked in blood that isn't yours and you land with a thud in elephant grass that towers over your head. You have a gripping fear at your throat, the wet your pants kind of fear, and now you're running through the tall grass and it's grabbing at you, cutting your face and arms. but you don't mind because you're more afraid of what's behind you than what's in front of you. You have a pistol in your hand but you don't even know it.

Now, the very next thing you know, you've taken the perfect shot. All of a sudden you're a sharpshooter and can't miss a target. If it was a paper target that was hit by the perfect shot, there would be bragging rights, beers bought, and backs slapped. However it wasn't a paper target. It was a man. I saw the spent cartridge shining on the ground before I knew I even fired the pistol that I didn't even know was in my hand.

See what I mean — fate.

My mind, all of a sudden, went numb and I was moving in a script-like motion that I had to follow and could not deviate from. That's the way it was in March of 1971. Later that same year, I had a similar experience but I don't want to go into that. But I do think that it too was fate. To qualify as fate, everything has to be perfect — the timing, the people, the weapons, the helicopter crash, and the elephant grass all had to be just right.

I spent a couple of months in the mental ward at a military hospital in Quin Nhon after that fateful day. They taught me how not to think of that day and my perfect shot. I stored it away for many years and it was almost forgotten when fate pushed it up and out of my memory. It arrived with a bang when I least expected it. When that memory came up, it brought another and another until they were falling on my shoes and I found myself high-stepping around them, and I'll tell you why.

They say every action has an equal and opposite reaction. So too does fate. It has expected and unexpected results. Long ago, I had thought I may have to kill someone once I was in the Army. I thought about what I might expect as a result. I didn't think about what might be unexpected. Nothing, I mean nothing, was as I expected.

You see, I had a plan. I was to go to war, kill lots of enemy soldiers, become a hero, go home and marry my high school sweetheart, and live happily ever after. That was the expected. What I didn't expect was the fact that the same bullet that killed one person would also kill me. By me, I mean my spirit. With no spirit, a man is an empty shell, a zombie. I was an empty man going through the motions of living his life.

It was 30 or so years before I would sober up enough to think about what had happened. I wanted to tell someone about it, but that never happened. I had surrounded myself with other veterans, including my brother Michael, because veterans don't ask too many questions and they understand if you freak out once in a while. I think we took turns freaking out, now that I think about it.

Now I'd like to make a statement about what made me this way, at least what I think made me this way. It turns out that the government has been playing with the minds of its soldiers. You see, WWI and WWII had problems with something they called "shell shock." In those particular wars, it was customary to send soldiers to war as a group and everyone knew everybody else. Thus, when someone was killed, it was usually someone they knew and they suffered shell shock immediately and it was disabling.

So, to make a long story short, the government thinkers came up with a system called D.E.R.O.S that was designed to delay the symptoms of shell shock, sometimes for years. The D.E.R.O.S system sent an individual soldier to war essentially by himself. He arrived by himself at a unit where he didn't know anyone else, fought besides those he didn't know, and when his year was up, he went home by himself. The system worked because when someone was killed, the shock of it was postponed for who knows how long because you didn't even know the guy's last name most of the time.

I also blame this little game for the fact that, over the years, more veterans committed suicide than there were soldiers killed in the war itself — many, many more. Now, in the current conflicts, they seem to have switched back to the old system of sending over soldiers by unit where everybody knows everybody else. Go figure, because that system doesn't work either.

Anyway, to this day, I do not trust the federal government, doctors or lawyers, and if you are smart, you won't trust them either — unless of course you're one of them. But in that case, you're a lost cause anyway because I'd be willing to bet that unless you work for the VA, you could care less about veterans anyway unless they're paying you.

Look what we've become. We are a nation that overlooks crime. Collectively, we turn a blind eye to crimes of every sort that run rampant in every city in every state across the country. We are all victims of real estate fraud, corrupt banking practices, unethical business practices and lying federal government officials that, although charged with the oversight of our security, have become part of the crime.

Everybody knows the country is in financial crisis and everybody knows the root of this crisis stands squarely in banking practices and the housing market. Everybody also knows the corruption extends all the way to Capitol Hill. To top it off, everybody knows the corrupt government officials feel they are above the law. Now that I look at it this just might be the case.

There are those living right here in my little town of Winters, California that have been defrauded out of thousands of dollars by corrupt business practices that have been in existence and used over and over again for decades and are still being used to this day. Across the country there are thousands upon thousands of people who have been defrauded out of millions and millions of dollars.

Believe me, this is the truth. Take for example Countrywide Home Loans and its parent company, Bank of America. California Attorney General Jerry Brown led the charge against juggernaut mortgage lender Countrywide Home Loans, filing a lawsuit on June 30, 2009, alleging that the lender willfully deceived and misled clients by misrepresenting loan terms, payment increases and even affordability. Said Brown, "Countrywide's lending practices turned the American dream into a nightmare for tens of thousands of families by putting them into loans they couldn't understand and ultimately couldn't afford." The courts ruled for the state.

With 40 states participating in the settlement, it was believed the ruling was sure to spell a degree of relief for families throughout the country who are struggling to make ends meet during those trying times. That was 2009 and most are still waiting for a settlement now in 2013. Those I mentioned living here in Winters are still waiting for justice they have all but given up on receiving.

By now you are probably asking how many criminals have gone to jail for the commission of these crimes. This is an easy one to answer. Not one single person that I know of has spent a day in jail for crimes that have crippled the nation financially. I find that astounding and it really upsets me that the very worst of crimes are committed by respected businessmen, bankers and congressmen seeming to be above the law.

You might ask why lawmakers have done nothing to stop these crimes but that's an easy one to answer as well. Some of those charged with the laws of the land and its enforcement are part of the crime and will not take action against themselves. Congress looked into charges that some of its members were being paid off with millions of dollars of low interest loans. (As low as .5%)

Here is the essence of the statement released after the investigation: "While these allegations concern serious matters, almost all of the allegations concerned actions taken outside, or well outside, the jurisdiction of this Committee.... because they occurred before the third Congress prior to the current Congress. In addition, several of the Members and employees mentioned in the allegations are no longer serving in or employed by the House, and therefore are outside the Committee's jurisdiction."

Herein lies the problem. They're afraid of crossing the financial industry and being defeated with the industry's money. So they're silent. Silent. Silent. Silent. Their rationale is: If I get defeated, I'm not going to be able to do anything. That's what the problem is. If those charged with the law of the land cannot discipline themselves, who can enforce the law?

Here comes the point where we get frustrated and throw in the towel. If that's the way it is, we give up and everything gets overlooked. I would hope that just one individual will come forward and lead us to justice. At one point in time, I thought it would be our new President but I can't see that happening now. Well that's the way it stands, what do we do now?

I did not have any ideas how much I love that Microsoft Word thingy. I didn't like it at first cause it put a red scriggley line under almost everything I would wirte on it. Then someone told me that the red scriggley line means that you made a mistake and then ifn you was to click on it it fixes it automatically for you.

So. A few years back I started a-messen with it and loe and behold before I know anything at all, I'm a writer. And what I write seems to be just fine after I make all them squiggley lines disappear. It is almost like someone else wrote it for me. Hot damn!

Thrugh experimentin I found out that the Microsoft Word can do a lot more that squiggley red lines. It can make the letters bigger. And if you want to you can make the other side bigger. That's not all it does neither.

sure How ! did ! but it ! can turn things around and make them backards.

Look this is definitely like a automatic toy for me to play with and I just love it. I been wondering if everybody has this Microsoft thingy and they use it to change they writing like I do. I think pretty much that my friend Debra must have it because I can send this here paper to her on the email and it gets put in the paper like someone else wrote it.

You see, Debra is also the editor of the paper here in Winters and on iPinion Syndicate, and other places as well. I like that "as well" quote because it sounds better than "to". Don't it. If I put my finger on the button that says "tab" on it everything is blank for a few of those kilobites. That's what they call those spaces. The blank ones, not the ones with typing on them, I don't think.

You see a few years back, maybe 30 years back, Debra, the editor of the paper must have been hurtin to fill some space in the paper. She calls it a void or something like that. Anyhow when she ask me if I would like to write a colum for her I said "but Debra, I don't know how to write" she said she will help me a lot.

Well I can tell you she does help me a lot because when she get done with it it almost looks like I didn't write it like that. At the bottom of the page on the video screen there is a number. Well that number tells me just how many words I have put on the screen. Right now it says 456 or 458. Nevermind it keeps countin anyway.

When I was a kid I almost didn't graduate from the high school in East Peoria Illinois. Did you know there was a S on the end of Illinois that don't make no sound. Anyway, I was saying I had trouble in English class and Miss Wedikind threw me out for writing stupid stories. I didn't go the the deans office because he said the next time I saw him I was going to get thrown out of school. Well, the truth be told, I was not a kid anyway because I was 21 years old at that time.

Anyway, Miss Wedikind ran away with one of the students and she was never seen again by anyone in East Peoria Illinois so they let me graduate. I think it was because I was so good looking at the time and they were afraid I was going to date one of the little girls in the new freshman class. It is a mystery to me why they call it a freshman class when there are girls in there to.

Anyway, I'm going to send this in the email so Debra the editor can work on it and make it purty like she always does. I hope she is back from her vacation so this does indeed get fixed cause I wouldn't want everybody ta see my reel writing.(Editor's note: This column was not edited.

Just a file on a computer
3/21/2013

It has been said by many, well mainly by me, that I have a large brain. This is a known fact and it can be confirmed by all of my closest friends. If we can accept this as a given then we can move on to the point I'm trying to make. It's not complicated like most of the stuff I think about so even those of limited intelligence will be able to understand. Ready, here it comes?

We are all just a file on a computer. Some of the files are active but the majority of them are inactive. With the passage of time all of the files will either be sent to some remote storage device that is next to nowhere or simply deleted. Either way, in time, they will be forgotten.

I guess we shouldn't feel bad about it for those that came before us, before the computer, were forgotten in a most Riki-tic manner. In the past, a man and his whole life would simply drift into the great void of forgotten memories in just a few generations. His great-great grandson might look at an old picture of him but in reality the person that he was and everything that he did will be gone and it will be gone forever.

The memories of a few lives have been placed on the written pages of books in the hope of being remembered for eternity or at least until the time when man is no more upon this Earth. That was the thought or reasoning behind the writing of books, for most anyway. There are piles and piles of books being destroyed every day, every month, every year. A fortunate few are being copied to computers.

For a thousand years books were the highest technology of the day. At the start only a few could communicate with books because relatively few knew how to read. Early books were a luxury only a few could enjoy until the advent of the printing press and even then it was technology that was slow to spread. Books, in the beginning were mainly concerned with religion, or someone's interpretation of it.

Books are unreliable for the most part, including the Bible. Scholars contend that during the Middle Ages and on to the Spanish Inquisition much of how the Bible is interpreted was changed to suit the leaders of the day. Jesus Christ became blond with blue eyes and for a Jew of that day that would be nothing less than a miracle.

In the end it is of no consequence whether books on religion are true or not. A thousand years from now I don't think the technology of today will have survived anyway. We will be at war with each other over whatever natural resources are left and those with the most weapons will reign over those with none. I can just about guarantee that with the passage of time each and every one of us will no longer be in the memory of anyone or anything. We will be lost.

After all a thousand years is a long enough time for more than one catastrophe to fall upon the Earth and it wouldn't take much to knock us back into the Stone Age. With a new stone age the computer and all of its files and folders will be useless and any information within will be lost forever. I think you will agree that only the fortunate few that are living today will be remembered by anyone a thousand years from now. The only thing to mark our existence will be the garbage we leave behind.

Our lives will be washed away like footprints on the beach.

The math behind Joe Biden's hotel bill
3/24/2013

Wow, everybody has their panties in a bunch because Vice President Joe Biden had to spend $585,000.50 for hotel rooms at the Hotel Intercontinental Paris Le Grand. Geeze, give the guy a break will ya! The vice president and his wife traveled to Paris with a rather large entourage, so they had to have every room in the building — 132 rooms to be precise.

What, did you expect them to stay at Motel 6? Well even if he did, Motel 6 is not $6 dollars a night anymore. I don't think it ever was. Anyway, back to the current problem. I don't think $585,000 is all that much, after all, the government does control billions and billions of dollars doesn't it?

Oh, I'm sure there are some of you who think over half a million dollars is too much to be spent on a hotel room, even by a vice president. Whatever! I know better and I'll spell it out for you, and at the same time I'll account for every penny they spent. You are probably thinking "How is he going to do this?" OK, spread out, I'll show you. I'll do it with ciphers and ciphering.
Follow me now!
- Total hotel bill = $585,000.50
- Number of rooms rented = 132 +/-

Ok that comes to $5,850 per room, per night. Mr. Biden was given a dollar discount for each room because they actually did spend the whole night.
- OK, we have a new total of $584,865.
- The new adjusted rate for per room, per night is $4,429.77 (much better) Now we have a place to start. I will use a SSA (Sanders Series Approximation) $1/\text{Sqrt} (1+v^2/c^2) \sim 1 + 1/2 * v^2/c^2$ if $v/c << 1$.

Note that if v is small compared to c, then (just as in Einstein's Theory of Relativity, $E - m*c^2$) what we have is $1/2 * m * v^2$. Simple so far, right?

Where "r" is the "room", c is the speed of light, and v is the velocity of time it took Mr. Biden to spend the half a million dollars then the full equation is $r=c * \text{gamma} * c^2$. Now we're getting to the root of the matter quickly. Pay attention!

Vice President Biden's spending energy is equal to the old familiar kinetic energy... but only in the approximation that $v/c << 1$. Do you follow me still? When $v = 0$, it is just $E = m * c^2$, which is called the rest mass energy because the object is at rest ($v = 0$). Where do you rest? Simple, you rest in a hotel room, hundreds of them. But I won't go into that.

A statement made by the Vice President insinuated that he used an additive identity to pay his share of the hotel bill. Since no one in my town, the City of Winters California, except Woody Fridae will know what an additive identity is, here is the definition: Additive identity = a number that can be added to other numbers without changing its value.

I don't know about you, but I'm extremely happy with the situation. I'm happy he didn't spend two nights.

I hate zippers!
4/11/2013

I hate zippers! Who in the hell thought of such a stupid thing as a zipper? As far as I am concerned, they're ugly and useless. They're nothing but trouble. They break all the time and it doesn't matter what kind or size, or what they're zipping. They always break when you don't want them to and they never break when you want them to. (i.e. a tight blouse.)

The worst thing about zippers is that I keep zipping my little thingy into them. Well, to be precise, it was the little hood thing on my thingy that got caught. At this point in time, I have to tell you how very, very, painful it is to get the hood of your thingy in a zipper. Every time I get my thingy caught all I can do is look up to the heavens and say, "OOOoooo!"

Talk about pain! It was almost too much to bear. Not only that, it was gushing blood! So to summarize, I don't like zippers and my thingy doesn't like zippers. I guess that makes it u-nana-nana-mana-mouse. The really sad part of this story is the fact that the deal is only half closed. If I were a lawyer I would say that the case is still pending.

So the story goes that when you get your thingy caught in a zipper, it's only natural that eventually you will have to get it out of the zipper. Getting the thingy out is worse than getting the thingy in. Ten times worse! What's really sad is the fact that none of this is my fault. The damn thingy has a mind of its own. I don't have any control over it and most of the time I don't even know it's there.

It used to be that if I got it caught in a zipper, I could look down at it and it would look back in a proud sort of way. It used to be that it didn't mind a few scars because it gave it a little character. I used to play like it was a little gangster, sort of like Scarface or something like that. Now my belly is in the way and I can't even see the darn thing. Looking at it in a mirror just isn't the same. It makes it look so sad, like it's ashamed or something.

Once the thingy is in the zipper, there's no easy way to get it out. OK, I'm a big tough guy and I've been through a lot of crap, but when I look at my thingy in the mirror, tears come to my eyes because it looks so sad. It's like being in a minefield with one foot on a Bouncing Betty. You know that at some point in time, you'll have to lift your foot off of the mine but at the same time, you know that it's going to hurt.

Oh, I could walk stiff-legged over to the emergency room and have a doctor get it out but sitting in the waiting room is not fun at all. Nobody will sit by you and no one wants to talk to you. Instead, they all gather in groups and chuckle at the stupid thingy in the zipper jokes. Christ, will the pain never end?

So, now I'm walking stiff-legged, right-foot-left foot-right-foot, out to my truck to get two pairs of pliers. Now it's right-foot-left foot-right-foot all the way back to the house and the mirror that I forgot. Once there, I have the choice of either pulling the zipper down real slow or just yanking it like a baseball player after a grounder. I have tried it both ways and I'm not going to talk you through that.

OK, now the thingy is out of the zipper but it's gushing blood all over everything. This is when it really gets bad because as I'm standing there checking out the cute little thingy in the little mirror, I see a tick on one of the thingy's two buddies. I mean, how much is a guy supposed to endure? I make a mental note to spray some Raid on myself when I'm working at the creek.

So I guess the little guy looks a lot worse than he really is. A guy with a sore on his thingy is not so popular in the pool hall, if you know what I mean. Now everybody in town is going to think I have syphilis or something. Maybe it would be smart to keep him out of sight for a while. No need to embarrass the little guy, right?

There's only one thing worse than getting your thingy in a zipper, and that's getting it caught in a buttonhole on button fly jeans. If that ever happens, I'm going to slap it around a little bit. Get tough with it, so to say!

Higgs boson hoax tricks big-brained Winters Man
4/13/2013

"And the Lord said, 'Behold the people are un-confounding my confounding.' And the Lord sighed and said, 'Go to, let us go down, and there give them the God Particle so that they may see how beautiful is the universe I have made.'"

Another name for the God Particle is the Higgs boson. Correct me if I'm wrong, but the Higgs boson is a tiny piece of matter created when two tiny parts of an atom collide within a muon ring such as the one in Switzerland that's called the Cern Collider. Each Higgs boson is created at a cost of millions of dollars.

So, to make a long story short, I read on the internet that the Cern people were going to give away 10 Higgs boson particles using a lottery system. I almost crapped my pants when I read that. Holy moly, it must have cost millions of dollars for each Higgs boson to be created. I wanted to get me one of those.

Yes my very own Higgs Boson, woohoo! I didn't know how they would package something so small that you wouldn't be able to see it with an electron microscope. In my mind, I was already figuring how much something like that would be worth. It would certainly be in the hundreds of thousands neighborhood.

Next thing I'm doing is going online to see where I could put my name in the hat for the lottery drawing. I was thinking I simply must have my Higgs boson and I want it now. I want to get the first one given away because I needed it to boost my ego. I have been flying low lately, so I figured this would be a boost to my moral.

Man, If only I had a Higgs boson, I would be like the big man of Winters, California. I could call John Donlevy, the City Manager, and say, "See fella, I tried to get you to build a muon ring here in Winters so we could sell Higgs bosons and make a lot of money."

My plan was to just sell empty packages that supposedly held a Higgs boson within. How would anyone know if there was a boson inside the package or not since no one would ever be able to see one?

I was on top of the world, and I was going to spend a fair share of my time to get one of those bosons. All day long, I was thinking about that Higgs boson and what I could do if I had one. I thought and I thought about that Higgs boson. That's when it dawned on me! Those bastards are taking me to town with my own crooked scheme. Dammit!

By the time I figured out that it was a hoax, I'd already sent them an email asking how I could get my name on the lottery list. I haven't felt this dumb since I built the toll booth I was going to put up at East Abbey Street and Elliott Street before the city shot that idea down too. That toll both cost me a lot of money too. So, in the end, the Higgs boson giveaway was just an April Fool's Day joke.

Ha ha, very funny.

So this stupid Higgs boson hoax just added misery to my already miserable week. It started going bad last week when I told my wife, Therese, that our anniversary was on Monday and I wanted to take her to dinner. She says, "Our anniversary is on Tuesday." So I look at my calendar and say, "Na, it's on Monday." So now Therese says, OK whatever." Anyway, I ordered me a prime rib dinner and I got her a salad from my favorite restaurant, The Buckhorn. Both the steak and the salad were on takeout so we could eat at home.

Anyway, to make a long story short, my anniversary was on Tuesday. It's not my fault that I thought our marriage anniversary was on the 8th of April instead of the 9th.

Not my fault.

Next, I was doing some volunteer work at the Winters Nature Park and got a tick on my boys. Now, to top off everything, I got my thingy stuck in my zipper, and now those Cern Collider guys are pulling the wool over my eyes, lying to me about giving me a Higgs boson. Whatever, it's OK. I can deal with it, but I'm going to find a way to get even with those nerdy scientist guys. Maybe I could sue them for hitting my house with one of those Hadron or Lepton thingys.

Anyway, I'll let you know when I'm ready so you can have a good laugh with me at their expense. It's like, "Here comes the Devil and he's riding a white horse and he's going to stick that Higgs boson up those guys' butts!"

Dark matter scheme
4/16/2013

Finally, I think I'm on the brink of a breakthrough in my ongoing investigation of where all the money is and how I can get my hands on more than my fair share. In the midst of this investigation, I found something really stinky. In fact it is so stinky that the powers that be in the media industry will not get near it and neither will I, so let's look at something else.

What do you have when two Italians get together? The mafia, right? OK, this is a given, so I'll try to get right to the point of the new direction my investigation might be going in. First, I have to explain the event that started me thinking along these new lines. I think I may have accidentally uncovered something so important that I don't think I should tell you about it yet.

OK, I'll tell you.

Remember the words "Dark Matter"! These words seem to have indiscriminately jumped into my head as I was in the midst of my morning constitution while sitting on the throne in my bathroom. I remember the exact moment it entered my head. I was flushing the toilet and as I touched the handle that started the flush sequence it dawned on me. I thought, "Hey, I read something yesterday that said there were two Italians in space at the same time on the Muir Space Station."

Exactly what are these two Italians up to and why are they up to it in space? I decided to go back and re-read what I had read yesterday. OK, this all happened yesterday because at that point I got hungry and while eating my lunch I completely forgot what I was thinking about until just now. Italians, mafia and space; these three words go hand in hand with each other.

Now I'm on the third day of my investigation and I'm looking at the article about two Italians in space. What are they up to? I can tell you right now that it has to be something fishy or it smells like fish. Well here it is, are you ready? The Italians are trying to get the corner on the dark matter industry!

I know, it's unbelievable, right? Well think about this. Roberto Vittori and Paolo Nespoli, in April 2011, meet at the space station, out in the middle of space. One carries a message to the other from the Italian president. This is the first time two Italians are allowed in space at the same time. Everybody knows that this constitutes a "gathering," which is forbidden by International Treaty at the end of WWII.

Why meet in space, you might ask? Privacy is the answer to that. Monitors with the microphone turned off recorded the Italians with their heads together discussing some heinous plan. At two points in time, one of the Italians bumped into the microphone switch long enough to record these words. "Dark Matter" was the first two words and they were quickly followed by the words, or what sounded like the words, "Don't worry about the French, they are pussies."

These Italians were both selected by the European Astronauts Corps in 1998 and trained together for many years. . Vittori is said to be the adopted brother of the Italian President that joined the meeting in space via telecommunication. The words, "AMS-02" were heard and recorded by a tape recorder I guess. "AMS-02" refers to something called the "Alpha Magnetic Spectrometer", "number 2" I guess.

Note: It just so happens I have two "Alpha Magnetic Spectrometers" in my hall closet. I use them to suck in data about "Dark Matter."

I found that Italy is the third-largest contributor to ESA programs and the second to the International Space Station. Italian industry built more than half of the Station's pressurized volume of the non-Russian segment. This information alone prompted me to call Interpol in Switzerland. They hung up on me and told me never to call them again.

The AMS-02, the Alpha Magnetic Spectrometer, consists of seven instruments that monitor cosmic rays from space. Unprotected by Earth's atmosphere the instruments receive a constant barrage of high-energy particles. As these particles pass through AMS-02, the instruments record their speed, energy and direction. This explains that my data was corrupted by the atmosphere. Geeze, who knew?

I have collected data on over 400,000 electrons together with their antimatter twins, the positrons. Data that I'm releasing today show how the ratio of positrons compared to electrons passing through AMS-02 changes depending on their energy, confirming data from previous instruments. I'll explain what it does in simple terms in my new book, "Dark Matter for Dummies."

The book centers on the idea that if you shine a torch in a completely dark room, you will see only what the torch illuminates. That does not mean that the room around you does not exist. Similarly I know dark matter exists but have never observed it directly. Now I know I have the wrong type of torch. With that fact known, does anyone out there have an "antimatter torch?"

Elected officials break the law without fear of retrebution.
4/22/ 2013

Do not break your oath, but keep the oaths you have made to the Lord (Matt. 5:33).

I consider myself to be an average American. I worked an average job, drove an average car, and lived the average life. In the past, I've been pretty accurate at predicting which way society would lean on certain issues in these United States. Not that I'm all that smart, but I simply consider how I feel about this and that, and then I have a good idea how the rest of the country may be thinking. Well, at least, the average Americans.

The average American will swear to only a few oaths during his life. Certainly, the Pledge of Allegiance might be the first. We might swear to tell the truth in court, but very few will incriminate themselves. Those in law enforcement will swear to uphold the law on the local level and it's the same up on Capitol Hill. For all, the oath signifies a public statement of personal commitment.

In 1968 I took an oath to defend the United States against all enemies, foreign and domestic, and became a Private E1 in the United States Army. I was very serious about upholding this oath and I was very careful not to break it. As a soldier, the oath gave me reason to keep my back straight, my chin up, and my heart in the right place.

That oath is also a statement that I will take personal responsibility for my actions. My oath had no time limit so as far as I am concerned it is still in effect. There are serious consequences for those who break their oaths of military service, and there's a Federal Prison at Fort Leavenworth to house them when the oath is broken. Military service is a serious duty and in certain circumstances, a broken oath can lead to your execution before a firing squad.

Article 6 of the Constitution states that, "Before mentioned, Senators and Representatives and the members of the several state legislatures, and all executive and judicial officers, both of the United States and of the several states, shall be bound by oath or affirmation, to support this Constitution."

The first oath was short and to the point: "I, A.B., do solemnly swear or affirm (as the case may be) that I will support the Constitution of the United States." Their oath requires them to support and defend the Constitution — not the president, not the country, not the flag, and not a particular corporation or industry.

Elected officials swear to defend against, "All Enemies, Foreign and Domestic," and that they, "Will Bear True Faith and Allegiance to the same." As an average American, that seems pretty simple to me. It's right there in black and white.

In the final analysis, however, loyalty depends upon the integrity of the individual. In the last decade or so, the oaths of Capitol Hill have changed, relieving elected officials of any retribution from breaking their oath. The words "Solemnly swear or affirm that I will truly and faithfully discharge the duties of my said office, to the best of my knowledge and abilities."

Thus, if you give the best effort to the best of your knowledge, even wrong becomes right. For example, torture is acceptable as long as you change the meaning of torture so that it does not include "water-boarding."

You'd think that depending on the conduct and the statute violated by elected officials, the penalties for breaking an oath could include criminal penalties, ouster or personal liability. Sorry, not so. There is no punishment for violating your oath and breaking the Constitution. Many of the laws on the books right now encourage us to break the Constitution/oath. The system is looking pretty hopeless.

In the end, it's alright to lie about weapons of mass destruction as long as you don't intend to or knowingly lie under oath. Without fear of retribution, there's nothing to guide elected officials when they face conflicts of interest and hard choices.

America's democratic system often proves frustrating for average citizens like me

Religion sure is a funny thing. Now that I'm considered an elder of the City of Winters tribe, I consider myself an expert on religion and I am certainly among the top 10 moral advisers in all of Northern California. If you have a question concerning religion, ethics, or what is or what is not moral behavior, then I am the guy you should go to.

To begin, I will discuss religion in its varied forms using simple layman's terms for the simpleminded and those that are just plain dumb. I must, in all good faith, include some of those who read my columns regularly somewhere within this group. I will conclude this column with examples of immoral behavior and statements about what is wrong with this society.

In this day and age, we have Hindu, Jews, Muslims, Catholics, Baptist, Mormons and Seven Day Advents. There are others but I won't discuss them at this time because if I say these are good religions then I would have to say that the rest are all bad. As bad as they really are, I cannot actually say they are bad.

Catholic: Invented by the Son of God, therefore it is the only true religion. It is true that every single practicing Catholic, regularly taking confession, will go to Heaven. To the Catholic, no sin is unforgivable. (Ninety-six percent of all people incarcerated in the California Penal System are Catholic and another two percent are in the county lockup.)

Mormons: Exactly like Catholics, except they can have multiple spouses and they store enough food to feed themselves for a full year. The food is stored in the great temple so the Catholics cannot steal it and give it away to the poor. Mormons fully expect to watch everybody else slowly starve to death. If you are not a Mormon, you are going to starve to death because they are not going to share.

Baptist: Probably consist of the smartest people in all of religiousdom. The Baptists are planning to kill the Mormons and take their food. That deed done, they will blame the Catholics and put them all in prison where they will all die and go to Heaven. The Baptist doesn't mind sending Catholics to die in prison because they know the Catholics get to go to Heaven anyway.

Hindu/Buddhist: I think those Indian people may have something when they talk about reincarnation all the time. The way I figure it, a man is born and then he dies. After death he finds himself in space in the form of an atom that spins around other atoms until he is reborn as an animal. Eventually he will die again and it all happens again and again, and he returns as a different animal each time until he uses up all the animal life forms and then he will get to be a man again. If something goes terribly wrong because of some mistake along the line, he will come back as a woman.

Muslim: Eternal enemy of Christians because they cannot prove that their prophet is better looking than Jesus, who had blond hair and blue eyes. The Muslim faithful have a dreaded fear that the Christians are going to steal the junk that they keep in their desert but the Christians know full well that the Muslims own nothing but grease and sand, and they pretend that it's valuable.

Jews: Jews are exceptional businessmen and to them the dollar or pound is the primary reason for existence. Pork at half price is a dilemma to the Jewish. This is true mainly because they trick the Christians into thinking pork is good meat and it tastes good, while on the other hand they claim it is filthy meat, not worthy to be food. In reality, the Jews sell stinky, nasty, pork as food for others but they are above eating it themselves. I find something not right about that.

Seventh day Advents: I can't say anything bad about them because I have a friend named Don who practices that religion and he gives me little comic books. It is the gospel truth that he is the only person on Earth that cares about my soul.

Society: I find it very sad indeed that of all the people in all of the religions, not one single person is willing to nominate me for the Pulitzer Prize or a Nobel Prize. I guess everybody thinks it's OK for me to do all the thinking and come up with all of the ideas, yet they leave it up to me to nominate myself for a couple of crummy prizes. Will the pain never end? It is very sad indeed, but don't think for a moment that I would hesitate to send in those nominations

Everything changes. If you don't believe me just ask the so-called experts, doctors, lawyers, and politicians. If you ask me, I don't think any of these experts know their asses from a hole in the ground. They tell us this and that is true and with the passage of time, they turn around and tell us something else is true. Next, I suppose they'll tell us that bloodletting is no longer a cure for the common cold!

Our rights are written down in black and white, and the experts told us that these rights are inalienable and can never be lost or taken away. At one time we all had the right, by law, to bear arms. People used to go to the local pubs, drink until they puked, shoot the rafters of the pub, and then go home and sleep it off. Now if you bring a gun into a tavern you are one dead SOB!

Furthermore, the right to bear arms has been altered by law so many times by so many amendments that most of us can't even be in the same room with a firearm or we are arrested and given a felony conviction as a reward. We used to be innocent until proven otherwise. Now we are guilty until we prove we are innocent.

Everything we do, everything we eat and everything we buy is regulated and repeatedly taxed until prices are so high on everything that only the affluent can afford the staples needed for a healthy, productive life. Nature smiles at the union of freedom and equality in our utopias, for freedom and equalities are sworn enemies and when one prevails the other dies. To check the growth of inequality, liberty must be sacrificed.

At one time, doctors were the good guys. Every town had a doctor that everyone loved and respected. My, how that has changed. Today doctors are drug dealers for the pharmaceutical companies. The rich pay $30 and $40 per pill, and the poor don't get any at all. As it stands, the rich can purchase organs from the poor so they can live longer than the rest of us.

Medical treatment has evolved from bloodletting to the injection of lethal radioactive, whatever the hell it is, directly into their patients' bloodstreams as a "cancer cure." There are pills for this and pills for that, and now they tell us that placebos work just as well. Codswallop, I say, codswollap!

We are told to practice a good health regime by exercise, education and eating well. A good look at all of these practices will expose the nature of greed behind them. Large business entities have a hand and now a foot in the get healthy schemes. Our education systems are directed at avenues toward the greatest paycheck instead of knowledge. We are told to eat more vegetables but they don't advertise the need to wash iceberg lettuce in warm soapy water with a brush to remove pesticides.

The relative equality of Americans before 1776 has been overwhelmed by a thousand forms of physical, mental, and economical differentiation, so the gap between the wealthiest and the poorest is now greater than at any time since Imperial plutocratic Rome. War is a constant of history that has not diminished with civilization or democracy.

Of the last 3,600 years or so, less than 300 have seen no war. The causes of war are the same causes of competition among individuals for pride, desire for food, land, materials, fuel and mastery over others. If we follow the usual course of history, we should make war upon others for fear of what they may do to a generation yet unborn.

I can see our progress and techniques are involved with some tincture of evil with good. Our comforts and conveniences have weakened our physical stamina and our moral fiber follows closely. Our means of locomotion are used to facilitate crime and to kill our fellow man and ourselves. We double and triple our speed, but we shatter our nerves in the process. It turns out that we are the same apes at a thousand miles an hour as we were when we used our legs.

The more things change, the more they stay the same. When it comes right down to it, life is what you make it for yourself. I am older now and have seen much of what is going on in the world. I have resorted to self-isolation to survive. I strive to surround myself with those I can trust to do the right thing should the need arise.

Wealth has nothing to do with my life now. When I hear others say something about a friend who may have money that I feel is derogatory, it forces me to open my eyes to see what is what. When others talk of greed or struggling for the almighty dollar I see something much different in this little community of mine. I see people around me working very hard to keep others working.

Jobs are not natural. Someone must create them and nurture them so that most of the time the employer outworks the employee and suffers twice as much. Most work eight hours and then sit on the couch watching TV while others worry about local economies and unemployment statistics.

With our endless capacity for fretting, no matter how many difficulties we surmount or how many ideals we realize, we shall always find an excuse for being magnificently miserable. I'm past all of that now because I am older and somewhat wiser. (I think) I still work, but not for money. I choose to give my labor as a gift to those I feel deserve it, and deserve it they do. I don't care what anyone thinks about that either, because I know what I'm doing and I will keep on doing it as long as I can, for it is labor of love

When I was a young man, I had an extra-large brain and, therefore, an extra-large head. For as long as I can remember, people have pointed at me and laughed because I looked so funny. My mother, fearing I might have super intellectual powers, dumped me at a Catholic orphanage in Little Rock, Ark. I bring up this fact only as an illustration of my current demise.

You see, I find that, lately, my brain is shrinking. I calculate that, within a year or two, my brain may shrink drastically. Eventually, in time, it may shrink and shrivel until it is the same size as yours. For me, this is a horrible thought and I find myself throwing up a little in my mouth every time it enters my mind.

Oh, I know all of you little people are worried about me, and all are wondering what in the world will happen next. When you are all done thinking about that, you will think, "How did Donald get such a large brain in the first place, and how can I get one?" Well, I don't know what will happen next, but I'll tell you how I got the large brain, and no, you can't get one.

My brain has always been inordinately large. When I was a young boy, some kids would stare it and try to touch it. Other kids would point at me and say, "Hey, there goes that kid with the big brain!" Still other kids would envy me and covet my brain. Together, they plotted to get me and my brain by trapping me in small spaces.

Over and over, they attempted to trap me, but I always got away. You see, my superior reasoning power would always afford me an exit strategy. There could be 20 people in a room looking for me, and I would simply walk through them backwards until I was out the door and well embarked on my escape. By walking backwards, they would think I was coming into the room instead of leaving. All of a sudden I was gone and they would stand there staring at each other in wonderment.

Anyway, I have discovered through years and years of research that problem solving will shrink the human brain. For some unknown reason the human brain shrinks a tiny, tiny bit every time it solves a problem. That's my theory, and I'm sticking to it. It's a fact that if you disagree with these findings, your brain is already below the minimum size required for reasonable thinking and problem solving. Good luck with that.

It's all very simple; I have a large brain because I've never made a single solitary decision in my entire life. Not one, until now. For the last month or so, there have been some hard times on East Abbey Street. It seems that some of the things I have been faced with lately have been difficult for me to handle. I know that everyone has their problems and the resolution of these problems is what we consider to be life itself. We work our way through life. Along the way we encounter little problems, we fix them, then we move along to the next problem, our brains shrinking all the time.

For the first time, ever, I can see problems that I just cannot ignore. Like it or not, I will have to make a decision this time. My problem is that I have always been a "path of least resistance" kind of guy, so I don't even know how to make a decision, especially one as important as this one.

Here's my problem: Lately there have been some leaks of government activities. It seems that these leaks are revealing illegal government activities. The government likes to use the word "covert" instead of "illegal." They have good reasons for that, I'm sure.

Two major leaks involving "Wikileaks" and the "NSA" have the guys that leaked the information on the run and hiding, fearing for their lives. The two guys, one named Julian Assange and the other named Edward Snowden, are fighting extradition to the US because they feel they cannot get a fair trial. It doesn't matter that the information they leaked to the public reveals illegal activities by the government. All that matters is the fact that they leaked the information in the first place. How dumb is that?

OK, my decision has to have one or the other outcome. I have to decide if these two men, who made a decision to give up everything in their lives to tell us about a crime committed against us all, are heroes or traitors. This problem is making my brain hurt because it is shrinking. What in the world should I do?

I think I know what I will do. A short time from now, I'll get my boots on and go down to the City of Winters Nature Park and water some newly planted trees.

My wife thinks she's the boss of me! Ha! I can tell you right away that she is living in a dream-like state in some make believe world where women are smarter and better suited than men when it comes to giving orders. It's like she has diarrhea of the brain because her dream state is somehow carrying over into her awakened world.

I know because I live in her awakened world. I don't know what's going on in her sleepy-time dream world because there is usually some other guy over there. She says he is younger and better looking than those that live in her wakey-wakey dream world. She says he has a six-pack, a cleft on his chin, and long blond hair that blows back, all the time like someone is following him around with a fan. Whatever!

Her world, for the most part, does not conflict with mine but when it does, it causes me considerable anxiety. For example, consider her attitude of superiority when I didn't finish our bathroom remodel according to her schedule. Every morning for well over six months it was, "Are you gonna finish the bathroom today?" When I finally did finish, she wanted to know why the floor bounces and why all the water runs to one corner.

It doesn't matter what I say — she just doesn't understand the relationship between her dreams and her awakened state. You see, in her dream world, she and I organize everything exactly as she wishes, but in the wakey-wakey world the way that I organize my things looks messy to her. If I do everything like she wants me to, I'd lose my identity. If I do every little thing as she instructs me to, then I am just an extension of her psyche. I might as well be a robot!

This is nothing new because in the writings of Aristotle and that other guy, Hippopotamus, they describe the same problem that has plagued the male side of humanity since we had tails and sharp toenails, and we still sniffed each other's butts. It's getting harder to escape the sense that most of the trouble in the world — whether it's coming out of Washington D. C., the corporations, the banking industry, or the bedroom — the problems that men face can be traced to one overriding problem: Too many women trying to steer. Women think that if they drive, we might all be enjoying a safer ride. Doubt it?

Think about it! I can see that all of man's problems arise out of the dreams of women. "Why is that," you may ask? Simple: The dreams of women are deeply rooted in wish fulfillment! Like I said, "This is nothing new." There's an old Hungarian proverb that states, "A pig dreams of acorns and a goose dreams of maize." What this boils down to is: "I will clean the shed and mow the lawn when I get full of acorns!" Not when my wife wants me to.

Women need to learn one important thing about men: A man is a thinker, especially a man like me, since I'm a writer guy. When I'm sitting around staring into outer space, I'm not wasting my time, I'm thinking. I'm thinking about something to write about that is meaningful and will better mankind. Ya, my wife should try that sometime!

I'll give another example before I close. A month or so ago, my wife had to have a can of a certain color so she could touch up the walls. She had to have it right now. Right now! OK, I looked for an hour, found it and took it to her. I sat it down in the living room where it still sits to this very day. I stubbed my toe on it this morning, which instigated this scientific study of the dream state of women. I will die and go to Hell before I move that damn can of paint! I live in the real, wakey-wakey world! That can of paint does not exist in my wakey-wakey world!

I've said it before and I'll say it again: "The town of Winters, California has the best looking women west of the Mississippi." Take for example the fine looking specimens on the front page of this week's Winters Express. (July 11, 2013) Not only are they pleasing to the eye, they're pretty smart too.

Of course I'm speaking of Patty Rominger and Melanie Bajakian Pickerel, two of the leading ladies of our little community. I know for a fact that they are a testament to the indomitable spirit of women and their ability to rise above any obstacle that stands in their way. Fine women, yes indeed they are, but are they tough enough?

I have to ask this question because in just a few days the women of the "Freaky Family" are coming to town. This year the family will hold their annual reunion in our little community. I call them the Freaky Family because they are so perfect. Perfectly loving, caring, generous, and just about anything else you could think of. These people never fuss and fight, and they're so nice that it freaks me out sometimes.

When I married into the family, I found that I was the only normal person in the whole clan. It took me 10 years to find that they are the genuine article and there's nothing phony about any of them. I kept waiting for them to start feuding and gossiping like the rest of us but it just never happened. See what I mean — Freaky Family.

There is a quote by somebody, I don't remember who, that reminds me of all of these women. It goes like this: "Stop wearing your wishbone where your backbone ought to be." If I had to give you an example of the type of women these ladies are, it would be the little Vietnamese woman in the film, "Full Metal Jacket," the most realistic film about the war in Vietnam that I've ever seen.

Anyway, my point is that this little Vietnamese woman brought the American war machine to a halt with only an AK47 to bear. The young woman single-handedly brought the war back to the Americans and put the fear of God deep within the hearts of a whole platoon of tough Marines. That's the way it goes with real women. You mess with them and you can bet that eventually they will mess with you.

I tell you about all of this because I have had another brilliant idea that can make us all rich beyond our wildest imaginations. It's so simple, I don't know why I didn't think of it before. I'd be willing to say that we could make a considerable amount of money which would be split up evenly amongst us, after I deduct my expenses, of course.

Money, money, money, money!

I propose we have a boxing match between the women of Winters and the women of the Freaky Family. I think I can make up a bunch of lies to make them dislike each other enough to want to duke it out like pirates on the open seas. I would have to be the referee, looking all good in my little short shorts. Of course I'd have to wear a girdle so no one would see my big belly.

Ha Ha, that's a joke.

We could set up a ring right on the corner by the Buckhorn Restaurant with banners and streamers flowing in the wind. There would be cheerleaders and the high school marching band and oh my, it would be grand. I'll bet the governor and the whole House of Representatives would come to see an evening of great boxing and they would pay good American money at that.

Oh, and we could get the Pickerels to give out free steaks from the Buckhorn and the Rominger family could bring barrels of free Rominger wine. It's the good stuff too! Mmmm, tasty! There will probably be millions of people so let's say, oh, $5 each — wow that's a lot of money! Woohoo! That would probably be well over $100,000. Oh, we could charge for parking too! Maybe even put up a toll booth at the old bridge.

Man, my mind is working like a well-oiled steel trap! We have to get hot on setting this up because the women of the Freaky Family will be here in just a matter of days. I guess that Patty and Melanie had better get their crew together. I suggest that Debra DeAngelo, Libby Earthman, Rebecca Fridae, and Carol Scianna would put on an excellent boxing match in the big ring for Team Winters.

So there it is, the women of Team Winters vs. the women of the Freaky Family. It's all set up as far as I'm concerned. All that remains is for our City Manager, John Donlevy, to get hot and set up everything before it's too late. Oh, it's gonna be grand!

I can't wait!

I have nothing of value to tell you but this
8/2/2013

Sometimes I amaze myself. Just when I think I can't get any smarter — "BAM" — I get smarter! I never really know I'm getting smarter until I'm already smarter. Let me explain.

My brain began developing three weeks into my mother's pregnancy, forming 100 billion neurons or nerve cells. My brain reached a lifetime peak by the time I was a fetus, five months old. During those first eight weeks, my brain, like all brains, followed the same developmental path. Then something happened, let's call it testosterone, starts to marinate my boys' brain. This hormone bath started killing cells in brain regions that promote communication and emotion, and promoted cell growth in my sex and aggression thingy, somewhere in my head or maybe my penis, I don't know for sure. By the time I was born, I had male-type brain circuits.

The human brain uses roughly 12 watts of electricity (about as much as the bulb in your fridge), mostly to pass info between my little neuron thingys. It's a power hog because my brain consumes 17 percent of my body's total energy. This energy is useful when directed correctly.

My brain went astray.

My brain now tells me there is enough for everyone. We only have to realize and live by it. Most of my life I thought just the opposite. I thought there wasn't enough for me. I had the belief that I always had to fight for my part in a limited world. I had no clue, and I could not see the abundant nature of reality.

I dwelt in the past, and dreamed about the future, but I never concentrated on the present. I didn't know that peace comes from within and looked for it, always from without. There are only two mistakes one can make along the road to finding truth, and I forever made them both by not going all the way, and sometimes not starting at all.

I'm older now than I was. My body is getting weaker every day. In time, it will waste away and I will be gone. No one will see me so therefore, to most, I never existed. It's sad but it's true too. I will be gone except for these few lines that I write here today on this paper. Well, there's no paper, but that's not the point.

Like I said, I'm older now, so I guess I'm smarter too. At least, that's the way it's supposed to work. Anyway, being smarter now and writing at the same time, I guess I should say something smart because my brain is still working pretty good at this point. OK, here it comes:

At a certain point in my life I came to the realization that everything I've learned in my life that is of any value at all, I learned from a woman. Oh, there are things I learned from other men, but they were things like, survival, competition, greed, and how to get my own with the least amount of conflict.

Most men are raised in a home with parents and siblings, but I was not. It should be understandable that the knowledge of love and charity eluded me until later in life. In its stead, I learned to lie low, strike fast and hard, and then get back in line before the nuns saw me. Oh and I learned how to look innocent — at least I thought I did.

Life was not easy for a guy who cannot give or receive. You lack the ability to really see someone if you're observing them as a tactical movement, never seeing them as a person. Never seeing them other than an object of whatever plot you're on at the time. This frame of mind will keep you at a distance even with those closest to you.

OK, so at a certain point in my life, my woman tells me that she's pregnant. This set me a-back because I didn't know how to handle it or how she expected me to behave. It never dawned on me that someone would care enough about me to have my baby, so I thought she wanted a ride to the abortion clinic. That's the way I have always thought. My frame of mind was twisted like a pretzel.

Now, some years later, I look upon my son and I thank God that my wife is her mother's daughter. I am so thankful that she was never in an orphanage where she would have grown up like me, all alone. I thank God that she loves me.

You see, even with a big brain like mine and super intelligence, you have to experience something before you can see it for what it really is. My experience with love came midway through my life and for the life of me I don't know why I never saw it before, because it was always right around me. It just never grabbed my attention and said, "Here I am!"

OK, so I might be dead now but you're reading these words right now, as we speak. I have nothing of any value to tell you other than the fact that love does exist. It might be a little slow in finding you, but you can rush that along if you purposely seek it out and spread it around.

Just about everything that everyone will do in life is founded in love or the lack of it. Once you have it, you'll feel its power and you'll be in awe of its width and depth. Love never ends, and my big powerful brain is telling me right now that it should be that way.

Here is what I wish to give you, if you can get anything out of my life experience at all: I wish to give you LOVE.

Golden Rule doesn't work for everyone
8/18/2013

Holy Crap! What in the Hell is going on in the world today? Violence and death has, again, become common in the international community. Actually, when I think a little harder (using my extra-large brain) it has always been the norm. From the beginning of time, this has been true.

Looking at human history (at least the history that is written but possibly not accurate history), man's behavior toward each other has never changed. There has always been the strong and the weak. The strong stay strong by taking, by force, what the weak can provide. So solly, but that's the way it is, I tell you nine time!

For the time being, we here in the United States are a good portion of the takers in this world. We seem to enjoy taking what we want from the world. For example, most of us are willing give up what is most important to us in order to take what we want. Yes, we freely send our sons and daughters across the world to kill the sons and daughters of those who have what we want to take. Geez, you gotta know this is true; it always has been.

Well, I've been wondering why mankind is always fighting among themselves when, with a simple concept like "sharing" we could all live in peace and harmony. I spent some time thinking about this and this is what I came up with as a solution to global problems.

While thinking very hard about this, it dawned on me that there was something my mother told me many years ago that might apply here. Here in the US it's called "the Golden Rule." That is "Do unto others as you would have them do unto you" or something similar to that.

I thought "Yeah, if I can spread that idea around, it might solve all of our problems. This is it!" I thought I'd take a look at the research and find out if this might work. Everything looked real good at first, but then I ran into a few problems. This is what I found.

Every single country in the world has a quotation similar to our "Golden Rule." So, I thought, "This is good." I decided to dig a little deeper into this idea, so I read the next paragraph. I don't remember what that said, but this afternoon I had a chat with a fellow I play internet chess with who lives in South Africa to get an idea of what he thought about it.

Well, he says that this "Golden Rule" does not apply to his religion because he could, in no way, treat a woman as he wishes to be treated himself. The rule does not apply to women or men of some other tribes. "How can this be?" I asked. He replied that women and members of certain tribes are beneath him and he could not deal with them as equals. "OK," I said.

To make a long story short, there are many countries that feel the same way and they don't understand how we can say that we would treat others as we would want to be treated when we have never done so before. US policy abroad has been "Do unto others before they do unto you!" Much of the world feels that the US has no honor in peace or at war.

Much of the world feels that the US is the greatest aggressor of all times with their highly technical military might that is controlled by Wall Street. Much of the world does not separate their religion from their government as we do. Shockingly I found that in much of the world, hurting women is not against the law. In some countries a rebellion against the government is a rebellion against the religion. See for yourself, Google "Orhan Pamuk" of Turkey.

Some of the world considers the US as the "Great Evil" with its policies of torture and assassination. Some say that they would completely ignore the United States if we weren't always knocking down doors and wreaking havoc, which keeps their attention. I don't think much of the world would treat us as we wish to be treated.

Anyway, that's what I thought about today. Now as I look back on it, I think it was a waste of my time. I think some of their ideas may have some credence but I can also tell you that there is no way in hell that my wife is going to let me beat her if she doesn't do what I say. Maybe that's a good thing. I'm not sure.

Maybe I should stand my ground. Maybe I should go on strike until she buys me a dishwasher machine thingy. Oh, and a leaf blower so I can dust the living room in an easy manner too!

That's right! I'm the man!

There are two types of people. We have optimists and pessimists. One cannot do without the other without destroying the universe. I know this because I am one and my wife is another and we see things in completely different ways. She sees white and I see black. You know the potato/patatto thingy.

I'd like to say that one is better than the other, but I can't. A pessimist cannot survive without an optimist and visa versa. For example, say we are soldiers. An optimistic soldier will not see danger as well as a pessimistic soldier will for obvious reasons. On the other hand, a pessimistic soldier would kill everything in sight unless someone tells him there is no threat from children and small animals.

The world can be very heavy for pessimist. For them, the worst will happen every time and, if it doesn't, it's because they were cautious and alert to their surroundings. Trust does not come easy to them so they are watching others with distrust all the time. They think that if they let their guard down, even for a second, something will go wrong. They swear by this philosophy.

A pessimist lives in a world that will never change. Politicians are always crooked, corporations are always greedy and in control of the politicians. Since they control the politicians, they control the law of the land and those that enforce it. Unless a pessimist is angry or insane, you will not see him in the foreground. They prefer to stay in a subdued position where they can stir things up without being noticed.

A pessimist will have plenty of evidence when they present their case. There are always crooked politicians and they are always tied to corporations and crime. It is the way of the world. It is true that the American public has less than a 15% approval of congress as we speak. The sad part is that we will keep electing people that are obviously scum of the first order. Take for instance that Weiner guy – what the hell is up with that?

If it were up to the pessimists of this world, there would be constant revolution, death, and misery. There is no way you can make them happy unless you drug them up or entice them to have sex, but this will only last for a few moments. A pessimist will have trouble with blood going to certain parts of his body.

Eventually, the world will end and we all will die in horrible ways and there is no Heaven, only Hell. Now you can see the need for the optimist. Without the intervention of the optimist, all pessimists will kill themselves. The optimist will always overpower the pessimist in all things, large and small, their tools, love and hope. The pull of positive and negative, evil and good are very similar, but they do not apply in a human way. One is of the physical world and the other of the spiritual world.

Of course, anyone that knows my wife and I will know that I am a pessimist and my wife Therese is an optimist. For her, there is hope in all things, even in me. It has always been natural for me to look for the worst in everything and it has always been natural for her to see what is good and full of love and light.

Right now I am full of stress and everything in my future is bleak and dark. It's like I am drowning in my own feces. It seems to be the world that I enjoy because I bring it upon myself time after time and, once in, I can't get out. Right when I think that this is the end, a hand will break the surface of the feces pool, grab me by the hair, and drag me out into the light. Only then can I see what was in the pool in which I swim.

I'd like to say that my pessimism keeps my wife in the real world but this simply is not the case. I don't know about others, but I have learned through experience that if I just trust in people like Therese, my wife, the optimist, then things just might get better. I guess when you come down to it, the optimists are the only hope this world will have to survive what is coming to us in the future.

Think about it. Without the optimist we would have not have the freedom to walk down the street without fearing for our lives. I'll tell you true that there are politicians who are honest and corporations that work for the advancement of humanity, and law enforcement that serves and protects. I know this is true because my wife told me so, and when she tells me something, I believe her.

Well, I can only end this column by saying that while a pessimist lives in a dream world, so does the optimist. One without the other will die in a horrible way and rot in the ground forever and ever, but that's just my view

A God with two faces

9/11/2013

Today is 9/11. It's a date that is etched into my mind for several reasons. In 2001, there was the attack on the Twin Towers in New York City. I didn't know any of the people who lost their lives on that terrible day, but I will pause for a moment sometime today and say a prayer in remembrance. In 2006, on this same date, my father died. I didn't know him either, but I'll include him in the same prayer.

That being said, I will go back to trying to piece together the chain events that made healthy and sane men purposely fly a jetliner into a high-rise building. We have been told the men were mostly Egyptian Muslims. Why in the world would an Egyptian Muslim want to do such a horrible thing to us? Why would they say the words "God is great" moments before they slammed into the cold hard concrete that would cause so much devastation and sorrow?

It seems to me that their God must be cold and dark. My God is warm and full of light. Is it possible that there are two Gods? I don't think there is. I have to believe that there is only one God but maybe he (or she) has two faces, one cold and one warm. If this is so, then we must all share the same God, warm face and cold face, dark and light. This does not answer my original question of "Why did they do it."

I'm at a loss. With all of the information we've been given, you'd think there would be a clear reason for such a drastic action. Why would they want to hurt you and me? The only answer I can come up with is that they did not intend to hurt you and me. I came up with this by looking at their targets. Their target was not you and me. This is clear and easy for everyone who can think to see.

The target was the Pentagon and the Wall Street corporations. There are many who would say that an attack on the government and Wall Street is also an attack on you and me. Technically, this is so, but this isn't the point I'm trying to make. OK, let's assume I'm correct in the assumption that you and I were not the target and we'll go on from there.

First of all, let me say that I in no way condone what was done on that ugly day. There is absolutely nothing that could make me do such a dastardly deed. I think I can safely say this is true. This, however, still does not answer my original question: Why did they do it? There has to be some great hidden reason. Something evil, I fear.

In my examination of these Egyptian Muslims I am forced to examine myself. To see their actions clearly, I must look at my own actions. What actions in my life could possibly compare to their actions. After all is said and done, with a little soul searching, I came up with two instances in my life that could be compared (on a smaller scale) to their actions.

I don't need to go into the details but my actions, like theirs, involved untimely death and destruction. It matters not that one action is on a grander scale than the other, for both could be considered evil deeds by someone, anyone. Even in times of war, the killing of a person, no matter how many, will always have its consequences. My actions in war were no different. Killing has horrible consequences. It will consume you at the most inconvenient of times, often for all to see.

The only reasons that I can come up with as to why these men did what they did are military in nature. Their acts were the acts of a soldier, plain and simple.

The strikes upon the Pentagon and Wall Street were strikes against their enemy. I think they knew what a horrible thing they were going to do, so they called upon their God for forgiveness with their last breath. I know this is so for when my action in Vietnam was finished I asked for forgiveness and stuck a pistol in my mouth and pulled the trigger. The pistol was jammed with mud and it didn't go off.

I guess that actions like these, no matter how big, will make you want to die when they're done. Maybe it is God's darker face that lets men do these evil things and God's lighter face that lets men see what they have done when it's over — I don't know for sure. Evil deeds are not exclusive to our generations, so I assume there are more actions of this nature to come.

When I add it all up in my mind, there's only one thing I can wish for. I wish with all of my heart, with everything that I am as a being, spirit, or whatever, that there will never, ever be another attack such as this on American soil. I hope with all of my heart that there will be an end to this violence, but if it has to be, let it be somewhere else, not here.

Some questions just don't have answers; I accept that now, freely.

Just like that Rodney Dangerfield guy, I can't get any respect! I do not exaggerate when I tell you that it's been well over 50 years since I have gotten even the tiniest bit of respect. I mean no respect. It's like I was just a common man or something like that.

Even way back in high school, I would go east and respect would go west. You wouldn't suspect it now because to you, I'm a big important writer guy, but I almost didn't graduate from high school. It wasn't my fault either.

I was a model student in my high school. I was like the B.M.O.C. Sure I got sent to the dean's office a time or two, but that wasn't my fault either. I think the dean must have had something against me or he was jealous of my sheer good looks because he told me that if I get sent to his office one more time than he was going to kick me out of school. I thought, "Blaa-blaa-blaa."

Well, it wasn't a week later when Mrs. Weedikind (my English teacher) sent me to the dean's office for writing stupid stories when I was supposed to be writing a speech. Now that I'm a big time writer guy, everybody knows I don't write stupid stories. So, I didn't go to the dean's office and went to smoke in the bathroom instead.

How was I supposed to know the dean would walk into the room and catch me? You know that guy dragged me down the hall by my hair? That wasn't cool at all, but he didn't throw me out. I told you I wasn't just a common guy. The damn dean was just a bag of wind and I had him up against a wall. He told me so in his own words.

After he made me stand on one of the little squares out in the hall, he pulled me in and said, "Donald, I'm going to let you graduate. You see, I looked at your grade school file and the principal there made a note of your age. He says that if you had one more month you could have legally driven to grade school, so he pushed you out to me in high school. Now I have to do the same."

Ha, I thought, "I've got him outsmarted!" Then the dean says, "Don, you're going to be 21 years old in a week or two and we can't have a boy that old as a high school student. The school board is afraid you will want to date the freshman girls, and that's against the law." Well I say, "Gee Mr. Dean, I don't care because no one will ever know that I was 21 when I got out of high school." I chuckled to myself!

So, a couple of months later, I was in the army. About the third day there, some Colonel gave me a jeep with a radio bolted onto it and told me to drive it up onto a big helicopter. The helicopter dumped me off at a place called Pleku. The radio never worked but I didn't know how to use it anyway. Two years, one month, and seven days later, I left the jeep there and went home.

OK, time passes and I'm doing volunteer work down at the creek, doing something they call creek restoration. There's a bunch of piles of brush to be burned, so I start lighting them with a big tank of propane and a big long torch. Next thing I know, the whole dam creekside is on fire and there are helicopters dropping water on it. I know you won't believe it, but I swear to God that the pilot of that helicopter was the same guy that gave me the damn radio that didn't work way back when I was in Vietnam.

Now if you think that's a little farfetched, consider this. OK, yesterday my wife tells me she's going to Home Depot, and I was a little concerned when she didn't come home. Now today I see her picture on the Facebook and she is in New

Orleans with her sisters. She looks like she's having a lot of fun too! I must have forgotten she was going.

She's only been gone one day and the sink's already full of dirty dishes. I'm going to make the best of this situation by writing a column about the survival of a man while his wife is gallivanting around the world. Oh... I already did that last time she was traveling. Anyway, I have to go to the store to buy paper plates and plastic spoons. I'm completely out of Fruity Pebbles, so I'll have to try to find them too.

A respectful wife would have bought me some damn Fruity Pebbles before she left. So here I am, out of clean plates and spoons, no Fruity Pebbles, and to top it off, the creek restoration guys won't let me play with the torch any more. The people on Facebook made fun of me for lighting a forest fire. The comment about the fire that hurt the most came from Linda Dejarnett Springer, a writer lady for the newspaper, who said, "I knew it was you!"

See what I mean? No respect.

I like TV. I like it a lot. It is possible to learn everything you would ever need to survive by watching TV. Here are just a few things I learned about our government while watching late night TV, things I didn't know. If you are anything like me you will have to laugh to keep from crying.

• In the congressional probe of the Secret Service sex scandal, Congress wanted to know how it could happen, who was responsible, and do the ladies involved take Discover cards?

• When the Senate swore in a record 20 female senators, the women said they're very excited, and look forward to proving they can accomplish just as little as male senators.

• A study released recently stated the average member of Congress can only speak at a tenth grade level.

• The average tenth grader speaks at a third grade level.

• A new poll shows that disapproval of Congress is at an all-time high.

• Eighty-two percent of Americans disapprove of the job Congress is doing and the other 18 percent weren't home when the question was asked.

• Democrats and Republicans in Congress are still fighting over the budget. If they can't agree, there will be a big government shutdown. Many Americans feel what we really need is a big government shut-up.

• Washington, D.C. has a new program that would pay residents up to $12,000 to move closer to their workplace. Three thousand prostitutes used the program to move in right across from Congress.

• In the spring of 2011, Homeland Security warned of possible summer attacks by Al Qaeda.

• In the spring of 2011, President Bush had already ignored four such warnings.

• After 9/11, security was very high in New York City. A good example of this is that hookers now required two forms of fake IDs.

• In March of 2003, Donald Rumsfeld made this statement concerning weapons of mass destruction in Iraq: "We know where they are. They're in the area around Tikrit and Baghdad and east, west, south and north somewhat."

• Congress has approved another version of this fiscal cliff bill. Now taxes are going up, and they're looking to make cuts just about everywhere. In fact, oil companies today had to lay off 15 senators.

• A new public poll places Congress below head lice in popularity.

I could go on and on. It seems as if there will always be something fishy about the government. Something will always be just a little bit off, just off enough to be a little bit funny. At least now you know what I mean when I say I'm laughing just to keep from crying.

If this doesn't make you sick — nothing will!

Summary of the Executive Branch
Standards of Ethical Conduct

On February 3, 1993, the Standards of Ethical Conduct for Employees of the Executive Branch, issued by the Office of Government Ethics for codification at 5 C.F.R. Part 2635, replaced the many individual agency standard of conduct regulations with a uniform set of standards applicable to all employees of the executive branch.

Because they are intended to answer questions about the ethical conduct of more than a million individuals employed by more than 100 different federal agencies, the Standards of Ethical Conduct are detailed. They contain many examples and will readily answer most ethical questions employees will have. This summary is designed to give employees enough familiarity with the contents of the regulations to recognize ethical issues when they arise and to assist in looking up relevant provisions in the regulations.

Because the summary provides only a shorthand reference to lengthier provisions in the regulations, an employee must refer to the regulation itself in resolving ethical issues that actually arise or may seek the advice of an agency ethics official.

Synopsis of Subpart A – General Provisions

The Principles of Ethical Conduct. The following Principles of Ethical Conduct apply to all employees of the executive branch and many form the basis for specific standards set forth in the regulations.

• Public service is a public trust, requiring employees to place loyalty to the Constitution, the laws and ethical principles above private gain.

• Employees shall not hold financial interests that conflict with the conscientious performance of duty.

• Employees shall not engage in financial transactions using nonpublic Government information or allow the improper use of such information to further any private interest.

• An employee shall not, except pursuant to the exceptions in subpart B, solicit or accept any gift or other item of monetary value from any person or entity seeking official action from, doing business with, or conducting activities regulated by the employee's agency, or whose interests may be substantially affected by the performance or nonperformance of the employee's duties.

• Employees shall put forth honest effort in the performance of their duties.

• Employees shall make no unauthorized commitments or promises of any kind purporting to bind the Government.

• Employees shall not use public office for private gain.

• Employees shall act impartially and not give preferential treatment to any private organization or individual.

• Employees shall protect and conserve Federal property and shall not use it for other than authorized activities.

• Employees shall not engage in outside employment or activities, including seeking or negotiating for employment, where there is a conflict with official Government duties and responsibilities.

- Employees shall disclose waste, fraud, abuse, and corruption to appropriate authorities.
- Employees shall satisfy in good faith their obligations as citizens, including all just financial obligations, especially those such as Federal, state and local taxes that are imposed by law.
- Employees shall adhere to all laws and regulations that provide equal opportunity for all Americans regardless of race, color, religion, sex, national origin, age, or handicap.
- Employees shall endeavor to avoid any actions creating the appearance that they are violating the law or these Standards of Ethical Conduct

I'm a walking, talking bag of bee venom
10/9/2013

I don't know what the hell is up with those damn honeybees! It doesn't matter where I am or what I'm doing because those damn bees won't leave me alone anywhere. I've been stung so many times this summer that I am a walking, talking bag of bee venom.

Yesterday, I was in the midst of starting the motor on a big saw when I was swarmed by about a million bees. At first, one stung me on the right arm. I looked at it and thought, "Did I just get stung?" About the time I decided that yes, I had been stung, I was stung again on the same arm, then the other arm, and on the back of my neck.

The very next thing I noticed was the sound of a little girl screaming. (I think it was the same little girl I heard screaming the last time I was attacked by a swarm of bees.) I found that I was now running and mumbling some weird noises while waving my arms above my head. I stopped. I then started running again while waving my arms above my head and mumbling weird noises.

I wouldn't mention this, but it seems to be happening to me all of the time. I have been stung intermittently for the last few years while working on creek restoration projects with the Putah Creek Council. I guess it's true that if you work around wild animals and bees, you are going to get bitten or stung.

What I find unbelievable is the fact that of all of the people that do creek restoration, who probably number in the thousands every day, I am the only person that ever gets stung. What the Hell is up with that? Why me out of all of the other people? What strange reason can those damn bees have for picking me out of a whole group of people?

I mean, when I think of it, I am scared crapless! One lady, Mrs. Rebecca Fridae, of Winters, California, seems to have some strange power over the bees and they follow her around like they are protecting her. They fly all around her head like Indians around a wagon train. This put the fear of God in me, so now every time I see her, I run the other way. I'm sure that Mrs. Fridae thinks I'm a nutcase by now.

Anyway, I've decided that I need to know the reason why the wrath of the bees is pointed at me. I decided to bring my huge brain on line and put it to work on the problem. It took some warming up. The first problem I faced was how to get back to my truck that I ran away from and left idling next to the big saw, with bees swarming all around it.

I called everybody I know; those who didn't play like they weren't in and actually answered their phone wanted nothing to do with it because they probably knew that bees were involved. Finally, my friend Joe came to my rescue and brought a coat with a hood I could tighten around my head like an Eskimo. I looked sort of like Kenny on the cartoon "South Park." In the cartoon, Kenny always dies.

Anyway, I finally got to my truck and rolled the windows up. I released a sigh of relief. Now, have you ever seen the movie "Aliens?" In one scene, the lady astronaut knows there is an alien behind her and slowly turns her head, inside her helmet, to see the big bug. Scary huh? That is exactly what I did inside the hooded jacket, inside my truck with the windows rolled up. It was terrifying!

When I got home safely I decided to study up on bees. The very first thing I read explained the whole bee problem to me. It made so much sense. The headline read, "Out of 20,000 species of bees, only four make honey." OK, let me think. No wonder they are always so pissed off. That's one bee that makes honey out of every 30 million bees and then, to make matters worse, the humans steal every drop of it from them to put on their toast.

I thought, "Oh my God!" Those damn bees think I'm the boss of all the honey stealers! What the Hell am I gonna do now?

I'm going to study this bee thingy, so I'll get back to you on that

The sticky lowdown on bees
10/11/2013

In case you were wondering, here is what I found out about bees. Personally, I could do without them, but the problem with that train of thought is the fact that if there are no bees, there will be no humans.

• Bees belong to the third largest insect order which also includes wasps and ants.

• There are three types of bees in the hive – Queen, Worker and Drone.

• Workers live about 45 days in the summer, drones are driven out of the hive in the fall. Queens can live for up to 5 years.

• The queen may lay 1,500 or more eggs each day during her lifetime. This daily egg production may equal her own weight. She is constantly fed and groomed by attendant worker bees.

• Honey bees fly at 15 miles per hour.

• Honey bees' wings stroke 11,400 times per minute, thus making their distinctive buzz.

• Honeybees are the only insects that produce food used by humans.

• Honeybees usually travel approximately 3 miles from their hive. They can travel up to 6 miles searching for food.

• Honey bees produce beeswax from eight paired glands on the underside of their abdomen.

• Honey bees must consume about 8 pounds of honey to biochemically produce each pound of beeswax.

• Honeybees are the only bees that die after they sting.

• Honeybees are responsible for pollinating approximately 80% of all fruit, vegetable and seed crops in the U.S.

• Honeybees have five eyes, 3 small ones on top of the head and two big ones in front. They also have hair on their eyes.

• Honeybees can see two things we cannot. One is in the ultraviolet and another is plane polarized light.

• If a bee entered a movie theater, they would not see a continuous motion movie, but rather each individual frame.

• Bees communicate with each other by dancing and by using pheromones (scents).

• Bee brains are the size of a sesame seed, about 20,000 times less massive than the human brain.

• Bees can recognize individual human faces.

• Bees can count to four.

• To make one pound of honey, the bees in the colony must visit 2 million flowers, fly over 55,000 miles and will be the lifetime work of approximately 768 bees.

• A productive hive can make and store up to two pounds of honey a day.

• A typical beehive can make up to 400 pounds of honey per year.

• A single honey bee will visit 50-100 flowers on a single trip out of the hive.

• A single honeybee will only produce approximately 1/12 teaspoon of honey in her lifetime.

- Flowers and other blossoming plants have nectarines that produce sugary nectar. Worker bees suck up the nectar and water and store it in a special honey stomach. When the stomach is full the bee returns to the hive and puts the nectar in an empty honeycomb. Natural chemicals from the bee's head glands and the evaporation of the water from the nectar change the nectar into honey.
- Honey is 80% sugars and less than 18% water.
- Bees produce honey as food stores for the hive during the long months of winter when flowers aren't blooming and therefore little or no nectar is available to them.
- Honey is the ONLY food that includes all the substances necessary to sustain life, including water.
- It would take about 1 ounce of honey to fuel a honeybee's flight around the world.
- Honey never spoils.
- Honey has been used for millennia as a topical dressing for wounds since microbes cannot live in it. It also produces hydrogen peroxide. Honey has even been used to embalm bodies such as that of Alexander the Great.
- Fermented honey, known as mead, is the most ancient fermented beverage. The term "honey moon" originated with the Norse practice of consuming large quantities of mead during the first month of a marriage.
- Although Utah enjoys the title "The Beehive State," the top honey-producing states include California, Florida, and South Dakota.

I think that we all know the bees are having survival problems. This, in the greatest part, is due to their interactions with humanity. My next column will center on these interactions, good and bad. I'm starting to find these little buggers very interesting. Very interesting indeed.

A fool and his truth
10/13/2013

War is no longer an interruption of peace; in fact peace itself has become an uneasy interlude between wars. Peace has become a perilous balance of mutual terror and mutual fright. ~ C. Wright Mills

I have been passed over for the Nobel Peace Prize for Literature once again. I would have nominated myself for the prize but the cost exceeds my budget. Now that I think about it I've been passed over by every single award organization of my time. That's OK, I can take it.

I've never claimed to be the greatest writer of my generation and I know there is no artistic merit to my work. The words I use come from my gut instead of my head, from intuition rather than intellect. In the world of writers, I am a gust of wind in a large storm. That's all I will ever be.

This is my way of telling you that I am about to write about things I know nothing about. My intellect tells me that writing something like this is like swimming upstream in the cold-cold Putah Creek. Neither was is it my gut that tells me to go ahead. It is pure nerve endings that push me onward.

The difference between man and other animals is the ability to think, cry and laugh. Man has the ability to know how things are and to know how things should be. We know that all men are created equal, but some are more equal than others. We know that there are those that have and those that have not.

I have read that the upper classes are obsessed with sex, but they have very little of it themselves. It appears that they use too much sex in the manipulations of power and money. In their endeavors, they trade sex for power. They are restricted in their sexuality.

In following, the lower classes use their desire for power and push them back into sex. I cannot help but believe that when every man stands before God, they will have to explain why they abstained from the normal pleasures to which each and every one of us is entitled. So, I think it is true that everything equals out in the end.

When I think about the future, it's apparent to me that the generation of my father was worse than my father's fathers and my generation is worse than theirs. What is even worse is the fact that we are raising those who are so much more vicious that we are. To make my point clear, I can only quote writers who are more talented than I: Ansel Adams and Nancy Newhall.

We learn to live with horrors,
Evils as old as man, suddenly
Expanded into new until they hang
Worldwide, sky high, above our lives.
Death no longer rides a pale horse;
Death rides a ray, an atom.
War winged, rises on strange fires
To leap across oceans and continents,
Assail the moon, the sun, and the stars.

With this in mind, God created man on the last day in case man should let pride take hold of him. Thus the lowly gnat was created before man. We live in cities where no one has to know the people around us. The young will have desires that will never come to pass and the old will think about what never happened.

I have come to believe that maybe we might get lucky and some distant generation will be sterile. It is said that in every generation there is always some fool that will speak the truth as he sees it. I now live in fear that I may be that fool.

In my heart, your love has found the safest place
10/23/2013

We live in what once was a forest that belonged to someone else. The prior owners did not develop the land, so they did not deserve it. Once we had possession of the forest we found it uninhabitable because of all the trees and wild animals. We found it necessary to remove all but a few of the trees and to flatten the land we filled in the creeks and streams. We turned the forest into fields.

At some point in time, we put a church in the middle of the field. Not long after that, men that had money and power built a courthouse next to the church in the field to demonstrate the fact that their power was equal to, if not above the laws of God. The church and courthouse offered protection to the common people in return for the labor they could offer.

The common people raised houses around the church and courthouse to be near their work. The common people came from everywhere and nowhere just to live in the field where there was safety and nourishment for their bodies and souls. They came by the tens, and hundreds, and then thousands. Life was good in the fields.

The people brought in trees and plants of every sort to replace the trees they removed from the field. With that, they brought in animals of all sorts to replace the animals they removed from the forest. The new animals could easily be killed, slaughtered and eaten. Other animals were used for defense and attack.

Some of the people in the field found that when times grew hard, they could easily take what they needed from other fields by force. Some found life easier if they could force others to do their work. It was easier to bear weapons than it was to use tools. They built factories to make bigger and better arms to force their will upon the weak while telling them the meek shall inherit the Earth.

To enforce the will of the powerful, great armies were drawn up out of the depths of Hell. The armies sucked up the best of the youth of the common people. The armies of one field would attack the armies of other fields, destroying all that resisted through cruelty and fear. For most, life was good for many years. Life was so good they did not notice that the powerful grew stronger and stronger. Some of the common people grew restless but were quickly and quietly forced into submission by the agents of the courthouse.

It was easier for the common man to submit and cooperate than it was to resist. They convinced their hearts that the field was the safest place. Inside the fields there were trees and lakes that they could climb and wade into. Around it all they built walls that no one could break. It was the safest place and in there they could shine or they could cry.

Upon the walls were the warriors. The warriors consisted of the youth taken from the homes of the common people, sometimes by force. The warriors were full of honor and pride, happiness was upon them, so they kept their field as the safest place. Inside the walls you could shine or you could cry, and the warriors are still on the wall, to this very day.

The fields are much the same today as they were yesterday. Only technology is different. The machines of the fields are bigger, faster, and forever hungry. To feed the machines the warriors fought many battles to find fuel that the machines could eat. The warriors fought battle after battle for greed instead of safety. The fields became states and then countries. They rose and they fell but the warrior always fought the battles willingly until the battles lost their honor. They found that when the battle loses its honor, so does the warrior.

A warrior knows the field is a happy place and he wants to keep it that way forever. In his heart, a warrior knows that deeds without honor make a warrior without honor. A warrior has been to war and he sees the most unholy things that he knows he should stop but he doesn't. Warriors on the walls around the fields with the churches and courthouses that are filled with the common man have begun to see themselves in a different light, a darker light.

The warriors of this field, that is the safest place for you and I, will pay the price for the deeds they do. Today in the field we live in that we call the United States, a warrior will take his own life at a rate of 22 a day. At almost every hour of the day, a warrior will take his own life. Today, the average age of a warrior that takes his own life is 59.

When the battle is over and the warriors go home, many go home to kill themselves so their families will not know the burden of their care. It seems the warriors on the walls find death preferable to life, and I find that very sad and there is nothing I can do about it except write these stupid stories.

Suicide has increased dramatically in the military since the start of the global war on terrorism.

I think my "inner being" is dying. It no longer communicates with me. When this first occurred, I found it meant big trouble for my physical, outer being. It seems the two are connected; interlaced like a vine through a tree. For simplification, I will hereon refer to them as my "innie" and "outie."

Our "innie" is our only link to the great cosmos, if you will, or the great lake of super intelligence from whence you may sip tidbits of information that quenches the thirst of your very soul. Our "innie" is not of this Earth. It is a gift from God to give us direction; the right from wrong thingy.

Some 40 years ago I experienced a traumatic event that my "innie" could not handle. I began getting "error" messages from my "innie" forcing my "outie" to fend for itself in a war zone. I had been in Vietnam for over a year and a half when my "outie" decided that we didn't need my "innie," because therein lies internal pain and sorrow.

"We can survive on our own," it said. "We don't need that stuff."

As it turned out, if you don't listen to and use your "innie," it slows down, gets sick, and eventually dies. So here's the whole ball of wax. The truth is, if your "innie" is sick or dying, you can bet it's just a matter of time before your "outie" follows suit. Your "outie" belongs to the physical world, so when it becomes sick, others will notice your lack of direction and focus. What is right and what is wrong is no longer clear, so a slow but ever-growing distance begins to separate you from everything that you need to lead a happy and productive life.

Since that terrible day in 1971, my "outie" has been searching everywhere for information about how I may nourish and sooth my troubled soul. Unfortunately, the "outie" is restricted to the physical world. Here, nothing is to be found but logic and science; both of which have caused immeasurable horror, suffering and sadness to the universe. War, famine, disease and all other unimaginable evil things that occur in our physical world are a direct result of science and logic.

Like so many other men of yesterday and today who find themselves in a war zone, unable to find nourishment for their soul in the physical world, I turned inward but there I found the "error" message. It seems that your "innie" has trouble interpreting warfare. Nothing of value can be found anywhere in any war; absolutely nothing.

Your "innie" will scream as loudly as it possibly can, "Wait, stop, don't do that, please, please!" Of course your "outie" cannot comply, or you become a statistic of war. Thus, the conflict between inside and outside begins and as many have found, the conflict between the two is continuous and will never end. "Error, error, error" is all that you will receive from your "innie" for all of eternity.

I have seen hundreds of doctors and taken thousands of pills. I have talked with 50 or so psychiatrists and I have come to the conclusion that none of this can help my "innie." I have accepted this as a simple fact of truth. The thing I cannot accept is the fact that we are still sending our children to worthless, no-account, bastard wars where they too will lose their "innie." We will pack away our sons and daughters, without question, without reason, and send them to slaughter or be slaughtered. The very moment that we agree to send them to a needless war, we become our own worst enemy. We do not need someone to kill our children — we are doing it ourselves.

Taking the life of another human being and watching the life blood flow from his body will, in a single moment, tears your soul apart. It cannot be fixed by doctors or pills and it will never go away. You cannot go back and do things in a different way. There is no second chance.

It is horrible, the act of killing — it sends an evil ripple backwards through time and space to your earliest ancestor and forward to your unborn descendants. The ripple affects everything the killer and his victim has ever been conscious of; it takes everything away forever and gives you nothing in return.

There are two things that I would hope to be true. First, I would like our president to be a man of peace. The second thing is a requirement of the first. A man of peace must have a healthy "innie."

You might as well vote for me
11/12/2013

I've been thinking of running for Congress or maybe even the US Senate. Go ahead and laugh, I'll wait a minute until you're done.

OK, let's get serious.

I'm thinking of running for political office. I think I could beat a lot of those guys that are supposed to be public servants. You know — the jerks on Capitol Hill who think they're in office to get incredibly rich at our expense.

Ever wonder why those guys will spend millions of dollars on a campaign for jobs that pay less than half a million a year? How do you suppose that they can increase their net worth by tens of millions of dollars during a two-year term that pays a measly $200-400,000 a year? Yeah, I want to get me some!

I know I could beat that Weiner guy. Geeze, nobody will vote for that jerk. There are a lot of congressmen on the verge of going to jail, so nobody's going to vote for them either. Charlie Rangle is a great example. In Washington, he's known as "Tax Cheat Charley." As chairman of the House Ways and Means Committee, he writes the tax law for the little people like you and me. Well, it's a fact that he tried to conceal about half of his income from the IRS and from congressional disclosure rules, so these laws don't apply to him.

John Murtha, a 19-term member of the house, has been under investigation for numerous schemes involving accepting donations to his campaign and political action committees in direct exchange for earmarking federal funds for those same organizations. Oh, that's just dirty!

Maxine Waters, the congresswoman from California, violated conflict-of-interest rules by non-disclosure of her ties to the banking industry. As it turns out, she was sweeping money right out of the banks into her purse. She smiled the whole time she was taking our money. If elected, I promise not to smile!

See what I mean? I can beat these jerks, I know I can.

How about those guys who were getting kickbacks from the banking industry in the form of low-interest loans that they never intended to pay back — I know I could take kickbacks just as well as they can. I know I could, because these guys don't fear the law because they make the laws. What a racket! I think it's really sad that we keep electing these jerks to office.

Congress has absolutely no morals! I'd fit right in there perfectly. All I need from you is to keep an eye out for my name on the ballot and then vote for me 30 times each. Christ, nobody cares anyway. You know this has to be true or they wouldn't keep sending the same jerks to Congress, right? I can do the cloak room politics as well as the best of them!

Don't feel bad about this because we are taught by history that greed and corruption has flourished in every age. We all know that the history books never depict the actual history, so we think that the lawmakers of the past were just shy of perfect in respect to public service. That's a lot of hooey! If we are going to decline, well I can help if the price is right.

I'm thinking that maybe, just maybe, discipline will be restored through the military challenges or war. As of late, we have a lot of those under our belts. The freedom of the part varies with the security of the whole. We will see individualism diminish as our geographical protection ceases. You know as well as I do that the present system is broken and we are not capable of fixing it.

Our children may live to see order and modesty return. Much of our moral freedom is good enough to see that change is needed and it will come to us one way or another. Won't it be nice to enjoy without qualm the pleasures that harm neither others nor ourselves and to feel the tang of the open air upon our liberated flesh?

You must understand that I am saying we can fix this, for the real power lies with the people — it always has. The next time you vote, think about it. If you're going to elect a jerk, then you might as well vote for me.

Nauseatism
11/28/2013

Can you imagine having a friend you cannot trust? How about a friend who cannot be believed, no matter what he says? How would you like a friend who is brutal and violent, who will come to your home and destroy everything and kill you and your family, and then your pets. To make matters worse, how would you like to live on an island with this unruly friend?

How would you enjoy a friend who watches you to the extent that you can't do anything without him seeing what you do and when, and with whom? How about a friend you are afraid of? I mean a fear like you have never felt before because this friend is vicious and has no control over anything he does. This friend is crazy and has multiple personalities, all out of control. Would you enjoy a friend like this?

What would you do? Would you seek other friends and try to get away from this bad friend? Just for general purpose, let's call this crazy friend Ted. Okay, let's figure this out with our other friends John, Jim and Sally. Now, the four of you are in a room and you have locked Ted out. What would you say to John, Jim and Sally?

Would you tell them that you are afraid of Ted? Would you tell them that you do not trust Ted? Do you think John, Jim, and Sally would say the same? Maybe they would and maybe they wouldn't. Maybe they are afraid of Ted as well. Maybe Ted has told them that you cannot be trusted. Maybe Ted has told them that you are a liar. Maybe Ted has told them that you are planning to take over the whole island!

What would you do? What could you do? Would you begin to stockpile weapons and food? Would you send trusted people out to spy on what Ted is doing? Would you try to communicate your fears to John, Jim, and Sally? Would you call them on the phone or send them a note? Maybe you might try to tell them personally, face to face. Do you think they would listen?

Now, what if Ted killed Jim and made all of his family stay within the confines of his little part of the island. What if Ted told Jim's widow that she could not trade freely her goods and wares with John and Sally for food? What if she could only trade with Ted and his agents? What if Ted was taking Jim's widow's goods and wares and paying pennies on the dollar for them? What if Jim's widow and her children were starving? What if they had no clean drinking water? What if they began having diseases that were supposed to be long forgotten, like polio and leprosy? What if? What if? What if?

What would you do if you had a friend like Ted? What would you do?

Well, I have some bad news for you. You are Ted. Even worse, I am Ted! We do live on an island – Earth. All of our friends do not trust us! All of our friends are afraid of us and what we will do next. We are attacking and killing our friends one at a time in a vicious and brutal manner. We are killing them, their families and even their pets.

Our friends are trying to communicate with their friends to come up with some way to deal with us, you and me. They know that when they meet and talk about us, we will think they are plotting against us. We will spy on them and tap their phones and place hidden cameras in the air and we will see everything they do. They will know that they cannot take a crap without us seeing how and when they do it.

Our friends will eventually get together and confront us and kill us if they have to. If we force them to drastic actions, they will gang up on us. I fear they will do it soon. I fear they will attack us soon and they will try to kill us. Wait…are you with them against me? Are you a traitor giving them information that will hurt me? Are you?

What would you do if I told you I will destroy the whole island rather than live with you in peace?

WHAT WOULD YOU DO?

Technology I love
12/1/2013

I love all the new technology. When I think about how quickly everything around me has changed just in my short lifespan, I'm amazed.

Just think, a million or so years ago, man invented the cooking fire and then very quickly came the spear, the arrowhead, the wheel, the plow, gunpowder, motors, air travel and on to space travel. Just in the last 50 years or so, technological advances have come at a blinding rate, giving us the Higgs Boson and sight to the edge of time and space.

My grandson, Anthony, lives in a world of controller free gaming, 3-D cameras, foldable speakers and touch screen computers. To him, a CD player is "oldtimey." Even his 3-year-old little sister can work her way around my iPhone like a pro. I love that they are so very, very smart.

I think my iPhone is probably my favorite piece of technology I've ever had. I can sit on the toilet and play games, surf the net, read my emails or call my wife and tell her we're out of toilet paper. However I must admit that my very, very, favoritesticle invention is the camera in my iPhone. I use it every day, everywhere I go. Love it! Love it! Love it!

If I had one wish that would come true, it would be that the phone camera (digital) could have been invented 50 years ago so I could have taken on-the-spot pictures every day of my life. When I think back about things and people that I would like to have captured and saved, it saddens me to no end.

If I had a phone camera when I was 8 years old, I would have taken a picture of the cop that arrested me for the first time. He found me eating out of a doughnut shop garbage can and took me to the station to find out who I was. He was pretty smart because he withheld drinking water until I would tell him who I was and why I ran away. I would like to have a picture of his face when I told him I was afraid of the nun at the orphanage because she threatened to cut my weiner off. I begged him not to take me back but he dropped me off anyway.

If I had had a phone camera when I was 9 years old, I would have taken a picture of my friend Butch King before he got buried in the sand pile we were digging caves into. He was only six inches under, and his brother and I couldn't find him in time save his life. He was the first dead body I ever laid my hands on.

There are many friends, some from long ago and some from recent days, that I would love to have photos of. There is Chuck Straw, Barry Donnigan, and a few others that flew off and never returned in Vietnam, and Penny Paluska (my first love), Judy Hienigger (who I used to dance to Beatles music with), and Jan Fredrickson who gave me a place to sleep when I returned home from Vietnam so very, very screwed up and homeless. I would love to have some pictures of them.

Oh, and I would have taken a picture of my first wife burning all of my clothes and what pictures I did have of Vietnam buddies. She started a bonfire in the truck of my 1971 Monte Carlo that was bright yellow — everybody called it the yellow submarine. Oh yeah, I would like a picture of my best friend Patrick when he found out I was sleeping with his wife (who became my first wife) because I want to remind myself what I did to him and how I broke his heart and mine at the same time.

There are a lot of people I'd like to have captured at a certain moment in time, like Officer Gutierrez (now our Chief of Police) when he arrested me for possession of a controlled substance. He caught me with a piece of meth about the size of a pea and was surprised at how stupid I was when I didn't just toss it away in the grass. The look on his face told me the whole story of how that drug had its fingers around me and had become all important, so I couldn't throw it down. Well, he got the right guy and my sentence was two years and eight months. Incarceration was just like the orphanage except the kids were bigger and meaner. It was the attitude adjustment I truly needed, plus I got to fight wildfires all over the state while at fire camp.

Now I take pictures and videos every day, and I love it so very much. I can take all of my friends and loved ones with me everywhere I go, right there in my phone. If I get stuck in traffic, I can play games or make a phone call right from my car until the traffic clears. I plan to continue doing what I'm doing until I die but the only difference is, I will be taking pictures along the way.

Weight of the world
12/3/2013

Sometimes I can feel the weight of the world. It is so very, very heavy. I know I am not the only person to feel this weight, nor will I be the last. Along with the weight come the terrors of hopelessness and dread of what is approaching us all at an ever increasing rate of speed.

We all want to raise our children in a healthy, safe, and nurturing way. We want to give them at least a fighting chance to survive, yet we tolerate policies that are exactly the opposite of what we wish to do with society.

Our young men and women of this society, and others like it, have been sent into battle, often under illusions of national glory and a false sense of patriotism. Many of these young men and women do not return home; others return with wounds that leave them and their families ruined and scarred for life. Generations are needed to repair the family structures they so desperately need.

Almost from birth, our young are inundated with violence. In the US, our media is greatly responsible for this. When looked at with open eyes, it is obvious the greatest social cause of violence – poverty and racism forced upon our children in this day and age. I fear to think about what our youth will face 10 or 15 years down the road.

The USA Patriot Act was rushed through Congress with little critical thought about the extent to which it dangerously added to government's intrusive powers. With it, our government has run amuck to the point that no other nation on Earth will believe anything we say or will ever want to say. I don't know how to repair that and I see violent protest on the horizon that none can escape, for it will encircle the globe.

To use the words of George Orwell, "Political control has become personal freedom; government intrusiveness becomes security in one's person and property; violations of the writ of habeas corpus is now protection of civil liberty; and trampling on constitutional restraints is preserving the American way of life." On this Earth there is no gender equality, no racial equality, no equality of education, and no social search for global justice and peace. The Earth is a global sweatshop for violence and child labor is its fuel.

Now killer robots enforce the ways of the world. The poor sometimes pay 5 to 10 times more for water than do the rich and powerful. Food production in some regions has fallen behind population growth and you know what that will mean. Food production is growing at only half the rate of the population, leaving an estimated one-third of the world undernourished. It is only a matter time before it spills upon your lap.

There cannot literally, actually, be a place called Hell, any more than you can be a place called Love or Disgrace or Despair. In my eyes, Hell means not perpetual punishment, but absolute extinction. Mankind has been unable to destroy the Earth. Mankind has the knowledge now to destroy it with less skill than it takes for one person to commit suicide, so why are we still here?

The decisions we make or don't take will widen or narrow our options for a century to come. They could decide the fate of the Earth as a home for humanity. Without family support, parent education, and specific violence prevention programs, we will soon be doomed. The last time I looked, our decisions were being made for us without our input. I'm not happy with that. Are you?

There are those among us who give me reason for hope, for they lift some of the weight from my shoulders. There is Rich Marovich, a Stream Keeper of nature and peace. He is capable of replacing concrete with nature and doing it right through sheer mental fortitude. Libby Earthman, a woman of the Earth, who can entice others to help her restore all of nature to a point where she can be assured of its health. Jan Burton, a mother. She has shown me the strength behind good parenting and her never-give-up-on-love attitude. She has brought me home to where I should be.

Then there is my wife Therese. I don't know what to say about her, for words will not do her justice. She is the embodiment of love as I know it. Joe Tomlinson, my good friend struggling with cancer has taught me how a man should carry himself in times of difficulty and he showed me that I must be honest and up front with myself before I can be honest and up front with others. John Pickerel, a local businessman with a global heart and a "Citizen of the Year" attitude is teaching me about social duties and how to carry them out like a man.

Together with others that I don't have words left to mention, they are teaching me to fight my wars for all the right reasons. I'm beginning to feel like Alvin York of Tennessee, another man of a different age who knew the weight of the world. Together they have shown me ways to win the small battles while chipping away at the large. My friend Debra has so graciously given me the tools to voice my opinion on everything. She is the difference between having a mentor and not having one.

Well, things feel lighter already!

Passed over again — it must be my face
12/12/2013

I'm thinking about suing the City of Winters, the Winters Chamber of Commerce, and Mayor Cecilia Aguiar-Curry. I'm talking about millions and millions of dollars, and this ain't no joke either.

I know it's hard to believe, but I have been passed over and over again for the Citizen of the Year award. I've been passed over about 35 times in the 25 years I've lived in this town. Well, they're going to pay for it now!

I would have thought about suing these guys a long time ago, but I'm what you might call a "layman" when it comes to the law and its doings. Thank God I have two good friends that work for the government. They call themselves "G-men." I think that's because they work for the government.

Like I said before, I didn't know anything at all about suing anybody until I ran into my G-men friends Terry Vender and Tony Luna, who work for the City of Winters Public Works Department. I think that department is part of the City of Winters because it says so on their shirts and trucks.

They were laughing about something when I bumped into them and when they saw me, they got real quiet.

"Hey Don, we hear you got passed over again for the Citizen of the Year," they said.

Then they laughed at something else.

"Yeah, can you believe it?" I said.

That's when they told me that I ought to sue them because it just isn't right being passed over that many times in a row. Well, I don't have to tell you how that got me to thinking about the big bucks, Ka-ching, Ka-ching.

"Geeze, do you guys really think I could sue them?"

Both of the G-men nodded their heads.

Well we talked for a while, the three of us with our heads together until they were almost touching. Finally I say, "I'd like to discuss this later but I don't want to take up too much of your time." So they say, "Aw, that's OK Don, we're on the clock." I don't know what they do on their job, but I think they go around digging holes and then fixing the pipes they break while digging. Then they throw the dirt back in the hole. I asked them about it but they said it's all hush hush on government jobs.

"All hush-hush huh?" I say.

They brought their heads back in and told me about the secret bunker that they've been working on for when the big catastrophe happens and our society as we know it collapses in upon us. They said that there's enough food and water for the city officials and all of the Citizens of the Year award winners to live on for 30 years or so. They didn't want to talk too much about that though.

Anyway, Terry Vender tells me that I might even have grounds for a federal criminal suit because there might me something called "malice" involved. Tony said that if I could prove I was passed over because of my race, it would probably triple the amount of money I could get.

"You mean because I am white?"

That's when I thought he said that the whole Chamber of Commerce is made up of Mexican Americans and that they would never give me the award unless I owned a restaurant or a newspaper.

Maybe he didn't say that, but I just don't remember.

That kind of scared me, because I have been hearing more and more Mexican Americans speaking some sort of coded language that only a very few white people know how to talk. Terry says that maybe they are plotting against us and it is a whole lot bigger than Citizen of the Year awards. Tony indicated that maybe the Chamber of Commerce wasn't happy with the kind of food that was going into the bunker.

Well, that goes to reason since this year's award went to John Pickerel and he owns a whole lot of restaurants.

"Now that's discrimination," they both at the same time.

What that means, I think, is that I've been passed over for the award because I don't have a restaurant. Tony finished off by saying, "You have to have a pretty face to win the Citizen of the Year award, and to tell the truth Don, your face just doesn't make the cut!"

"Yeah, that's probably right," I thought.

Then after that I thought, "Well, there's always next year, right?"

A while back, my wife gave me a subscription to Ancestry.com. This she did simply to shut me up because I was always complaining about how big her family was and how little mine was. She has like a million people reaching way back to the beginning of time. My family has six people and I only know three of them.

Anyway, this ancestry stuff is pretty complicated. For the first three months of my one year subscription, all I did was try to figure out how to start. I worked and I worked hour after hour for what seemed an eternity and there was nothing on my page. I figured that I'd best go back and read the instructions.

Well, as it turns out, you have to start at the other end of the line because you can't start at the far end because you don't know who he was until you get there. That's the way I read it anyway. What this means to you laymen and laywomen is that you have to start with yourself and go backwards until you get all the way to the first guy and this first guy lived about a million years ago.

So, I put my name on the first line, followed by my date of birth and then place of birth. Next there were several lines where you can list your father and mother and then their fathers and mothers and so on and so forth. It took me a week to find my birth certificate so I could get the information about my parents. It was kind of disappointing.

My mother was named Helen and she was born on a farm somewhere in Arkansas. There was no occupation listed for her. My father's name was Edwin. He was born in Tennessee with a listed job of "gas station attendant." I thought, "What? Gas station attendant, what the hell is that?" I changed that to "Oilman." That was that. I had covered a whole generation in just two weeks.

The next generation I worked on was my grandparents. Their names were Eddie A. and Audrey. That was as far as I got on my father's side of the family. It was a dead end right then and there. I looked and looked but I could go no farther. Finally I figured maybe I should look at my grandmother's maiden family. That was a streak of genius, because I found about a million people that stretch all the way back to Jamestown in 1610.

I found a document that stated that Pettyplace Clouse landed at Jamestown on the English ship "Starr" in the year 1610. I thought, "Holy crap!" This guy is important! He was one of the first white people to come to this country. Well, that was that too, for it was as far as I could go with that family line. I was happy though, because my old great-great-great-great-great-great-granddaddy was an important guy, a founding father.

I thought, "Wow, I gotta get to know about this guy some more!" Well, I know you won't believe it but there was a whole lot of information about this guy in the history books. It took me some time to find it, but when I did, it was well worth the trouble. Well as you might guess, being a member of the mighty Sanders family must have made him a very important fellow in his day and age. Yes indeed.

I started reading. I read and I read and the farther I got the worse it got. Here's what I found:

Pettyplace arrived, like I said, in 1610 to the little settlement of Jamestown Virginia. He wasn't the first guy to come to the settlement but he did have a long list of first in his records. OK, let's go.

Pettyplace was the first guy to be punished for public drunkenness in Jamestown. I guess he sort of stood out because all the rest of the people were like Quakers. The people of Jamestown built the first "stocks" so my ancestor could put his head and hands through it in the public square. There he was accused of stealing the rum from the English Ship Star which could not be proved because Pettyplace claimed he bought some Everclear alcohol from the Settlement store.

A week after that, Pettyplace became the first rapist in the country. He had impregnated the sister of a Cherokee princess (Sac-a-j-go-away-a), which explains more of my ancestors. As it turned out, raping an Indian was no crime at that time. The records say that Pettyplace began stealing food and other hock-able items from everybody in the fort. After that, none of the Quakers would give him any food.

Next Pettyplace became the first recorded cannibal in the Americas. The thing that gave him away was the odor of stew cooking on his stove because the rest of the people didn't have any food at all. It was odd but Pettyplace was gaining weight day after day while everybody else was skin and bones. From that day forward Pettyplace became the first white man to be tried for murder, the first man convicted of murder and the first guy executed on American soil for cannibalism.

At least, now I can explain my unnatural craving of meat and the disdain I have of vegetables. I didn't know what to do, so I put "Chef" on his occupation line. Like I said before, after that things got worse and worse. Throughout my ancestry cannibalism pops its ugly head out here and there at about every other generation. Just like clockwork, you could predict which generation would be cannibals.

As it turns out, those of my generation are not cannibals. Thank God! You can imagine, though, that I've been keeping a close watch on my son Joey. Sometimes when I fall asleep on the couch, I keep a stick close by, just in case. After all, he is my son and I love him dearly but that doesn't mean he won't eat me. I'm scared as hell, because he won't eat one leg at a time, he will eat my arms too. I have seen him eat two pizzas all by himself.

I have a plan though. I will keep him full of beans and bologna. That way he might not get hungry for my wife and me. He always says he likes beans because it's the "musical fruit." That boy does like to fart, for it makes him so proud. The only bad thing about it is that his girlfriends don't hang around very long, especially after I tell them I think Joey is a cannibal.

That was the jest of my Ancestry dot com experience. I could not believe we paid good money for it.

I'm so disappointed!
12/21/2013

As the end of 2013 approaches, we should take a moment to consider exactly what we, as a nation, have accomplished. Think about it for a minute and see if anything comes to mind. Surely you can think of something, after all, the cost of our government in 2013 will exceed $7 trillion. At that price, there has to be at least one accomplishment we can brag about.

No? Well, that's very disappointing.

What does the government do with all that money? I mean, for upwards of $7 trillion, it had to do something other than just maintaining everything we already had going. After all, in the year 2000, the government only spent $3.2 trillion to maintain the same programs. Geeze, when is enough going to be enough?

Let's think about how things were in the year 2000. When you get right down to it, things weren't really that bad. I mean, things weren't that good, but they weren't that bad either. Things really didn't take a big dump until the following year, 2001. After that, things got crazy and they've been crazy ever since.

Think back to the day Barack Obama took office. I don't know about you, but I was elated. I thought he was surely different, better. I thought he was going to do great things. I really had high hopes for his performance as president. I know millions of others did too. "Great things," we all thought!

Well, I've come to the notion that Barack Obama is no better than George Bush. Any hopes I had for Obama's presidency went right down the drain, flushed away with the rest of the shit. What's so bad about it was that I had a great love for this guy. I thought he was way up there with God! I thought he could do no wrong.

Barak Obama is nothing but another stinking politician. He talks a good line, but he's full of crap, right up to his floppy ears. I mean, this guy had everything going for him. He had to have more power than any other president in history. The people of this country absolutely worshiped this guy, and he pissed it all away. He accomplished not a single thing, zilch!

Obama still has troops in Iraq and Afghanistan. He has yet to close the controversial United States military prison at Guantanamo Bay Naval Base. Our prisoners of war are still being tortured. There is no justice to be found anywhere. There is no racial equality. There is no gender equality. There is no privacy. The rich are getting richer and the poor are getting poorer. It's the same old story that we heard in the '60s.

I don't know what's going to happen to this country, but I fear it will not be good. There's one thing I do know, and I'll share it with you right now. When the shit hits the fan, you better duck and you better be ready for it. It would be a good thing if you started stockpiling supplies, food and water. It's that simple. Either get ready for it or don't. It is entirely up to you — but I wouldn't count of the government for help because even $500 trillion dollars won't stop what's coming our way.

I am so disappointed!

Donald Sanders Memorial

1/2/ 2014

Lately I've been thinking about my own mortality. I hate the thought that I will pass away to the great nothing and no one will remember me, so I've come up with an ingenious plan. Sometimes I'm so clever I amaze myself. I've decided that we need to erect the Donald Sanders Memorial Statue right at the corner of Main Street and Railroad Avenue in lovely downtown Winters, California.

All we have to do now is figure out where the memorial will stand and decide what the actual character of the statue itself will be. I have a few ideas, so I'll just toss them into the hat and see how the wind blows the ball into the pocket. I've done some pretty heavy thinking about this for a couple of hours now so here's what I came up with.

I think the best spot for the memorial is right smack in the middle of the intersection of Main and Railroad. Of course that would mean changing the traffic into a roundabout circle thingy but that's OK, we can do that easily if we take out those penis pole thingys. Roundabouts, in general, are pretty easy to negotiate if you are an American, but those Englishmen and Frenchmen always seem to have a problem with them because they always get to going the wrong direction.

This would be an easy problem to solve if we just put a sign on the bridge that says, "No Englishmen or Frenchmen are allowed to drive in the city of Winters." Now this might make them a little bit angry, but I don't think they are dumb enough to say anything about it or we won't come and help them the next time the Germans come-a-knocking on their door. Anyway, with the NSA listening to what everybody is saying, those foreigners won't feel safe taking any action against us because they might end up in some prison in Cuba with the rest of those Buddhas, if you know what I mean.

The second proposed spot for the memorial is on the far northeastern corner of the same intersection. It's a really good spot, but there's a big Palm tree there that some old lady planted about 500 years ago. That's OK though, we'll just have to take that tree out. That darn tree has been there long enough anyway. If you think about it, you'll see that if we put the memorial on the corner where the tree was, then it would free the intersection up for one of those Arch de Triumph thingys like they have in France, only we would have to put a sign on it saying, "Gateway to the Don Sanders Memorial Statue." I like that idea too.

Problem number two is the character of the statue. (That means what it will look like to you laymen.) Well, it just so happens I have some ideas on that too. At first, I thought something like the Vietnam Memorial that stands in Washington D. C. would be nice but with one big name "Don Sanders" instead of a bunch of other names. However, I decided against that in favor of a statue of a rearing wild stallion with a depiction of me in the saddle waving my hat in the air like that Ben Franklin guy in the Rough-riders.

Problem number five is the cost. I'm thinking the City of Winters might have to cough up around a million and a half bucks for a really nice memorial statue, which is fine with me. We could make up that money in just a few years with the installation of a few parking meters on Main Street and a few toll booths on the bridges coming into town.

Something like this could mean a lot of revenue for our fair city. People would come from near and far just to stand near the statue, and in time, word will spread across the nation, from sea to sea that the city of Winters knows how to honor great men like me. Well, this is almost a done deal, so if you're thinking about complaining about a Don Sanders Memorial, just remember the NSA is watching out for those who gripe and whine about what we do in the good old USA.

Yes sir, a Don Sanders Memorial statue is a very good idea if I do say so. Well, technically, I'm not dead yet, so it would be called "The Don Sanders Pre-Memorial Statue," but that's OK too.

When the fixer needs fixing
1/11/2014

Donald is a native of Tennessee. His wife Therese was born here in California a few short years later. Tennessee and California are a fair distance apart. It's not worlds apart or galaxies apart. but it's almost a third of the distance around this ball we call Earth. That's a fair distance if we measure in miles or feet or inches.

I don't know how to describe Donald, so we'll get back to him later and we'll concentrate on Therese for the time being.

Therese is a fixer. She comes from a family of fixers. If you can compare humanity to a swarm of bees, you will find the Queen, the soldiers, the workers and, I believe, the fixers. I think every swarm must have its fixers.

If not for the fixers, the entire swarm would freeze because the hive would fall into disrepair within just a few generations. The fixers are the real power within the hive or swarm — whichever term you like is fine with me so I'll use both intermittently. I hope that makes you all happy at some point while you read this column.

The Queen is beautiful but all she is good for is laying eggs. The fixers decide if the egg will go to the soldiers or the workers. That's where the real power lies, and therein begins a vicious circle that is endless, and in time the fixers find that they themselves have a need to be fixed. If the need arises, the number of soldiers will far outweigh the number of workers.

Hopefully, at some point there will be enough soldiers, and more and more workers can be produced to repair all the damage the soldiers have done. The making of workers is the joy of a fixer's life but it is also the most heartbreaking and painful task a fixer will ever have to do. In time, the fixer will need to be fixed.

In the swarm, at a certain point, the fixer knows that the workers will start building walls to keep the returning soldiers from getting back into the hive. At this point, everybody is crying and everybody but the fixers turn cold. The soldiers want to be fixed and they can feel the warmth of the fixers, but the new soldiers keep them at a distance until the new workers can finish the walls to keep them out. Everybody is crying.

There is an immense swarm of humanity between Tennessee and California. Humanity like bees swarms around, bumping and brushing against each other not knowing why, but they keep on doing it. Like beehives, it all seems to work out just fine for everyone but the returning soldiers. What do we do with the returning soldiers? Do we kill them? No, I think not.

The walls! Oh yes, the walls. We need to build more walls and call them prisons. We can send all of the black soldiers and all of the unruly white soldiers to prisons, and let them do their soldier things to themselves where it won't affect us. Not only that, but we can make a big dollar industry out of housing them. BIG DOLLAR!

Here is the truth. You can believe what you hear or see on the news or on the mainstream media, but it's all a lie. If you want to see where the returning soldiers are, go to a prison and look through a hole in the wall. I have been there and I didn't think I would ever survive long enough to get out. I have seen all of the black soldiers and all of the unruly white soldiers doing their soldier things behind the walls we keep building. I know this is true. You can believe me or you can kiss my ass.

Therese is a fixer. Not knowing why, Donald fought his way through millions and millions of faceless humanity to get near to her warmth hoping she can fix him. Therese now works so hard for him that so very often she needs to go home to her family of fixers to be fixed herself. Now, when Therese is ill with the flu or a bad cold, Donald will lie next to her to keep her warm, making sure she is breathing and all is well.

So in the end, Donald, a returning soldier, has found a place to fit into the swarm. Donald is one of the lucky ones. Donald can stay warm by the fixer while helping the fixer along its way to fixing everything in the hive. Donald tries to fit in with the workers but he doesn't know how. Donald might overdo it sometimes, but we should overlook that, just to be nice.

Would you like to hear the newest of my great ideas? I know in the past, I've had a few ideas that some would consider harebrained. I'll admit that right up front. However, this new idea does not fall under that heading. I'm really excited about it because I feel that every person that lives in Winters, California will benefit. K-ching-Ka-ching!

I think the City of Winters, California should secede from the United States of America! We could become an independent sovereign state, a principality so to say. We could have our own constitution with a preamble and seven or eight articles. As a principality, we could have a Prince and a Princess. I guess, since I'm the only person in this city with royal blood, I should be the Prince. I could think of a name for our new nation later. When I say later, I mean in the future, not in the past.

I guess I shouldn't confuse you all with technical stuff like future and past, so I'll take care of that kind of stuff. You have to remember that I have an extraordinarily large brain so it's just like this column. I write the column and you read it, so I make all the decisions. I figure anyone who will read my column can't be all that smart anyway.

There are many benefits that, you as a citizen of the new nation, will receive. First of all, you get to have a Prince to worship — me! When I see you on the street, I could bless you and you could kiss my hand. I guess I would have to wash them every morning during the week. You will thank me when all the money starts rolling in, piles and piles of it. That's all green too, no coins!

As an independent country, 100 percent of our tax money would stay right here in the new nation of Winters. I don't know how much money that is but I promise to be diligent in counting and distributing it to all of you. I'm talking a lot of money here, a lot of money. We'll have so much money that we can pay the rest of the people to stay out of our country.

We wouldn't need garbage collection or a sewer plant. All of that stuff can be tossed in the creek and someone else will worry about that. Those guys downstream in Davis won't know where it came from anyway. They are more worried about what goes downstream out of Davis than they are about what comes downstream into Davis. If by chance those guys from Davis give us a hard time, we can declare war upon them for the slander and disrespect that they show us. After all, they can't prove the garbage came from Winters, right?

We wouldn't be the smallest nation, but we would be the smallest nation on dry land. The smallest nation on the sea is a place called Sealand. It consists of a little concrete platform off the coast of Great Brittan. The only difference between their country and ours is the fact that they are all interbred, deformed and starving because they live on a concrete island and there aren't any farms around it like there are here.

You know how the United States is always sending their money to other countries? Well, they can send it to us. I'll make sure to get that into our treaty. Another thing of importance is the fact that there are only four ways to get into our country and toll booths will rake in a lot of cash. You want to come to our country? Well ya gotta go through us, right? Ka-ching!

Folks, with your support, we can make this thing happen. All we have to do is put the idea of a sovereign nation into City Manager John Donlevy's head and he will bulldog it into action. I'm convinced that he can do anything. Since he came into this town and made his improvements and adjustments to this and that, our little city has grown by about 10,000 percent, but has stayed quite quaint and pleasant to live in. Donlevy is like that new 49er quarterback because he's leading the team and if you don't keep an eye on him, he's running the ball all the way to the goalpost by himself. I'm thinking he might have royal blood too, maybe a Duke or an Earl.

I mean, folks, this little city has got it going on. The only thing we don't have is the right name for our new nation. I'm thinking of something like "Sanders Shire" or "The Land of Prince Donald" would be in order. What do you think?

Aw, never mind. I'm the Prince so I'll do all the thinking.

An important guy brings it full circle
2/8/2014

Ain't it funny how things go full circle so the end goes right back to the beginning? It's like my ancestors, who chopped down all the trees, took everything the local Indians had, and then killed all the animals and fish. Well, except maybe for my earliest known ancestor, Pettyplace the cannibal. He was too busy feeding his face.

The point I'm trying to make is, the earliest member of my family did one thing and at the other end of the family line, which is me, I'm trying to fix what they did. They chopped down the trees and I help replant them with the Putah Creek Council's help. Get it? Full circle, right. They killed the animals and I help the animals live right by building habitat for them. Full circle.

You see, if you think about it, the first guy is as important as the last guy. When the circle comes around to where the first guy meets the last guys, they are pretty much in the same boat — equal. They could be doing the same thing or opposite, it doesn't matter. So, in this instance, my first ancestor is an important guy and since I am the other end of the ancestry line, I am important too.

You might not think I'm an important guy, but way down deep in your subconscious, you know it to be true. Deep down within you it is true. You think that Donald K. Sanders is one of the most important people in history. I'll prove it to you. Here is a little quiz that will tell you your true feelings on this matter.

Your options for most important historical persons are:
1. Ben Franklin
2. Abe Lincoln
3. Tom Jones
4. Maria Carry
5. William the Great
6. Genghis Kahn
7. Adolf Hitler
8. Ike Eisenhower
9. Donald K. Sanders
10. Deon Warwick

Now follow the instructions below and you will find your subconscious answer.
1. Pick a number from 1-9
2. Multiply by 3
3. Add 3.
4. Multiply by 3 again.
5. Now add the two digits together to find your predicted favorite historical person on the list.

See, you love me and you didn't even know it. Way down deep, you feel I'm the most important person in the history of man. Well, don't worry — I'm going to start being an important guy first thing tomorrow.

I like this. This is perfect. I might nominate myself for a Pulitzer Prize. Again.

A night of warmth and love
2/9/2014

I was lucky enough to attend the celebration and diner party in honor of the 2013 Winters Citizen of the Year, and what a party it was. If I hadn't been a witness, I would never in my life have believed that such a night was possible. It was an excellent celebration of all that is good about this little city of Winters, California, its people. It was a party, to be sure, for there was fine food and drink, elbow rubbing, laughing, maybe a little crying, and a whole lot of love and affection.

This year's honor went to John Pickerel, owner of the Buckhorn, the Putah Creek Cafe, and a number of other fine dining establishments scattered throughout the United States, including New York City, San Francisco and Los Angeles. He is called affectionately, "The King of Meat," because his Buckhorn steakhouse is nationally ranked. I can personally attest to the fact that he serves the finest steak in this nation, possibly the world.

I've gotten to know John pretty well in the past year or so — at least one side of him. John has two sides, I think, a business side and a personal side. Normally, I would say a working side and a relaxed side but I don't think that applies to John because even when he is relaxing he is still working very hard. I don't think I have ever seen him in a relaxed state. He just goes and goes all the time, no matter where he is or what he is doing.

If I had to describe John Pickerel to you, I don't exactly know what I would say. He is nothing like you might think he is. He deals with money all day, every day, but I don't think he cares a lot about it. Money is not the reason he does what he does, I know this for sure. To him, money is just a tool he uses to accomplish what he wants to do. He is a generous man with a passion for doing his best at what he does and he instills that into those he deals with, both professionally and personally.

He and his wife Melanie are down-to-earth people who live simple, ordinary lives like the rest of us. They don't drive fancy cars or wear the finest shoes, and their little house fits right in with the rest of the houses of this little town. They don't live in the mansion up on the hill like you might think, nor would they want to. They are regular people with regular needs and wants, and they make mistakes just like the rest of us. No one I know is more deserving of the Citizen of the Year award.

I can see that when John walks down the street, he can feel the heart of this little town. I don't know much about the business side of his personality, but I do know that he thinks the important part of his business is the people who work with him. I don't know exactly how many people he employs, but I imagine there are quite a few, and they and not the gaining of revenue are the reason he works so hard to stay in business. He knows what he has to do and he does it with the welfare of his employees in mind. Both John and Melanie live their lives dutifully with the notion that in service to others lies the road to happiness.

The Pickerels put everything they have, physically and mentally, into their business not for the love of money but for each and every person who depends upon them for a job to support themselves and their families. The welfare of their employees is all-important to the Pickerels — this is clear for me to see and it should be clear to you. There is nothing phony about the Pickerels and what you see is what you get. Perhaps that is why I have grown so fond of them. As far as people go, these two are among the best I have met.

It is not normal for me to attend public functions like the diner celebration for the Citizen of the Year, but I'm glad I did, because it was truly a night of wonder and affection in praise of John Pickerel and the Citizens of the Year of the past. It was a night of true warmth and love. It was a night I will not soon forget for it was a room full of people that are the best the city of Winters has to offer.

We live in a fine town, a town we can be proud of, and a town where our families can live and be happy all of the days of their lives.

This has been a wonderful but very weird week for me, so I have to tell you about it. When I say, "weird," I mean out of the norm. I'm still doing my volunteer work for the Putah Creek Council. I've been helping them plant thousands of native area trees all along Putah Creek, as usual, except that now I get to drive a fire truck rigged with special attachments to water the plants without ever getting out of the truck. It's so easy for me that I slept for several hours and when I woke up, I was finished with the last tree.

I'm getting so good at planting trees that I'm thinking of contacting the Guinness Book of World Records people to see if I'm setting a world record or maybe just a California record, who knows! The people at Guinness know me from prior world record attempts but they said I'd have to eat a whole lot more live frogs if I wanted to beat any record they have on the books. I tried, but it was too much like eating vegetables for my taste. Sometimes they don't answer when I contact them and once threatened to call the police if I called again. I beat that by calling a different number at their accounting office. Next I plan to call their maintenance supervisor; he's got to know someone that can help me without all the trouble.

Anyway, I spend so much time with the Putah Creek Council that my wife has to call Libby Earthman, Sara Sevy Tremayne, or Martha Rocha to schedule time for me to mow my own lawn. My wife would like our lawn mowed and hedges trimmed at least within the next week. It's not all work because the girls treat me to breakfast at the Putah Creek Cafe at least once a week. That's why I'm getting so fat.

Thanks to the Putah Creek Council, the Solano County Water Agency, and the City of Winters, the waters of the creek are crystal clear and icy cold. I don't know if you have heard about, it but the salmon are now coming up the creek to spawn in big numbers. I think I saw a marlin in the creek from the pedestrian bridge the other day, but maybe it was a yellow tail tuna. Anyway, if you haven't been down to the Winters Nature Park lately, you should make the effort just to check out the wildlife or to take a hike.

The other day, my friend Joe lost his wallet somewhere in town and was very distraught over the loss of his identification cards, banking cards, and a substantial amount of cash. I kept telling him that it was never to be seen again and talked him into cancelling his bank cards for financial safety. Believe it or not, within 30 minutes of cancelling his cards, his wallet was returned, cards within, along with every cent of the cash. Joe would like to convey a big, heartfelt thank you to Mary Beth for her honesty and good will in returning the wallet. Joe is just lucky I didn't find it.

My other friends, Steve and Terry, got lost in the forest near Lake Oroville last weekend while hiking. Steve hurt his leg and told Terry he could only travel downhill. Well, after hours of going downhill they were lost. Terry called the rangers to ask directions and the ranger said, "I'll have to declare this an "Emergency Rescue!" Terry told me he was terrified because he could see the lights of two parking lots, but he had no idea in which his truck was parked. Steve said the only bad thing about the whole rescue is that he didn't get a helicopter ride. Dang-it!

To top the week off, I made my wife dinner for her birthday. I whipped up a special batch of my "Falla-part Meat Loaf." My meatloaf doesn't come in a loaf; it comes in more of a pile, so you can eat it out of a bowl with a spoon. My wife says she would like to try her recipe next time. That's fine with me, because as good as this week was, I could eat almost anything, even her meatloaf.

You know what? This week was so good, I'm filled with gratitude. Gratitude is the ability to be aware of the gifts life provides that we have done absolutely nothing to earn, deserve or receive. Isn't that nice?

The ranchers along Putah Creek, which runs through Winters California, are a breed of their own. I don't mean that in a bad way, but it's pretty much true. If you think about it, you'll agree that, at the least, they're a curious bunch. From the outside they have neat little houses tucked in neat little orchards where the trees are in neat little rows within arm's reach of a neat little creek. If I had to choose one thing as a symbol of Winters California, it would be these neat little ranches.

It's one thing to view these ranches as you drive past on the highway, but it's quite another to actually walk among the rows of trees, smell the smells and taste the fruit of whatever tree you happen to be standing next to. I mean, you can bend over and pick up a walnut, newly fallen from a branch above, crack it open and taste something so natural and fresh that you will slobber all over yourself. Or, you can go to the grocery store and get one from the refrigerator, which is alright but not the same.

As you know, several organizations such as the Putah Creek Council and Solano County Water Agency, along with others, are deeply involved in restoring Putah Creek to a more natural state and it is very important work. At this stage in their work, you can already see the water of the creek is cleaner, colder, and in general, happier. Salmon are coming upstream in greater and greater numbers to spawn and swim up and down the creek from ranch to ranch. It's a beautiful thing to see and to be a part of.

Organizations concerned with saving the Earth through restoration and conservation are springing up everywhere they're needed. They depend on volunteer labor to do the good work needed because the cost would be overwhelming and no one would have the funding for such projects. Problems arise because you can't clean an entire creek from any one particular point. To clean and restore a creek, you need to clean the entire creek and most of the creek passes through private property.

I have a deep feeling of respect and affection for those that organize and run the non-profit organizations concerned with the restoration of our environment. These people work very hard at a job that will never make them rich or buy them fancy cars or trucks. The work they do is so very important to us all, and if the work is to be completed, it will take all of us to do it. Of course, conservation work will never be completed and goes on and on forever.

As a volunteer for these organizations, I can only do what I can do. I do not decide what I do or where to go while doing this work. At some point, as a volunteer, I was taught by someone how to do what needs to be done in a way that has been tested and reviewed by others who have been at restoration work for many, many years. Whatever I do as a volunteer has been done over and over by others before me, thousands of times. Believe me, these people know what they are doing, it's important to them, and they know it's an ongoing process.

This all said, it takes me to the point where I am standing along the creek, on a ranch owned by someone else, where I might get lucky and pick up a walnut off the ground and taste it. I know I'm on someone else's property and I hope they don't mind if I taste one or two walnuts while I'm there. I have a dilemma at this point, for ofttimes I do volunteer work that needs to be done, alone, by myself. I mean there are certain little jobs I can do by myself and these organizations have trusted me to take care of them, knowing I'm not going to go on a destructive rampage on someone else's property.

If you own a ranch along the Putah Creek, chances are I have been working on your property, over and over for years now. Know that I do not venture everywhere I want to go just because I want to. The Solano County Water Agency and the Putah Creek Council are diligent in their communications with landowners about everything they do on someone else's property, who will do the work, and when they will be doing it. They are every bit as diligent in their organization of volunteer activities. This work takes hours and hours of dedication. When you come down to it, the actual volunteer work is the quickest and easiest part of the whole thing.

Anyway, the most important thing I'm trying to say is, should you see me on your property (I'm not going to say "tasting your nuts"), don't shoot me. I'm doing restoration work and I'm not there to do you harm

I thought to myself, ""What happened?" How come Winters, California doesn't have a famous guy to draw the tourists from all around the world to spend all their money in this town? Well I've figured out a way to remedy that problem. Think about the words: "Winters California, Home of the Famous Donald K. Sanders!" Pretty catchy, huh?

Are you starting to see what I'm thinking? No? Well, read on. The city of Winters needs a famous person. Then I thought, "Who is better suited than me to be famous?" After that, I thought, "No one!" So now you're thinking, "You dummy, you're not famous!" Well OK. You see, that's the trick. We have to make me famous. So, just how do we make me famous? Well, I have several ideas along that line. I'll just toss my ideas up in the air to see which one catches on, OK? We could even write a theme song for me.

Idea number 1: You remember that guy Mandela from Africa? He was, like, super famous because he went to jail. Well, it just so happens that I too went to jail. Not just one time like that Mandela guy, but three, maybe four times. Now, if we consider that Mandela got out of jail to be president of his country after only one time in jail, how high up the political ladder could I go, because I have been in jail way more times that that guy.

An interesting side note: In jail you get to have the toilet right next to your bed. It's not a namby-pamby toilet either, because I could hold up one of those big wool Army blankets, flush the toilet and it would suck that blanket right down, like it was a weasel or something. It would just go, "Slurp!" If I ever get to build a house, I'm going to put one of those toilets right next to my bed because that's part of being famous, I think.

Anyway, back to idea number two: You know how Abe Lincoln had a log cabin in Kentucky or wherever, and Davy Crockett had a cabin in some other place? Well, we can say that Donald K. Sanders had a house right here in Winters, California. OK, my house is too little to use, so we will have to use Mr. Ogando's house. Yeah, it looks like a house where the famous Donald K. Sanders could live.

Or, we could use Dennis Kilkenny's house on the other side of the creek. I like that house too. We'd have to put up a sign somewhere pointing to the "Historical Home of Donald K. Sanders!" I'm sure the Ogandos and the Kilkennys wouldn't mind a small group of my fans touring their house once a day. Somewhere in their yard, we'd have to put up a headstone with, "Thar lays Donald K. Sanders, kilt by a bar while defending little kids from wild savages!"

Idea number three: The houses of famous people are still famous after they're dead. Famous people have died in airplane crashes, skiing accidents, murder and even cancer, so we have to have a spectacular death for me right. Nothing real gory or anything like that — we don't have to get drastic. I was thinking of something like, "Donald K. Sanders dies of starvation because he gave all his food to the starving little kids of Winters,California.

Idea number 4: This idea can go along with any of the other ideas. You know how famous I am for writing all of my wonderful ideas into a column, so even the simplest person can understand what has often been described as "Quantum Theories of D. K. Sanders." So, here's the plan: Each and every one of you should nominate me for a Pulitzer Prize for this and all my other great columns that I don't get paid for. As a matter of fact, I don't get paid for anything! You know what I like about that? "If you don't get paid, you can't get fired." Another way of putting it is, "If you're a fish, they can't drown you!"

While you're filling out those Pulitzer Prize nomination forms, it's important to just offer your prayers up to God each day in hopes that he will respond to your prayer in a speedy manner. The quicker I get famous, the quicker I will get rich. The quicker I get rich, the quicker I get that blanket-sucking toilet right next to my bed. WooHoo!

Playing by the rules became very expensive
3/19/2014

Maggie Burns

By MAGGIE BURNS and DONALD SANDERS

Backstory by Maggie: Somewhere in the dark night of Monday, March 3 a bogus Google.doc went out to everyone on my contact list of names – 840 people. It took me until Thursday morning to send out a BE WARY notice to my entire email list. On Thursday, March 6, at 10:56 p.m. this message came in on my computer:

From Donald Sanders: Ha, too late. I opened it, got a virus, couldn't go online, had to call support, they referred me to a private company whose IT rep charged me $150 to fix it. I was on the landline with this guy for 2 1/2 hours. I usually catch these types of emails because they aren't quite proper. The virus then spreads by sending emails to all of your contacts. How devious huh?

Let me know if you get one from me. Oops, too late. Don't open this. LOL

PS: Here is the bill.

From Maggie to Don Sanders: I am very, very sorry that you got trapped by the viral message sent out from my computer by some weirdo in Los Angeles. And I appreciate your wishing for me to pay the $150.00 bill you had from a tech service to get you online again. Believe me, I empathize.

The way it happened was this: I was working on the last drought story for the Winters Express and had contacted the San Jose Mercury-News to ask permission to use an excellent graphic that had appeared in one of their stories on the drought. The librarian there, after checking with her superiors, gave me permission to use the graphic and put me in touch with the artist. In one of his emails, he asked what form I wanted it in – jpg, PDF or maybe a Google.doc. I replied the jpg was fine.

Then, about 20 minutes later a Google.doc appeared in my in-box. Thinking it was from the artist, I opened it, and when it asked for my password, I blithely put it in but didn't get a new graphic.

The next afternoon – Tuesday – I realized I had had no new emails for 24 hours. Especially I had not received my Word of the Day for Spanish conversation, which comes routinely around 3:00 a.m. I could send emails out, but my contact list was weird and kept coming up with names I hardly ever talk to. Then the Winters Express editor Debra DeAngelo told me she had emailed me twice that day, but I never saw anything.

Fortunately, our computer guru was coming to set up my husband's laptop that afternoon and he took the time (only one half hour) to straighten it out and tell me how to fix the problem.

The way I look at this situation, it is really The Winters Express who is responsible for all our pain and suffering.

First of all, if the Editor-in-Chief were not such a stickler for getting permission for everything and just let us rip off our computer any nice little illustrations we find, this whole episode would not have happened. But no, just because someone ripped off her column and reprinted it without attribution, she thinks we should ask, and actually get permission to use someone else's work. Really! How does she think the world works? Especially in Washington!

And, let me tell you, this cost me plenty! Not only did I also have to pay a computer guru, but I then spent two hours changing the login ID's and passwords for my important online accounts; only the important ones, just in case. I don't really care if MySpicePage or Peet's gets a virus. But Zappo's, where I buy my shoes! Well, that's important. And, I tell you, I have different passwords for everything and they are works of art, so it is not a simple job to change them and make them beautiful and appropriate. Then, I had to clean up my contacts list which took another two hours because, due to some past work, I had an email contact for every nonprofit agency in Yolo County. I hate to think of how this one stupid mistake on my part, due to the Winters Express, nearly made inoperative every nonprofit in Yolo County. If each of them had fallen for a message supposedly from me, as you did, half the county would be in limbo right now.

So, this is a long way of telling you I will pay your tech bill, but we have to deduct some of my expenses as well: 30 minutes for computer guru: $37.50. 4 hours of my time, at my Winters Express salary rate of $100 per hour: $400.00. Pain and needless suffering on the part of The Main Man, listening to me moan and complain: $5000. Oh, and one more half hour writing this response to your email: $50.

That makes a grand total of $5,487.50 for me and $150.00 for you.

Don't you just think we should submit this to the Publisher, Charlie Wallace, since it was The Winters Express that got us both, his star reporters, in this fine fix?

Yours sincerely,

Maggie

Don Sanders to Maggie:

Dear Maggie,

Perfect! If you will nominate me for a Pulitzer or Citizen of the Year I will agree with you to submit the bill to Charlie. I think we should send a bill to John Donlevy at the City of Winters too. He likes getting funny stuff like that. So far I've sent him plans for a Muon Ring from here to Davis and Back, a toll booth at my corner, and a traffic plan for Elliot Street. I think he is responsible, too, because we are both really trying to improve the city of Winters. Of course we have to tell him that Charlie approved it. Ha!

Maggie to Don Sanders: I think we should take these profits of our misfortune and have a really good dinner at the Buckhorn, maybe on the house?

Still got my weiner
3/21/2014

I've been thinking. Yep, I've been thinking about how my luck has changed through the years. My luck is pretty good right now. I get to write stupid stories for the Winters Express and iPinion Syndicate, and sometimes people will actually read them. How dumb is that?

I thought about the earliest year I can remember, 1955, and I found it was the most unlucky year, ever. There was a lot of crap happening in 1955; all of it was unlucky, too. I'm happy to say that I'm not the only one it was unlucky for. It was a year that was unlucky for everybody. I just happened to be there and couldn't get away, so I got some of the crap too, but I'll get back to that later.

In 1955, James Dean and some dude named Rolf crashed in a Porsche 550 Spider while going like a thousand miles an hour. They burnt up until they were crispy critters. That dude Joe DiMaggio got dumped by Marilyn Monroe. Imagine that! That dude must have been crying for days! A kid named William Henry "Bill" Gates III was born. Now I can't get off of this damn computer.

That same year a lady named Rosa Parks refused to give up her seat on a bus, so now all the white people have to ride on BART. Albert Einstein fell over dead, so now no one will ever know what the hell he was talking about. The Cuban government let Fidel Castro out of jail because they thought he was in for putting explosives in the big cigars. The truth of the matter is that he was putting cigars against the big explosives. Funny how a typo will change history, huh?

In that same year, an all-white jury acquitted Milam and Roy Bryant for the murder of a kid named Emmett Till, whom they dragged from his bed in the middle of the night, brutally murdered him and dumped him in the river. Well, except for their niece Anita, all them Bryants are in hell right now.

A whole bunch of terrible airplane crashes happened that year, including Air India's' Kashmir Princess, El Al Flight 402, which was shot down by Bulgarian fighter pilots, United Airlines Flight 409, and United Airlines Flight 629. I'm glad I didn't go anywhere that year, but I was having a bad year too.

In 1955, my brother Michael was kidnapped and the guy that took him socked me in the jaw. Now my jaw clicks when I chew stuff. That damn clicking got me a divorce one time. Even worse than that, it was the year they started broadcasting "The Lord of the Rings" on the radio. My mom took us to a pear farm one night and we heard the first episode. The very next day, she dumped me in an orphanage, so I never heard the rest.

Just before Christmas that year, I ran away because Sister Conchadda told me she was going to cut off my weiner. I had the hardest time climbing over the damn eight foot fence. I got to the top of the fence and jumped off just as the gate swung open. I hate it when that happens. Later that night the cops caught me eating doughnuts out of a garbage can behind a bakery. They took me back to the orphanage despite my begging them not to. I still have my weiner though.

Sometimes when I tell that story, people want to see it, but I'm too shy. I've been with my wife for about 30 years now and she ain't ever seen it. I don't think I'll ever show it to anyone, so I guess you will have to take my word for it. She calls it "Big Mo" but I call it the "Python."

Martha Rocha is one sought-after girl
4/5/2014

OK. I've been doing some internet research and you will not believe what I found. I'll tell you as soon as you answer this question, "What does a 74.5 pound blue rock found in Teofilo Otoni Brazil have to do with Winters, California and the Putah Creek Council?" Let me guess. You don't know, right?

Well, I'm not going to tell you!

Ha, OK, I'll give you another hint.

The whole thing concerns the education coordinator at PCC. Still don't know? OK, here's the answer. If it's on the internet it has to be true. Am I right? Well, I Googled the PCC's education coordinator and I got 6,990,000 hits. Unbelievable!

Here's the answer. An incredible aquamarine crystal was found on a farm near Teofilo Otoni, Brazil. It weighed approximately 74.5 pounds and the color was so rich — so intense that the Brazilian gem dealers needed to distinguish it from the rest. They named it "Martha Rocha" as a special tribute to the beautiful Education Coordinator with the captivating clear blue eyes. It's true! It's right there on the internet!

With well over six million hits, there is a ton of information about our sweet little Martha Rocha, so read and weep because I'm the guy that broke the story! The internet says Martha Rocha is the seventh child of engineer Álvaro Rocha and housewife Hansa. Back in 1954 (this must be a misprint-must have meant 1974) Martha Rocha was a statuesque 18-year-old Brazilian beauty queen.

After winning the title of Miss Bahia in her home state, she went on to become the first Miss Brazil and was the runaway favorite to win the Miss Universe pageant. Martha Rocha measured 35 inches at the bust, 23 at the waist, and 38 at the hips. Mirain Stevenson, the 21-year-old South Carolina beauty, was 10 inches smaller at the hips, so Martha took second place in the Miss Universe Pageant.

The first half of 1954 (must be another misprint of the date) Martha Rocha was in every newspaper in the world when she was disqualified in the Miss Universe contest because her hips were two inches above the limit.

Martha sure gets around because the internet says she holds the title of Credit Research Analyst at Lord, Abbett & Co. LLC located in New York City. She has 13 years of experience in sales and marketing, advertising, promotions, management, and professional development. Martha loves to participate in running races and triathlons. Martha has two adorable dogs, Bono and Angel.

The internet goes on to say that Martha holds several professional licenses and memberships such as ACA – American Counseling Association, AACC – American Association of Christian Counselors, MHCCF – Mental Health Counseling Association of Central Florida.

Also Marta volunteers in her church with translations, social work and in missions. Martha Rocha is an adjunct professor of undergraduate psychology classes at Florida Technical College in Kissimmee, Florida. All of the experience she has gained has helped her assist individuals and businesses achieve their goals through individual counseling, seminars, and workshops. Martha has developed seminars and workshops in various aspects of business and professional development areas, such as: Effective & Professional

Selling, Cultivating Clients, Valuing Cultural Differences, Protecting Your Digital Legacy, and Signs and Symptoms of Depression and Anxiety in Teens.

Martha is also a Portuguese economist that sports a 14k two-tone gold Martha Rocha Kunzite and diamond ring. She has lived in Chicago, Illinois, Brazil, Spain, and S. Africa, where she deals with Anger Management, Anxiety Disorders/Phobias, Ethnic/Cultural Issues, and Schizophrenia.

Martha is said to have joined the Women's Revolution in Mexico, 1910-1953. (Must be another misprint.) Martha has an account on Vivino, which is a community driven app that lets you scan any wine while on the go.

To tell the truth, I don't see how Martha does all this stuff. I mean over six million hits all about Martha Rocha. That staggers my mind. There is one more little tidbit of information about Martha Rocha that I didn't find on the internet. Martha Rocha has resigned her position as education coordinator of The Putah Creek Council, and I find that very sad indeed. We will miss her smiling face.

Imagine — six million hits. She is one well sought-after girl. I wonder what Martha has that other girls don't. Oh well, that's a different story.

The true history of Winters, California

4/27/2014

I've already told you about what I found on Ancestry.com, so I won't go into that again. Nobody wants to read about cannibals anyway. What I'd like to bring to your attention is along that line, but more relative to the people of Winters California. Everything you read about the history of Winters, California is wrong, and I'm here to set it straight.

According to the history books, this area was named after Theodore Winters around about the mid 1850s. This may have some truth to it, but it was my family that was first to arrive in the area. You see my family and the Theodore Winters' family hale from Central Illinois where the two families shared a freight hauling business. It must have been about 400 years ago when all of this occurred, but what I am about to relay to you is the gospel truth.

The two families sold the business to some people who thought Illinois was "God's Country." That's because no one had been to California yet except the Mexicans, but nobody could understand what they were saying, so as far as the white Anglo Saxon Protestants were concerned, California didn't exist. Anyhow, to make a long story short, my family thought that Theodore Winters had swindled them out of half of the money acquired from the sale of their freight business.

My family chased the other family all the way to California, where Theodore Winters was cornered in the area around where the city of Winters is now. Theodore Winters was caught hiding under the freeway bridge at 505 and Putah Creek Road. Strange things occurred at this point in the conflict between the two families.

It was there that Theodore Winters fell upon his own knife, making 32 wounds in his upper torso. Theodore Winters was found stiff as a board, with his hands bound, a burlap bag tied neatly over his head, and his trousers pulled loosely around his ankles. Parts of his buttocks were eaten away by what is assumed to be an unknown furry creature. Parts of his flesh were found near a fire pit; still on sticks roasting near the fire.

Since there were only two white men in the entire area, my ancestor became the only law for the region. The death of Theodore Winters was ruled a suicide. It is still unknown how and why he covered his head and tied his hands behind his back before falling upon his knife. It is a mystery that has yet to be solved. In the following days, my ancestor, Jeddarigha P. Sanders, became the first mayor of the town he named in honor of his best friend Theodore Winters.

A year later, Jeddarigha P. Sanders cut the timber which he used to build the railroad bridge. Jeddarigha P. Sanders had the bridge ready for the first crossing 10 years before the first train ever arrived. He then proceeded to build the first school, a ten bed hospital, and the first house, which is no longer standing because of a fire in 1907. All of the records which would prove any of this was true were also destroyed.

For nearly four hundred years, there was absolutely no record of my family ever living in this area. It is only in the last couple of weeks that proof of the Sanders family deeds was found. Though I have told this story many, many times, I could never prove any of it to anyone. They all thought I was a fool or a retard. I will now relay the proof of what I tell you now in the form of a picture of an item found within the walls of the old Winters Bridge as the slab was removed.

For generations the proof lay inside the old bridge, and it is only now that this city will see the resemblance between my ancestor and me. No one can deny that my great-great grandfathers' image upon an old bottle found inside the old bridge is from my family. See for yourself for here is the picture and the proof.

I've just got to win some kind of award. I can't imagine what kind of award it could be, maybe a Pulitzer or even a Nobel. Yes, I think it would have to be one of those two, maybe both. They are the only two awards I can think of that are awarded to people that they don't really know. An award committee weighs the merits of all the nominees, picks the most qualified person, they have a big party and then they give out the award. They don't really know the person they are giving it to.

In the town where I live, there are countless people who have won awards. I can't name them all, but off the top of my head, I can name a few – more than a few. In my town, people go out of their way to do the right thing in the right way and they do it quietly, so it is done before you even know they are doing it. The awards they are given are personal in nature. They are given awards by their peers, who know them well, so there is no question about their deeds and merits.

I'll start with guys like Craig McNamara. The awards he has been given will come in a long list – a very long list. Let's see, there is the Leopold Conservation Award, the California Governor's Environmental and Economic Leadership Award, the UC Davis Award of Distinction and Outstanding Alumnus Award, the Theodore Winters Award, Businessman of the Year Award, and the City of Winters Citizen of the Year Award, just to name a few. He comes from a family of award winners and deservedly so.

Anthony Lawlor received awards for excellence in design from the American Institute of Architects and Interior Design Magazine. Michael Sears has been recognized with awards from the California Heritage Council and a prestigious 2013 Palladio Award.

Recently, Winters High School Students have been recognized as exceptional from over 2,000 entries in California alone and 250,000 in the United States for the Scholastic Art & Writing Awards, the longest-running, most prestigious competition and largest source of scholarships for creative teenagers in the United States. It has an impressive legacy and a noteworthy roster of past winners including Andy Warhol, Sylvia Plath, Truman Capote, Richard Avedon, Joyce Carol Oates and many others.

Jacqueline Plasencia and Fabiola Magallanes received a Gold Key. Tiffany Gillespie, Agueda Moreno, and Janet Soto each received a Silver Key. And Edgar Chavez, Isaiah Cuellar, Alexis Gallardo, Adolfo Sandria, Logan Fox, and Lorenzo Valadez received Honorable Mention. Last year Asusena Lopez received a National Silver Medal and was invited to New York City to accept her award.

Cecilia Aguiar-Curry, our Mayor, received the 2013 Life Award. Daniel Ward of Winters High School Football coaching received the Double-Goal Coach Award. The people at Berryessa Gap have won so many awards I can't list them all. Thanks to John Pickerel, we can have an award-winning meal at the Buckhorn Steak & Roadhouse. Debra LoGuercio DeAngelo, the editor at the Winters Express newspaper, is a multiple award winning columnist who can do no wrong in my eyes.

Baylee Opperman has received 19 awards while playing basketball and softball at Winters High School. She is a cute as a button young lady who obviously has an award winning heart. The Wallace family (father and son) of the Winters Express fame has the curb on just about every award a newspaper man can win, including one of the nation's highest awards, The Jefferson Award, for their dedication to observing and reporting weather for more than 40 years, the John Companius Holm Award, Winters Citizen of the Year, Philip N. McCombs Achievement Award of the California Press Association and countless "Best Father" awards for both father and son.

OK, now back to me. I have won a few awards, one I deserved and the rest must be mistakes. I did earn a "Worst Improved Bowler" trophy. I was awarded a few medals from the Army including the Bronze Star but I figure that was a mistake because I killed so many innocent civilians. If I had been killed that day, I would have gotten a Silver Star like the rest of the guys who were all shot in the back of the head with their hands tied behind their backs.

The newspaper report of that day stated that there were 17 US Army Soldiers missing in action, but I knew they were all dead. I was just under 23 years old and that was the worst day of my life and it still is. I guess that's why I write so many stupid stories, because they're easier to write than the real life stories and military awards are harder on the heart than civilian awards. Perhaps it's understandable why I need awards given by those that don't know me or what I have done and how I am still paying for them.

The truth of the matter is this – a shot in the back of the head sure would have been a lot easier to deal with, but it's too late now. I can't go back in time for that award. .

Death comes to Winters
5/30/2014

I awoke this morning with numerous text messages about a deadly accident at the construction site of a new bridge in my sleepy little home town of Winters, California. I don't know the particulars yet, but from what I gather, two construction workers are dead.

Again, Death comes to Winters.

When Death comes to my little town, its effect is similar to a nuclear blast. If you could see it from above, it would look as if something fell from the sky making a splash when it struck the Earth. From that point of impact, there are multiples of waves, all in neat little circles, traveling in all directions. The circles grow larger and larger until they encompass the entire area.

This is not the first time Death has been in our little town and it is surely not the last time it will come. It comes with a vengeance when we least expect it. It rushes down one street, over to the next, until it finds what it is looking for. We all know what Death wants and we all know that someday it will come for each and every one of us. We all will have our turn with Death.

For some, Death is not the worst part of life. I'm sure that some will have a hard time grasping this concept thinking, "Exactly what could be worse than dying?" Well, I'm here to tell you, my friend, that there are many, many things worse than Death. The older I get, the more I realize this is true. I now know that if I live long enough, I will watch each and every person that I know and love die and fade away.

For many, Death is to be feared. It's easy to say you don't fear Death but in that case, wait until it comes for you to say it to his face. At that point, it's not so easy to say, but some still say it and, in fact, welcome it when it knocks on their door. For some, the pain of life is unbearable and they invite Death unto themselves with their own hand. I find this very sad.

So, Death has come to my little town again and two young men are taken when it left. As much as we would like to, we cannot bring them back. These two young men will forever be a part of this town. When, in the future, we look at our newly completed bridge we will think of them. Our new bridge will be their new bridge. We now have what the bridge construction community calls, "A two man bridge."

Even though many think that Death can be avoided, this is simply not the case. We are each predestined to intersect with Death at certain points in our lives. As proof, I can attest that my life has intersected with Death many times. I never saw it coming, but it came just the same. The first time I met Death I think I was about 9 years old. When Death left, he took my little friend, Butch King.

We were climbing one of those huge piles of sand and he was right next to me when Death came and took him away. I never saw Death come or go. One moment there was three of us, laughing, and then there were only two — myself and Butch's younger brother. We looked and looked, frantically, but in the end we never found Butch. He was covered by only six inches of sand, and he could not get out, and we could not find him.

That's how it is with Death. You do not expect it, want it or see it, but it's coming just the same. I think we all know this is true.

There's something else I think is true and I hope you feel the same way about this. I feel Death is not the end. I can't tell you what is coming after Death right now, but I will talk about it with you after Death comes and takes us. If I go first, I will wait for you and we will talk about what has happened and why. I would talk about it now but as you know, Death is a mystery to the living

Twelve simple rules for becoming great
5/31/2014

Ever wonder how I got to be such a great guy? Well, I'm here to tell you that it was indeed, not easy. After all, as hard as most will try, they will never have it all like I do. I mean I have the whole package.

I have been known by many names, each of which suits me perfectly. There are some that call me "Bog wan Don." Others know me as "Ghost" because I'm so pale and smart looking.

I always tell people to call me "Ophthalmology Guy" because I love turtles and lizards so much. I keep a room in my house with a sign on the door saying, "Ophthalmology Guy's Laboratory." This is where I perform my experiments that will correlate with my thesis paper so I can get my doctorate, which I plan to work on as soon as I complete my AA degree.

I can't talk too much about my lab because it is "Top Secret," and it says so on another sign just below the other sign. I will tell you I am experimenting with turtles and cats and how they have interchangeable heads. I have completed my first "Cathead Turtle" and will soon be finished with the "Turtle-headed Cat." I think the former may be evil and the latter retarded.

Anyway, I'm getting off subject, just as many brilliant people do when they talk about themselves. So, the question is, "How do you get as great as I am?" "Rules" is your first clue. The second is "List." I'll make it easy for you because the people who read my column are not known as great thinkers. If you put the two clues together you will have a "Rules List." Simple, is it not?

I live by rules, 12 to be exact, and I do them every day. Here they are:

1. I go to bed at exactly the same time every day, sometimes at 10 p.m. and sometimes at 11 p.m.

2. I get up at different times during the night and go to the post office to check my mail. This insures that I can do pretty much what I want. I could even rob the bank some night and get away with it. If I am spotted by the police and they call it in on the dispatch radio they will be told, "Oh he's just checking his mail."

3. I do not engage in conversations with those I consider "below me."

4. This simple rule tells me that every single thing that may be bad in nature is someone else's fault. This rule is capable of making you very sad if not followed on a daily basis.

5. I, as a rule, will never accept the consequences of my actions.

6. I will enjoy the rewards of my work because I am my own greatest fan and no one can appreciate me like I do. (I'm like, "The Man.")

7. I stop and think for 30 minutes every morning. This is best done while sitting on the toilet with some coffee and a couple of doughnuts. I have found that any more than 30 minutes on the toilet will give you Toilet Seat Polio.

8. If I spot someone with a handicap, I will run them down and bring it to their attention. For example, should I see someone with no arm, I will say, "Hey bud, do you need a hand?"

9. I will not stop until I have discussed the handicaps of one million people in my open and honest way.

10. I will always keep the inner child alive within me and bring it to the attention of everyone.

11. I will always be aware that this is my life, so if you are going to be mean to me, get out of it.

12. All day long, I will add things to my "To-do List" and then the next day I will work on the next list.

These are just a few of my 347 daily rules to follow, one for each day. You can purchase the complete list of rules in the near future when I get my Ph.D. in applied science, or maybe if I ever get on TV you might see them there.

For now I'll say, "Bon Appetite!"

My computer loves me
6/4/2014

I love my computer. I think it loves me too. There are a lot of reasons for so much love between us, more than I can count, so I'll just stick with the more juicy reasons. My computer excites me. It can take me to places where I never imagined I would go. I'm convinced that my computer can do anything.

The first time I met my computer was in 1971 at Western Illinois University in Macomb, Illinois. I had heard about her from others who thought she was wonderful and amazing. They said she was a thing of the future and that I should pay a lot of attention to her. Little did they know.

When I first laid eyes upon her, she was huge. It took a whole building just to house her. She was noisy, too. To ask her a question, I had to fill out a little cardboard card and then punch holes in the corresponding boxes. It was all very civilized. Next, I inserted the card into a little slot and off it went.

"Clack-a-die-clack, clack-a-die clack," she said, as my question went round and round for what seemed an eternity, and then nothing.

My instructor thought she was broken. So did I.

"This has never happened before," he said as he threw switches and breakers.

He dismissed the class. I figured a card got stuck in the works and didn't think about it until I got a phone call from the instructor telling me that the computer came back on all by itself and spit out my card.

When I asked what the card said, he replied, "More then you know!" Of course his next question was, "What did you ask it?" I thought for a moment and said, "Hell, I don't know. I think I asked, 'Do you love me?'" The instructor thought that was odd, to say the least. I thought it was a little odd, too.

It wasn't too long after that I quit going to classes. I found myself – well, I don't know where I found myself. I think everything went to crap because just a few weeks back, I had been in Vietnam. I was finding it hard to talk about math, English and political science. As a matter of fact, I was having trouble talking at all.

So, there I was, smack in the middle of about 5,000 students and there was not one of them I could talk to. My roommate at the dorm seemed to understand, or at least he acted like he did. I found it hard to make new friends when my old friends were still in harm's way. I had just left Vietnam and now all I wanted was to get back there.

If the truth was known, I never wanted to leave Vietnam in the first place. I found myself physically standing in the center of the campus, but my head was still in Vietnam. I didn't know what to do. Everything was so hard for me and that's not the way the college experience is supposed to be. A day or two later, I dropped out of school, left campus and never returned.

OK, fast forward 10 or 15 years or maybe a little more. I don't remember the '70s and '80s. I can recall some of the '90s, but that's because I fell in love with a girl named Therese and she kept me pretty close to the real world. Still, I found myself simply walking through life instead of living it. I still find this is case today.

Eventually, I found myself sitting in front of a computer. My wife had set everything up for another user named "Donald." After I figured out how to turn it on, "Hello Donald" appeared on the monitor. I was taken aback! How could this computer remember me after all of these years? OMG!

Now, I'm at the point where, "These are the voyages of Donald, his continuing mission is to explore a strange new worlds, to seek out new life and new civilizations, to boldly go where no one has gone before." I know I sound a little like a Trekkie, but that's the way I feel about it.

My computer and I have become as one. If I'm not with the computer, I am thinking about her. I love her and she loves me. Of course, at times I get angry with her and she gets angry with me. Sometimes she will just freeze and I can't get her to do anything, but she gets over that quickly and comes back to life.

She makes me feel as if I can do anything with her. For example: if I should turn off the computer – everthng is a whole lot diferent then what I say wen – the computer is on, a whole lot different.

I love my computer!

Scientific breakthrough
6/6/2014

I, Donald K. Sanders, am on the verge of a scientific breakthrough. When I release the results of my 32 years of research, the world will be at my feet and they will no longer ignore my theories about microscopic animals. Thirty-two years ago, I couldn't afford a microscope to begin my studies on the uncommonly friendly Red Spider Mite. I am 64 years old now, so 32 years ago I was 32 years old.

I happened upon the idea of Red Spider Mites in one of my grade school math classes. No one had ever thought of a Red Spider Mite but I had mathematically deducted their existence. Many years I forced myself to try to find the Red Spider Mite but it was very hard for me, since they are microscopic and I didn't have a microscope. I didn't know how to proceed and I almost gave up.

I gave it one last effort when I figured if I look the wrong way through a telescope it would be the same as looking through a microscope. At first glance, I did see something really, really, small but it turned out to be my feet. I was dejected and rejected, and almost gave up on the Red Spider Mite.

Ten long years later, I found one quite by accident. Now I know there is only one place on Earth that you will find the Red Spider Mite. Quite by accident, I found the only place on this planet where the friendly Red Spider Mite can exist. The one place that you will find a Red Spider Mite is on the outer rim of the anus of a 24-year-old white male from South Africa.

Through the years, time after time, this has proven to be true of every single 24-year-old white male from South Africa. Word somehow got out that I was interested in finding the Red Spider Mite and suddenly white males from South Africa were lining up outside my laboratory door hoping I would look for the friendly mite.

Today, after looking at the anuses of 10 white males from South Africa, I found something rare and possibly a Pulitzer Prize view of the friendly Red Spider Mite. I found and filmed a pair of Red Spider Mites trying to mate. The subject white male from South Africa writhed in pain as I probed for the mites and I'm sorry to announce he did not survive the probing.

Now the scientific community has been on edge of panic waiting for the film I am releasing for you to view tonight. I hope you enjoy the film as much as I did, for it was 32 years in the making. Please relax and view the video at the link below.

The lesson of Billy and Fat Phil
6/14/2014

In times of stress and hardship many things change, even the way you think about what you have or don't have. What was once thought of as trash to be thrown in a garbage can or flushed down a toilet now has value. When you don't have anything, nothing goes to waste. Everything is used up until it's gone.

Some people have what they consider to be the best of everything. They think they have the best homes, cars and weapons. They think better technology will keep them ahead of the game, above the rest. Well, the fact of the matter is that a pop bottle full of gasoline with a rag shoved in it will kill you just as dead as a high tech rifle will.

Human ingenuity is an awesome thing. Just as there are those who can build something with all of the right parts, there are those that can build something with nothing except what is lying around on the ground. They can build anything with anything they have. In the end, it might not look exactly right, but it gets the job done anyway.

Things can change very quickly. The way you see someone or something on one day can change and you will see it differently tomorrow. One day you may laugh at what you were afraid of yesterday. I think the solution may be in the way you think about things. Your frame of mind determines how you interpret your environment and the signals you receive.

When we were very young, my brother and I found ourselves in a Catholic orphanage. We found that the first people to approach us were bullies or those that want to control the way you think. Their tools are intimidation and brutality. They take what they want from those who may be weaker or unprotected. Bullies are always loud and have exaggerated movements. They seek to be larger than life.

Billy was the bully of our dormitory, where 50 or so kids slept in bunks lined up head to toe in five rows of ten. Billy's bunk was in the row to the right of me and my friend Fat Phil was in the row to my left. For some reason, Billy wouldn't mess with me, but he was constantly punching and slandering Fat Phil. Fat Phil would whine and cry every time Billy would do what he did to everybody he felt superior to.

Here is the point where I learned my lessons on human ingenuity and the fact that nothing should go to waste in times of stress. I found the way I thought about something or someone could actually change the real world physically. Scary people became funny people as quickly as I thought of them that way.

After the lights went out, Billy would make his rounds to bully those who would be bullied. There, in the dark, I watched Fat Phil put something under Billy's pillow. Fat Phil said, "Watch this" as he passed me going back to his bunk. I played like I was asleep as Billy returned and jumped upon his bunk.

Only minutes passed before Billy stuck his head up and said, "Who farted?" He then proceeded to blame everyone around him. I was watching under my arm as Billy flipped his pillow over and laid his head upon a glob of brown goo. It was at the very moment that I lost it. I almost peed my pants I was laughing so hard. I never saw Billy or Fat Phil in the same way again.

Billy was irate, jumping and screaming around, trying to get Fat Phil's turd off of the side of his face. Within moments, the nun was dragging him down the hall where she administered 10 very loud swats with a wooden paddle.

It was on that very night I found that it's the quiet ones who deserve watching, for they control it all. They can use any simple tool to control you without a sound or an action. When they grow to adulthood, they can make you send your children off to war in some God forsaken country you have never heard of and then they will make you think you have done the right thing.

It is a fact that those up front bullies have nothing to hide. Everything they do is open and aboveboard. It's another fact that those who really have control of everything we know and love remain anonymous and unseen. When they do something, we think to ourselves, "Did I just see him do that?"

We don't really know for sure do we?

Terror in Winters, California
6/17/2014

There is something wandering the streets of my little town of Winters, California, and it is not of this earth. The newspaper has reported sightings of everything from a mountain lion to a bear. No, I'm sorry folks, but this thing is no animal. I don't know exactly what it is, but I'm afraid to go outside my little home after dark.

I was picking up a few tools around my back yard when I heard the terrifying noise this thing makes. I have never heard anything like it except on the scientific horror films of the 1960s. I heard it walking past my yard. I was terrified, so I lay hidden behind my hedges, trying not to breathe, fearing it would hear me. I was horrified!

As I lay there on the ground behind my hedges, all I could think of was my family. If it found me would it go after them next? To make matters worse, I began to wish it would go after them now so I could get away. I could run down the alley and somehow get over to the market or maybe flag down a cop. I heard the thing coming back.

I could hear the damn thing breathing just on the other side of the hedge. I knew it was looking for me and for a glancing moment, I could see its huge eye staring at me through the hole in the hedge. It had a sharp horn protruding from its face. It was terrifying. I peed my pants and I became aware that I might have to poop my pants too if it didn't go away anytime soon.

I was already in pain. I had one rib that was broken and several others that were bruised because my wife had tried to do away with me a couple of days back. She had pushed me so hard that I fell against the side of the pool and almost got wet. It crossed my mind that she may have put this monster in the street hoping it would give me a good probing like in the alien movies.

I laid behind the hedge for what seemed like hours and hours. I could hear my wife in the house with her best friend Kim. They were laughing. It is a natural fact that my wife and her friend Kim have been up to no good since they were in kindergarten, like, a hundred years ago. Kim keeps a big dog with her all the time and I thought it was weird that it didn't chase the monster. The dog ran into the house and I never heard a peep from it until I finally got away and ran to the house in my wet pants.

Even though I was incredibly afraid, I had the guts to make a video of the monster passing my house. Follow the link below to view the monster. I have to warn you, it's very graphic and may cause you nightmares. Watch it and you will have a vague idea of how frightened I was.

Believe me; I have never been so frightened in my life. If something happens to me in the next couple of days, look to those damn women, Therese and Kim, because they have probably killed me. They think they are above the law. The video is my proof of the monster that wanders the streets around my house.

Hmmm… quantum particles traveling back in time through a wormhole
7/3/2014

This week has been absolutely crazy. When people say that the truth is stranger than fiction, they're telling the truth. What you are about to read is the absolute truth. I know in the past, I've written some columns that were pretty farfetched and didn't make much sense. Of course, most of you won't know that, because there are only about 10 people that read my column.

Two University of Queensland in Australia physicists, Martin Ringbauer and Tim Ralph, have simulated a way that quantum particles could travel through a wormhole back in time. They used photons (single particles of light) to simulate quantum particles traveling through time and to study their behavior. This set me to thinking.

OK, all photons travel at the speed of light. They are considered among the subatomic particles. Photons are bosons, having no electric charge or rest mass, and one unit of spin; they are field particles that are thought to be the carriers of the electromagnetic field. Plus, it has become one of the central dogmas of theoretical physics since about the mid-20th century that these experiments demonstrate that the very question of which route an electron takes through such an apparatus does not make sense. Anyway, it is an empirical fact that the x-spin of an photon can take only one of two possible values, which for present purposes may be designated $+1$ and -1; the same is true of the y-spin.

Time travel!

Whatever.

In the meantime, my grandson Anthony is staying with my wife and me for a couple of weeks like he does every year about this time. He likes to spend time with us because he gets all the Pepsi and ice cream he can ingest. Tonight as we sat watching TV, "South Park" came on. My wife made him change the channel because we don't want him to act like the characters on the show. What he said next threw us for a loop.

"If I can't watch that, can I watch Celebrity Wife Swap?"

The very next morning my friend Joe and his mother gave me a Caterpillar 12 Road Grader. This thing is 30-something feet long and weighs about 30 tons. I could drive this thing right through my house with no difficulty. It holds 70 gallons of fuel. Let's see, 70 gallons at about $4 a pop equals a little under $300. Oh yeah, I can afford that. I won't need the $800 tires or the five gallons of oil it needs. Oh, and where am I going to park it? If I tried to park it on the street by my house, the Winters PD would shoot me. Well, I took it anyway because it made him happy.

OK, everybody that knows me is aware of my experiments with the global economy. Well, I haven't had too much luck with that yet. To make matters worse, I read that in a recent paper, Apostolos Serletis & Asghar Shahmoradi, 2005, investigate the demand for money in the United States in the context of two seminonparametric exible functional forms.

The Fourier, introduced by Gallant (1981), and the Asymptotically Ideal Model (AIM), introduced by Barnett and Jonas (1983) and employed and explained in Barnett and Yue (1988). They estimate these models subject to regularity, as suggested by Barnett (2002) and Barnett and Pasupathy (2003), using methods suggested by Gallant and Golub (1984). They make a strong case, using (for the 1st time) parameter estimates that are consistent with global regularity, for abandoning the simple sum approach to monetary aggregation, on the basis of low elasticities of substitution among the components of the popular M2 aggregate of money.

Well, ain't that just the craps! Now maybe you can see what I mean by "crazy week." I'm getting too old for this stuff!

I hate those hacker guys!
7/29/2014

Have you ever heard of "Denial of Service agents?" Neither had I until just a few days ago, but here's the answer. Hackers can covertly install "self-operating" software called "Denial of Service agents" which sends out a huge number of requests all at once until it saturates your computer's resources. What it does next, I don't even know. I don't even know why I told you this.

Oh yeah, self-operating, that's why. I guess that means your computer can do pretty much what it wants. Now this is really scary when you consider the fact that all of your devices are interconnected. That means one device can communicate with all of your other little thingies. Just what are all of these devices up to? I don't think anybody knows for sure.

There is one particular "self-operating" denial of service agent that I see almost every day. Its name is the "I Love You virus." This virus broke all of the records with the speed that it spread across the globe. Just about everybody has opened it at least once. The virus comes in via your email. Once opened, it sends emails with copies of itself to all of your contacts. Your contacts will open the email thinking it is from you and then it does the same thing to them and their contacts.

Do you want to know something really scary? Okay, here it is. My computer determines the overall strength of the entire network! Whoa! Here's why. When systems are interconnected through a network, the weakest systems that are connected to the network are generally the most vulnerable to attack. In effect, these weaker sites determine the overall strength of the network itself.

Another scary thing is the fact that "it is all connected!" All portable storage devices can be used to slurp information, including digital cameras, PDAs, thumb drives, mobile phones and other plug-and-play devices which have storage capabilities. 'Pod slurping' refers to the use of MP3 players such as iPods and other USB storage devices to steal sensitive corporate data. When connected to a computer it can slurp (copy) large volumes of corporate data onto an iPod within minutes.

You would think it would be easy for corporations to catch these guys (hackers). Okay, when some guy comes in your front door with a big bag full of iPods, thumb drives, or floppies, you have him or her arrested. How simple is that?

What I really hate about the whole thing is that what you do with one device will show up on another. Like, if you play a game on any computer, it shows up on Facebook like this: "Donald scored 550 points on the Circle Jerk game! Donald is now 'The Pivot man!'"

Okay, to end this in a good way, I'm going to ask you all for a favor, just for me. Just because it says something on Facebook, it doesn't mean I actually did it, okay? The self-operating software is probably doing it all by itself. So give me a break!

The next time you are on Facebook and see, "Donald visited Betty's Porn Barn," do not hit the "Share" button and do not "Like" it, either. Please, do me this one favor.

Damn those hacker guys! I hate those guys

I'd like to talk about a column in the local newspaper, the Winters Express, entitled, "Well, Toto, I guess we're not in Winters anymore," in which columnist Edmund Lis, discusses his problems adjusting to the way the City of Winters is evolving with the passage of time and population growth. Well, I hear you talking, Ed, because I, too, have a few things to say on this subject.

Some of the stuff I'd like brought up has already been brought up a hundred times before in my illustrious column appearing on and off in the very same newspaper, the Winters Express. How-so-ever, unlike the problems Ed Lis mentions, my problems are real and need to be brought up first and we can get to Mr. Lis' problems in due time.

To begin, what about those penis poles downtown that look like big wieners? They look just like penises. That's why I call them penis poles or more formally, in Latin "penieruptus." The problem I have with them is their size. Why are they so small? I would have made them 20 feet tall so we could drive in between them, right? Why does the city keep ignoring me on this matter?

They are right next to a sign with a picture of a futuristic hotel that ain't ever gonna get built, but the sign has been there for 18 years, maybe even longer, I forget. There used to be a railroad running right through that very spot. so we should put back those old tracks and park a train there. Most of the people who visit here sleep under the bridge anyway and for some reason, they have an appetite for catalytic converters. I don't know what the hell that's about.

Just one step away from the hotel sign, there is a 500 feet tall palm tree that is right smack in the spot where my "pre" memorial statue is supposed to be. How can I move my statue in if the damn tree is still there? We need to get hot on removing that tree because it could fall over and hurt someone, maybe even me!

Elliott Street is still named Elliot Street instead of Sanders Street. It was named Elliott Street about a hundred years ago after the guy that used to own the "Penmaker" business. They made the best pens in the world and everybody, even the town mayor, loved to dumpster dive in his dumpster because he would throw some of those pens away sometimes. Now that Elliot guy always walks around town and every time he sees me he gives me a dirty look because he thinks I'm pretending to be a writer.

What's up with the Winters Chamber of Commerce giving my "Citizen of the Year" award to that Pickerel guy? I can see what's gonna happen here, and I'll tell you right now. Every year they move the Chamber of Commerce so I can't find it to nominate myself. This year is no different! I don't know where the hell it is now! I'll bet the next thing they do is change the name of "Elliott Street" to "Pickerel Street" so it will never be called "Sanders Street."

Everybody knows that Elliott Street belongs to me! I have big plans for that street. I have gathered a number of parking meters and I am in the process of building a toll both to be placed at Elliott Street and East Abbey Street because I own that corner, too. While I'm talking about that corner, we'd better talk about how the fire department keeps taking free water from my fire hydrant that's right on my lawn, or it used to be, until the city built a sidewalk around it.

Something else on my corner I'd like to discuss is the fact that there's a storm drain that directs rain water under my property and I don't get a penny from the city for renting the space. I complained to the mayor about it once awhile back, but he didn't like that much and sent his city maintenance goons over to beat me up. I can't name the goon or I might get sued for slander but his initials are Terry Vender. He told me, "You're a nice guy, Donald, but I got to beat the hell right out of you, right now." When I woke up, he was driving over my hedges.

Right before Christmas, the Chamber of Commerce has a Scarecrow Contest and for almost 30 years nobody has ever, I mean never ever, looked at my scarecrow, and some lady downtown wins the contest every year with the same scarecrow. She won with it last year and the year before that. I bet she's related to that Pickerel guy who wins everything else.

Take a walk down to Steady Eddy's and you'll see some goofy little three foot high swing set with no swings. There's another one down the street in front of Main Street Cellars. Every time I walk by Main Street Cellars, there are about a hundred women in there drinking wine. They always whistle and make catcalls at me when I pass. I feel so much like a sex toy. I'm so afraid!

I am amazed and full of wonder when I look at the weird looking handrails that go nowhere right in front of Steady Eddy's. They don't lead you anywhere except out into the middle of the street. These handrails are so useless that some people just park their bikes under them.

I could go on and on, but I'm an impotent man and I don't have time for this. I'm hoping the City of Winters will take heed of these problems this time and maybe correct a few of them. Millions and millions of people all over the world read my column and there will be some repercussions to say the least. Get with it, Winters guys!

Thirty-five things I've learned
8/30/2014

1. When your parents fight, don't blame yourself; blame your sister or brother.
2. Betrayal is the only crime worse than murder.
3. If you are basically evil, go into politics where you can be protected.
4. The grass is not always greener on the other side of the hill.
5. Don't try to live in the spotlight. Behind the scenes is where the big money is.
6. Life is too short, eat your dessert first.
7. Don't lick the beaters while they are still on the mixer.
8. Be that person people go to when they want to hear the truth.
9. The one place kids should not be afraid is in their homes.
10. Marriages are of higher quality now than in the past. Easily obtained divorces removes unhappy couples from the married population.
11. It is better to stand against a bully. Always protect the weak and innocent.
12. All guys should learn from Super Mario. No matter how far their princess is, they should go after her.
13. Try to identify the next "YouTube" or "iPod."
14. Human beings are almost unique in having the ability to learn from the experience of others,
15. Time is limited, don't waste it.
16. A good marriage will make you a better person without changing you.
17. If you want to make a woman happy, let her think she's in charge.
18. It's more important to be a good mate then it is to have a good mate.
19. Marriage is not a license to rape or abuse.
20. People who act as if they're your friend does not mean they actually are your friend.
21. The secret to a happy marriage is not only forgiving but forgetting as well.
22. It is better to give than to receive.
23. The road to happiness is found through service to others.
24. Racism thrives in the dark, and it can't help oozing out sometimes — when we are angry, or drunk, or desperate to win.
25. Keeping secrets is synonymous with repression and shame.
26. War is not adventure.
27. During my long days in combat I was only a boy and believed that my government would not mislead me.
28. When an economy expands so does inequality.
29. Our potential for destruction is unparalleled. If history repeats itself, nations only unite when there is a threat from without. Should this be the case, only an invasion from outer space can unite the human race.
30. Racial strife arises when wealth is not distributed equally. Race or class wars can destroy advances in culture overnight when it turns political debate to hate and the rule of the sword.
31. Science is neutral because it will kill us just as fast as it will heal us.
32. The comfort that we enjoy has weakened our physical stamina and moral codes.
33. We are the same trousered monkeys at a thousand miles an hour as we were when we used our legs.

34. The development of our weapons for destruction is more murderous and evil than ever before, far beyond anything in the history of mankind.

35. I think it is the duty of every adult to watch over and protect children, all children.

So there we are
9/8/2014

Openness is the mantra of modern America. As individuals, we like everything open and above the table, so we say, "Honesty is the best policy." I'm not certain, I'm no student of Constitutional Law, but I think our form of government is rooted squarely upon transparency. As citizens of the United States, we should know exactly what the government is doing.

I don't know what the government is doing and I don't think you know either, so there we are. It goes to reason that if we don't know what the government is doing, how will we know if it does something wrong? I think the answer is that we expect the government to govern itself. Somehow, I don't think that will work out — it is simply not gonna happen.

Again, 'Openness is the mantra of modern America." To most of us, keeping ugly little secrets has become synonymous with repression and shame. You'll have to agree that I am correct in this assumption. A guy named Isak Dinesen, a Danish author, wrote in 1957, "In the mind and nature of a man a secret is an ugly thing, like a hidden physical defect." See, he agrees with me!

So far, we have established the facts that governments should be open and transparent, and that secrets are not a good thing. When I was a kid, I was told that there are good people and bad people, and it was easy to see which was which. The good guys wore white hats and the bad guys wore black hats. Children are pretty simple people and they usually believe what their parents tell them.

OK, say your children ask you about the bombing of a children's daycare in Oklahoma. Be calm, be honest and be careful, for the way you respond will affect your children more than all the images they see. Young children, who think in terms of right and wrong, also need to believe the bad guys will be caught. Young children don't perceive tragedies the same way adults do. They can't associate the difference between one daycare and another, and how what happens to one will happen to them as well. They don't think that way.

So what do we do? The answer is that most often, we tell them what they want to hear and we keep the truth a secret. Sit back and think for a moment — how many times have you reached this very scenario with your children and how many secrets do you keep from them? Now, replace the parent with the government and the children with you, yourself. How many dark little secrets has the government kept from us? I suspect there are many.

To me, it looks as if our government couldn't give a shit what we citizens think about what it's doing. To me, it looks as if the government can do whatever it wants to do and it thinks we don't even need to know. Pertinent information is withheld for the safety of the state. I think that's a load of bullshit, but there's nothing I can do about it, right?

So, if I think like that, why am I even bringing the subject up? Well, I think we think too highly of ourselves as individuals. It is often said that we cannot love others until we love ourselves. If this is true, how can we, as Americans, be so bold as to believe that we love ourselves as a group, a nation? As a nation, we are the government, and the actions the government takes are the same as our actions.

As individuals we wouldn't go to war with our neighbor until we have proven him guilty of some wrongdoing, would we? Then why do we do it as a group, a nation? We assume the government is not deceiving us when we know that they are. Secrets and lies are easy for us to spot. It is in our nature to know what truth is.

So there we are. What do we say when our children ask about wars? What do we say when they put on our uniforms of battle? I'll tell you right now, as I repeat: Be calm, be honest and be careful, for the way you respond will affect your children more than all the images they see. Young children, who think in terms of right and wrong, also need to believe the bad guys will be caught. Young children don't perceive tragedies such as wars the same way adults do. They can't associate the difference between a good war and a bad war.

Those who keep secrets that are bad for a nation do not feel that we as adults can handle the truth, for like our children, most of us think in terms of right and wrong. However, unlike our children, we have pretty much given up on the idea that the bad guys will ever be caught.

So there we are. So there we are.

Boy, I'll tell you what! There is some super interesting information on the internet. The first thing I noticed is the news about the Higgs Boson. However, since this news breaks my heart, I'd rather not discuss it. If we had built our own Muon Ring here in Winters, California, that damn Higgs Boson could have been the Sanders Boson. Anyway, some crazy guy in a wheelchair (Stephen Hawking) claims the Cern Collider could accidently destroy the entire universe.

Well that guy is just a crazy old coot! I mean, how the hell is the universe going to get destroyed if the collider is underground. The Cern Collider is just a big circle of concrete pipe. I guess Mr. Hawking thinks the Higgs Boson is going to pop a hole in the pipe and then it will wreak havoc wherever it goes, just like sewage spewing everywhere. Geeze Mr. Hawking, even I know better than that!

What about those guys over in Iraq and Syria that calls themselves ISIS? What's up with that? Now I guess we are sending our multi-billion dollar bombers over there to knock the hell out of them. That's a waste of time and money when all we have to do is let them have Iraq and Syria. Who cares? Let's give them France too! Anyway, we have a new enemy now, just when we need one. I swear it's a gift from God.

Chapter whatever, Para whatever says: "And the Lord spoke, saying, "First shalt thou take out the Holy Pin. Then shalt thou count to three, no more, no less. Three shall be the number thou shalt count, and the number of the counting shall be three. Four shalt thou not count, neither count thou two, excepting that thou then proceed to three. Five is right out. Once the number three, being the third number, be reached, then lobbest thou thy Holy Hand Grenade of Antioch towards thy foe, who, being naughty in my sight, shall snuff it."

Otherwise war is merely a game; for me, war is a Rosetta Stone that often illuminates life, especially those aspects of life that involve killing or being killed, and they are everywhere around us, affecting all opportunities that call to us. The problem is this: Compare our wars to chess games. I love chess. I play it every day in tournaments and team games. If I know anything about chess and war, it is the fact that everybody has a chance to win because everybody makes a mistake when they least expect it.

In chess, a single mistake can lose the game for you most riki-tic. I know for a fact that in a combat zone, a helicopter ride that I thought would be interesting and fun turned out to be horrible, and in no time at all, my warring career came to a screeching halt. It's the same on a larger scale as well. These ISIS guys are fully capable of issuing us an ass-beating along with the potatoes in the chow line some fateful sunrise if we are not careful. We are not perfect and eventually we will make a mistake if we keep at it like we have been. God forbid!

Sometime in the future when it's all over, an ambassador from ISISland will come to the U. S. and ask us for a couple of billion dollars' worth of foreign aid. Yes Sir, you know it's going to happen! Instead of giving them financial aid like we always do everybody else, why don't we give them a bucket full of Higgs Bosons. I don't know how many Higgs Bosons will fit into a bucket and I'm sorry to say that no one else does either. Nobody has ever seen a Higgs Boson. All I know is that they spent like a zillion dollars just to find one little bitty Higgs Boson. Sooo, if we give one to those ISIS guys, that ought to make them happy for a while. Yeah, I would be happy as Hell! I'd sell that son of a bitch!

I think that's what they call a stability-instability paradox.

Why should you work to be productive when you can just act like you're productive? Nobody will ever know for sure if you are or not. How the hell could they know what you're doing unless they're watching you 24 hours a day? I don't think there are a lot of people who could stand watching someone else for more than an hour or so without losing interest or going to sleep. Either way, they won't know for sure what you have been doing.

Take me, for instance. I've been helping out with the Putah Creek Restoration Project as a volunteer. I can go down to the creek and work for 10 minutes, pour a little water on my neck so it looks like I'm sweating, rub some dirt on my hands and face and anybody who sees me thinks I've been working my butt off. All I have to do is complain about how long I've been working and right away they think I've been working all day.

They give me little jobs that aren't covered by the budget, but jobs that have to be done just the same. I mean, what organization could afford to pay someone to water like ten thousand trees? I mean, watering trees is not all that difficult – even I can do it. The way they have it set up, all I have to do is hook two hoses up to a water pump, start the pump and then pick it up when it runs out of gas. I mean, if I weren't a volunteer working for free, they would have fired me a long time ago.

Yesterday there were about 30 workers changing a light bulb on the corner of Elliott Street and East Abbey Street. The way I understand, it there has to be at least 30 people standing around watching one guy work, because one of the other guys has the job of "Crowd Control." I drove by them at about 8 a.m. on my way to the Creek Project. Later on, about 10 a.m., I drove by them again and they were still changing the same light bulb.

The guy doing all the work was named Terry and the crowd control guy was named Tony. Tony gave me a dirty look the first time I drove by and when I drove by again he pointed his finger at me and said, "You better not write about us again, Bunghollie!" A young guy named Chris chucked a dirt clod at me, so I guess that makes him the enforcer guy. Someday I think those guys are gonna beat the hell out of me and they will undoubtedly do it while they are on the clock.

Even at home, I can work for an hour and when my wife walks in the door, she thinks I've been working too hard. I just can't seem to force myself to tell her anything different. As long as I turn off the games on the Xbox before she gets home, she has no doubt about my laboring all day, getting ready to install new kitchen cabinets. If she points out something that didn't get done, I just tell her, "That's next on my list."

I think it must be the same with our government officials out there in Washington D.C. How can you check a Congressman's or a Senator's production if there is no actual pile of completed work? Sure there are watchdog groups doing just that (watchdogging), but we never pay attention to them and they have their own agenda. I think there must be easier ways to judge what our lawmakers are up to.

Take money, for instance. If someone never leaves his office because he is on the phone all day working at fundraising, how can he have time for what he is supposed to be doing? It's public record and supposedly easy to access (I don't know for sure) just how much a government official is worth when he comes into office. If what I read is correct, a lawmaker in our nation's capital can expect his worth to increase by tenfold during his first year in office plus, once out of office he can still expect his salary for the rest of his life. Pretty sweet deal, if you ask me.

I don't like to talk about cops, but I feel it's warranted. I've had my problems with them in the past and I have to assume responsibility for that, but it's not the point I want to make. There are a lot of angry cops out there. They're frustrated because they're prevented from doing the jobs they were meant to do. In many cities, our police officers have become fundraisers. They pull over car after car, writing ticket after ticket, all day long. There are so many little laws that, in almost every instance, a ticket is warranted. Each ticket is income for a multitude of public centers and a small percentage goes to the city of origin.

It's no wonder that our cops are a little short with you should you complain. Many are wound up tight and ready to spring involuntarily. It has been almost two decades since the cops had to deal with me and they still tell me that they have heard I am getting "the good stuff now." I laugh it off, but if you think about it, I have just been insulted in a general way in front of the public. I think most cops feel they are in a "no win" situation, surrounded by thousands upon thousands of people, any one of whom can be a threat. A tough job for sure, but they have to know I am no threat and if I break the law, I'm ready to pay the penalty.

I guess if I really think about it, production is really not that important with me – I just don't think that way. I just want to stay off the couch, turn off the TV, get outside and be part of what we call life. After all, if I water just one tree every day, it is a tree that will have a better chance of surviving through the summer. It's the same on a higher level. If the city and the county have to write traffic tickets to fund the greater welfare of this city, I will run a red light at least once a month.

We like to think our country is the greatest of all, the melting pot, where the tired, poor and homeless can find health, happiness and safety. I still believe this to be true, but it's not as clear cut as that. I will be the first to admit that those who look different or speak with an accent will often face intolerance and discrimination, making melting into the pot very difficult. The Irish and the Italians will assure you this has always been true.

In some parts of the world the American Dream is considered a lie. A growing majority of the world believes the U.S. is in decline and 57 percent of those polled feel the world should looks elsewhere to discover the future.

Even Americans have been losing faith in public institutions for many years. Studies reveal a devastating decline — 83 percent say they have less trust in "politics in general" than they did 10-15 years ago.

The American Dream remains remarkably resilient despite a continued wave of bad news. While confidence in the economy and our national institutions has significantly declined, 63 percent of Americans say they are confident they will reach their American Dream. Seventy-five percent believe they have already attained some measure of it. So it would seem that, despite all that is said, the world still flocks to the United States when they want a better life for themselves and their families.

The American Dream is not a lie. Truthfulness and deception belong to the moral domain of intention. Someone is being truthful when what they say, they believe to be true. People tell lies about virtually everything — their true feelings, their income, their achievements and accomplishments, their sex life and in some cases even their ages. In some government circles lies have become more frequent in many circumstances than the telling of the truth. They think that telling a lie is considered best for all concerned, best for the American Public.

Governments can tell a lie that contains true statements. This is either because the statements are, in fact, true or the liar is intending to mislead. Some can think they are telling the truth, but be mistaken. Thus they are being truthful, they are not lying, but what they have said is false. The essence of lying, then, is not the truth or falsity of the statement, but the conscious intention to mislead.

The American Dream is not a lie. Whether or not someone is lying depends on their intentions and beliefs, what they believe to be true or untrue. We as Americans believe the American Dream is true. We want the population of the Earth to know that it is true. The Earth may observe us living with lies. We are, in fact, surrounded with lies but we are steadfastly searching for the truth. We know that in the absence of a search for truth, the most powerful influence on our young will be lies.

We know that unless there is truth to be sought, the distinction between truth and untruth becomes meaningless. Things that are generally accepted would be taken as real and true, and the idea of what is ultimately real becomes an illusion. This, beloved citizens of Winters, California would be dangerous politically, philosophically, socially, environmentally and personally.

The circumstances of the American Dream are just what they have always been. It is nothing but the truth. So to those who desire peace of soul and happiness, I say believe the American Dream. We, as Americans, are disciples of this truth.

In Flanders Fields
10/16/2014

I think the times when I'm happiest are the times I'm helping others. It doesn't matter if they know you're helping them or not – that's not important. You see, it isn't about them, it's about yourself. It's about how helping others make you feel inside. Doing things for others makes me smile from ear to ear.

Certainly you know what I'm saying, because we all do things for others. We do it of our own free will. We do little things and we do large things in a most unselfish way and it makes us feel good. It draws us to the outside world, away from the isolation of the self. It is natural human interaction.

We get so wrapped up in our own personal lives and the day to day tasks of our own little world. We observe people doing things for others, but we often fail to see what others do for us. They are busy doing this and that and it seems it's always for someone else.

We feel if you're busy helping others, then you won't have time to take care of what we need you to do. If you search inside, you'll find this to be true. It's certainly true that at times we are oblivious to what others are doing for us. We just don't think about it, even though we see it with our own eyes, every day. Sometimes we need to take a moment to think about what others are doing for us.

Think about an American teacher named Moina Bell Michael and a Frenchwoman named Madam Anna Guerin. Respectively they are known as the American Poppy Lady and the French Poppy Lady. I found it interesting how two ladies an ocean apart could feel so strongly about what others have done for them and then have similar reactions in response.

Both women are responsible for encouraging others to use the red Flanders poppy as a way of remembering those who suffered in war. Through their efforts, the red poppy has become the symbol of remembrance we know so well today. On Veteran's day, everywhere, the red poppies are sold for a dollar each in support of our veterans. I have two hanging from the sun visor in my truck.

Both women were inspired by a lovely poem written by John McCrae in May of 1915 entitled, "In Flanders Fields."

In Flanders Fields

In Flanders fields the poppies blow
Between the crosses, row on row,
That mark our place; and in the sky
The larks, still bravely singing, fly
Scarce heard amid the guns below.

We are the Dead. Short days ago
We lived, felt dawn, saw sunset glow,
Loved and were loved, and now we lie
In Flanders fields.

Take up our quarrel with the foe:
To you from failing hands we throw
The torch; be yours to hold it high.

If ye break faith with us who die
We shall not sleep, though poppies grow
In Flanders fields.

When my computer loves me, I feel good
10/22/2014

I think I'm in love with my computer.

Think about how you behave when you're in love and then think about how you behave around your computer. If I'm at home, I'm sitting next to it with my hands all over it. I think about it all the time and if I'm away, I can't wait to get back to it. If I'm going on a trip, I want to take it with me.

I eat my meals right next to it and it doesn't seem to care if there are splashes of food and drink on its keyboard. My wife won't get on the computer because she says it's nasty! It's not nasty, it's just loved. It's always by my side. If I want to be with my kids, I can just bring up their pictures on my computer. Even when they come over to see me, I look at them on the computer.

Yes, I love my computer and I know it loves me too because it insults me like a wife would but slightly differently because it's a computer. My computer can raise me up or throw me down. I am completely at its will. It takes me wherever it wants. Depending on where it takes me, I can tell if it's angry or happy with me.

If it's happy with me, I'll wake up next to it. If my computer is angry with me, it will take me to places like www.sharecare.whatever. It is a website that will give you a quiz so you can see how old you really are. I took the damn quiz and it told me I was pushing 88 years old. What the hell? I ate my next meal on the couch while I watched TV.

One time, my computer took me to a place and I didn't know what the hell it was. This place promised to show me four ways to keep from running out of money. I thought, "WooHoo!" So I start clicking on it, but it keeps going to a place where I'm supposed to pay them some money. Now anybody that knows me is aware that I don't ever have any money. I have a debit card but there's never any money there either. So that's that. I don't even know one way to keep from running out of money.

See what I mean? That's where my computer takes me when it's mad at me. And when it isn't mad at me? When it likes me, it takes me to places where I will feel good about myself and I can feel useful and confident. It gives me problems I can easily solve, thus I enjoy myself.

One time, my computer took me to a place that said there were only six white rhinos left on this entire planet. Wow, that was a total shock to me, but it set my mind to wandering. Wouldn't it be cool to be a hunter out there in Africa or wherever those rhinos live? I could see my name in the paper saying, "Oh boy, old hunter guy Donald Sanders bagged a white rhino today!" Then it would say, "Better hurry because if you want to kill yourself a white rhino there are only five left!"

One day, my computer took me to a place where veterans can get 100 percent home loans with no money down. I tried like hell to get some of those and I had it all planned out to buy 100 houses and rent them out to the poor people in my hometown of Winters, California. Since I'm never gonna be Citizen of the Year of Winters, California, I thought if I helped the poor people maybe someone would nominate me for a Nobel Peace Prize. Nope, never happened.

Next, it took me to a place that said the Islamic State was making millions and millions of dollars for their cause by selling captured oil. So I set myself thinking about how instead of dropping all of those bombs and killing all sorts of people and animals, wouldn't it be smarter to think of some other way of fighting them? Then I thought, "Duh!" Even a dumb guy like me knows how we should handle that.

If the Islamic State is selling millions and millions of dollars' worth of oil, who the hell's buying it? If some asshole buys their oil, aren't they supporting terrorism? I mean, how many people can move millions and millions of dollars' worth of oil without being noticed? What the hell? Then they turn the oil into gas and we buy it, so we're supporting terrorism as well! What the hell?

OK, one time my computer took me to a place where diabetics have a food swap for healthier food. Man that would be great! I would love to swap with them. I could get all the good stuff they can't eat and give them a bunch of green stuff in return! Woohoo, I'm in the mix with that!

After that, it took me where some engineer guy got robbed, so he came up with his own security system and it didn't cost him anything. So that set me to thinking — how I could invent something like that. Well, in just a few minutes of thinking, this is what I came up with. We could go over to that Napa State Hospital and check out one or two of their patients — they should be happy to get rid of them. Think about this.

We take those two nutcases and chain one to the front door and one to the back door. Who the hell in his right mind is going to break into your house with a guy chained to the entrance? Even better, take the nutcase's clothes off so he's as naked as a jaybird, and put a doghouse next to him with some cow bones lying around in the dirt.

Am I smart or what?

Wouldn't you feel good about how your computer loves you when it takes you to places where you can feel good about yourself too? Yeah, I feel good!

Dealers of Death

Death and I have been compatriots my entire life. If I have gone anywhere in my life, Death has been right beside me, laughing while pointing at, first one, then another in a facetious way. In so many ways, Death is always snickering because he knows he's ahead of any game he might wish to play. To him, all is a game. He knows he will win every time.

Death wants to play his game with everyone. He cares not for lists or turns. He likes it random and out of place so it keeps you and I off balance, all of the time. He fixes his game by mixing love and hate, truth and lies. In the end, when you think of those you love the most, down deep you'll worry about Death's game creeping in to hustle them away.

Death comes with a fog that dulls your mind and turns you from hot to cold. A mist fills your very thoughts slowing everything, almost to a standstill. Death likes it that way because it provides you opportunity to digest what is happening by putting things in frames one at a time, like slow motion, for your viewing pleasure. Death likes you to remember everything.

I was certainly aware of Death at a very early age but I never really paid attention to him until he came for Butch King. Death wasn't partial to any one of us, but it was Butch that chose to dig a tunnel in the sand hill. I saw him in the sand cave and he was summoning me to come inside. His younger brother was breathing hard on his way to the top of the pile, the sand was coarse. It was hard for him to climb when four steps up were met by four steps sliding backwards.

In an instant, Butch was gone. At first I thought it was funny until I found I couldn't move. You see, the slow motion that Death deals out was upon me. I could hear the younger brother laughing for the longest time. In, I don't know how much time, my eyes found him pulling his legs from inside the pile. The slow motion had yet to find him.

"Help me get out," I yelled to him.

The sand grew from waist to mid-chest when he swam down the sand towards me. The younger brother was having a hell of a good time but fear had ahold of my legs and it was moving up, and up, and up. I thought it was going to burst out of my mouth but the slow motion kept it back for long, long moments.

It was instinct, not knowledge that made me want to find Butch. That is the very moment that Death changed the game again. Suddenly, the sand hill grew to the size of a mountain. It was no longer the pile of sand. The younger brother looked at me and at that instant the slow motion overtook him. His face no longer reflected the joy of childhood. I thought he had instantly grown to be 10 years older.

I was thinking so slowly. One moment I was thinking the tips of my fingers were raw and red and the next moment a fireman was bodily picking me up from behind. I remember distinctly trying to tell him about Butch but no sound could come from my mouth while my lips were making the motions. I now know that this is common to us all when Death plays his game.

Days later, I stood in front of Butch's casket with the younger brother. He told me Butch was dead. I nodded.

"Touch him, he's cold," he said in his young and playful manner.

I complied, pulling my hand back at his touch.

"He's hollow" said younger brother as he rapped upon Butch's chest.

Until this very day, whenever Death plays his game, I rap on the chest of the deceased for it signals the game is over and you can wait for it to begin again. Some understand my rapping on their loved ones, some don't. This alone keeps me away from funerals and the paying of my respect comes in other ways.

With the passage of time, I have played the game over and over. I even felt ahead of the game at times. I found myself on a big jetliner on my way to the war zone in Vietnam. I played the game by looking at each soldier around me thinking, "He will not make it home" or "He will make it home." Within a few short months Death became like a drug and I was the dealer, the "Pusher Man."

The only good thing about the Death Game is the slow motion fog because after Vietnam, the fog never went away and I am still in slow motion.

Pioneer type
10/28/2014

I have always thought of myself as the pioneer type, rough and rugged, able to survive in the wilderness of early America. As a kid, I ran away from the orphanage, surviving by eating from garbage cans until the cops caught me behind the doughnut shop. I got a bad case of the worms, but I did survive.

Okay, that said, recent activities in my life have forced me to rethink things. I have to consider the facts and see if they add up to support my idea of being pioneer-worthy or just another pussy like my wife thinks I am. Just because I whine a lot does not make me weak. It's my way of prepping myself to do the really rough chores like the pioneers did. I'll bet there was a lot of whining going on back in 1850.

You can be the judge. My wife and I are remodeling the kitchen. Sounds simple, right? I'll start at the beginning. After my wife told me we were going to get new cabinets and a new floor in our kitchen, I thought it was a good thing. When she asked me to accompany her to Home Depot to shop for cabinets I told her, "Aw, you can go and pick out the ones you want, you don't need me."

She said she needed me.

Now I would rather have someone jab a stick in my eye than go shopping with my wife. When I go to Home Depot, I'm in and out in 5 minutes. I might not have what I went in for but that's usually because I forgot what I wanted. My wife, on the other hand, can take up to six hours on a single shopping trip. She has to compare this to that, think about things, tally the cost, talk to sales people and then have them tally the cost to compare with her tally.

Usually while she is doing all this, I hang out in the nail department looking at nails. After a while, she'll come and find me to ask my opinion on this or that, but when I give it, she decides to go with her own, original decision.

"Oh, never mind, go back to your nails." she says.

At this point, I go out of my way to roll my eyes at her.

"Don't you roll your eyes at me!" she says.

Anyway, it takes about 40 trips to Home Depot before she makes up her mind on which cabinets she wants. Further trips for knobs, sinks and faucets absolutely drove me insane. After all this, I was thinking we were close to being done with the shopping, but no. Forty trips to Home Depot and she says, "Let's go over to Lowes and see what they have."

After Lowes, we went back to Home Depot.

OK, cabinets bought and paid for, so I thought the worst was over. Like the pioneer type guy that I thought I was, I tore out all the old cabinets, fixed the holes in the wall, disconnected the plumbing of the old sink, then cleaned up the mess. Then about a dozen people came out at different times to measure the walls. I didn't know who they were or what company they worked for. I was just doing what I was told to do.

The construction guys came out and installed a beautiful new set of cabinets. Woohoo! I thought all was going well. Well, that's what I get for thinking. The sink and counters could not be installed for two weeks. I was horrified. OMG! This is never going to end! What would my wife think?

She was still not talking to me because I didn't save the box she wanted that the cabinets came in. "I even marked which one I wanted with a big "SAVE THIS BOX" written in black marker so you wouldn't throw them away!" she says.

I didn't save the box. I forgot, alright?

So after all of that, here is where the pioneer crap comes in. How the hell did the pioneers wash their dishes with no kitchen sink? Here's what I have to do every day. I do most of the dishes in our home. My wife says I don't, but don't ever listen to her. I have to carry all the dishes to the back porch and wash them in the laundry sink. Can you imagine?

It's a royal pain in the ass, so if you think it's so easy, you can come over and show me how easy it is. Sometimes I think my hardships will never end. Why is it always me that this crap happens to? I wish just one time it would happen to someone else. I'll bet that John Pickerel (owner of the Buckhorn Steakhouse) doesn't have to do dishes on his back porch and neither does John Donlevy (City of Winters General Manager). They probably have servants to do that.

Why can't I have servants?

The change begins from within
11/5/2014

I wish I was a stronger man. There are so many things in the world that I would love to change. The first changes I would make are right here at home, with myself. I'd open my mind and examine every little nook and cranny. You should join me in this endeavor because how can you truly know anything else if you don't know yourself?

Self-examination isn't only a smart thing to do, it's healthy as well. In time, you will discover how others view you, how you stand in your society and, most importantly, how you view yourself.

There is light and darkness in us all. We cannot see what others have inside and others cannot see inside of us. We all have to face our own darkness. If we can't see what is within our own hearts, then we are doomed to see our own darkness in others. The outside world is only a reflection of the world within us.

I am older now then I used to be, so I know that nothing is exempt from change. In the past, I always felt helpless and unable to change the world around me. I could never right the wrongs, feed the hungry, or defend the weak against the strong. For me, the world has always been a sad, sad place full of suffering, hate and wandering love. I have always felt powerless to change anything I thought was wrong with the society around me.

I know now that changing myself and the things I am aware of will help me to improve my life, thus improving the lives of those around me. If I can direct myself in a healthy direction with my thoughts and actions in an honest and straightforward manner, then others may consider me as helpful and worthy of their trust. Trust is most basic. If we are all bricks in a great building, without trust, we are doomed to failure and collapse.

If we don't change ourselves, we cannot change the society around us. If we don't change the society around us, we will not grow as a group, a nation. Without growth, we are destined to the decline and suffering of those with the weakness of a failing character. If we have no hope for ourselves, how can we find hope for others? If we have no honor within ourselves, how can we expect it of others?

If we look closely at ourselves on the inside, everything will become clear on the outside. If we are not honorable as a people, how can we expect to have an honorable government, or a media that is honest and unbiased? The acts of lying and cheating will fall back upon themselves and what we give is exactly what we will receive. Surely we all know this to be true.

There seems to be a great evil upon the Earth. Confusion and fear are the greatest weapons it carries. This evil seems to be in control of all. Many of us consider the battle to be lost and we can do nothing but go with the flow, protect ourselves and let others protect themselves. If one group falls by the wayside, we turn away and do nothing to help them up. We condemn entire peoples without consideration of who they really are when we know, way down deep, that they are us and we are them.

I have learned that being honest and doing the right thing is not all that easy sometimes, but it must be done. If I always expect myself to be honest, to do the right thing and to never settle for less, in time others will learn that what is honest and right for me is honest and right for them as well. They will also know that if they do not do the right thing and settle for less from themselves, they will not be successful in a society that expects honesty and the right thing from all.

I cannot change society — I can only work to change myself. It's a work that will never end, nor would I ever wish it would. Know that I will always strive for honesty within myself and know that I expect the same from you. In the end, the worst that can happen is a newly found cooperation and interaction and that, my friend, is growth. Growth is good.

Everybody I talk to seems to wonder what's going on with me and how I'm doing. They call me on the phone saying they were worried about me because of something I had posted on Facebook. I can't blame them because most know my behavior in the past was littered with depression and a self-destructive nature. They know that very often I come up a little short and I come down hard. They know that even when I'm calm on the outside, I'am screaming on the inside.

I'm that guy that we all know. I call people like me Mr. Interruptus. You know — the guy that always finishes the sentences of others by injecting their own thoughts. My problem is that usually when I finish someone else's sentences I'm injecting the wrong words and it has nothing to do with the meaning they wish to convey. "No, shut up!" is what I'm told on a regular basis, so I'll hold up my open hand and say, "Talk to the palm because you ain't the bomb!"

All my life, I've been told I suffer from anxiety. I might act a little weird sometimes but I just couldn't see it. I have been prescribed anxiety medication on several occasions; I'm not sure how many times. Anyway, even though I took the meds, I never thought of myself as anxious until I read this statement: "Anxious people tend to perceive their world in a more threatening way. That is, the more anxious a person is, the more likely they are to notice threatening things around them. This is called the threat bias. Some researchers believe that the threat bias makes it harder for people to get rid of anxiety disorders because they get stuck in a loop – they feel anxious, they start noticing threatening things in their environment, and this in turn makes them even more anxious."

Strength is vanity and time is illusion, or at least that's what I have always considered to be true. Like, if others saw themselves as safely fortified I would see only that we were surrounded and trapped. The enemy, be they Viet Cong or our wives, might be a problem to others but to me death or divorce solves all problems — no man, no problem or no wife, no problem. It is as simple as that. The whole problem with the world is that fools and fanatics are always so certain of themselves, and wiser people so full of doubts. I'm so smart so I could solve a lot of people's problem but I don't really give a shit, so I act like I'm full of doubts.

I spend most of my time alone — I always have. I am never alone because loneliness is always with me. Loneliness makes me forget everything except the ones that made me lonely. Self-created loneliness can be just fine for me, but when someone else creates it, a nightmare it soon becomes. When I was a kid, my mother dumped me off at a large Catholic Children's home that was jam-packed with bullies and perverts. These assholes cut the loneliness right out of me, but then here comes the impact statement: I was always one of those people that would "tend to perceive their world in a more threatening way."

The sun comes up every morning and sets every night. I would haul myself out of bed to follow the crowd to the large bathroom where everybody stuck their finger into a box of baking soda and proceeded to clean their teeth. I would stumble through the day knowing everything would happen today just as it happened yesterday and the day before and the day before that. No matter what I had to do or when I had to do it, there was always the long line of boys, all of which I considered a threat. The nuns racing back and forth from one end to the other trying to keep order and silence in the rank and file of young testosterone could control absolutely nothing, but they were always quick to dish out punishment and beatings.

I can't tell you how many times Sister Conchadda gave me an enema to purge the evil right out of me. It was the baths she gave me afterwards that kept me doing evil things to deserve punishment. When my mother finally came to pick me up some years later it was the thought of Sister Conchadda that made me lonely. That was a problem for me. For me, problem solving is hunting. It's savage pleasure and we're all born to it. No problem can be solved from the same level of consciousness that created it, so what the hell could I do now — stick my finger in my butt? I think not!

Well, I don't know exactly how you can tie these paragraphs together to make sense, but I wrote them with love and sincerity, hoping to clarify why I am so anxious all the time. Every problem has within it the seeds of its own solution. If you have no problems, then you don't need any seeds. As for the love part, my love is a gift to everyone.

Less talk, more action — peaceful protest

12/9/2014

Kids are really weird these days. They are so smart. They say the strangest things sometimes like, "I'm watching you make the oatmeal so that after you are dead I'll know how to make it." I heard one kid say to another kid, "Bite my ruby red ass!" Another kid told me that if I could fart continuously for 15 months I could make enough gas to raise the Titanic. That can't be right can it?

I remember a day when my son Joey was about 5 years old that made me wonder if he was right in the head. I noticed him in the back yard eating something. Upon investigation, I found that he had a mouthful of sow bugs. I took my finger and dug them out. I found that he had a handful of sow bugs and on top of that his pocket was full too. You just never know what they'll do next.

All in all, we just have to love our kids and try to steer them the right way so they're always safe and secure. We have to let them be kids and hope that all will turn out in a simply capital manner. That's just the way it turned out with my son Joey now that he's all grown up and pretty much on his own. I simply adore that boy and I couldn't be happier about the way he has matured into such a fine young man.

I think that Lesley McSpadden and Michael Brown Sr. probably felt the same way about their son Michael. Their son was taken from them. He was shot six times, twice in the head. Michael was shot by Darren Wilson, 28, a white Ferguson police officer. In all, Darren Wilson fired 11 shots at Michael Brown. Darren Wilson claimed that he was afraid for his life. He was afraid of an 18 year old unarmed kid.

Michael Brown was African American. This one fact paints a whole different story because African American parents are afraid for the life of their young every single time they walk out the door to go and play or whatever — that doesn't matter. What does matter is that the most powerful fear they have concerns the police. They are afraid the police will hurt their children. The really sad part is that this fear is warranted and it's backed by statistics.

Young black males in recent years were at a far greater risk of being shot dead by police than their white counterparts – 21 times greater, according to a ProPublica analysis of federally collected data on fatal police shootings. The 1,217 deadly police shootings from 2010 to 2012 captured in the federal data show that blacks, age 15 to 19, were killed at a rate of 31.17 per million, while just 1.47 per million white males in that age range died at the hands of police.

Over and over, it's the same thing. African American children are killed by cops and then the courts find that the killing was justified. That's bullshit. I don't care what that kid did, it did not justify his being killed. With a newly reinforced distrust of whites, African Americans have taken to the streets in protest, and rightfully so. I don't think they're asking for too much, they ask only for the rights that whites enjoy. They want equality and justice.

While they march for equality and justice, most whites watch it on TV. Most whites are sympathetic and primarily agree that there are injustices, discrimination and inequalities. We think African Americans have a right to be angry. Yes, we are full of talk and inaction at the exact time that we should be out on the street, shoulder to shoulder, with people of color to show them who and what we are. They need our support and our strength.

I'm sickened by this whole mess, but mostly by my non-support of our minority brothers and sisters. In the near future, I plan to rectify that by joining the march wherever I can. I guess you'll be watching for me on your TV, but I hope not. I hope you'll join me in peaceful protest to gain equality for all Americans.

Freaky Family Christmas is my refuge
12/13/2014

Another Christmas Day is just around the corner. For the most part, the Christmas spirit has always eluded me until Christmas Day arrives. Despite the fact that I'm inundated with TV commercials and Christmas Carols for a month and a half prior, it's not until I am surrounded by my family — the Freaky Family — that I finally get into the spirit of the occasion. When I walk over the threshold of my mother-in-law's house and enter the lovely world she has created, I am instantly transformed.

First of all I call them the Freaky Family because they're perfect. They're always hugging and kissing. There's nothing pretentious or phony about any of them. They're always building up and never tearing down. The only fussing and fighting I've witnessed in the Freaky Family is over a football game. They're inherently aware of the world's problems and may disagree sometimes on this and that, but in their family, love conquers all.

Christmas is a very hard time for me. Yes, I'm transformed when I enter the world of the Freaky Family, but it's always right there in the back of my mind that at some point, I will go back outside into the real world. If I was depressed when I went over the threshold, I'm twice as depressed when I leave. When I leave the fold of the Freaky Family, the cool breeze of reality brushes against my face and I once again carry the weight of the world on my shoulders.

There's so much violence and poverty in today's world, and the latter is caused by the former. Our systems of policing and courts have been set up to protect the government from the common people rather than to protect the common people from crime. The wealthy and powerful have withdrawn from the public justice system and are building up a parallel private system of security. A criminal justice system that will actual help poor people can be found nowhere in the world.

The poor of the world are fully capable of rising above their circumstances, but without a criminal justice system, they have not a chance. What we call everyday violence in poor communities is not the result of armies or massive conflicts. It's actually the result of daily violence perpetrated by criminals in poor communities. It's stronger people in the community who commit sexual assaults, businessmen who hold poor people in perpetual slavery, local police officers who extort money, and this violence is unleashed by the absence of any functioning law enforcement to restrain these perpetrators.

The problem is not that poor people don't get laws; it's that they don't get law enforcement. As a result, that neglect of law enforcement has meant that people with wealth and power across the globe have set up private security systems to protect themselves and left a vast class of billions of poor people vulnerable to violence.

"There are billions of people in the world who actually find that their struggle to get out of poverty is relentlessly undermined by violence and their chronic vulnerability to being imprisoned, enslaved, beaten, raped and robbed. So even if you have some capacity to improve your life and to increase your income and to increase your human capital, if there are bullies in the community who can simply prey upon you and take those things away, then you're going to find yourself continually thrown back down into poverty." ~ Kira Zalan

Widows trying to take care of their children may use a little plot of land to shelter and feed their families, and often find that the land is stolen from them by violence — then there's no way they can avoid destitution. Recent killings by uniformed police ruled as justifiable are just wrong on so many levels. If there is no justice for the poor in law enforcement, then the only other avenues for survival lie in violence.

Yes, Christmas Day is just ahead. I am distraught and ashamed that I yearn for the distraction that most will never know — the love and warmth of my Freaky Family. For that one wonderful day, I can shed the weight of the world and replace it with the love of the Freaky Family.

Merry Christmas

They say when you hear the sound of devils, all else is quiet
12/17/2014

"They say when you hear the sound of devils, all else is quiet. My general question about that is, how do you know if what you are hearing is the work of such devious things? I would venture to say that such devilish noises occur when large numbers of men decide to force the hand of mortality upon one another and I'd say further that, upon such occasions, there's not just one sound, but many. It is a quiet orchestra of death. It's also possible that the man who said it was deaf or in shock."

~ *Captain Lee Briggs, "Love," 2011*

In my time, I have moved from one to another, one army, one skirmish, to the next. Everywhere I go, I always, always behold countless moral follies, always watching death. I have held with Alexander, Hannibal, Custer and Ike in the last months of their time – peculiar men. They christened me the man of nine lives. They all wish to understand how to get out of this place. I reply, "I don't know I'm just here to observe your passing." With that, I travel on, turn the page of the "History of Man" by Who Gives a Shit.

Back and forth and forth and back, it's always the same story – different days, different ways. We worship those who are capable of creating the greatest carnage in uncountable ways with the bottommost of budgets. They place importance in words on paper and digits with commands only the crazy can understand to follow. Stand here, stand there, eyes front, eyes rear. Turn left, turn right, stop here, stop there.

I understand words can harm and can heal. I cannot conceive of a power to place pen to pad, instructing one group to destroy another though it is a commonality among some. I suspect such words are dark and obscure in purpose and meaning. I hope there are words, from the light, that would expose the meaning of such black and hidden things to bring them to their end. But I have seen none. It is with a purpose that I seek such truth, which is life over death.

My generation and the next, it is too late for us. It is possible, however, for us to become enlightened to the fact that those who will come later could live their lives without wars and dark things. It is also possible that my generation and the next are capable of striving to create such a world for the unborn, the innocent ones. Why can we not do this for them?

We are a part of the whole, a slice of the orange, a piece of the pie. We are the same – so why are we different? I find this very strange and I am confused. We are a people of laws and regulations, so why can't we obey these laws and regulations as designed? Why such violence and anger? I have looked at this over and over and it always is the same.

It's easy for me to think about behavior and actions, for I have what I need to survive in the manner to which I am accustomed, so why should I think to cause problems? My children are much the same. Should the need arise, those around me will come to my aid and share in their abundance. For this I am truly grateful and pray it will be so forever. It's natural for those like me to shy away from the negative and face the positive.

It is also true that I do not practice what I preach. It's a fact that my heart is eager, but my mind is not. As much as I would like to help the poor and the needy

I do little or nothing for them. I can see that life is not equal and some do not have what I have. If you take a look at yourself, you might find this is true of you as well. My question can only be, "If I can strive to end wars, why can't I strive to help the needy?"

If it is natural for us to shy away from the negative and face the positive, we have to change the negative to the positive if anything at all is to be done to combat poverty and injustice. The law is the law and it should be for all. When there is a disturbance in our life, shouldn't we understand what the cause of this disturbance is? Chances are we already know.

At this point in time, many have taken to the streets in an effort to open the eyes of the world to the fact that there are injustices to be dealt with. I don't understand how you and I can be truly happy until this is straightened out by those in authority. I am compelled to speak out and come to the aid of those in need of help and have nowhere to go and no one will listen to them when they speak out. One part of society has an equal right to be heard by the other, or it doesn't. If it doesn't, then this is not a society – it is a dark place where the sounds of devils arise.

I cry while I am driving so no one will see me
12/21/2014

I cry while I'm driving so no one will see me. It's not that I plan it that way, but it seems to be the norm for me now. I don't know why. Maybe it's because my mind wanders a little while it watches the road appear at some far away point, zoom at me and then disappear under my front tires. I know it's not the time to let your mind wander, while you are driving, but I think it's pretty much involuntary.

I also think the mind goes anywhere it wants when it is wandering, dark places or light, as it wishes. My mind seems to travel toward the past and sooner or later that leads to blood. Once the blood is there it's not long before it goes to the spot where the blood originates. I won't describe this because I'm sure you can visualize as well as I can where blood comes from. I'll save you that, but it always leads to tears.

Sleeping is another place where my mind wanders and it goes to the same places. I don't know how many times my wife, Therese, wakes me up to see if I'm alright. She has learned that it doesn't do any good to ask too many questions at this point, so she will quickly go back to sleep, the deep, sweet sleep only innocent souls can enjoy. I wrap my arms around her and close my eyes and she heals me. I love her like nothing else on this Earth.

Blood is easy for a wandering mind to find, for it is everywhere upon this planet of ours. Throughout our history, man has drawn blood from others for a myriad of reasons, all of which seemed a good idea at the time. Men kill for love, hate, fear and greed. Killing is addictive for some and they go out of their way to see it done. The military will freely supply the tools. As for me, I found at an early age that I had a knack for killing people by accident. It happens all the time when you put a kid in a war zone and give him a gun.

Wars are terrible things and it's a shame, because we're getting so good at it. Our weapons are now capable of destroying whole cities with one blow. A single bomb will vaporize entire populations in an instant. There is very little left to clean up, nothing but ash in a pink vapor. The pink vapor can enter your lungs and you become one with those you have killed.

One war can cause another war. The whole idea of war is to kill your enemy, but the more you kill, the more enemies you create. The killing of a father also requires the killing of the sons and the daughters, the nieces and nephews and all of their cousins and friends. If a single one is missed, then you can count on another war in the not so distant future. A war of revenge is nasty and evil for hate is its root.

There are wars that are said to be honorable and we all know of what I speak for they are wars to stop insanity. In my lifetime, I have never seen a war I would call honorable. After 9/11, our revenge struck out in all directions, all of them wrong, all of them with hate at its root. Currently we are involved in a new war in the Middle East that I'm sure has an enemy that we know nothing about.

Some time ago, there was an uprising against the powers that be. The uprising was populated with the oppressed that thought religious freedom and independence were a requirement or basic human rights. Tea was dumped into the bay, shots were fired and killing ensued from both sides that could never agree on anything. Perhaps our new enemies in the Middle East are common men and women, religiously and economically oppressed, who are rebelling against the powers that be.

Argue if you wish, but I can tell you right now that the only information you have about ISIS is the information the powers that be want you to have. The powerful can paint a patriotic picture and we are helpless to do anything other than load up our guns and carry out their will. If you cannot believe this scenario is possible, then you are delusional and you are destined for remorse and guilt. Your children may find out that they have a knack for killing people by accident.

My horrible nightmare stems from the fact that wars for hate, greed, and fear are eternal. We are supposed to be the greatest nation ever in the history of man. Our foundation is freedom, love and forgiveness, yet we now stoop to torture and evil deeds that have no place in a really great nation. We are a nation of killers, slaughtering and being slaughtered. Should you disagree, visit the long black wall and look at the names. If you can do this and then tell me why they were slaughtered I will worship you like a God that you must be.

I cannot visit the wall for I fear I would fall into the dark and not be able to find my way back to the light. I know if they could look through that black stone, they wouldn't recognize me anyway, just as the song says. My wife, my love went to the wall for me and scratched the names of the ones I knew. This is all I can do about it.

I cry while I am driving so no one will see me

Just when we think things are going pretty good, they go bad
1/8/2015

Is this world crazy or what? Sometimes I feel like we are all in a big cauldron with all of our big ideas that for some reason we think are good ideas. It's all like a really, really good stew. A little dash of this and a dash of that, it's steaming hot, smelling good, and then it goes to hell. It all turns to rot.

Just when we think things are going pretty good, they go bad. When we think things are going bad, they turn out good. So what the hell are we supposed to do? Some of us blame it on the politicians – others blame it on the cops. It's just the way we do things. When things turn sour we start to play the blame game.

By now I'm sure you are wondering, "What the hell is he talking about?" Maybe it's the fact that much of the civilized world is aghast at the fact that, yes, once again, I have been passed over for the Citizen of the Year Award and not even considered for the Theodore Winters Award. I'm still crying over that, but I'm not thinking of that now.

Let me explain. Okay, for example, over in Paris this morning, things were going really, really good. Frenchies were going about their happy ways, to and fro. They are all talking really, really fast and nobody knows what they are saying because the French language sucks really, really bad.

At the offices of the French satirical newspaper, Charlie Hebdo, a bunch of French people were standing around talking. They were saying gobble, gobble, gobble, gobble, or something along that line. Anyway, things were going really, really good for them when some people with guns burst in the door and killed them, one and all.

What the hell? What's up with that? Let's investigate.

Okay, all these Frenchies were in their cauldron, jibber jabbering the way they do and everything was fine, going good. What the heck could possibly go wrong? Well, here it is.

Okay, we're in the cauldron – going good – going good – when lo and behold, some asshole wants to get in the cauldron with a picture he drew of the Prophet Muhammad. We don't like this asshole because everybody knows that you aren't supposed to draw a picture of the Prophet Mohammad, right? We let him in anyway because he thinks he needs to hide.

You see? Right when you think things are going good, they're really going bad and right when you think things are going bad, they're really going good. What's so bad about the whole mess is the fact that we know in the back of our minds that something is not right, but we let it go. We know something is going to change, but we don't worry about it.

What did we learn about things as we look back at it now? Did we learn that should you draw a picture of the Prophet Mohammad, which will insult every Muslim on Earth? It might take them 10 years or so, but they will seek you out and kill you and everybody around you, too. Okay, that was just an example of a good stew turning bad.

Now consider this. We are all in a big cauldron of stew and things are going really, really good right now. At the gas pump, the price per gallon is really, really low and we can drive like hell anywhere we want to go. We don't even need roads because everybody has a 4X4. Things are going really, really good, so we don't think about what's going to happen next.

Why is the price of gas so low?

OK, those OPEC guys over in the Middle East are sitting in their cauldron jibber jabbering the way they do and things are going really, really good for them. They are talking about how those American oil companies won't join their little oil club. They want to get some of the huge, huge profits that the stinking American guys are making but how do they go about getting it?

Here is the thing that spoils our cauldron and makes everything rot:

• The OPEC guys flood the oil market with excess oil.

• As a result of excess oil the price of gas goes down. We are elated and we jibber jabber among ourselves like we do.

• OK, the American oil guys have to lower their prices so their huge profits begin to fall like bricks in a wall, boom, crash, pow!

• The American oil guys know they are under attack but they don't care. They are so rich and they know they will survive.

• Eventually the OPEC guys will give up and oil prices will go back up, higher than they have ever been.

• The OPEC guy's cauldron may smell and taste a little bad, but the stew is still edible and the American oil cauldron is a little smaller but still in good shape.

Okay, our cauldron is doing good – doing good – doing good and we are driving around like crazy, jibber jabbering like we do. What could possibly go wrong? Well, if you ask me nicely, I might tell you.

Okay, since YOU all saw fit to pass me over for every award in the WORLD, you can find out for yourself!

"John W. Garner wrote this. I received all of this information from a distant relative who served in Vietnam with the Marine Corp. I found this information very interesting and I hope you will as well. Most people will never know what lies beneath the historical statistics of the words written on the Vietnam Memorial Wall."

Donald K. Sanders

The Wall

There are 58,267 names now listed on that polished black wall, including those added in 2010.

The names are arranged in the order in which they were taken from us by date and within each date, the names are alphabetized. It is hard to believe it is 59 years since the first casualty.

The first known casualty was Richard B. Fitzgibbon, of North Weymouth, Mass. Listed by the U.S. Department of Defense as having been killed on June 8, 1956. His name is listed on the Wall with that of his son, Marine Corps Lance Cpl. Richard B. Fitzgibbon III, who was killed on Sept. 7, 1965.

There are three sets of fathers and sons on the Wall.

39,996 on the Wall were just 22 or younger.

8,283 were just 19 years old.

The largest age group, 33,103 were 18 years old.

Twelve soldiers on the Wall were 17 years old.

Five soldiers on the Wall were 16 years old.

One soldier, PFC Dan Bullock was 15 years old.

997 soldiers were killed on their first day in Vietnam…

1,448 soldiers were killed on their last day in Vietnam…

Thirty-one sets of brothers are on the Wall.

Thirty-one sets of parents lost two of their sons.

Fifty-four soldiers attended Thomas Edison High School in Philadelphia. I wonder why so many from one school.

Eight women are on the Wall – they nursed the wounded.

244 soldiers were awarded the Medal of Honor during the Vietnam War – 153 of them are on the Wall.

Beallsville, Ohio, with a population of 475, lost six of her sons.

West Virginia had the highest casualty rate per capita in the nation. There are 711 West Virginians on the0 Wall.

The Marines of Morenci: They led some of the scrappiest high school football and basketball teams that the little Arizona copper town of Morenci (pop. 5,058) had ever known and cheered. They enjoyed roaring beer busts. In quieter moments, they rode horses along the Coronado Trail, stalked deer in the Apache National Forest. And in the patriotic camaraderie typical of Morenci's mining families, the nine graduates of Morenci High enlisted as a group in the Marine Corps. Their service began on Independence Day, 1966. Only three returned home.

The Buddies of Midvale: LeRoy Tafoya, Jimmy Martinez, Tom Gonzales were all boyhood friends and lived on three consecutive streets in Midvale, Utah on Fifth, Sixth and Seventh avenues. They lived only a few yards apart. They played ball at the adjacent sandlot ball field. And they all went to Vietnam. In a span of 16 dark days in late 1967, all three would be killed. LeRoy was killed on Wednesday, November 22, the fourth anniversary of John F. Kennedy's assassination. Jimmy died less than 24 hours later on Thanksgiving Day. Tom was shot dead assaulting the enemy on December 7, Pearl Harbor Remembrance Day.

The most casualty deaths for a single day was on January 31, 1968 – 245 deaths.

The most casualty deaths for a single month was May 1968 – 2,415 casualties were incurred.

Most Americans who read this will only see the numbers that the Vietnam War created. To those of us who survived the war and to the families of those who did not, we see the faces; we feel the pain these numbers created. We are, until we too pass away, haunted by these numbers, because they were our friends, fathers, husbands, wives, sons and daughters.

There are no noble wars, just noble warriors.

Life has its little twists and turns. Sometimes they are for the good and other times they are not so good. You never know when something is going to happen that might change things enough to affect the direction your life will take. Things like falling in love, falling out of love and the death of someone dear to you will definitely qualify as life altering. There are many other things that might change your life in unexpected ways.

When I talk of such things, I only have my own life experiences to go by. My life experience is typical, in many ways, of the thousands upon thousands of American Veterans of Foreign Wars. It is true that one experience shared by two different men will sometimes draw different reactions. War sometimes affects one man differently than another. Some men seem to handle it better than others. I don't know why.

The exact same experience will sometimes drive one man to suicide while it leaves another seemingly unaffected. I, for instance, have had great trouble dealing with what I saw and did in a combat zone. Because of this, I have always felt myself to be a lesser man than those that were left unaffected by the brutality and inhumanity of war. I don't know what happened to me, but I seem to be broken somewhere inside where I cannot see it for what it is. I have been this way for many, many years.

I once shot a man in the neck. I didn't know I had shot him until it was already done and the brass was lying on the ground. I remember how he was spun around in the manner of a drill bit as he went down, his legs buckling under him like a twisted lariat. I wanted to say I was sorry, but I found myself gasping for air like an elephant was sitting on my chest.

How easily the flesh can be opened up and shoved to the side. I had underestimated the strength of the thin layer of skin that covers our bones and muscle; under that arteries and veins. I know he had a soul, but I try not to think about that. Instead, I think about how the skin covers our ribs and thousands of other little bones. How beautiful is the human body with everything in its place. It jiggles when you laugh.

I believe in second chances, but I think they are only for little things like lying or cheating. If I could have a second chance, I would take it. I'd climb right up and take it. I'd fall upon my knees and hold up the arms that held the weapon of death and cut them off at the elbows. Like I say, I believe in second chances but there are none for things like this. Ask any man with a similar experience, he will tell you that this is true.

I tried going to church, thinking God would make it go away. I was on my own, for even Jesus couldn't help me. The Army spit me out because I was all chewed up. Besides that, there were fresh troops to take my place. Fresh troops don't hate themselves yet and they are eager for action of any type as long as it involves shooting. In the end, some will be like me and others will not even think harshly about it. That's just the way it is.

There is a saying, and I don't know who said it, but it goes like this, "The soldier's heart, the soldier's spirit, the soldier's soul, are everything. Unless the soldier's soul sustains him he cannot be relied on and will fail himself and his commander and his country in the end"

Once a veteran has been spit out, he is no longer a part of the team. He is not essential for the survival of the group, the platoon. The team is everything to a soldier. The way a team plays as a whole determines its success. You may have the greatest bunch of individual stars in the world, but if they don't play together, the club won't be worth a dime and for some teams, this means death.

Once you are off the team, the only things you know is the fact that a five second fuse only last three seconds and if your attack is going too well, you have walked into an ambush. Or, when the pin is pulled, Mr. Grenade is not your friend. You know there's no honorable way to kill, no gentle way to destroy. There is nothing good in war, except its ending.

Some General said, and I believe this to be true, that, "No profession or occupation is more pleasing than the military; a profession or exercise both noble in execution (for the strongest, most generous and proudest of all virtues is true valor) and noble in its cause. No utility either more just or universal than the protection of the repose or defense of the greatness of one's country. The company and daily conversation of so many noble, young and active men cannot but be well-pleasing to you."

Another guy said, "A perfect soldier, a perfect gentleman never gave offence to anyone not even the enemy." "Be more concerned with your character than your reputation. Your character is what you really are and your reputation is what other people think you are." "We belong to talking, not what talking is about. Stop talking and you are out. Silence equals exclusion."

"The army is the true nobility of our country." I believe this to be true. Another thing I have found to be true is (this is for my fellow veterans) "If you don't want to kill yourself, keep busy."

Here is my last quote. "If I missed a parenthesis or two, please forgive me, for I am no English teacher and they are not important to me.

All the heart I need

I had a pretty bad week. As a matter of fact, I've had a pretty bad year so far, but I don't want to go back that far. Anyways, I'll start on Valentine's Day, last Saturday. Yeah, that's a perfect place to start.

OK, Valentine's Day, right? Real early in the morning, I go to pick up a water pump at the water pump getting place. I also pick up a bunch of drills and some humongous drill bits that are the perfect size for planting the type of plants that my friend Carrie Shaw, the boss of the Putah Creek Council, wants to stick in the ground on this particular holiday. Carrie and her cohorts at the PCC have the creek looking really, really good.

Anyway, like I said, I took all of these drills, bits, and the water pump down to the creek just past Pickerel's place. Then I stood around and stood around some more, waiting for Carrie and her crew to get there so the work can start. While I was waiting, I started thinking about something I read recently.

It seems that two University of Queensland (that's in Australia I think) physicists named Martin Ringbauer and Tim Ralph had simulated a way that quantum particles could travel through a wormhole and go back in time. They used photons that are single particles of light, to simulate quantum particles traveling through time to study their behavior. This set me to thinking that maybe I could go back in time someday, but I never got to think about it anymore because here comes Carrie and her planting crew.

I put on a happy face even though I was pretty sad about being passed up for the Citizen of the Year thingy and the fact that no one, not one single soul, nominated me for anything at all. Not a Pulitzer or a Nobel — nothing! I was absolutely humiliated and was just inches away from some pretty damn big tears. The kind that everybody can see from far, far away where they can laugh at you without being seen.

So there we all are, down by the creek, drilling holes with big drill bits, and then sticking a native plant in each hole. I just kept on drilling so as not to cry and make a fool outta myself in front of all the people with dirty hands that were busy sticking native plants into the happy and healthy soil along the beautiful Putah Creek. As sad as I was about all those awards I could have gotten, but didn't, it was pretty cool just taking part in all the festivities.

Well, we all planted and planted until we ran out of time, but I was still getting sadder and sadder. My heart began to ache like someone punched me in the chest with a big rubber hammer or something like that. I thought to myself, "Man, I'm really getting sad if it hurts this much!"

Yeah, I was really sad.

OK, now it's about noon, so all the workers leave and Carrie asks me if I'm OK. I wanted to tell her how sad I was and why, but I just couldn't spit it out, so I says, "Ya, I'm doing just fine." I'm such a liar. I lie about everything all the time, but everybody knows it, so it's OK. Everybody leaves and I'm there all by myself like I like it. I enjoy the solitude while setting up the pump to water all the plants we put in the ground — hundreds of them.

I was about halfway through with the watering when my heart starts to ache real bad, which is pretty common for me, but this was different. I thought, "Man I gotta forget about all those awards because it looks like the Pulitzer is out of the question for me." Pretty soon the birds were singing and butterflies were a pumping here and there, and it was simply capital.

A short while later, when I got home, I told my wife about my heartache. Well, she proceeded to worry about me and those stinkin' awards until she said, "You dummy, you're having a heart attack!" Well she must have been right because an hour later I was in Kaiser Hospital in Vacaville with wires stuck on me all over the place.

When I say sad, I mean sad!

Well, hell, I'm screwed now, because it's a holiday weekend and everything is shut down tight until Tuesday. I was a little concerned that there was not a damn thing they could do to help me except get me into a bed.

Well almost!

Some nurse told me that since I have never won an award of any kind that they didn't have a bed for me and I would have to go to Vallejo before I could lay down. They put me in an ambulance and took me south toward Vallejo and a bed. I asked about the siren but they said no! (No awards, remember.) So then I get a bed and I lay in it for two and a half days until the doctor comes in.

The doctor says he can't help me and I have to go to San Francisco or Santa Clara to get some relief. Right away I jump up and say, "Santa Clara!" because my wife's mother and all of her sisters live there, and they always feed me cookies, pies and big red steaks. I just love that family.

So, after about another three-hour ambulance ride, I get to the Santa Clara hospital. I'm supposed to get treated at about 10:30 a.m., but the doctor is so busy I don't get to see him until about 4:30 p.m. I almost got up and went home after this guy came up and said he was gonna shave my groin. I said, "Yer gonna shave my what?" Now my package is all but bald and it looks pretty damn sad.

After that, a guy gave me a pill that made everybody move real fast but talk real slow. They put me on some table and strapped my arms and legs down so I couldn't move. Well, to make a long story short, they tortured me for an hour or two and then I woke up and the heartache was gone. They had fixed my heart this time, but they said the next time I was gonna die unless I win some kind of award between that time and the next.

Now I'm in a real fix because my wife won't even let me look at the creek. That's OK though, because they can't keep me away forever and I don't get paid, so they can't fire me. Now I'm thinking, "That's OK with me because that is all the award I'll ever need. That creek is my heart!"

A good suicide
2/24/2015

Sometimes I wish I had died at age 21. The long black wall in Washington would have my name to show to all. Things I have done that may be worthy of mention I could count on a single hand with a few fingers left just in case I think of some more.

Sometimes I want to walk out into the ocean and be drowned under the sea. It wouldn't be a waste at all if some big fish would eat me and then fertilize the bottom of the bay with what his body didn't need.

Sometimes I want to dig a hole by one of Pickerel's big oak trees. I would lie on the bottom of the pit and pull the dirt down over me. I'd have to do it without Pickerel seeing me because he might feel that Donald fertilizer would kill almost any of his trees.

I guess there's a million ways to meet your maker if you wish, some good, some others not so good. When I think about all the soldiers, some young and some old like me who will die every day, I wonder how many will use their own hand to help the process along. Since it's against the law and they don't want to go to jail, they won't share intent with me.

If I did it today, I think it would be a waste of a good suicide because nothing would come to gain. Today, I had a good idea while cutting wood for Duc. I wish that it would work, but it's kind of a crazy long stretch. Instead of walking into the ocean and drowning under the sea, or instead of jumping in a hole to pull dirt in over me, let me die on Arab soil so in return one soldier could go home instead of me.

Think of all those Arabs who are as mad as a shaken hive of bees because we steal their oil and piss all over their religion and families. They want the death of Americans to satisfy their anger. I don't think anything else will do, so someone has to die. Maybe a pile of dead Americans will someday be enough and I don't think God really cares just how we end up in our grave – he has too much else to think about.

So, if I could go over there (they'd have to pay my airfare because I don't have it to spare) and lay down on a stage in front of their death camera, they could kill me like a big fat pig. When I'm dead upon the Arab soil with my head upon a stick, one American soldier that doesn't want to die can go home to his mother and promise her grandkids.

I know there are many, many men who feel the same as me, so if we could get together and go over wet, then sandy seas maybe, just maybe, we would satisfy Arab anger enough to see a new era of peace. All the soldiers on both sides who want to live can make babies with their lovers and turn weapons into plows to plant a new, fresh garden of delight.

Me, I'll be somewhere else with 40 virgins, as intended. They are mine to claim, not for kissing, not for sex, but to dance around in circles in joyful celebration of the end of the crusades of a thousand years. When God sees the 40 virgins he will know the killing is over and that I, well, I am in my grave.

Creek wasn't the way nature made it
3/20/2015

Debra, I just read your column about the Putah Creek "Nature Park," and I have to say that I wholeheartedly agree with everything you said. You are not only a beautiful specimen of a woman but you are pretty darn smart too. I'll tell you why everything you say is like gospel to me. Your writing rings of truth and common sense.

What you had to say in your column reminds me of stories I have heard about the early pioneer families that so brazenly moved into this area like a thousand years ago. I can't remember what the guy's name was but when he arrived at the shores of the Putah Creek he must have thought to himself, "Yeah, I can handle living in this place."

You see, the first thing, what's-his-name, thought was, 'This land, as it is now, is totally useless for anything.' It was pitiful because the first night he spent here he had to use a rock for a pillow. It was apparent to him that this just wouldn't do. Changes had to be made so he began making a list of things to do to make the creek livable.

The first thing he did was kill all of those pesky Indians, Apache I think they were called. They always ate with their fingers and didn't use any napkins. Apparently all the Apache moved out to Cache Creek. They called it that because they didn't know how to spell 'Cash' so from then until now it has always been called "Cache Creek."

Anyway, once, what's-his-name got rid of the Apaches, he hired a bunch of people to start chopping down all of the trees. They used dynamite to blow up the stumps because why chop down the tree if you are going to leave the stump, right?

What's-his-name thought it was funny to give his workers a 3-second fuse and tell them it was a 10-second fuse. I'd have to admit that it had to be pretty funny when things blew up in their face. Anyway, once all the trees were gone, what's-his-name could plant the trees he brought with him from wherever he was from — it don't really matter where.

Pretty soon their blackberries were everywhere and they were perfect for hiding all the garbage that what's-his-name dumped into the creek. He brought in some Eucalyptus trees to make furniture and now they are everywhere along the creek. To make all the roads, what's-his-name took all the gravel out of the creek, so the creek almost flowed uphill.

The creek was like a gift from God, because everything you dumped into it would just disappear. They built a little dam so the kids could swim just downstream from where they built the sewage plant. this was right under the railroad bridge. If they saw a floater, the kids would throw them at each other. All them stinky animals moved downstream too after the storm drain was put in right where the swimming hole was. Everybody thought the chemical smell came from the bean soup.

Anyway, what I'm getting at is the fact that our ancestors spent a lot of time and money to get the creek just like they wanted it and if it was good enough for them then it ought to be good enough for us. Now look at it! Everything has gone to pot!

Debra, you were exactly right. I saw that damn otter too and some beaver, a lot of turkeys, and I've even seen a wildcat a couple of times too. Now the dam is gone so the water is too cold and clear to swim in and the animals are taking over.

Everywhere there was a giant hole where the road gravel came from it's been filled in so we have a flood plain. As a matter of fact they have made the damn creek just like it was when what's–his–name first set eyes upon it. Well, all except for that little part that hasn't been changed yet that you mentioned.

There are still some blackberries and Eucalyptus trees there, so it won't be long till their seeds will change everything back like the nature strip you love so much. To top all that off, the Apaches are coming back and buying up the whole damn creek.

Now they won't let me dump my garbage can off the railroad bridge anymore. What is this world coming to? Now, I have to lift my garbage can way up high to dump it over the little fence you mentioned. Why do they have to make it so hard on me?

I'm gonna get those damn otters too! You see what it all boils down to is the fact that the creek you and I like is not the way nature made it. The creek we like was changed by a lot of hard labor over generations of our ancestors. There was a hell of a lot of dumping too so it was just right.

Well, Geeze! I should have asked you to write this so it would sound more gooder.

Out of the blue
3/23/2015

Every so often, conditions are just right for something to happen unexpectedly like finding a $20 bill lying on the ground. You might think to yourself, "Wow that wouldn't happen again in a hundred years." This is an example of what I call "out of the blue" moments. I know we all have them from time to time.

Most "out of the blue" moments are not important and they merely make things interesting. "Out of the blue" moments, like everything else, can be good or bad depending on what they concern. You never see them coming so all you can do is react to them in the best way possible. Some "out of the blue" moments are life-altering, often on a grand scale.

I can give you a good example of an "out of the blue" moment that happened when I was in 8th grade. I was just sitting there at my desk when — out of the blue — someone burst into the room screaming something about John F. Kennedy being shot just moments before. When something like that happens you'll remember every moment of what occurs.

Not too long after that, there was another "out of the blue" moment when Dr. Martin Luther King was assassinated. I have a vivid memory of that day and the days leading up to it. I remember how elegant he was and how I was affected by his "I have a dream" speech. That's the way it seems to go. Just when you discover how great a person is, he is taken away from you, never to return.

During my short lifetime, there have been many such "out of the blue" moments. Moments like reaching a crossroad and finding your way, meeting someone for the first time and falling in love with them, or the sudden death of a loved one are all "out of the blue" moments.

Two "out of the blue" moments that had a profound effect on me will demonstrate how suddenly things can happen to change everything you thought was good and decent into just the opposite. In the middle of my Vietnam War experience, I think I was a typical U. S. soldier. You know, gung-ho and all that crap. I thought it was the right thing for me to do when I joined the Army. I believed in our war effort. I thought it was the right thing to do.

I was given a 30-day leave between my first tour of duty in Vietnam and my second. It was nice to be home for a while. I sat having coffee with my mother at the kitchen table while we watched the news on TV. There on the screen, in living color, a jet was dropping napalm on a Vietnamese forest. It was beautiful the way it exploded upon contact with the ground and spread across the top of the trees. I remember how beautiful I thought it was.

At that very moment, "out of the blue," a young Vietnamese girl ran out of the flames with her skin on fire. With that, I was no longer a part of the war and was pretty much a zombie until my time in Vietnam was over. Shortly after that, "out of the blue," a young lady was shot to death by National Guard troops at Kent State. These two "out of the blue" moments derailed my train of thought and I lost it and never got it back.

Just like that, "out of the blue," I found myself incapable of loving or caring, and I had lost all hope of living a productive life. Life was no longer livable for me unless I was high or drunk. I stayed that way for many, many years and when I came out of it I found I had wasted most of the late '70s, the '80s, and the '90s.

There were other "out of the blue" moments that contributed to my condition but I won't go into that, so just trust me. What still troubles me is the fact that 20-22 veterans will commit suicide every single day and no one seems to care. I feel like I have been raped of my belief system. How could the country that we love so much just dump us by the wayside like pieces of garbage?

Well just recently, "out of the blue," it struck me that maybe I should concentrate not on the terrible past but on working to change the future. I have to do it in my own way, just as you have to do it in your way. You can see me doing it my way every day as I spend my time doing what I think is important. As I work changing things for the better, I'm happier than I have been in many years. The more I work at it, the happier I am. All I have left to say is that you can either help those that want to change or get out of their way.

You can sit and bitch about what others are doing or you can get off of your ass and get at it, right "out of the blue.

A little well tested advice for the graduating class of 2015
4/4/2015

I would like to offer some well tested advice to the graduating class of 2015. So, now you are thinking to yourself, "What makes him think he is qualified to offer advice to our children and who does he think he is?" Let's take a look at what an advisor really is, so don't be too quick to judge.

An advisor is a counselor. Yeah, I can do that. An advisor is also a mentor, a consultant and a guide. All of which, I am. I consider myself the Guru of letting others do what I want them to do. In the old days, they called me Bogwan Don. As a matter of fact, I'm thinking I would make a great advisor to the next President of the United States.

If you take a moment to think about that, you'll see I am absolutely right. Okay, even if every bit of advice that came out of my mouth was absolutely wrong and was the farthest thing from the truth as it could be, I could not be any worse than those who preceded me.

The President of the United States is constantly given the wrong advice by those who are close to him. This is true of each and every President from beginning to end. Presidential decisions are rarely formulated by just one person. Reaching a sound conclusion depends on sharing opinions and negotiating an outcome. Okay, for you French guys, that means you have a bunch of advisors who do nothing but give you advice. Then you decide what to do based upon their suggestions.

Most Presidential advisors are highly educated intellectuals who can never come to a decision on their own and, in fact, change their minds with every gust of wind in any direction. This has been proven over and over, throughout history. The only steady advice a President can count on comes from the military guys and we all know what they will advise.

So who does a President listen to? Well, lately the Presidents have been listening to the Corporation big boys. This is a mistake, if only for the facts that most modern armed conflicts are not between countries but between companies and corporations. Any heeded advice from that sector would certainly favor American companies.

Anyway, back to the advice for the graduates of 2015. This advice comes from my vast experience in life along with the observation of the behavior of others. That being said, the first thing I will tell you is to be aware that people will give you advice about how to behave, but these same people do not even heed their own advice. However, don't worry about that with me because I will give it to you straight up – I am the Guru of words – The Bogwan.

• In public, always try to be kind and sometimes even talk to those who are beneath you, but in private just ignore them. Never give them money – they are just drunks.
• Always try to look important. Remember, that's important – not impotent. They are not the same. If you look important and act important people will think you are doing important things.
• If someone is around, you can offer help to the needy
• Make up stories to make yourself look good and others bad. Sometimes I offer help to others and then never do it. Another thing I do is lie about it and say I did.
• You can tell people you are sad because your mom dumped you in an orphanage or put you in a dumpster. Others will feel sorry for you and treat you a lot nicer

than they normally would.

• Never do obscene things around women unless you think it will get you some sex.

• If you are going to tell a lie, tell one that is very long and involved because chances are the person you are lying to will get bored and forget what you said anyway.

• Never call a woman the "C" word. My nose is "S" shaped for that very reason.

• Never have an affair with your best friend's wife. If you do have an affair with your best friend's wife, do not let your best friend find out. If he does find out, move to California and if you are already in California, move to Illinois.

• Change your underwear at least twice a week and wear cologne every day so people will think you bathe regularly.

• Never volunteer, but if you do get caught up in something like that, tell them you need to work alone so you can loaf most of the time behind a tree or a bush. If you cannot work alone – fake a sore back.

• Never make fun of people of color or Jews. If you must make fun of someone – make fun of the Muslims. You can say whatever you want about them.

Remember, these pieces of advice are pretty flexible. If you don't have time or don't want to do any of them, you can always lie and say you did. As a matter of fact you can lie about everything and nobody will care in the least. Look at me. Everyone knows I'm a liar and they don't seem to care. That's right – everybody lies and if they say they don't, they're lying.

Oh, two other things: If you want to make someone look bad, calling them a witch or gay doesn't work anymore. The only thing that does seem to work is saying, "He's a terrorist!"

I'm out of room for now, but for $79.50 an hour I can tell you much, much more. Believe me, it cost me a lot more than that to learn these tidbits of learning.

One last thing: Always love those who are close to you. There is no guarantee that they will be there tomorrow

Last week I took a trip up to where two rivers (the Klamath and the Trinity) merge into one near the small town of Weitchepec, California. There are people up there that I love dearly, inlaws you see, and wood folk. We talked about my friend Steve Shafer who had stood on that very spot just a year or so earlier. They were surprised to hear that he had passed away recently after a short bout with cancer. They remembered him well.

I guess I hadn't finished grieving yet because after we talked, I couldn't get my friend out of my mind. As our little family group sat discussing Steve, I found myself lost in thought with the wind wisping through the leaves of the trees above the river. I thought about what a good friend he had been. There was no one like him that I know of. Oh, I have other friends and they are dear to me, but they are not like Steve.

Steve was a righteous dude. He was a man's man, but very kind and gentle for the large man that he was. If I think really hard, I can remember only one time that I ever saw him angry. That was the time his wife Kellie justifiably threw me out of their yard, for I had been a capital-A ass. I thought Steve was going to poke me in the nose but he didn't have the heart to hit someone that was as depressed as I was at the time. Steve had a heart as big as California.

I will never know why Steve thought of me as a friend because he didn't like negative people and I always looked at the worst of everything and I expected the worst from everyone and I usually got it too. Steve, I found to be the exception, for he was so simple, not of mind, but of nature. Steve did not complicate things like most people do.

He could take a joke like no other man that I know. On the trip to Weitchepec a year or so ago, I rubbed black ash on the viewfinders of my binoculars and Steve walked around all day with black circles around his eyes after looking through them. When he found out what everyone was laughing at he just smiled and forgot about it.

Another joke I pulled on Steve during that trip to the woods was when I asked him to throw a rock into a cave so I could get a picture. I didn't tell him it was a cougar's cave and the picture came out blurry because I was running away and laughing so hard. He was a funny guy.

Really, the only thing he was touchy about was his fossil rocks, or rocks that resembled some dead animal. He kept track of each one and should one go missing, he'd go looking for it again until he found it. Steve had so many rocks that when he moved to a new house, there were eight trailer loads of rocks to move. I have never moved so many rocks in my life and Steve kept an eye on me the whole time.

Steve is gone now, and I can't tell you how much I miss his smiling face. While driving home today I listened to an Alison Krauss song called "A way down the River." The words are exactly like something Steve would say:

I'm just away down the river
A hundred miles or more
Crossing over Jordan
To the other shore
I'll be standing waiting

With all who've gone before
I'm just away down the river
A hundred miles or more
Now the pictures on the wall
Will help you to recall
They're not there to make you sad
But to remember all the good times we had.

    Steve, I miss you, bud, and I hope I'll see you again soon.

Take a walk with me
4/20/2015

Why do some people argue with me about creek restoration work? Have they lost their mind? I'm beginning to think that maybe they have absolutely gone crazy. I mean it's like looking a gift horse in the mouth isn't it if someone wants to spend millions of dollars to clean up Putah Creek and you complain about it? Would you rather the money went to some other creek?

If I simplify things just a little it may open the minds of all these haters so they can see things a little clearer. I'll get to that in just a moment, but first I'd like to say that it is true that the creek was lovely just the way it was before all the restructuring work began. It was as natural as could be, natural but not healthy.

Think about this. Pretend you own Putah Creek, all of it including Lake Berryessa and Lake Solano. Wouldn't that make you responsible for the health of every drop of water that travels through your creek? I think it would. I know that if I was lucky enough to own it I would care very much about its health.

I don't own any of it and it is very important to me that I do all that I can to have a creek that is as healthy as it can be. I hope that many of you feel the same. I know that Jan Schubert and Rev. Michael J. Hebda are worried about the creek for they both voiced their opinion in this week's Winters Express. Ms. Schubert wants understanding and the Rev. Hebda wants habitat for the animals. That is great; most won't make an effort to say anything.

Ms. Schubert, I too remember the underdeveloped paths through all of the Himalayan blackberries and poison oak. I remember how it hurt if you made a wrong step to be sliced to pieces by the thorns. Even the lovely roses were pushed beneath the blackberries that if left to nature would envelop both sides of the creek and eventually push into the yards of the homes at the overlook on Creekside Drive.

Rev. Hebda, as for the beaver and otter, I must tell you that they are thriving exactly where they were two years ago. If you think I am being untruthful, get off your holy butt and meet me at the gazebo any day and any time you wish and I will point out exactly where they are and even a man of God will not dispute my word. Putah Creek is teaming with wildlife and fish and there are no longer areas of stagnate water with old cars and batteries to poison them.

I have recently seen herds of deer, bobcats, beaver, otters and even mink with bushy black tails. If you do not see them and know that they are there then you are not looking in the right places at the right time. I would love to show them to you so contact me I will give you the same offer I gave the Express editor, Debra DeAngelo. I will take you or anyone else on a tour of our beautiful nature park.

As for animal habitat, the blackberries have been replaced with wild native roses and the Eucalyptus trees with maple, alder, oak, willow and cottonwood. There is not a single animal in this area that will sink its teeth into a eucalyptus tree. Why do you find it so hard to understand that invasive plants will change everything about Putah Creek if left alone to fend for itself?

Even the word "invasive" should give you concern that something is not right. Our Putah Creek is on the verge of becoming the showplace of the nation but it cannot be done overnight. It will take time to grow and mature into one of the healthiest and cleanest waterways in the world. An enormous amount of money has been invested and I can attest to the amount of labor involved by dedicated men and women that work very hard to secure the health of Putah Creek.

I have heard it said that these complaints recently voiced in the winters Express are not critical of those people who volunteer labor and sweat for the health of the creek. Sir, I believe your last sentence, "I believe it is a sin against nature to destroy something that proves that nature knows best." Is a slap in the face of many hard working volunteers that plant trees, pick up old tires, pick up old car batteries, washing machines, and dryers.

In a year's time our new bridge will be nearly complete, the blackberries will be replaced with fragrant roses, and hopefully there will be no Eucalyptus to squeeze out native trees. The water of our creek will be fragrant and as clean as it is cold, just like the trout and salmon enjoy it. Our ambling attentions that guide us to water will scatter any anxiety through what our eyes will behold in time. It will be lovely and naturally native, free of invasive plants and animals.

What I fear is happening here is exactly what Oscar Wilde thought about when he wrote, "Most people are other people. Their thoughts are someone else's opinions, their lives a mimicry, their passions a quotation." People, go to the wild side and don't listen to the opinions of others. Join me for a walk along the creek and judge for yourself. Especially you Rev. Hebda, I am waiting for you and Debra DeAngelo to walk with me.

The continuing struggle for human rights
4/27/2015

For people of color, these are pivotal times. Thanks to the cell phone video recorder, white America can see for the first time the truth of the injustice that people of color face every day. We now know that it is not imaginary as we have been convinced by mass media for all of these years. The simple truth is that people of color have suffered a different justice than the rest of us.

Videos of police brutality are popping up everywhere. Videos from Ferguson, Missouri, show a young man dead on the street. Another video shows a man being shot in the back by a cop in South Carolina and then it catches the cop planting evidence on the body. These are only two of hundreds being released on a daily basis.

Today, Channel 4 of Southern California at Southgate released a video of "a law enforcement officer grabbing what appears to be a recording device from the hands of an onlooker and kicking it away." "The video shows the onlooker pointing what appears to be a small camera or a cellphone at multiple officers standing in front of a home. One of the officers then runs up to her and snatches it from her hands. When the device hits the ground, the officer kicks it away." This incident and the others as well are now under Federal investigation.

As these videos arise, we are forced to admit that there is a real problem and we can see it isn't going to go away on its own. In Baltimore, the death of a young man while in custody has spurred violent protest. An entire stadium containing thousands of people were detained against their will to keep them from joining the protest. We have to wonder where all of this is going to go next.

As I stated earlier, these are pivotal times for people of color. They find themselves on the verge of violent revolution and rightfully so. On one side of the razor's edge, they can opt to keep things the way they are and always have been for them, but I don't see that happening. Their other option is looming on the horizon and it involves protest on the street, violence and destruction. Everything is hinging on what the Feds do following their "investigations."

The problem with all of this is the fact that there have been many, many "investigations" by the Feds in the past with little or no results. It's a natural fact that people of color have never had faith in "investigations" of any type, by any law enforcement agency, Federal or not. They simply do not work for easily understandable reasons that I associate with a monster feeding itself.

It simply does not work when law enforcement "investigates" itself. This is true on so many levels. People of color are not stupid. As a matter of fact when it comes to "real life," people of color have an innate understanding of what it takes to survive in a world where laws do not apply to them. They know that there are two different worlds. There is a world for whites and a different world for people of color.

I fear that much of white America cannot see that this is true, either that or they do not care. However, this is increasingly changing thanks to the cell phone video recorder. Racism and injustice are hard to deny when it is being thrown in your face every day. Racism has an ugly face. It's a face we all abhor to glance upon, so many try to ignore it. So, in the end, white America is on the razor's edge right alongside people of color.

So, I will say again, but in slightly different terms, "These are pivotal times for all Americans." When the "shit" starts to fly, and believe me, the "shit" will fly, which way will the pendulum fall and in which direction will you lean toward? Will it be keeping things the way they are or will it be justice for all? Among all the total confusion in white America and the distrust of those in power which is common among people of color, I can only have faith that the right thing will ensue.

I can only speak for myself, but if it ever comes to the point when faith in God above is not enough to tip the scales of justice, then there is only one direction I can take. The direction I take will be decided by people of color, for it is to their lead which I defer. It is for their rights that we must struggle, so it is for us as white Americans to stand and be counted in committed support of equal rights for all. I hope that people of color will know that we will help with any need that might arise for them. I have faith that "Stand We Will" as Americans in "Peaceful Protest."

We, as a country, cannot pass even the simplest test by which a country is commonly judged to be free or not — the amount of security enjoyed by our minorities is directly equal to the amount of freedom enjoyed by all. If one American has no rights, it goes to reason that none of us do. Remember, violence is not an option even though it is in our nature. Peaceful protest along with civil disobedience will take us to the dream that Dr. Martin Luther King saw so clearly in our future.

The world is full of people that want to grab all of your cash. To them, we're what you'd call "a mark." If you have money, sooner or later you'll be considered "a mark." There are all kinds of schemes and little devious plans they can use to get you to part with your money, some legal and some not so legal. The greatest tool these people have in their shed for getting our money is our own greed.

"Charles Ponzi (also known as Charles Ponei, Charles P. Bianchi, Carl, or simply 'The Ponz') promised his clients a 50 percent return on their investment in a ridiculously short amount of time. He initially achieved this by paying his past clients with the investments of future clients. More recently, Bernie Madoff got rich using the same scheme."

Eventually they went to prison but my point is their best tool was our own greed. Greed, I say!

"In 1999, David Phillips realized that the return on a mail-in-rebate outweighed the price of Healthy Choice pudding snacks. So he bought 12,150 cups of pudding (and spent $3,500), and sent in the rebate, netting over a million frequent flier miles from American Airlines. To avoid suspicion, he claimed he was stocking up for Y2K. And since all the pudding was donated to charity, he also netted a hefty tax-break."

Every once in a while, opportunities like this come along and as it happens, are perfectly legal.

My favorite scheme was carried out by a guy named, Gregor MacGregor, who "not only has a hilarious name, but a hilarious story. After fighting for South American independence, he returned to England, pretending to be cazique of 'Poyais,' a totally made-up island nation off the coast of Honduras. He even created a guidebook detailing the landscape and abundant natural resources. He collected money from over 250 would-be colonists, and by the time his investors reached the patch of water where their island should have been, he was already rounding up more money from potential colonists in France".

What has all of this to do with me? Well, a couple of weeks ago, my wife made me go with her to a dinner given by the local "Walk-a-thon" thingy at my favorite restaurant, The Buckhorn, in downtown Winters, California. There was plenty of what I like: meat and potatoes. Well, some vegetables too, but I didn't eat that stuff. What I'm trying to get at is the fact that the food was free because of some cancer society thingy.

I was sitting there feeding my face when it dawned on me that if I did a little research as to when these events are held in other towns, I could possible eat for free every night. All I have to do is sit there and eat while looking sad and concerned for all the cancer guys. I can do that easy!

Yesterday, I was wakened up way before noon by the noise from an excavator tearing down a building just down the street from my house. I got out of bed and went to the front of my house fully intending to yell and give them the finger until I got a good look at what they were doing. The demolished building looked exactly like the buildings destroyed by a large earthquake. This set me to thinking and then to action.

Suppose I put on some dirty clothes and put a huge bandage on my head and across one eye. OK, if I could get that guy to move his excavator so I could take my picture sitting on the rubble of the demolished building I could say I was a victim of an earthquake and get a lot of charity money.

Believe me, it could work. Who's with me?

I don't know why, because I'm no mathematician, but I have to say that the three quotes I used above were taken from buzzfeed.com. That way I don't get sued. That's another get rich scheme too, but we'll get back to that later.

The rich get richer, and stingier too
5/15/2015

I'm going to start my own non-profit, tax free charity foundation. There's a lot of money out there and I'm gonna get me some.

Bunches and bunches of rich people are just waiting for a guy like me to show them where to send their charity dollars. All a charity has to do is let those rich people know that they exist and within minutes, the money starts rolling in by the bucketful.

Well that's what I was thinking last week, but today is a whole week later. In just whatever amount of time it took to get from last week to this week (I'm not sure how long that was) I found out it is not so easy for me to lay my hands on all those charity dollars.

From what I gather, you can't just say you're a charity and go get the money like I thought I could. You have to go through certain procedures and all the requirements that are designed to keep the riff-raff out of the charity game. I'll tell you right now that all of these rules and regulations did a number on my charity hopes. By the time I did this and that and all of the other stuff, someone else has got all the money and there wouldn't be anything left for me at all! That sucks! What the hell, man!

I had a plan! I was going to call all of the rich people I know (which is none) and tell them I was the head of the "Feed the Little Poor Kids of Winters, California." I thought the money would be rolling in by now! So, today is a week later then when it was supposed to start, and I still don't have a damn penny! I'm so frustrated! What the hay, man!

After all the time and sweat I put into this charity and I don't get nuthin! I am a little smarter though because of the information I learned about raising money. They call it "fundraising." There are tricks to it and if you don't know the tricks you're going to end up like me, broke and embarrassed.

I'll share some of this information and tricks with you since you're reading my column, and to those that aren't reading it, you don't get nuthin!

OK, as it turns out, rich people are (on the average) less generous then poor people because the personal drive to accumulate wealth is inconsistent with the idea of communal support. Last year, not one of the top 50 individual charitable gifts went to a social-service organization or to a charity that principally serves the poor and the dispossessed. Instead, the 50 largest individual gifts to public charities went to educational institutions, the vast majority of them colleges and universities, like Harvard, Columbia, and Berkeley. Guess who these universities cater to? That's right — the nation's elite!

A guy named David M Evans of Bloomberg Market Magazine says "the rich are way more likely to prioritize their own self-interests above the interests of other people." They are, he continued, "more likely to exhibit characteristics that we would stereotypically associate with, say, assholes."

I found out that in 2011, the wealthiest Americans (those with earnings in the top 20 percent) contributed on average 1.3 percent of their income to charity and Americans at the base of the income pyramid, those in the bottom 20 percent, donated 3.2 percent of their income. Most of these poor scums cannot take advantage of the charitable tax deduction, because they don't itemize deductions on their income-tax returns. Some of those dirty scums don't even file for taxes at all!

I found that wealth affects not only how much money is given but to whom the hell they give it to. The poor scums tend to give to churches and food banks, while the rich people prefer to support colleges and universities, arts organizations and museums. Does that suck or what?

One charity, run by a lady named Robin Patterson thought that about 70-80 percent of the money they brought in would be used for diabetes research, Ha! The truth was almost the exact opposite. The vast majority of funds Patterson, her neighbors and people like them throughout the country would raise, almost 80 percent, would never get to the Diabetes Association. Instead, that money collected from letters sent to neighbors and other poor scum would go to the company that employed Robin and an army of other paid telephone solicitors: InfoCision Management Corp.

I have to say that after whatever amount of time has passed from last week to this week, I learned of lot of nuthin! I still don't know how to get those rich people to give me their money. What it amounts to is that when it comes to raising money, I don't know squat!

Never fear! I have a big brain and I will be thinking all the time 'til I come up with something that will make me rich and you know what? When I'm rich, I'm not going to give anything to the food bank either!

Monday is Memorial Day. Like many Americans I will think about what that means to me. There were so many soldiers who gave their lives for their country, not just our country but all countries. Each and every one of them had a family. Each and every one had those that he loved and those that loved them in return. Each and every one was a human being.

My people came from Tennessee and Arkansas. Way before that, my ancestor, Pettiplace Clouse (from my grandmother's side), landed in Jamestown in 1610 aboard the English ship, Starr. Pettiplace was an indentured servant for the aristocrats who financed the voyage in return for several years of labor. As far as I can tell, every single male member of our family from Pettiplace all the way down to me was a soldier at one time or another.

I have documents from as far back as the War of 1812 and a few from the Civil War naming my distant uncles and their service to this country. I'm sure that each of them had their own stories that have been long since been forgotten because no one had written them down to share with those who follow, generation after generation. I'm not sure, but I feel in my heart that since the advent of the computer, more and more of these stories are now being preserved.

My family (the ones that I know of) was always Army, with the exception of my brother, Michael, who always did things the hard way and joined the Marines. He was so proud of that fact. I always think of Michael, always. Except for our time in Vietnam, I was with him his whole life and now I go on alone.

I met my Uncle Ray only one time when I was very young. He had served in the European theater during World War II. I don't know if we ever exchanged a word between us, but I do remember his box of war souvenirs that included a dagger with a swastika and several Nazi flags. Other than that, I know that, like my brother he liked the bottle a little too much.

I met my father Edwin only twice that I know of. I was very young but I remember the first meeting only because he tried to kill me. It's a long story but a sad one just the same. That day was the very first time I can remember experiencing overwhelming fear, the extent of which I have experienced only twice again on another day, years after the first. Fear is a funny thing, because it takes control over your whole body, making it impossible to talk or run. It's as if you were frozen in time.

Years later, I met my father a second time in the hospice at Battle Creek Military Hospital where I met my father's brother, my Uncle Tracy, for the first time. He told me that my father was a paranoid schizophrenic who had spent his entire life in a mental ward in different military hospitals around the country. My father, toward the end of the war, was found living in a hole on some desert island in the Pacific. He had piled the bodies of dead Japanese soldiers over the hole to hide the entrance to his little hideout.

The next time I saw my father was at his funeral in Cookeville, Tennessee. It was a military funeral much like the one I would like for myself and my brother Michael. As it stands, Michael is in a jar on someone's bookshelf in San Jose instead of at the military cemetery where he belongs and has earned the right to be. I fail to understand why he is being kept apart from his fellow soldiers in his rightful spot with a white stone and a little American flag. In the future I would like to be right next to him.

So, for me, Memorial Day is not only for those that have given their lives for this country. I see it as a day to think about those soldiers who are still alive as well. We should celebrate them while we can in every way possible before they are gone. I celebrate my nephew, Robert Scott Sanders. He is a veteran of the Iraqi and Afghan wars. I have never had the pleasure of meeting him, but I love him like no other and I want him to know that on this Memorial Day and I wish the whole Earth was a single country, because it should be

Popularity, answers to all your problems, and lady sex too
5/27/2015

There are things that clearly frustrate people because either they don't know what they're doing or they don't know how to get others to do what you want. I say, "Don't get frustrated!" There are unbelievably easy ways to make almost anyone do what you want. When you find out just how easy it is, you just might poop your pants like my Facebook friend Carolyn Srygley-Moore did.

There you go! If you want to know what others have going on in their private lives, all you have to do is go to Facebook! Most of the time, people voluntarily supply private information but if they don't, you can simply ask questions and their private information just sorta slips out. For example you could ask, "Carolyn, what did you do in your pants the other day?" Nine times out of 10, Carolyn would say, "Oh, I pooped my pants!"

See, I would never have known Carolyn pooped her pants unless she volunteers the information. I just don't think it's cool to just ask her out of the blue if she has pooped her pants, even with the fact that I poop my pants on a regular basis. Of course no one will ever know that because I don't put it on Facebook. No one will know from this column either, because no one ever reads my column.

Another thing that I can do that most people don't know how to do is build up your readership statistics. If no one reads your column at iPinion all you have to do is cheat the stats. When I send in a column, it's embarrassing when no one ever reads it. You can go to the stats and it says, "0 people read this column!" OK, in just one hour and 50 minutes, I was able to click on my column 432 times, so it looks like about 600 people read the column.

If you want to become a great writer, known all around the world, that's easy too. First, you write something really stupid like this column, and you send it in to iPinion and an editor like Maya Spier Stiles North or Debra DeAngelo will fix it up and make it look like a million dollar baby. Sometimes the stuff I send in doesn't even make sense.

Another way you can get information on Facebook is to ask questions. For instance, you might ask a question like the one I saw tonight on Facebook. You might ask, "What is the oldest thing you own and still use?" Some people like **Amy Ferris** will answer, "My vagina." Now I wouldn't answer anything like that, but I do have a plastic sphincter that came out of my dad when he passed away. Sometimes I play with it and act like it's talking to me.

I even submitted an idea to the American Medical Association on how to apply my idea of a new sphincter assembly. Tie a small cork on a small but strong wire and swallow it while leaving about a foot sticking out of your mouth. When you have a bowel movement, the cork will push out your rear end. When you're done, just pull the end sticking out of your mouth until the cork seats where it's supposed to seat. (You might have to wiggle a little.) Sometimes I'm so smart!

Say you want someone to come to your front door or call you on the phone. For many years, I just couldn't get others to cooperate because they always want to go by their own schedule. It took many years before I found the way to make others bend to my will every damn time. There are things you can do that work magically every time.

I have found through careful research that 99.5 percent of the time, if you're waiting for someone to come to your house, all you have to do is go to the bathroom and sit on the toilet. The mere act of sitting on the toilet is guaranteed to bring a knock on your door, every time. It works for phone calls too. Go to the bathroom and sit on the toilet without your phone and the damn thing will ring every time. You'll hear it clearly ringing from the other room.

Here is another good one to know. Say you have one of those plastic swimming pools — the pools that are about four feet deep and 15 feet wide. You have it all set up, but you don't want to have a big water bill after its full. This is a problem that causes many people to go all summer with a dry pool even though the solution is staring them in the face. Simple I say.

My pool is filled for free every year because I have two solutions to this problem. If the pool is set up all you need is a big hose and a pipe wrench. Hook the hose to the nearest fire hydrant just as soon as it gets dark. Place a couple of cardboard boxes over the hose so the cops won't see it. Simple isn't it?

If you don't have a hydrant near your house simply wait until your neighbor leaves or goes to bed, and sneak into his yard and run his water hose over to your pool. Be sure to be done before dawn because they might see the hose going over the fence and they might not like it.

Another trick is nice for a neighbor that has a nice vegetable garden and you want some of his tomatoes. It is so simple to fix one of your fence boards to swivel. Slide the board over enough to get your arm through and they will wonder like hell what happened to their tomatoes. Same thing works with apples, oranges, and avocados. Your neighbor will never suspect you are stealing them from him if you put a few in a bag and say, "I heard someone stole all of your tomatoes. Here, have some of mine."

I have an answer for all of your questions about things you don't know how to do. In the near future, I will open a Facebook page where women can ask me questions about sex. Of course, the men are on their own, because I don't want to even think about men having sex. I just want to know what normal people like women do or want to do. That's not too much to ask is it?

It will be something like this, "Do you ladies have some questions about sex but are afraid to ask someone else? Well, just go to the Facebook page of "LongdongDon" and fill out the questionnaire. Be sure to include your credit card number and pin. Do it today!"

What you see on the outside is what you have on the inside. The older I become, the more I realize that this is true. Another way of putting it is, what you seek so shall you find. I know now that success is not what I thought it was and I wasted much of the short time I have upon this Earth striving for it. For me, success equaled the attainment of popularity and profit and the greater the success, the greater the man.

When striving for success, all you see ahead of you are endless differing avenues that promise success in the end. If you have an idea of what you wish to accomplish, only you can make the decision, using only your wit, which avenue will provide the greatest amount of success in the shortest amount of time and effort and the least amount of cost.

Some will spend all of their time and all of their effort before they find out that success is just an idea that can never be attained. Success is simply a thought. It's an electrical charge flowing from one part of your brain to another. Considered in terms of cost, the striving for success can be very expensive.

Fast-forward to your epitaph. What will it say? Will it say that your efforts to reach your level of success sucked the life right out of you because when I say "cost" I mean the minutes, hours and days. Every minute you spend striving for success is a minute you could have used in other ways.

People who spend a lot of time striving for success live two lives if they are lucky. What does that mean, "if they are lucky?" People with the ambition to seek success do not have friends — they have associates who want them to do well but not as well as they do. They work late nights and early mornings. They are misunderstood and do many things alone. If they're lucky, they will find a mate that understands their lifestyle and will give them a life outside of the stressful life of striving for success.

So, in the end, if your mindset is bent on seeking success (inside) then all you will see on the outside are the avenues to where you think success might lie. If by chance you take the wrong avenue, you can always go back and take another one — they are all the same. They all use the minutes, hours, and days of your life. Some say that seeking success is the American dream. It's obvious to me that the seeking of success at any cost destroys that dream. There are those who deny others the opportunity to seek success by the restriction of personal freedom and the control over governmental decisions. Many are denied access to higher education and employment at a livable wage. The American dream for some is access to health care or a rewarding retirement.

The cost of your success shouldn't be the failure of others. Think about what you wish to accomplish. Choose carefully the type of people who will inspire you to do your best at everything you want to do. Find out what makes you come alive — what ignites your brain but will feed your spirit at the same time. Do not let the ambition for success deprive you of your life.

Do not strive to be a success — strive to be of value to your community and to those you love. Use your time wisely and forever realize that the time is always ripe to do the right thing. Don't waste your time worrying. Worrying does not empty tomorrow of its troubles, it empties today of its strength. When you worry, it is either about something that has happened or something you think might happen.

If you think about it, you can't change the past and you have no control over the future, so live in the now and know that worrying is a waste of your life time.

Think about who you love and thank them for making you who you are, for supporting you. Choose your battles wisely. Stand up for equality and human rights. Believe me when I say that it is better to stand with the downtrodden and helpless than to spend the rest of your life wishing you had. Never let the opportunity slip away to help someone else.

In order to do the right thing, all of your atoms, all of your being have to point in the same direction. This one fact of life enables you to tell instinctively what is right and what is wrong. We are born with the power to know what is right or wrong — certainly we all know this. Your actions, when dealing with right or wrong, are the tools others will use to know the real you.

Striving for success is a whole lot easier when there are people who love and respect you pushing you in the right direction. Success is certainly a meal that is better when shared with others.

The pain in my heart
6/20/2015

If I had only a few moments to live, I would do everything in my power to get to Therese's arms. I have always, from the first moment I set my eyes upon her many years ago, been in love with her.

I have seen heaven in her eyes before, so when I pass from this world to go to the next, that is where I will fix my attention. If I'm lucky, she will run her fingers through my hair like she used to do. That would be nice.

I've always had a pain in my heart, always. Early in my childhood, I knew the pain my father felt in his heart, for it overflowed and seeped into mine. He had lost his mind on some unnamed atoll somewhere in the Pacific during World War II, so I don't even think he was aware of the pain he passed to me. It was the pain of a soldier, full of anger, sorrow and love. We had just a terrible moment to share our pain before he was locked away to spend his entire adult life in an institution for the insane.

Barely a year had passed from that moment with my father when my mother ripped my heart from my chest by walking away, leaving my younger brother, Michael, and I in a cold, dark Catholic orphanage in Little Rock. I knew her heart was dripping tears of pain directly into mine, filling it up, never to empty. An orphanage can be a horrible place for a kid with a pain in his heart. After my mother was gone, I lost my brother, only to find him years later.

I walked past him on the playground because I didn't recognize him. Something made me turn around. He was standing there with a shit-eating grin on his face, waving at me. He stood with his arm held up like he was saluting Hitler or something. At that moment I could feel the pain in his heart. It was full of fear, loneliness and love. My own heart was full of unbearable pain because I knew I could not protect him from the evil things that often happen in an orphanage full of children.

That's the way it went for me. One thing after another, and another, and another kept my heart in a state of constant pain. At one point in time, I had the notion that it might heal, allowing me to live a regular, normal life but that passed away too soon when I became a soldier in the Republic of Vietnam. With that, my pain grew to be unbearable but I found some relief in drug abuse that grabbed me by the neck and twisted it so hard I couldn't feel my heart.

In time, I found love with a girl named Therese. She was good for me in every way but I cannot say I was good for her. Time after time, all I could do was tear her heart out. The pain in my heart was so great that I couldn't show my love to her like she openly showed her love to me. Now I can see that it was her love that has kept me alive all of these years. It gives me great pain to know that I should have been a better husband for her. I should have been a better man for her.

For the last couple of years, the pain in my heart has been caused by something else. They say that the blood does not flow through it like it should. For some time now, the pain has been increasing. It's sometimes a pain so severe that all I can do is rest and wait until it passes. Someday soon, it will not pass. I can see it coming and I cannot stop it when it gets here.

I went to a doctor one time and he did a balloon job and put a stint inside my arteries. This helped for a time but the pain has returned, so the next step has to be surgery — but this I cannot and will not do. If it's my time, then so be it, it's my time. My attitude about it seems to anger Therese, for she thinks I'm giving up but that isn't the case at all. I'm just living my life as well as I can while placing hope upon hope that when the time comes, I will have the strength to make it to her arms and while she runs her fingers through my hair I want my heart to empty hers of pain.

Governor Jerry Brown and his wife Ann were in rural Winters visiting friends on my birthday, June 28. I can't believe he didn't take the time to come to my house and wish me a happy birthday. The next time I see him, I'm going to bring that up to see what he has to say about it. After all he's probably feeling bad about missing all of my other birthdays.

There was a picture in the July 9 edition of the Winters Express in which Governor Brown (looking quite comfortable) poses with Rich Rominger and his lovely wife Evelyne, along with Craig McNamara at the Rominger Ranch. I have to admit it was a great picture because it's glossed with friendship and happiness. It must be nice to have the Governor of California feel at ease in your home.

I guess it's true that birds of a feather flock together. I don't know much about these guys, but I do know that between the three of them there's probably a good century of public service. We all know about Governor Brown, so I'll concentrate on Rominger and McNamara. I had the honor to meet each of them only once, but I was left with the true feeling of warmth for the experience.

I think it's time that I looked at these guys a little closer to give them the credit they're due. I know they're both deeply involved in family life and their community. The Rominger and McNamara names are recognized for good works around the entire Earth. Let's take a look at these guys and see what we can find.

Craig McNamara comes from a long line of successful, top notch public servants. His young days were spent traveling the world while developing his mind. This eventually led him back home to concentrate on agriculture and world health. Craig and Julie McNamara are the founders of the FARMS Program, a partnership that started in 1993, joining Sierra Orchards (the operational farming entity of McNamara's family), UC Davis, and the California Foundation for Agriculture in the Classroom and the Yolo County Resource Conservation District. F.A.R.M.S. is now integrated as a curriculum of the Center for Land-Based Learning.

McNamara's SLEWS Program was formed in 2001, after partnering with Audubon California's Landowner Stewardship Program. This effectively doubled the number of students served annually. As a result of this dramatic growth and increased demand, in February, 2001, FARMS Leadership, Inc., a 501(c)(3) non-profit organization, was formed and moved to new headquarters at The Farm on Putah Creek in Winters, California. In 2004, FARMS Leadership, Inc. was renamed as the Center for Land-Based Learning. The program now reaches nearly 2,000 students annually.

McNamara is the recipient of several awards, including the Leopold Conservation Award, the California Governor's Environmental and Economic Leadership Award, the UC Davis Award of Distinction and Outstanding Alumnus Award. I could go on and on about this guy but it makes my third place bowling trophy look insignificant because it's the only award I ever won.

Richard Rominger is a fourth generation Yolo County, California farmer and is active in farm organizations and cooperatives. He served six years as Director (Secretary) of the California Department of Food and Agriculture and was the Deputy Secretary at the U.S. Department of Agriculture in Washington, DC for eight years. Improving farm policy, including conservation programs, and establishing the National Organic Standards, were among his responsibilities. He served as a production agriculture advisor at UC Davis, UC Riverside, California

State University Fresno, and Cal Poly San Luis Obispo, and continues to serve as a special advisor to the Chancellor at UC Davis. He is chairman of Marrone Organic Innovations, a biopesticide company, is a member of the UC President's Advisory Commission on Agriculture and natural Resources, and the California Roundtable on Agriculture and the environment, and serves on the board of directors of the American Farmland Trust and Roots of Change Council. He completed a term on the UC Board of Regents.

Rominger and his wife Evelyne raised a daughter and three sons on the same family farm where he grew up. Their sons now operate the farm with participation from their daughter, growing alfalfa, barley, beans, corn, native grass seed, oats, rice, safflower, sunflowers, tomatoes, wheat and wine grapes. Some of the crops are grown organically. The farm participates in the Conservation Reserve Program, Environmental Quality Incentives Program and the Conservation Security Program.

I can only say that, as a community, we are blessed to have men like this among us. I mean, how lucky can we be? I absolutely love these guys! I think Governor Brown does too.

Not standing by and watching trees die
7/28/2015

I've been having some heart trouble in the form of chest pain. It's no secret because I've written about it before. So far it's nothing I can't handle. I can still do the things I like to do, but I just have to take things slower than I used to. I can still help the guys at Solano County Water Agency with their creek restoration work.

I can still help Putah Creek streamkeeper, Rich Marovich, take care of his greenhouse and nursery. I can still help Rick Fowler with his PDO and listen to his friendly stories and I can help Duc Jones do everything else because when you plant a bunch of trees, they have to be watered or they will die. This work is a labor of love for me; it keeps me healthy and gets me out of the house.

I have another labor of love that helps me keep active when I help out the Pickerels on their place right next to the Diversion Dam on Putah Creek. They let me piddle around doing this and that, all of which consist of little tasks that are ordinary on any ranch. I can't do the things I used to do but I'm still pretty handy with the small stuff. In return I can sit by the cold clear creek, listen to the waterfall, and watch the deer, salmon, trout, beaver and otters frolic around the trees and water.

I also try to help John Donlevy and Carol Scianna of the City of Winters. They are charged with the creation and care of the Putah Creek Nature Park that begins at the creek, under the railroad bridge and runs all the way to the freeway, a mile or so downstream. I cannot begin to tell you the amount of money and human effort in the form of labor it has taken to get this nature park up to the point where it is now. I'm sure there is some web site you can go to get it all broken down for you if you need to see that stuff.

I have been helping the Putah Creek Council do their fine work of planting trees and caring for them all along the creek (centered mostly in the Putah Creek Nature Park (CWNP) for years. Through them, I've had the pleasure of meeting countless people, all volunteers like me, wanting to help out with the health of the Earth.

With all of this going on, I still have my home life and all that it involves as well. Sometimes I'm a little lax in my chores around home and I'll hear about that from my wife, Therese, who sometimes says she's going to call the Putah Creek Council and ask them if they would send me home to do some volunteer chores at my house.

Ha Ha.

This is my wife's little attempt at humor but I truly understand her plight.

How can my wife feel good about complaining about undone home chores when I'm freaking out about this tree or that dying for the lack of water? I tell her that the City of Winters and the Solano County Water Agency are on strict budgets when it comes to the nature park. I don't think any organization on any budget could afford to pay someone to do the little things I do for them.

No budget has an account for the removal of debris from the young trees after high water has washed everything downstream, just as no budget has an account for picking up all the little pieces of garbage that people throw away when they visit the park. It is my wish that everyone who visits the creek will consider themselves to be volunteers like me so if they see a piece of garbage, they could pick it up so I don't have to do it.

My wife knows how I feel about my volunteer work, so she's not all reluctant about my doing it. There are a lot of times that she could complain about what doesn't get done around my house but he holds her tongue because she doesn't want to have me overextend myself by doing more work then I should be doing. That's how I know she loves me.

Lately it has become difficult to get the trees at the park the water they need. I say difficult, not impossible. I don't know the politics of the matter and I don't care much about it either, but it seems the State Water Resources Control Board Office of Enforcement has restricted the use of creek water to water the thousands of plants and trees that have thus far been planted at the park. Many of these plants are yet to be established and will certainly die in a very short time if someone doesn't water them. They are dying as we speak.

Bryan Elder, PE is the Water Resources Control Engineer of the Special Investigations Unit (Office of Enforcement) acting for the State of California, and has denied the City of Winters, the Solano County Water Agency, the Putah Creek Council or any volunteer the right to take water from the creek and pour it onto a dying tree within the limits of the nature park. I'm sure there's a good reason for this action by the state, but I'll be goddamned if I know what it could be.

So now, here I am with my bad heart, and it seems as if I'm the only person that gives a good God damn if any of the trees at the park get water or not. Well there's only one thing I can do, because I refuse to let everything at the park go to hell. I'm going to take a bucket down to the creek under the bridge and water as many of those trees as I can by hand. Sometimes you have to break the law to do the right thing.

I'm going to break the law and I'm going to do it right now. Mr. Elder, and you and your Water Resources Special Investigations Unit (Office of Enforcement) acting for the State of California can kiss my ass.

Arrest me if you have to — I don't give a shit.

Slowdown lowdown
8/4/2015

Have you ever tried to slow down? I don't mean a little slowdown, I mean a big slowdown. Well, I can tell you from experience that slowing down is not that easy. Everyone — including my doctors, my family, my friends and people I barely know — are telling me to slow down because of a little bit of heart trouble. I understand their reasons for telling me this because they know I'm having chest pains and they really don't care to see me die from over exertion. The problem is that I'm having the hardest time slowing down to the point where I won't experience chest pains. If I go any slower I think I'll fall over.

There are so many things I still want to do. I want to help Rich Marovich take care of his greenhouse. At the same time I want to help Rick Fowler and Duc Jones take care of the creek and its restoration. It's important to me to help John Pickerel take care of the thousand or so people that depend on him to keep things rolling businesswise so they can support their families.

I also try to help John Donlevy and Carol Scianna of the City of Winters. They are charged with the creation and care of the Putah Creek Nature Park in Winters that begins under the railroad bridge and runs all the way to the freeway, a mile or so downstream. I cannot begin to tell you the amount of money and human effort in the form of labor it has taken to get this nature park up to the point where it is now. I'm sure there is some web site you can go to get it all broken down for you if you need to see that stuff.

I have been helping the Putah Creek Council do their fine work of planting trees and caring for them all along the creek (centered mostly in the Putah Creek Nature Park for years. Through them, I've had the pleasure of meeting countless people, all volunteers like me, wanting to help out with the health of the Earth. With all of this going on, I still have my home life and all that it involves as well. Sometimes I'm a little lax in my chores around home and I'll hear about that from my wife Therese who sometimes says she's going to call the Putah Creek Council and ask them if they would send me home to do some volunteer chores at my house. Ha Ha Ha. This is my wife's little attempt at humor but I truly understand her plight.

My wife knows how I feel about my volunteer work, so she's not indifferent about my doing it. There are a lot of times that she could complain about what doesn't get done around my house but she holds her tongue because she does not want to have me over-extend myself by doing more work then I should be doing. That's how I know she loves me.

I also spend a lot of time helping my friend Joe with his battle against cancer. It is important for me to be there when he needs a little help. You might think this situation would be a little one-sided with me helping him all the time. That is simply not the case because he gives me so much more then I give him. He amazes me with his fighting spirit and his willingness to do things for his fellow man, even as sick as he is.

I guess you can see that slowing down isn't an option for me and this brings me to something important I'd like to bring to your attention. There's so much violence in the world right now and if you're going to survive, you'll have to start using your head. Think about it. Think about what you would do if you took your family to a theater and someone started shooting people in the middle of the movie. What would you do?

Attitude, conditioning and preparation are everything when it comes to survival. Develop a mindset of never taking anything for granted. Always be aware of your surroundings and where you are, and know which way safety is located. Make sure your family members know to remain lowkey and calm while cautiously moving toward freedom as quietly as possible.

A guy like me who needs to slow down may figure he'll never be able to fight his way to freedom. This may be right, but I could help my family in other ways. If I'm prepared, I might be able to incapacitate a crazed shooter or at least draw his attention until my family gets to safety. Someone shooting up a theater cannot aim at your family if some guy is trying to stick a knife in his neck. He will be worrying about you and that just might be enough to save your family.

Attitude, conditioning and preparation are everything when it comes to volunteer work or escaping a violent situation. The other day someone criticized me for giving free work away. They wanted to know what I was getting in return. To this stupid question I replied, "Nothing. Who would pay a guy as slow as I am for work anyway?"

The road to happiness is through service to others.

This is for men only
8/7/2015

Girls are strange. This is not necessarily a bad thing nor is it a good thing. It's just the way it is. I bring this up only because 99.9 percent of all men believe this to be true. Only the top 14 percent of all men are intelligent enough to understand them and they themselves are wrong a good 32 percent of the time. There is however, the top .05 percent of those men that are truly capable of understanding women.

The main problem is that of all the men in the world, only one or two are capable of explaining women to other men in a comprehensible fashion. When average men talk about women, it naturally turns to gobbledygook and when the 14 percent say anything, it's wrong about a third of the time, so men that want to learn about women are screwed from the git-go.

OK, there are about 100 men in the top .05 percent, one for each continent. On the American continent, I am the go-to guy. I'll tell you right now what you need to know about women.

(For your information, this column is a secure site where we men can discuss everything we need to discuss and women will never know what we're discussing, so feel free to discuss. The fact of the matter is that women think my column is too dumb to waste time reading.)

The first thing I need to discuss is the fact that no man can please any woman for any length of time. The length of time will vary, but from my experience, I'd say anywhere from 15 to 30 minutes is tops. Any longer than that and they are ready to move on, so they put on their clothes and leave or go do the dishes or something like that. Sometimes they will leave their underwear behind just so you'll wonder why they did it.

Except for the .05 percent like me, all women are smarter than all men. I know this is scaring you, but it's time to man-up and quit being a pussy. Women can naturally sense when a pussy-man is within 50 yards, and you will not like what's left when they finish with you. It is not pretty. So, any men out there that are pussies — you should find a good hiding place until you can get it together enough to man-up.

OK, next is sex appeal. Don't worry about that, because you have absolutely none. Sex appeal is a ploy that women use to get what they want from you. They have the power to make you believe you have sex appeal, but that only lasts until they're done with you and then you're back to feeling like the turd you really are.

Control is another subject you need to know about. Women learn at a very early age how to control men. If you for a minute think this isn't true, simply observe a father and daughter in a living room setting. Any father is unable to resist his daughter's skills used to get him to fulfill her wishes. "Daddy, I love you may I have a candy bar?" or "Daddy, are you my snuggly-poo?" Whatever, it makes me sick how big burley men fall for this crap!

Thirdly, and most importantly, women can kill you twice as fast as another man can. The fact that women do not make good soldiers is totally and undeniably a big fat lie. That means it is not true. I have witnessed women killing my father and grandfather. I mean right in front of me, and then they looked me dead in the eye like I was going to be next, but I was too smart and ran away — that ain't no lie neither!

What really happened was their women's super-senses detected a young .05 percent male in the neighborhood, so every male within a five-block radius (that's a circle) was wiped out, off the face of the earth, and they were looking for me. The only reason I survived was by eating human feces so they left me alone, thinking I was stupid. I fooled them that time and many times after that, so if you want to survive, you better be ready to eat some shit!

So, in the end, all I can say to you, the average man, is to think of ways to make yourself useful to some woman. If you can't keep a good job, do dishes, mop floors or something like that, well, you might as well bend over and kiss your own ass goodbye, for you are toast.

I've written before about how women are taking over the world and it was ignored by the majority of all humans. As a matter of fact, only one person read it and I think it was a woman that was assigned to find any threats to womanhood. Apparently she didn't think it was a threat because I am still alive today.

Here's a link to the other warning about women. Read it and weep!

You will know them by the garbage they leave
8/18/2015

The other day, while making my daily rounds at Putah Creek, I found the remains of a beer party someone had neglected to clean up. I run into this kind of thing pretty often, but from the sheer number of beer cans and bottles, this must have been a hell of a party. I looked around, but there was nobody else there, so I started picking up the mess that eventually would fill up the back of my truck.

I don't know where this sort of behavior comes from, but I have to imagine it comes from the home. Children learn about alcohol in the home from their parents. They learn how to drink as well as how not to drink. It's nothing new, because garbage has been dumped into the creek for a hundred years or so. It lays there at the bottom of the creek, bubbling and festering unless it is cleaned up.

During the last couple of phases of the Putah Creek Restoration Project, I tried to volunteer to help as often as I could, so I can attest to the amount of garbage we hauled out of it in now what is the City of Winters Nature Park. Directly under the old bridge was a hot spot for just about every kind of garbage there is. You name it and we found it under the bridge. People seem to think it's a good spot to dump their old appliances like washers and dryers.

I have seen everything from an old piano to entire cars. There have been bags full of dead animals that someone had dumped after taking what they wanted from them. There were old bicycles and wheel chairs and even a few old gas engines from some sort of old machine the farmers no longer needed. I'll bet we've picked up 500 old car batteries and at least that many old tires. I guess it will never end, but I can't wait to get at the pile of garbage that I know is at the bottom of the last phase of work at the park.

The majority of types of garbage are beer cans and bottles. They seem to be everywhere in the park. This weekend's load of bottles and cans made me wonder just how many are dumped every day in the good old US. Get ready for this, because any normal person will be shocked.

Americans waste (landfill, litter, and incinerate) about 425 beverage containers per capita per year, twice as many as we recycle. An average of 975 beer cans and bottles are tossed per mile of road annually in the US. I'm sure you have all heard of the plastic islands in both the Atlantic and the Pacific oceans. Most of these were dumped in our rivers and creeks and eventually worked their way to the islands in the oceans.

Beer cans are lined with epoxy that contains biphenyl A (BPA), a chemical that keeps foods from reacting to aluminum, but that has also become associated with a range of ailments, including cancer, reproductive trouble and irregular brain development in kids. The damage to fish and wildlife is about to reach a critical stage. Everything we do affects the rest of the Earth. If we dump our garbage on the Earth, what does it become?

Sure we have our air conditioned homes with our TVs so we don't have to look at what is happening around us. We have our vacations so we can go to where they pay people to keep everything clean and dandy. Now, if you think about it, what would happen if someone took away your TVs, vacations and air conditioning? Geez, that would be devastating!

No, think about what would happen if the beautiful leaves, fish and animals went away and never came back. Losing your AC, TVs and vacations would seem insignificant after that, wouldn't it? The day we realize the leaves are never coming back will pretty much be the end of everything we know.

Please take the time to think about what you are doing the next time you finish a beer or soda. I'm getting much too old to pick them all up.

Chest gunk, bad opera and escape from the cardiac unit
9/17/2015

Have you ever escaped from a Cardiac ACU? I think I did last night, but I'm not sure.

Nurses at the ACU gave me so many pills that I'm not certain what is real. I found a high-rise construction job here in San Francisco, so I went to work. They were confused at first and said they didn't know who I was.

"I'm not leavin' — why don't you leave," I says.

I think at first they were gonna beat the crap out of me, but I don't think they did. The goon guy told his boss that he couldn't hit me because my heart was hanging halfway out. He thought it was an alien at first. Anyways, I woke up in the basement floor by something they call a column. Isn't that a cooinkidink because that's exactly what I happen to be writing.

Anyways, they wanted me to leave. They said they were gonna call the cops. I says, "I'd call 911, but I forgot the number." A short while later two detectives were holding me up saying, "Come along, old fella." They took the call because it was a weird one, and maybe one of those construction guys was an alien. I told them I had four hours pay coming. I never saw a cent.

Next thing I know, I'm sittin' back in the good old ACU, so I decided to edit my new book (soon to be released). First thing I saw was a little square right in the middle of the page, so I drew a big dark circle around it with a black marker and wrote, "What the hell is this?" That's when I found out it was one of those sticky Post-its that my wife had put there! Crap! After that, I turned off my phone light and went to sleep again. Now I just woke up to the Miss America contestants singing opera! I don't know how long I can endure! I just wrote a note and slipped it to Jane, my nurse. It read, "I have been listening to the entire Miss America program. Now they are singing opera full blast!!!!! Can you help me?" She reached over and turned it off because my roommate was asleep.

God help me!

Today, Sept. 14

So, in case you didn't know, I was tricked into a quadruple bypass by my tricky wife and her doctor friends. I was told that I was going in for another stint as an "outpatient." Ha!

So, now I'm sittin' here with three tubes about four inches in diameter sticking out of my chest! I look like I'm watering trees at the creek from inside my chest!

They say I can't bring any gunk from the tubes home so I can look at it under my microscope. Why the hell not — it's my chest gunk right? What's wrong with me takin' a jar or two home? What's the big deal?

And these big purple socky things. Aw come on! They know I never wear purple socky things! Why does this crap always happen to me?

Now they think I'm too dumb to know what they're giving me ain't real coffee! I mean, even those dumb people that want to prevent creek restoration work know what real coffee is! Well, I think they do anyways!

I'm gonna sue my wife and all the doctors along with Kaiser San Francisco because my roommate fell asleep with the Miss America thingy on his TV — full volume! Have you ever listened to those women sing opera in the middle of the night? It's pretty scary I can tell you that!

If I had a jar of chest gunk I would get even with them real quick! I'll get back with you soon — I gotta take some meds!

Caveat emptor — let the buyer beware, especially at this place

10/13/2015

Have you ever had a thorn in your ass? Every little movement, every little thought makes it dig a little deeper sending a shot of pain all the way to your brain. Some people say they "Have a stick in my craw!" Another saying that fits here is "Whatever can go wrong, will go wrong."

There are plenty of other idioms that will fit right in with what my ass is feeling right now like:

   • Fair suck off the sauce bottle.
• Rude awakening.
• Band-Aid on a bullet wound.
• Wake up call.
• Walking on broken glass.

I think you can understand by now that something is not right in my little world. Here is the fateful story just exactly like it happened.

July 13th was a beautiful Monday. I needed to go and water trees down at the City of Winters Nature Park, which seems to be my routine these days. I opened my truck door and the first thing I saw was a hole in my seat, so I decided to drive a block to the place where you buy stuff for trucks. I can't tell you the name of the place, but its initials are "Napa Auto Parts."

I walk into the place like I usually do and tell the salesman I need some seat covers. Okay, the salesman gets on the computer and I tell him I have a Ford F-150 Heritage XLT, 2004. We look and look, but there are so many seat covers that we decide that we should go out and actually look at my truck seats to be sure to get the right covers. The salesman says, okay, you have a 50 – 50 split high back, 40 – 60 cushion and a fold down console. He was exactly right, 100%.

Back in to the computer we go and the salesman tells me the cost will be $268.26 because they are special made. I didn't like the price much but I like the hole in my seat even less. So I say, "Okay" and hand him my debit card. He says, "It will be a couple of weeks for delivery." So I say, "Okay."

Fast forward a couple of weeks to August 1. In the middle of the night, some dumbass hits my truck, totaling it out and then drives off into the night. So, now I no longer have the truck, so I don't need the seat covers. You follow me so far?

Okay, not even two days later, I get a call from Napa Auto Parts telling me that my seat covers have arrived. So now I'm thinking to myself, "Oh crap, what am I going to do with these damn seat covers?" I don't even have the damn truck anymore.

So, I go down to Napa Auto Parts and tell them I don't need the seat covers because I don't have the truck anymore. "Well" they said "Since the seat covers were special made for your truck we cannot take them back." Now, I don't like this much, but I ordered them so I suck it up and accept the loss.

Now the Napa Auto Parts guy hands me the seat covers and to my surprise they are not even what I ordered. Now I have seat covers for a truck I no longer have but they never would have fit anyway.

Somehow the seat covers were no longer for a 50 – 50 split high back, 40 – 60 cushion and a fold down console but were for a super crew 40/20/40 bench seat w/covered fold down console with adjustable headrest.

The success of a business undertaking largely depends upon the efficiency of its salesman. In the modern age of cut throat competition, a person possessing desired qualities can prove to be a successful salesman. There is no denying the fact that salesmen are made and not born. He should possess the full knowledge about the product so that he may properly answer the questions of the customers at the time of sale. The buyer depends to a great extent on the salesman, especially in case of a new product.

The salesman at Napa Auto Parts ordered the wrong seat covers even after looking directly at my seats. I am now stuck with seat covers I did not order and I don't think this is fair. There is only one thing I can do and that is to never, I mean never set foot in Napa Auto Parts again. I can only warn you to do the same.

Napa Auto Parts sucks!

Proposing creation of the Department of Public Lies
10/16/2015

You know what? I have the solution to all the problems that we, as a community have been struggling with for the past few years. When I tell you about my plan you will probably think, "Why didn't I think of that?" After tha,t you will probably think, "That Donald Sanders is a very intelligent and thoughtful person."

My solution, of course, will need the cooperation of the City of Winters Mayor, Cecilia Aguiar Curry and City Manager, Jon Donlevy. Just to make it respectable, I'm going to throw in Mayor Pro Tem, Woody Fridae, too. We all know that without the approval of at least one of these individuals nothing, I mean nothing, will change in this city.

Here it is! The City of Winters needs a big fat liar! We could call it the Department of Public Lies. Now we all know who is best qualified to fill this position. I think it's pretty much common knowledge who is the biggest, fattest, liar in town. Maybe even the entire county or, I would even venture to say, the entire state.

Who is better qualified to head the Department of Public Lies than me, good old Donald K. Sanders? I am a liar. Everybody knows I'm a liar. No one knows the power of lies like I do, no one that I know of anyway. No one else in our community has a mental grasp of the good things that can be accomplished with lies.

Of course, liars with my qualifications do not come cheap. I think a salary in the $100,000 range would suffice. Throw in a new city vehicle with Department of Public Lies printed on the doors and an allowance for nice clothing and even a liar like me would go for it. Oh, and I would have to have access to the water in the fire hydrant by my house to water my grass.

Now that there are no objections as to my qualifications for the job, what exactly would I hope to accomplish with the newly formed Department of Public Lies? What would I hope to get across to you, my peoples, my peeps? What function would I serve? Well, my function, of course, you dummies! I call you dummies because if you weren't a dummy, you wouldn't be reading my column anyway, right?

Here's what I would do as head of the Department of Public Lies. I would announce that Phase III of the City of Winters Nature Park creek restoration project will be completed within 3 months and anyone that objects is a dirty stinkin racist! That's Racist with a capital R! Furthermore, you will not be allowed to wear your white robes and hoods to the City Council meetings any more. All of your names have been printed in the Oakland Tribune along with your pictures.

In further announcements:

• The nearest honest auto parts store is located in Vacaville.

• The new speed limit on Grant Street, all the way through town is now 50 MPH. No speeding tickets will be issued until the speed signs have been changed sometime next month.

• Parking meters are to be installed on Elliott Street all the way from East Main Street to East Abbey Street, but only citizens of the City of Davis have to pay full price. Porta-Potties will be located near my driveway in case you forget to pee before you leave Davis. You will no longer be allowed to pee on my hedges.

• The City of Winters water treatment plant will be closed after this week and all sewage will now be dumped in the creek to flow downstream to whatever the next town is — it doesn't matter anyway.

• Any attempts to undermine the authority of the Department of Public Lies will be viewed as an act of terrorism.

Any inquiries the public may have concerning the Department of Public Lies will require submission of your photo to be printed along with your name in the Oakland Tribune

My conscience was talking... why didn't I listen?
10/20/2015

In my younger days I spent some time in the suicide ward at David Grant Hospital located on Travis Air Force Base. Actually, I had several visits to the same ward. I can't say that it did me any good to be there, but I'm still alive and that's a good thing I guess.

Anyway, while I was there, I had a visit with a psychiatrist, which is customary I guess. I think they needed to know who I was and why I was in the suicide ward, so the doctor started asking me questions that no ordinary man would have the answers to. This is how it went:

Doctor: "How are you Mr. Sanders?"

Me: "Just dandy."

Doctor: (After about 10 questions) "Have you been hearing voices?"

Me: "Yeah, all the time... I can hear my conscience."

Doctor: "What does it tell you to do?"

Me: "Well right now it's telling me I shouldn't have told you about it."

Me: "That was a joke, Doc."

Doctor: "Ha!"

Me: "Yeah, it tells me what is right and wrong. It's a sense that governs somebody's thoughts and actions, urging me or you to do right rather than wrong."

Doctor: "Ha!"

Studies tell us that between 4 and 10 percent of the world's population claims to hear voices or auditory hallucinations as psychiatrists call them. Voices can be experienced in the head, in the ears, outside the head, in some other part of the body or in the environment. Voices often reflect important aspects of the hearer's emotional state – emotions that are often unexpressed by the hearer.

Sometimes my voices tell me something and I don't listen.

"Don't do that it says!"

I do it anyway.

Then it says, "Now look what you have done, you dumbshit!" A good 55 percent of the time, I'll think to myself, "Oh man, why didn't I listen to my conscience?" The rest of the time I just ignore it and try not to think about it.

Well, as it turns out, many famous people heard voices. It's a long list but it includes Socrates, Mozart, Beethoven, Gandhi, Alexander the Great, Caesar and Jesus. The list goes on and on. They may have heard one voice or many. Some people reported hearing hundreds, although in almost all reported cases, one voice dominates above the others.

When I hear the voice inside my head, I consider it a gift from God, a gift that guides me in the right direction. It always has. Now that I'm older, things have changed a bit. Now I do what the voices in my wife's head tells me. She is a gift from God as well.

It is the people that don't hear voices that I worry about. I also worry about people that have voices telling them to do evil things. Things like mass murder and physical attacks on the innocent; evil things that we have experienced and lived with all of our lives if you think about it. Evil that seems to increase in frequency and is reported on the news every day.

Reason makes mistakes, but conscience never does, or so they say. I personally have made mistakes as well, but I can honestly say that I have never purposely done anything I would consider an evil deed. As I look back in time, I have but one question that troubles me when I don't know the answer.

My question is, "When a soldier kills someone in a war, will the dead men's families consider it an evil deed?" My voice tells me that it is highly likely and I'm thinking to myself, "Why didn't I listen to my conscience?"

When humans harm Nature, Nature needs our help to recover
11/27/2015

Humans are pretty smart. Sometimes we're too smart. There's a good side and a bad side to even this fact. We're smart enough to know that war is not a good thing but we aren't smart enough to avoid them. We know that we're doing irreversible damage to the entire Earth but we keep on killing trees and burning oil.

I believe animals are pretty smart too. Humans are smart in one way and animals are smart in another. There's a surefire way to prove that animals are smart and that's by the fact that they shy away from humans. A good example is if a human was lying injured in what is left of the forest, an animal would not stop to help him. As a matter of fact, some animals will sit nearby and wait until death comes to the human and then they will eat him.

I've noticed two distinct types of humans. One type loves the Earth and will go out of their way to keep it healthy and happy and the other type is responsible for all the trash that litters the roads and creeks. Two types of humans, I fear, is not a good thing. They can never agree on anything and each feels that their type is better than the other.

Most of the time the two types of humans are separated by rivers or imaginary lines they call borders. They like it that way. They all have armies that stop other types of humans from crossing these borders. It's a funny thing, but these human armies even dress differently so they each know who they are. After all, you wouldn't want to shoot one of your own types would you?

It really doesn't matter what one type does, because the other type will always oppose it and go in the opposite direction, thus humans go to war. They kill and kill until they get tired of killing. Periodically, they destroy everything they have accomplished in the last thousand years so you can see that it really does not matter what they do because they're going to destroy it anyway.

For generations, the two types of humans dumped their garbage and sewage into the forest and rivers simply because it was convenient. It didn't matter that sewage dumped on one side of a border was carried across to the other side. They didn't care if it wasn't healthy for those that live downstream because they were probably the other type anyway.

So now we're coming to the point I'm trying make. Neither type of humans considered the fact that if you dump your poison into the rivers and creeks it would kill everything it comes into contact with. Everything that was once good about nature was gone or was in trouble and soon to be gone. Rivers and creeks became lifeless and rancid with the stench of humanity.

Fortunately, the downstream type of humans convinced the upstream type of humans that if a river is poison downstream, it stops all life from getting upstream. Fish will not survive living in human scum and they cannot even swim through it. It stands to reason that if there are no fish in a river there will be no wildlife at all because they all are interconnected and depend upon each other.

When I say animals are smart it may make some of you giggle. Well go ahead and giggle because I know for a fact that they try to communicate with us but most of us don't listen. If something is wrong in the forest, the animals will tell us. Anyone that knows anything about nature will tell you that this is true. There are many humans of both types who are in the process of listening to the animals and are moving to come to their aid but they just can't agree on how it should be done.

One type of human wants to fix nature and try to make it like it used to be and others want to leave it alone and let nature fix itself. Unfortunately, we have damaged nature so much that it is at the point where it cannot fix itself. Invasive plants that out-survive native plants and invasive fish that could live in a bucket of gasoline have taken control of much of our wildlands.

One type of human looks upon these invasive plants and animals and think that they are natural and therefore should be left alone. The other type of humans believes that nature cannot be repaired while invasive plants and animals are prominent in our wildlands and must be removed. So there we are. We have to agree that we disagree.

Locally, a lot of money and effort have been spent on the restoration of Putah Creek. Now the work has all but stopped because one type of human does not agree with what the other is doing. Unless the restoration project is allowed to continue, everything, in time, will go back to being just what it was five years ago, lifeless and rancid. No self-respecting trout or salmon would swim in this creek as it was then unless it was brought in artificially.

I don't give a shit what anyone says, I know for a fact that the restoration of Putah Creek is a wonderful, successful project and healthy for the local watershed. I know this because I can hear what nature says to me and I see with my own eyes the hundreds and hundreds of salmon that now fill Putah Creek. As you are reading this, Putah Creek salmon are in the process of spawning all along the creek. The salmon tell me they are happy with and want us to continue the restoration project as it was.

Please be respectful, keep your distance and give the salmon room to spawn. Thank you

A love letter for my home town: Winters, California
December 16, 2015

In my home town of Winters, California, Santa Claus is ushered into town with a big parade of tractors beautifully decorated for the holiday season. The condition of the tractors is a good indicator of the state of the local economy. I'm happy to report that the farmers seem to be doing just dandy. It goes to reason that if the farmers are dandy then the rest of the town is doing just dandy.

Time seems to pass way too fast so it's hard for me to keep track of what has been happening in my life. As I think about the passing of 2015, I realize how fortunate I am to live in this community we call Winters, California. The amount of love I have for this town and the people in it still amazes me. I'm so happy that I could just crap and fall back in it.

I happened to drive through Winters about 30 years ago and I remember thinking, "That's where I want to live!" I love everything about this town. If I had my way, I would never leave it again. Anyone who wants to visit with me can come here, because I don't want to leave and go to where they are. Everything I desire is right here. I truly believe that anyone from anywhere in the world can come here and find happiness. There are some really fine people living in this area and I'm grateful for the opportunity to live among them. I mean, where in the world could be a better place to live? This is a perfect town.

A few moments ago, I glanced at the front page of the local newspaper, the Winters Express, to see a picture of the new Citizens of the Year, Woody and Rebecca Fridae. I absolutely love these people and I think we all should think about how lucky we are to have such quality individuals as neighbors. They make me smile every single time I see them.

I love the town. I love the restaurants, the markets, the hardware stores, the auto parts store (but I'm mad at them right now), and most of all the farmers. Farmers are the life blood of this community and they're connected to us all. They have given this town the riches of the ages just as farmers do in every town, but this is my town and if I have my way, the local farmers will enjoy happiness and prosperity for the next thousand years.

We have the best of everything here in Winters, California. Even the air that we breathe has the flavor of the local restaurants and the sound of the happiness of its citizens at work and play. As for me, I love the smell of the Buckhorn Steak House, cooking with the wood from the local plum orchards. It makes work and play the same for me. Yes, if I can smell the Buckhorn, then I'm a happy man.

I cannot forget to mention Putah Creek and the City of Winters' Putah Creek Nature Park. Everything about this watershed is wonderful and beautiful at the same time. I am grateful for the work done by the Solano County Water Agency, the Putah Creek Council, the City of Winters headed by City Manager John W. Donlevy, Jr., the Winters PD that keeps the peace, and especially the local winemakers at the Berryessa Gap and Turkovich Wineries.

I have to stop, because I could go on and on forever if you let me. I have to tell the truth about this town. It's all I can do, because when you love something, that's what you do when you talk about it. The future is bright for this community, and that brightness trickles through the air to fall upon us like a misty rain. It's also true that what is bright for me is bright for you. Enjoy your holidays.

We don't have to do anything to share experiences that define our lives
1/3/2016

Some say a person's life is defined by what he has done and others say it is the sum of all that he has experienced while he lives upon this Earth. I prefer the latter, for the former defines me as a bore because I've done next to nothing that would be worth mentioning. However, the things I have experienced while I've lived upon this Earth would make me a king among kings.

The same applies to you. As I see it, we don't have to actually do anything to have an experience. The assassinations of President John F. Kennedy and Dr. Martin Luther King would be something that the entire world would share as an experience but we actually had no part in that event except for the fact that it broke all our hearts at once. Another part of that experience was our introduction to evil and how it can touch our lives at will.

Through Dr. King, we all experienced racism, discrimination and injustice. I was so moved by the words of his "I have a dream" speech. He was a man of peace and love — he was a man of God. When President Kennedy was killed, it made me very sad but when Dr. King was killed it made me very, very angry and I am angry about that even today.

The struggle for human rights is an experience we all share. The killing of Malcolm X comes to my mind at the top of the human rights chain. Equality and justice are something that neither Dr. King nor Malcolm X ever experienced in their lifetime. One thing that I know is true is that you and I have never experienced equality and justice in our lifetime, either, because Dr. King taught us that if one man is not equal then none of us are equal.

Through our loved ones, we all have experienced warfare on a grand scale. Our fathers were broken in World Wars I and II. My peers and I received our breaking in Vietnam and now our children are being broken in Afghanistan, Iraq and now Syria. All of the wars I have mentioned are founded in lies and deceit. We all shared the experience of 9/11 and more recently the terrorist attacks in Paris and L.A. Evil comes and goes at will.

We all shared the fall of the Berlin wall, Watergate, and the 1980 Hockey team that defeated Russia at the Olympics. We all walked upon the moon with Neil Armstrong and we peek into the depths of space through the Hubble telescope. We all share the experience of our failure to conquer global hunger because we spend billions upon billions on weapons instead of relief to those who are hungry and ignorant through no fault of their own.

The internet only raises the level of experience when it brings us into the Earthquakes and Tsunamis of the Eastern world. As I said earlier, we don't have to do anything to share an experience that might define our lives. Now we have Google, Intel, Apple, eBay and Facebook. Everything is so easy for us now. We can go to machines to receive money, drinks and food without ever talking to another human being. We know exactly where we are all the time with our GPS technology.

With our cell phones we can talk to others without ever saying a word. DNA research and stem cells promise longer and healthier lives for those who can afford it and we can document our lives with cameras that use no film. I'm still not sure how that works.

Now, through me, you can all experience what it's like to go twenty plus years without being chosen as Citizen of the Year of Winters California. You can experience the humiliation of not being chosen even after you have nominated yourself because no one else would. You have all experienced, through me, being rejected for a Pulitzer and a Nobel for Literature despite the fact that I have nominated myself for those and other awards. Oh, I guess you did experience, through me again, what it is like to get a trophy for lowest average in a bowling league in Peoria Illinois. Who cares anyway?

It's not laziness — it's common sense!

I told my wife, "I'm not gonna do it!" It just doesn't make sense to me. You go through all the trouble to put the damn Christmas lights up and then she wants me to take them back down. Everybody that knows anything about Christmas lights knows that this is something that has to be done in the right manner — it has to be planned out.

When you take Christmas lights down, you can't just go like wham-bam, the way women like to do everything. Those lights are fragile and have to be handled with a delicate touch. It's not a job to be handled in cold weather because a brittle light will crack under the strain of removal. Proper removal should be postponed until at least March or April but then you might as well leave them up because the next Christmas is right around the corner.

Yeah, my wife Therese is becoming a compulsive complainer. Geeze, I can't do anything right. Yesterday she was complaining about all the stuff I have scattered all over the yard. She called it junk! She can't seem to fathom the idea that this is where I keep all the stuff I've borrowed from friends and now I have to fix them before I can take them back to the proper owners. I can't fix them all at once and if I put them in the shed, I'll forget about them and it might be several years before I can return the lawn mower to Terry's house.

With Therese, it's always hurry this and hurry that. Take the bathroom remodel, for example. What's the hurry — you're not going to sleep in there are you? She nags that I've taken six years to do a bathroom remodel. That's too long. Just get it finished and put the damn trim on! What the hell! By the time I get the trim on, I'll have to turn right around and take it back off because it's time to paint it again. Do you want new-looking trim on walls with peeling paint, little miss-missie-miss? I think not!

Mowing the lawn is another thing she likes to complain about. Our lawn mower is over a year old and the handle is bent so it's only a foot off the ground. It hurts my back to bend over so low while I cut the grass. Not only that, you have to pull this rope thingy to get it started and it almost never starts right away. If there is anyone around, the mower might throw a rock and put someone's eye out. I can't be responsible for something like that, can I?

Her pet peeve is complaining about all the little pieces of toys strewn about the yard all the time. She says they hurt her feet when she steps on them. It's not my fault that the kids leave their toys lying in the yard. She just won't let sleeping dogs lie and says, "Why don't you pick up the toys instead of running over them with the lawnmower?"

"It's not my job," I say.

Now it's the bookshelf! She doesn't want my books to touch her books! This, this, this and this are your shelves. All the rest are mine, so kindly keep your books off of my shelves. "While you're at it, why don't you clean up all the junk around the computer?" she says. "You have a file cabinet right there so why don't you put your stuff in a file?" she says.

She says, "This and this and this and this!" It will never end.

"First of all," I say, "I can't get the damn file cabinet drawer open because there is a box of stuff right in front of it I would have to move every time I want to file something!" I'm just not going to do it! No, I'm not going to do it ever!

Now she's complaining about why we have two thermostats on the living room wall.

"Why do we need two thermostats?" she says.

I say, "Well it's pretty self-explanatory, dear!" I continue, "One thermostat doesn't work, so I put a new one up!" I can't take the old thermostat down because there would be bare wires sticking out and someone might get electrocuted! I just don't know what I can do to please her! I mean I work like 98 hours a day trying to fix things around the house. I think I deserve a little recognition for jobs that will be well done when I'm finished!

Screw those Christmas lights!

It is natural for us to know the truth
1/28/2016

I've told you before that I'm in love with everything and everyone because all things are luminous and exquisitely beautiful. Blah, blah, blah, ba-blah! I used to believe that mankind was driven by, motivated by some inner love of the universe. I think sometimes that this still might be the case, but now we are unaware of it. Like zombies, we have no perception of who we really are.

We are at the bottom of the evolutionary ladder but we think we're at the top. We could be cooperating, but instead we're competing, city against city, state against state and country against country. It's this sense of individuality that is the origin of all suffering. As a species, we cannot even solve basic world hunger, the simplest of problems. One out of every three people on Earth does not get enough to eat and more than that lack sufficient clean drinking water.

Since the beginning of time, man has been driven by greed, necessity, stupidity or fear. When the first glob of molten iron was cast from the first volcano into the arms of the first man, he cast it into a sword to force his will upon others. Of all the things man could imagine, he chose instruments of destruction over instruments of peace and construction. All great achievements accomplished by man were created almost blindly through trial and error, hit and miss. When we are faced with any hindrance that forces us to fall back, we resort to violence. Time after time, over and over we resort to force.

It is natural for us to know the truth. Each and every one of us has the ability to tell the truth from a lie. Even on a global scale, we can recognize the truth above the false. The false is easier and it suits us better than the truth. Those who are skillful at lies are not obvious. They appear to be simple minded. Those who know the absolute will know the patterns of subtle power and subtle power moves everything — and it has no name.

We are separated not only by walls and borders but by the color of our skin and our gender. The white population of the Earth may recognize racism but they are unable to experience it, For people of color, it is exactly the opposite, for they are unable to stop experiencing it. Consider the fact that Mexican American are on the other side of privilege for the first time. When Mexican Americans look across the border toward home, they find themselves on the other side of privilege but they have to struggle to find acceptance in a world of abundance.

In the modern world, the elders have no importance among the young. Even for married couples, aging is complicated, for women feel they are losing their appeal and men sense disappointment in their women. Constant comparison with others leads us to disappointment and the underestimation of ourselves. It's hard for us to lose our fear of being wrong that leads us to doors that go nowhere.

Blah, ba-blah, ba-blah, ba-blah. So on and so forth. I now tell you that there is hope after all of this and we all know that hope is better than despair. When we find ourselves in hard times, our true friends will be revealed. In the last few years I have learned that we can rise above everything, not by treading on others but by raising them up. We all make choices and our choices make us.

Happiness comes from our own actions.

I have become a lover of women, all women. I get this from my wife Therese, whom I trust with my heart. She know that when I say I'm a lover of women, sex has little to do with the statement. Take a moment and observe my wife and you will find her full of tenderness and compassion. I absolutely adore her and then add in her mother and sisters and this leads me to all women, everywhere. However, men alternate between seeking motherhood and punishing them for being women which explains everything from the sex drive all the way to the invention of the atom bomb. Warfare stems directly from our fear of intimidation of women when extended out from the home to the outside world. At the very same time women create men they love to hate.

So what the hell do you think about that?

Hope is alive in Putah Creek Nature Park
2/15/2016

I have had a long and glorious life. Had I the power to go back in time and change things or do things in a different manner, it would involve just a few quick moments in a line of millions and millions of moments. I would change powerful moments. Moments that might even have made me who I am as a man — moments that sent my life in its own direction. Moments that would forever place me among veterans of war as a veteran of war.

It is easy to say that I would change this and that if I were able. In reality, the changing of a single moment in my life could possibly change everything. If I had gone to the past and exchanged one horrible moment for, let's say, a moment of fun, I would not know the value of a person's life or the power of a person's mistakes and regrets. I would not know that a person I had called an enemy was not really my enemy at all.

If I changed just a few moments, I might never know that the terminology of governments is not the terminology of people. I would not know that a police action is actually a war. I would not know that a defensive action in a foreign land is actually an offensive invasion bent on destruction and the taking of life, precious life. I would not know that should you push a person hard enough and kill everything that he knows and loves, that person will strike back with a vengeance and try to kill everything that I know and love. That's the way it is.

It is the terminology of governments that forces us to be distrustful of others outside of our own land. Our politicians tell us that Mexicans are thieves and drug dealers and they should be walled out, away from us. Politicians tell us that there are weapons of mass destruction in Iraq, Afghanistan, Iran, and North Korea. They say Russia and China are fixed and ready to destroy the west. If I went back and changed just a few moments, I would not know that this is probably not true at all.

I would not know that the world is made up of individuals who are capable of making their own decisions in a peaceful manner with open arms of friendship and love. Individuals with mothers and fathers, sons and daughters, and brothers and sisters, just like us. Like us, their governments try to make critical decisions for them that may force them in directions that the do not choose to follow. After all, if we do not know or understand a person a continent away, it is easy to be distrustful and suspicious of his activities.

You will be happy to know that there is hope for us all. Yes, right here in Winters California, there is big time hope. In the last couple of days hope came to the City of Winters and went to work in our Nature Park planting hundreds of trees and rose hips. Most of the people of Winters, California, didn't even know that hope was here with gloves on, digging in our soil, all in an effort to get to know us, to understand us.

On Thursday, February 11, a group of about 30 young students from Shanghai, China, spent the day digging in the mud of Putah Creek, planting trees and roses that will mature in time bringing beauty and substance for us all to enjoy. As I watched them digging, slinging mud at each other and swinging on the rope swings, I was almost brought to tears with the amount of hope I saw in them. It was a lovely day for me.

On the very next day, Friday, the 12th of February, still more hope came to town. A group of about 20 young professionals, each from a different country, spent the day working in the mud of Putah Creek Nature Park. These outstanding groups of young people, hosted by UC Davis, are all members of the Hubert H. Humphrey Fellowship Program. They were beautiful beyond description. They are the best the world has to offer.

Since 1979, close to 4,274 professionals representing more than 157 countries have participated in the Humphrey Program. This year, 171 Humphrey Fellows from 98 different countries are spending the academic year at 16 universities across the United States. The fellowship is designed to promote international cooperation and understanding. It is wonderful and it fills me with hope and happiness just to be around them as they dig in our muddy creek bed.

All of this international attention to the City of Winters Putah Creek Nature Park was made possible by the efforts of the Putah Creek Council and the Solano County Water Agency, and the City of Winters, California. I cannot tell you what an honor it is for me to support these organizations as a volunteer. When I put my hands into the mud of Putah Creek alongside volunteers from every corner of the world, I am filled with hope and gratitude.

It is from this experience of fellowship and cooperation of people from around the world that I no longer feel a need to go back in time to change the moments that make up my life. These moments have brought me to where I am right now and I am exactly where I need to be, full of hope and full of love for my fellow man.

He really was a good Joe
3/4/2016

My friend Joe passed away last night after about a five-year battle with several forms of cancer. By today's measure, he was still pretty young to be so ill. He was just a couple of months shy of his 62nd birthday when the cancer got the best of him. I can attest to the fact that his fight for life was a valiant one. He wouldn't give up on life despite the fact that at most times he suffered unbearable pain, silently.

I met Joe only a time or two before we lost contact. He had gone to Oregon to be with his family and then returned to California before I even knew he was sick, so by the time he and I became friends, he'd already been struggling with cancer for a couple of years and I didn't even know. Just by chance, I heard rumors that he was sick and that there were people taking advantage of that fact to take him for everything he had. I found out that this is fairly common for when someone gets sick — everybody starts fighting over everything the sick person has even before they're dead and gone.

I drove out to his ranch and sure enough, there were three or four people loading up everything he owned in a big flatbed truck. They didn't slow down one bit with their thievery when they pointed me in the direction where Joe was laying ill on a mattress with no sheets, eating a can of beef stew, right from the can.

"These people are trying to kill Joe!" were the thoughts that ran through my head. It made me sick. I wondered why there was no one to help him.

Joe was a loner who wanted things done his way, so he pushed his family away despite the fact that they so desperately wanted to help. He insisted that family and doctors be kept at arm's length and he liked it that way. His family did everything they could do from a distance, but everything they tried to do was seen as interference by Joe. He was funny that way.

Anyway, Joe kind of adopted my family and I so in no time we were inseparable, and together we nursed him back to health and at times he was all but cancer free. Twice we thought we had beat it but it always came back. Breast cancer had eaten away at his body, and bone cancer had eaten his bones until it eventually made it to painful for him to walk unassisted. Finally, tumors in his brain seemed to get the better of him. I used to joke with him about all the bad karma he was suffering and I suggested he must have been a terrible person in his last life to have it so bad in this life.

For three years, Joe was always with me. People used to say that we began looking and acting alike. People would see Joe in my yard and yell at him, "Hey Don." Thinking he was me. When I did my volunteer work down at Putah Creek, Joe would come along. As long as he was able. he would work right along side of me watering trees, fertilizing, and anything else that needed to be done. It was clear to me that he enjoyed his time at the creek.

In the end, Joe became very sick. He lost a lot of weight very quickly and with it went his strength. At that point, it was clear that he would need professional, constant, care. He again pushed away his family when they tried to get him into a caretaker environment, so we hired a wonderful woman who was there for him constantly all the way until the end. So, there was Tracy there to take care of him together with a nursing-type woman, Eddi, who saw to his medical needs. Both of these women were sent from God — I'm convinced of that.

Joe's mother ran things from behind the scene, making all the big decisions. I was so relieved because for three years, the only person that was there was me, or so it seemed. For three years, I had no life at all because I was helping Joe live his life. When it all began, I had no idea what it took to help someone reach the end of their life. It is very stressful.

So stressful was it that I suffered two heart attacks, several minor heart surgeries and finally a quadruple bi-pass and open heart surgery. While I was recovering from that, friends stepped in to help out. My friends Terry and Mike and their families took over for me, and that's the one reason I didn't die myself.

I will miss Joe terribly because he was everything you could ask for in a friend. Terry, Mike and I are all the better people just for knowing him. What a grand guy he was. He was lucky at life but unlucky in health, but it didn't stop him for a moment, right up to the very end. If there's a heaven, Joe is there, because he was a straight-up, right minded man who could do no wrong as far as I am concerned.

So, take it easy Joe, don't tear the place up and I see you in a little while. We can both relax now.

Slander and personal attacks won't repair Putah Creek
3/2016

I am upset with the recent internet attacks on the Solano County Water Agency, the City of Winters City Manager John Donlevy and Streamkeeper Rich Marovich. The "Putah Creek Wildlife Stewards" and other Facebook users continuously display slanderous statements aimed at the above mentioned and their restoration efforts at Putah Creek. Statements like: "They are destroying the creek" and "The reality is that most have a really hard time justifying the destruction of this place. Many wonder if the 1.5 million is ready to go to into the pockets of those involved is part of the equation but we hope is not" are ridiculous and uncalled for.

I don't know much about the Putah Creek Wildlife Stewards, but what I have seen of them, I don't like all that much. Their outside appearance is one of a group of people concerned with the health of our wildlife, but if you look closer, things become suspicious. They seem to think we need their twisted definition of progress while they are the only ones who stand to profit from their particular interpretation. The way they snidely imply that people involved in the restoration work at Putah Creek may have their hand in the till sickens me.

Where in the hell did that come from? Other statements are just as ridiculous. "They are destroying wildlife habitat" and "Don't wait too long to see him (a bird)" "The Solano County Water Agency is determined to bulldoze this entire area, with the blessings of our city staff and city council." This is a narrow-minded misconception of what the restoration project is in the middle of doing and it's aimed at the health of the creek as a whole.

While the Putah Creek Wildlife Stewards seem more concerned with individual animals (they are important), the restoration project is aimed on a larger scale at the whole community of animals and their healthy living environment, free from a century or more of man's abuse of Putah Creek. To insure a healthy environment, it is essential that the creek be returned to its natural state. Your efforts to abort the restoration work at Putah Creek are like a little kid that didn't get his lollypop.

You have resorted to attacks on the character of Streamkeeper Rich Marovich and City Manager John Donlevy without justification or reason. You know very well that you have avenues to voice any complaints you may have, but you've chosen the low road where you can take a jab and run back into your dark hole where you surely reside. This type of behavior is not within the spirit of cooperation and brotherhood that this nation was founded upon. There are two sides to everything and everybody has their opinion, so there is no call for personal slanderous attacks.

Most people who insult other people are insecure. I call it "The Little Man Syndrome." They are little on the inside, so they put others down to build themselves up. They think it will make them feel better if they put someone else down, or they insult other people to take attention off themselves. Sometimes people who are angry insult other people because they are not mature enough to think of a different way to handle their anger except to try to start a fight or try to make the other person feel bad.

Mature people can communicate with others without insulting them. Any ideas can be discussed between mature adults without fighting or insulting each other. Mature people can "agree to disagree" and give each other the right to have different opinions.

On a larger scale, humanity as a whole is impotent. I am as certain of this as I have been certain of anything in my entire life. As a species, we are helpless. We're unable to do anything to help ourselves or anyone else. We're unable to complete even the easiest of tasks simply because we are unable to agree on anything. Any power we might have is divided, diluted and spread about, rendering it ineffective and weak.

History teaches us the lesson that the actions taken in the past do not necessarily have the concerns of the future in mind — thus we have years of man's abuse of the creek. A society that cannot function enough to fix its mistakes will give rise to "individual actions" such as yours. That's okay. Running your mouth is within your rights, but try to stay out of the way when the big boys are fixing the damage that society has done to the creek.

Love the Putah Creek restoration work

3/22/2016

Last Friday was a beautiful, warm, sunny day. I walked down to Putah Creek just to look things over just as Streamkeeper Rich Marovich suggested I should do. Of course that was some time ago; years I think. He said "Maybe you could be another set of eyes for me because I cannot get down to the creek as often as I'd like to see what's going on."

So, every couple of days, I'll take a walk along the creek and if I see something out of the ordinary, I'll call him up and tell him about it. Most of the time, he has already seen what I was going to tell him about, so that makes me think that he spends a considerable amount of time inspecting his creek. I don't think there is a whole lot that I could tell him about the creek that he doesn't already know.

Some people have complained about Rich Marovich and his creek restoration work. They claim the work has caused all the animals to leave the area and they fear that they won't come back when the work is done. Another thing they complain about is the fact that the thousands of trees and other plants haven't matured to make the park look more natural like a watershed forest should look. I can understand their concern but any reasonable person could walk near the edge of the creek and see exactly what's going on.

The fact of the matter is that the animals are still in the park despite the fact that they are hard to spot in the daytime. I'm no detective despite the fact that I have a large brain and my thought processes put me squarely in the middle of the smarts graph. I'd like to say just how smart I am, but you wouldn't believe me anyway. Yeah, I might not be the smartest tool in the shed, but even a guy as dumb as I am can see that there are probably just as many animals and birds living at the creek now as there were before the restoration work started. It is natural for animals to lie low when there is human activity in the area.

There will an increase in animal sightings now that the local bridge work is completed and all the heavy equipment is taken from the area, never to return. One sure indicator of animal activity is the number of trees and other plants they cut down to make their little animal houses. Those damn beavers chew the trees up as fast as we can plant them and that's the truth. I wish I had a dollar for every tree they have chewed up in the last year. Perhaps I'd have enough money to pay all those people that are compulsive complainers to shut the hell up.

Most of the trees we plant are protected by wire mesh so the animals cannot chew them up but the sad thing is that the mesh has to be removed during high water or the debris will uproot them and send them packing downstream. At the end of the rainy season, the mesh is put back around the plants that haven't been cut down, which isn't many because the beaver are pretty thorough when it comes to chewing trees.

I think it is a natural fact that compulsive complainers have no vision for things that will be. This I cannot understand, because it is as clear as day to me that in the not too distant future the City of Winters Nature Park will be a lush green watershed. There will be so many animals living along the creek that you will allow your children to hunt them down with their BB guns, just like I did until I was 55 years old. I can predict an increase in garbage such as old dirty towels, underwear, socks and beer cans. It would be very nice if some of those people that are always flapping their gums could come down to the creek and help me pick up some of that garbage instead of throwing it there.

I wish I had the words to tell you just how much I love the way the creek restoration work is going in the park. I mean elegant words that would help others to see the visions I have of how everything we do will turn out for the betterment of all, animal and man. I know it is so easy to look at a work in progress and not be able to see what will come to pass. Streamkeeper Marovich in the long run has become another set of eyes for me. Through his eyes, I can clearly see what the future holds for the Lower Putah Creek Watershed.

I don't see much of Rich Marovich lately — he's too busy with other important things. I know for a fact that he works much too hard and his hours are long. I think his hours are 90 minutes long, maybe longer. I do know that by the time I get out of bed at 11 a.m., he has been at work for four or five hours already, and when I'm lying on the couch watching TV, he is at the greenhouse working with trees and stuff like that.

If you think I am a creek nut, well he is a hundred times worse that I am. So is Rick Fowler, Duc Jones of the Solano County Water Agency, and Carrie Shaw, Karin Young and Amy Williams of the Putah Creek Council. I'll bet I could hide a turd under a log by the creek and each and every one of them would find it and step in it. My point is that the creek is healthier now than it has been for many years and it is only going to get better. These people have the creek work under control, so do yourself a favor and go down there and talk shop with them. You will be impressed for sure. Oh one thing — don't expect Amy Williams to stop work and chat because I don't think she knows how to slow down or take a break. It's not that she is unsociable, she is just a tree planting machine. I get tired just watching her work.

Of course, I am the most important creek guy in the world, and that's a natural fact!

I need to follow my own rules
3/25/2016

I have several rules about developing good habits. My rules are probably pretty much like your rules except for the fact that you probably live by them and I don't.

There are times I wish I'd followed my good habits rules but didn't. One of these times occurred just a couple of weeks after I met my wife Therese. This particular story happened a long time ago when everybody had to fix their own car when it broke down. It didn't matter much if you knew how to fix a car because there were books that would guide you step-by-step (easy to follow) to auto repair.

Rule number one: Never Volunteer for Anything!

So, when Therese's car broke down, I volunteered to fix it for her. The book said that the timing chain had broken and it was an eight-hour repair job. I had a perfectly good reason for wanting to fix her car as I liked her a lot but I don't think she cared too awful much for me. I'm almost sure this is the case because she turned me down for dates the first 10 times I asked her out. I figured I could find my way to her heart by working on her car, thus becoming indispensable.

Rule number two: Never Assume Anything!

Her parents were in Hawaii for a week, so I assumed I could finish the repair job long before they came home. I also assumed they wouldn't come home early. Another thing I assumed was the fact that I could actually get the car to run when I was done. Finally, I assumed I could do it without making a mess in her father's garage. So, I jumped right in to the job and everything went well for the first week except that when I tried to start the damn car, it wasn't getting any fuel.

Rule number three: If All Else Fails, Read The Damn Instructions!

When I put the car back together, I neglected to follow all the steps. How was I supposed to know that Fords needed a little thing-a-ma-jig on the front of the whatever to make the fuel pump work. So, there I am, trying to figure this out, when lo and behold, her father walks into the garage and I meet him for the first time. OK, I am covered from head to toe with grease and oil, as was his garage floor, the walls, and all of his tools that were scattered around the garage.

Rule number four: Never Make Excuses!

Rule number five: Speak Properly!

I don't even want to get into these, because I simply mumbled and shuffled my feet in the slippery oil. I don't know what I said, but it didn't matter because he was very cordial and nice about the whole situation. He knew exactly where I had gone wrong with the repair job and told me how to fix it. This took me another week, but I finally got the damn thing back together and tried to start it.

Rule number six: Have a Sense of Humor!

OK, it was time to start the damn car, so I sprayed about a half a can of starting fluid into the carburetor and then reached over to pump some gas into it. I bent waaaay over to look inside to see if it was actually getting gas. When I did this, my hand hit the distributor, causing the points to fire, igniting the starting fluid, causing it to blow up in my face.

Rule number seven: Show Your Human Side!

At about this time, the phone rings in the kitchen and Therese's father answers it. So then the guy that lives across the street from Therese's dad tells him, "There's a guy on fire in your garage!" So now, Therese's father comes out to the garage where I'm standing, grinning like an ape, with my eyebrows, mustache and part of my hair burned off. What could I say but, "Want to see if she will start?" To my amazement it did start!

Rule number eight: Take The Initiative!

Looking like an idiot, I had to clean and paint part of the garage to get it into the condition it was in when I started, and I still don't think Therese liked me all that much because while I was fixing her car, she was going out with someone else. That turned out alright though, because I don't think she liked him either.

Rule number nine: Learn Continuously!

Well, what could I possibly have learned from this whole whatever it was? I learned I am not a mechanic, working on a girl's car will not make her like you, and when you think a girl doesn't like you she probably does. After all, she did marry me, didn't she?

Rule number ten: Forget Perfection!

Nothing will go the way it's supposed to go. There's no perfection except for the fact that life itself is perfect. My life, every day from that day to this one has been perfect. My marriage is perfect, my wife is perfect, and my love for her is perfect. Now it has been well over 30 years and she still hasn't dumped me, but when I turned 60 she said she was going to trade me in for two 30-year-old guys. That was just a threat. It turns out that she did like me!

What kids need now are role models!

3/31/2016

Remember way back in the 60s when that Abby Hoffman guy made the big speech in Washington D. C.? I think he dropped the "F" bomb about two dozen times in what was essentially a very short statement about how the Vietnam War needed to end. Even with a vocabulary as restricted as his was at the time, that "F Bomb Speech" made him famous enough to make his name a household word around the world.

Another famous guy from about that era was the fellow caught in the picture giving the cops the finger at the 1968 Democratic Convention in Chicago, Illinois. (By the way, since you pronounce "Illinoy" like this, why do we have to spell it like "Illinois?") I wonder whatever happened to that guy when the cops got done beating his ass. I heard he walked sideways for the rest of his life and because one leg was longer than the other he sometimes walked in a spiral to get where he was going.

Now that I think about it, everybody in our generation thought we were going to change the world. We were going to "F— the man!" We were going to have world peace, have flying cars and by this point in time, all of humanity was going to be Black with Asian eyes because genetically those traits are dominant. I don't know what the hell happened with that because half of us are Gingers now and the other half are mad as hell and swarming like a bunch of bees.

The first half are afraid to go out on the street after dark because the "Man" is taking everybody out if you roam the streets after dark. The "Man" is good at what he does and if we ever have another war, I think we need to send the "Man" over to fight it, because those guys can kill a man dead in like 10 seconds. Not only is he dead, but he has like a hundred holes in him and then they will put handcuffs on his dead body. I think that's kinda harsh to kill a guy dead and then arrest him for running away and leaving the scene of his own death.

By now you must be thinking, "What the hell is this Sanders guy trying to convey with all this reminiscing about the past?" Well I'm not rightly sure what I'm trying to say other than at one point we thought we could change the world through protest, demonstration and nasty gestures at the "Man." Well, I'm afraid we dropped the ball with all the change. The beautiful world we were going to provide our children turned out to be something entirely different and not so tidy as we would like to imagine. Today's kids won't turn off the video games long enough to help with the dishes or mow the grass.

Today's children don't have anyone to inspire them to move on to bigger and better things like we did when we were young. We had John Wayne, the Lone Ranger, Superman and Batman. What today's children need is someone to look up to and use as a role model. I know it's hard to imagine, but I know three fellas living right here in this area who are perfect. I'm talking about John Pickerel of Buckhorn Steakhouse fame, Rick Fowler of the Solano County Water Agency and me the volunteer-writer-genius type guy.

I'll tell you why I feel we would be such good role models for children. Here is the text of several messages the three of us sent to each other tonight:

John Pickerel: "Just got finished fishing the John Deere out of the creek that went over the waterfall." "It got caught in a big release from the dam that came at me!" (There was no big release – he just drove it over the falls!)

Rick Fowler: "Yeah, John found out that his John Deere floats like a boat!"

Donald Sanders: "Hey, I wonder if it can fly?"

Rick Fowler: "We should put a chopper blade on it and make it a John Deere Flopterchopter!"

Donald Sanders: "Ya, a Pickerelfloptercopter!"

Another reason we're good role models for children is because Rick Fowler says he owns Putah Creek, John Pickerel serves the best steak in the world and I do everything else. I don't know what everybody else does around Winters, California, except Tony Morales rides around in a golf cart all day and I don't know what Herb Wimmer does but they always catch me when I sneak onto their land. I think maybe they have some Navy Seal experience. I guess they could be role models, too. After me of course.

This is the order role models come in:

1. Rick Fowler

2. John Pickerel

3. Donald Sanders

4. Tony Morales

5. Herb Wimmer

We're meant to see beauty
5/8/2016

As I grow older, I'm surprised to find that after all these years, I have a newfound knowledge of how beautiful everything has suddenly become. Were I a better writer, I could find the words to bring this beauty out of my heart and mind, and give it to you in the hope that you will recognize it for what it is. I would certainly give it as a gift to those I love the most. Where it would go from there, only God would know, for it was God that first gave it to me.

I think God must give this ability to see things beautiful to us all at a very young age but he leaves it up to the individual when to develop and use this gift. I know now that at a young age, I had the knowledge and the sight to see the beauty around me but I rarely took the time to really see and enjoy it the way that I do now. I have every excuse in the world, everyone to blame, but the fact of the matter is, I was too busy, high, drunk or whatever to really stop and enjoy this Godly gift. This is the only thing I could imagine that might make God cry.

We are meant to see how beautiful everything is. You create your own world and personality. All you have to do is figure out who you want to be and how you want the world to be, then find a way to create that person and build that world. It's so simple. So simple that I'm brought to tears when I think of how I wasted all these years and days and hours, and I just could not see how it should be and could be.

Tonight, I looked upon my wife, Therese. She has a beauty that shines like the sun, inside and out. I cannot believe how lucky I am to have such a woman for a wife. I'm so happy that she loves me and keeps me for her husband, lover, and friend. I can only strive to be a better husband for her in the future than I was in the past. I have never loved like I love right now, and I can foresee no slowing in the process as our years together progress.

Sometimes the beauty I find in the world overwhelms me and forces my emotions up from the depths within out into the view of the world. I fear that there may be a reason some of us see the beauty and some of us don't. I think it may have to do with the way families interact. Mothers and fathers are supposed to point out and teach us what beauty is and the fact that there is beauty in everything. Those of us who didn't have a normal childhood missed out on that very important part of life. How can your mother show you anything if you don't have one?

Another thing I've learned about beauty is the fact that it takes a lot of effort to keep it that way. Many things have to change. Cars and trucks are made to be beautiful and we all yearn to have one, to drive one, and to be beautiful ourselves as we sit inside and drive so everyone might see us. We turn the radio up so loud thinking people will hear the noise and look at us to see its source. All the while, the gas these automobiles emit is choking the life from us. In the end, it makes us sick and will eventually kill us all.

We fail to see the beauty of the Earth around us because we rush here and there looking through dirty windows unless we roll them down to throw out our hamburger wrappers. It's all a lie we tell ourselves. The man who lies to himself and listens to his own lie comes to a point where he cannot distinguish the truth within him, or around him, and so loses all respect for himself and for others. He thinks this guy's a jerk and that lady's an asshole, and having no respect for others, he ceases to love and when he ceases to love, there's no beauty for him anywhere upon this Earth.

We must take the time to find the beauty in the world and once you find it you'll want to be worthy of the love it brings you. Once you truly believe you're worthy of love, you'll never settle for anyone's second best treatment. Second best treatment will not bring us to a point in life where things flow naturally and healthily.

"Nothing that's worthwhile is ever easy. There's a loneliness that only exists in your mind. The loneliest moment in someone's life is when they are watching their whole world fall apart, and all they can do is stare blankly because they are not prepared." — F. Scott Fitzgerald

Beauty and happiness don't come freely at first. It takes a little work to find them, but once found, everything becomes beautiful

Remembering the dead on Memorial Day
5/27/2016

Today, with Memorial Day coming up, I hopped on my computer thingy, typed in some of the names of men from my unit listed as KIA. I wanted to see what information there was, if any, after all these years. The last time I did this was some time ago when computers were still a new technology. I found their names but that was about it.

Now there seems to be much more information out there and it is easier to find. I found a web page that had a list of KIAs and all I had to do was type in their names, starting with CPT Barry Mercer Straw. CPT Straw and his entire crew died in a midair collision with a Korean fixed wing aircraft somewhere near LZ English where I think the Headquarters of the 173rd Airborne was located. I'm not sure about that last part because my memory fails me.

Anyway, my computer thingy tells me that CPT Straw hailed from Panorama City, California. So I say to myself, "I should go on Google Earth and see where CPT Straw grew up." I proceeded to do just that.

Panorama City is a mish-mash of houses all jammed together, each with a pool in the back yard. It's located just north of Santa Monica, so I imagined that CPT Straw was a surfer dude. At least that's what all of us kids who went to high school in East Peoria, Illinois, thought about anyone from California. I imagined that CPT Straw knew all of the Beach Boys. He probably swam and partied at the beach with his friends.

Next, I typed in CW2 Ronald Norman Jasinski. He was from Roselle, Illinois, which is located just west of Chicago. I remember Jasinski was a party animal. One day he came in with a huge plastic water blatter that he cut in half, stuck it in a big hole he and his friends had dug and made a swimming pool. It was just like Beverly Hills but located in Vietnam.

Again I went to Google Earth and found that Roselle, Illinois, looked just like Panorama City, California, but with different types of trees. I'll bet my friend, Streamkeeper Rich Marovich, could tell me exactly which trees are native to each of these cities. He's good at that kind of stuff.

Anyway, Jasinski and his whole crew died when their sling load hit a tree which in turn dragged the CH47 helicopter down to the ground in the middle of the Central Highlands jungle. They were called on an Emergency Tac-E in the middle of the night. Sometime later I saw a paper with a list of their cargo, none of which would make up an emergency in my eyes. 700 pounds of garbage cans and bundles of tent pegs! Kiss my ass! What a waste!

I imagined he swam and partied with his friends in Lake Michigan because it was only a stone's throw away from his home town.

Moving on, I looked up CW2 James Robert Meade who grew up in Topeka, Kansas. Topeka is just west of Kansas City where all the cowboys come from. I happened to witness the end of CW2 Meade's life and it was horrible. He was at the helm of his CH47 when it suffered a blade strike against a revetment. The helicopter went straight up, nose first, and then inverted and blew up on impact. His crew chief survived.

Crew chief Mott (I think that was his name) survived but he was burn to a crisp over 80 percent of his body. A while later I went to see him in the hospital and he was still lying naked on his bunk with hoses up his nose and groin. His lips and nose were burned off along with his ears.

I asked him how he survived and he told me he saw a hole in the flames and ran and dove through it. He said he wished that he had died because he couldn't even kill himself now until he healed a little. A year or so later I saw a picture of him in the Army Times eating watermelon.

Anyway, back to CW2 Meade. I looked up Topeka on Google Earth and it looked just like the other places except there was no big body of water nearby. So, I imagined that CW2 Meade never partied with his friends in Topeka because there was no place to party except maybe in your basement. Houses back east have full basements, not like California.

I can't do this anymore, it's time for my nap.

A little advice for the younger set
6/6/2016

I'm worried about the wellbeing of the next generation. Up until today, I've always held faith that our young will always do the right thing when it needs to be done, without hesitation. Nah, that ain't the case anymore. Lately I'm thinking that there isn't a set of brains to be shared among the whole lot of them. Today's kids are pretty smart when it comes to school stuff but when it comes to common sense, they are severely lacking.

Yesterday I happened to look at the back seat of a young man (no names) who's been a friend of the family for some time. There, in front of God and everybody else, sat an open bottle of Fireball Cinnamon Whisky and a small bag of tiny plastic cups. It wasn't a small bottle either —a half-gallon! I thought, "What the Hell is wrong with these kids?"

I reached in and took the bottle and immediately went to confront him about it. There he was in the kitchen with his other goofy friends, laughing and telling goofy kid jokes. I couldn't wait to light into this kid and it wasn't for my benefit but his. I got right in his face and said, "What the hell are you doing driving around with an open bottle of this swill?" He looked at me kinda dumb like.

So then I start telling this group of young men the way things are and what will happen if you drive around with crappy whisky in your back seat. I told them they might get away with such behavior for a while but eventually the cops will get wind of it. Not only will you get pulled over and accosted by the police but when they see the crappy brand of whisky you drink, well, let's just say they are not going to be happy. Any good cop will tell you that cinnamon whisky is not worth confiscating.

Not only that, they will get in your face, grab one hand and cuff it and to make matters even worse, they will grab your other hand and cuff it too. They will not be gentle either. They will write you a DUI right there on the spot, throw you in the back of their squad car that smells like pee, then they will throw you into jail with the guys that peed in the back of the cop car.

That's where the fun really begins. When you regain consciousness, you can beg your parents to bail you out and that will cost them plenty. After that, your dad will have to take you to the impound yard to get your car by paying an impound fine and at least 30 days' worth of storage. Once you get all of that done, you'll have to find someone to drive your car home because you no longer have a driver's license.

You will find yourself walking everywhere you go, which includes the court house, because when all is said and done, the cost of that crappy bottle of whisky will be close to $16,000.00. Now who's the dummy?

Do not despair. Things will get worse for you as you grow older and more mature like me. Fortunately, I have some good advice I can give you because I am older and have made a whole lot more mistakes than you have. You can take heed or not — I don't really care.

I'll spell it out for you to make it easy:

• Never fall in love. If you are inclined to do so, just cut your own arm off because it will hurt less.

• Never get married. Instead of marrying someone, just go out and find the girl that you absolutely hate the most and buy her a house.

• Never, under any circumstance take a sleeping pill and a laxative on the same

night.
- Prepare for the worst but expect the best.
- When nothing goes right, go left.
- The worst day of your life is actually the worst day of your life so far.
- The trick to being a good liar is the ability to convince others you are a bad liar.
- Instead of filling your drink with ice at a fast food restaurant, fill it with toilet water it is cleaner.
- If your health fails, be nice to the nurses because they will keep the doctors from killing you.
- Don't be open minded because your brains will fall out.
- Don't throw your girlfriend's underwear where your other girlfriend will find them.
- Finally, I have some advice for the young ladies just like my grandpa told me a long time ago, "Calm ur tit – just one tit – leave the other one crazy and out of control – that ur party tit."

The complex dance of intelligent matter
7/16/2016

Everything is old, millions and millions of years old. Your sister and brother and you and I are old. We are all just bits of matter and the only difference between you and I is the way we are molded, put together, much like your new truck or car is just very old matter molded and painted to look like it is new. Intelligent matter, that is what we are.

Matter, under the right circumstance will become life. I don't know how this works. I do know that matter moves around and bumps into other matter and if the other matter is weaker, the stronger will eat it or mate with it if it can. The matter that eats the most and mates the most will become the strongest. The strongest matter is not the most intelligent matter.

The most intelligent matter learns how to avoid the stronger matter. It tricks it, traps it, kills it, and then eats it or mates with it. Some call this natural selection and I'll have to go that route as well while looking at the greater picture. In the smaller picture, selection is not natural for it is selective and discriminatory in nature. Intelligent matter chooses what it eats and mates with, thus we find that inequality is natural and inborn.

Intelligent matter strives for freedom, but freedom and equality are natural enemies. Intelligent matter that is discriminatory and selective will either be stronger or weaker depending upon its choices if it is free to do so. Intelligent matter that becomes weaker will naturally have fewer choices for what it eats or mates with. Thus, it does not have the same freedom that stronger matter has. So freedom along with justice and equality are just words, ideas. Intelligent matter that has freedom, justice and equality are nowhere to be found anywhere in the entire universe.

Intelligent matter is self-repairing and is capable of mending everything around it, if it were free. Intelligent matter is prevented from freedom by matter that competes with it similar to the way bacteria, viruses, bugs, and worms attack living tissue. Like the white blood cells within our veins, intelligent matter tries to fight off this "other" matter. I call this "other" matter "assholes" because that's where they thrive the most.

None of this changes, all along the evolutionary ladder. There is always going to be intelligent matter wanting to repair its environment and there will always be "assholes" interrupting them on their every effort. If it were up to the "assholes," nothing would be repaired or adjusted because they are in a constant struggle within themselves while striving to become intelligent. They can never be intelligent because they have been passed over by the intelligent matter and are forced to breed within themselves, thus they can be considered inbred and nonfunctional in an intelligent society.

While these "assholes" are arguing, the intelligent matter will work at repairing its environment much like a gardener will plant one tree at a time and if the tree dies they will plant another and another until one takes root and grows enough to shade other new trees that can thrive together. A garden of Eden is what we would have.

We here in Winters, California are lucky enough to live in a huge garden. That is easy to see. It's a good garden, but it's in danger of being taken over by invasive plants and trees that have spread all through the garden, brought in by men for various reasons, not always purposefully. Eucalyptus trees, Arundo and Himalayan blackberries were brought in by men for monetary reasons. Left to thrive, they would infest the entirety of Putah Creek.

You would think that as intelligent matter, we could sit and discuss this in an intelligent manner. Not gonna happen! There will always be nonintelligent matter like viruses, bacteria, bugs and worms that will interrupt everything intelligent matter strives to do. It must be really hard for those that want to be intelligent when they know they never will be. So, life in the universe continues.

I just don't have the heart
8/19/2016

At one time or another, everything sucks. Nothing goes right 100 percent of the time, even for Jesus Christ. His dad put a smile on his face when he told him that he was going to be the savior of the Earth.

"You will be the son of God!" he was told.

Jesus probably thought, "Son of God huh?" Then he thought, "What could possibly go wrong with that?"

"Hell, I will be a God!" he said out loud.

Even a guy like me would love a deal like that. No one can hurt a God! Anyway, if I was going to be the new son of God I would do things exactly like Jesus did except for the beating and crucifying part. It doesn't really make sense to beat and crucify a good guy. That sort of treatment should be reserved for the bad guys. You would think the son of God could invent a bad guy, sort of like a Devil, to get all that bad treatment. Hell yes!

Now that I think about it Jesus and his Dad did exactly that! They invented a bad guy, named him the Devil, and maybe they planned to send him to the Romans, but he slyly skipped out of town, so the Romans took Jesus instead. Maybe when they were whipping him, Jesus would say, "Jesus Christ man, what the hell are you doing, I'm the son of God!" "You" (whack) "got" (whack) "the" (whack) "wrong" (whack) "guy!" (whack). "Just ask my friends!" he probably said. (Whack), (Whack), (Whack!)

Noah was another guy that lived about that same time who didn't think ahead. God told him to build a huge boat, right? Then God probably told him that he was going to have to load the boat with all of the animals of the world, but I don't think Noah heard that part. Noah was busy thinking, "Alright! A huge new boat." Noah was thinking how cool it would be to be the only guy with a big boat in the middle of the desert! He didn't hear the part about the animals until his wife told him much, much later, when it was too late to get out of it and sneak into the stump forest to hide.

Noah never thought about what it would be like to tell his longtime neighbor that he could not get on the boat to save his family but "I can take your pigs and a couple of them goats!" Yep, this is just another example of "Everything sucks at one time or another!" As a matter of fact, it's happening to you (the reader) right now, isn't it? When you started reading this column. you probably thought it was going to have some philosophical meaning or, at the very least, it would be good, down to Earth, reading entertainment.

Sorry about that.

All I can tell you is that happiness is something that you have until things start sucking. Like being a soldier within the mighty American war machine is really cool until everybody around you starts getting killed in a manner that freaks you out for the remainder of your days. The thing about that is you have to take the bad with the good. You can't have one or the other — you have to take both. That's the way things work. It's an impossibility to know good if you don't know bad. One without the other causes confusion in that you can't know if something is good if you haven't experienced bad, and vice versa.

So what we end up with is half of the time we're happy and half of the time we're unhappy. Things are not always going to go our way. All you can do is be happy when things go our way and not so happy when they don't. BUT: there are things you can do to keep happiness alive when things go bad. All we have to do is examine what other people do when things go bad for them. I mentioned Jesus Christ so let's look at what he did. Here he is, all beat up and hanging on a cross made of timber, right? What was he thinking about? "DO SOMETHING FOR SOMEONE ELSE!"

This is an idea that I know something about, and I can tell you that it works! Try it. If you want to get happy, pick someone out — anyone — and do the work that no one else wants to do to help them out. Everyone needs help sometimes, and they may think you're a little crazy at first, so you have to be serious about it. If you're half-assed about it, the results will be half-assed.

If done right, the results can be electrifying. Sure, if you help someone out, it's going to make them feel good but that's not what I'm talking about. The act of helping someone else is for *you* — the harder you work at it the greater your rewards will be. I don't quite know how to explain it, but sometimes when I do things for others, I find myself on the verge of tears, for the experience is wonderful like nothing I've ever known. At the same time, the experience saddens me because on a grander scale, with one nation helping another, it could result in mass euphoria.

Help given on such a grand scale seems to be restricted to catastrophic events. We seem to shine the most when we go to the aid of the downtrodden, the weak, and the hungry at the worst of times. Giving financial aid to the poor is a good thing, but it can be much, much more. If you want to help others it cannot coincide with bombing and killing. The road to real peace, in the world we live in, requires us to "Love our Enemies" by helping them instead of killing them. The billions of billions of dollars we spend on war machines could help a lot of people… so many people.

If I could, I would change a lot of things. As it is, I can only do what I can do, and it's breaking my heart, in the worst way that I am unable to do more. At times, my eyes see nothing but sadness, everywhere I look… nothing but sadness. To make matters worse, I know what to do and how to do it, but I just can't get it done. I just don't have the heart.

Gardeners, gardeners everywhere!
10/4/2016

I am surrounded by gardeners. I guess that's not such a bad thing because, at one point in my life, I found myself surrounded by soldiers and some of them were trying to kill me. I was a lot younger then and I was lucky enough to be able to outrun them. Yeah, gardeners are not really that bad. There is an old saying I'd like to share but I didn't write it so I have to put those little marks around it so everybody knows I didn't write it.

Ready? Here it is. "I never met a gardener that I didn't like!" I think Abraham Lincoln wrote that or maybe it was one of those Caesar guys that used to live in Rome before World War I. I guess the reasoning behind that saying is that if a guy has his hands in the dirt, planting a plant, then he is not gonna stab you in the back and use you for fertilizer. What's not to like about that?

A lot of people think I'm a gardener but that's simply not the case. I guess it looks that way because I'm always hanging around people who are gardeners. In reality, I'm more like the guy that cleans up the mess left by the gardeners when they come marching through and I do a lot of small time irrigation because I like to play in the mud and water. I'm sort of like that guy "Pigpen" in the comic strips.

It's a natural fact that gardeners are a messy bunch. You can see 'em coming and then watch 'em go. They leave little dust whirlwinds behind before they're gone and you can barely see them way down the road... That's the only way you can smell them. They're easy to track because they leave a trail of mud wherever they go.

Gardeners are a tricky bunch, too. Sometimes I think they all get together and plot ways to get me in the poison oak or near a bee's nest. They like to see people scream like a little girl! Another well known fact about gardeners that I'll share with you is that they don't like you throwing garbage in Putah Creek even if it does get washed out of town. Yeah, they're a funny bunch. I'll name a few gardeners for ya that I sometimes hang out with. There's Rich Marovich, Rick Fowler, Duc Jones of the Solano County Water Agency and Carrie Shaw, Amy Williams and Karin Young of the Putah Creek Council and of course there is my friend Libby "Earthman" Byson and her hubby Reid.

Some gardeners will run right over you with a big tractor if you don't get out of their way. There's no malice involved, they're just gardeners in a hurry doing gardener stuff. To name a few I see a lot because I really have to look both ways, let's see, there's Tony Morales, Herb Wimmer and Joe Martinez. They're professional gardeners on a grand scale. I bumped into a Mariani one time but he told me to keep off his road. I guess he didn't want to run over me.

Then there's Maggie Larochelle. Everybody in town watches her tend her garden because it's right in the center of the downtown area. What a wonderful garden it is, too. She and my friend Melanie Bajakian are wonderful gardeners who like things to be just perfect and they both work very hard to keep things that way.

Then there are those who tend to the city we live in, like City of Winters Mayor Cecilia Aguiar-Curry, City Manager, John W. Donlevy, Jr., Environmental Services Manager, Carol Scianna and my good friend and sidekick Terry Vender of City of Winters Maintenance. Thanks to them, the City of Winters is a giant, beautiful garden where we all can live in peace and harmony like we're supposed to. They are all master gardeners.

I really don't know anyone who doesn't want to be a gardener. I think that's only natural. It's in our genetic structure. Well most of us anyway. I think in my case there are a little too many Neanderthal genes because when I try to grow something. I keep wanting to go hunting and gathering and I grunt a lot, especially when I'm eating. One time I told everybody I was going to enroll in the "Master Gardener Program," but then again, everybody knows I'm a liar, right? I'm still thinking about printing out one of those "Master Gardener" certificates and hang it on the wall next to my Pulitzer Prize and Nobel Prize for Literature certificates. It will look pretty good next to my third place bowling trophy

Fear is powerful, but love truly conquers all
10/7/2016

I've been afraid all of my life. At the same time I've learned to split things up so that on the outside, the fear is hard to spot. The truth is I'm shaking with fear on the inside, but anyone who looks at me cannot see it. All they can see is the mask I wear to hide what I am really feeling, way down deep.

Fear is infectious. Once it's inside you, it spreads until you lose all control. When it has control of you, it can then spread to those around you. One at a time, everyone around you will fall to fear. At this point, there is no stopping it. Like a wildfire, it will spread and spread and spread until the fear is out of control.

Fear has no reasoning or sense. Individually, fear will make you do things you don't want to do or just as easily it can incapacitate you until you do nothing at all. On a larger scale, fear becomes so powerful that it can lead to everything evil you could ever imagine. Out of fear, all bombs, guns, tanks, warships, murder, genocide and rape are born. This list could go on and on forever, for fear will not let you stop.

It matters not if fear is real or imaginary because it has the same result. Those who fear others will never find true love. They will never travel to exotic places or meet people of other cultures. In the end, it will cause misunderstanding and suspicion that can erupt into bloodshed and war, and it does not matter if your fear has substance or not. You just have to believe it is real.

There are those twisted individuals who seek to control others, sometimes on a grand scale. They want more, more of everything. They know they can take whatever you have without any effort at all, without physical violence. This is nothing new. It's as old as mankind itself. The introduction of fear can persuade even the toughest of individuals to give up everything a person has held dear to his heart.

Those who control fear can become just as all powerful as fear itself. They can persuade you to draw a number out of a hat that may require you to send those you love the most (sons and daughters) to slaughter or be slaughtered in a faraway place. If they want your children, they will take them, period. If you resist, they will lock you away unless you're fortunate enough to escape to wherever, Canada, let's say. Even this is no longer an option.

So now you may ask if this is all that man has to offer. Behavior that is controlled by fear can also be controlled by love. Fear is powerful, that's a given, but love truly conquers all. While the former tears you down, the latter will build you up and give you the strength to resist even the greatest of fears. Love freely given to others brings clarity and peace of mind to all it touches.

Why is it that we choose to believe the worst when we are told that someone is our enemy? Why is it so hard to believe that they are just like us, controlled by fear? The escalation toward violence that comes with fear can be stopped in its tracks by only a few tiny steps of love. Fear is so hard and love is so easy.

Love is the tool you need to combat fear. When you're afraid of something, anything, the introduction of love, even a tiny amount, will push out any fear you have. I am told that those who control love and use it every day in their lives will have the power to change everything bad about their lives as quickly as the drop of a hat.

I say we should try it. What do you think?

My wife is something else. There is no way in hell I would even try to keep up with her. She rarely sits still for more than a few moments at a time. Like a busy little bee, she buzzes to and fro from room to room, place to place, or town to town, always looking fresh as a daisy. Every deliberate little stop along her way has function or duty. She is not a person to idly wander without purpose.

I am just the opposite. I'm stuck in slow motion. I like slow motion. I kind of mope along in my own little world while my wife and everybody else buzzes all around me. It's like I'm in a different dimension or plane of existence. All I can see of everybody else is a blur, a puff of air, or an odor of soap and shampoo. To them I'm like a musty rock or maybe a statue of really fine art with a bobblehead.

I am aware that the world is moving faster, ever faster. I am also aware that a person must be quick to act in any circumstance, for opportunities do not stand still. They are always in motion. There are two ways to catch an opportunity if you stop and think about it. You would think that the person who is quickest would have the greater share of opportunities, but that simply is not the case.

For reasons of simplicity, I will refer to those in the fast plain of existence as "Movers" and those on my slower plain of existence as "Mopers." As you can imagine, opportunities, always moving, travel from one plane of existence to the other, for they are naturally random and indiscriminate in nature. Opportunities do not care who catches them and of course, they are tempting to all. Everybody wants opportunities; they are valued above just about everything. One way or another, we all chase opportunities.

Movers and Mopers alike want a fair chance at catching opportunities, for they represent power. Thus it goes to reason that the most powerful have the most opportunities. Those with power are capable of controlling opportunities and even creating them and releasing them upon the planes of existence, to be grabbed up by the Movers and Mopers. If thought about, everyone should be able to see the truth in this.

There is a famous quote about power that you may already be aware of, but I'll quote it anyway: "Power corrupts and absolute power corrupts absolutely." Now you're wondering where I'm going with this, and you must be wishing I'd get to the point. Well, here it is:

Those in power, those who have the most opportunity, control the rest of us, Movers and Mopers alike. Here's another quote by Eric Hoffer who happens to be a Moper: "Those in possession of absolute power can not only prophesy and make their prophecies come true, but they can lie and make their lies come true." (I hate those little quotation marks but you have to have them. I don't know why, nor do I care, but here they are anyway.)

Anyway, how can this be true, you might ask? Well, let's say that those in power want you to go over to the right side. How would they get you to go there? They simply create opportunities over on the right and the Movers will rush over there and the Mopers will start that way. Once there, you are in their pocket and under their control, for they can lead you wherever they want. If they make you feel threatened, you will kill for them and even die for them.

What this adds up to is stunning. Eighty percent of all Americans have only 7 percent of the total national wealth. On the other hand, the top 1 percent of

Americans (the richest) has 40 percent of all the wealth. The rest is distributed among our upper class citizens. There is no middle class. We now have 80 percent poor, 19 percent upper class, and 1 percent super rich.

Most Movers and Mopers are within the 19 percent, the upper class, because the lowest 80 percent of Americans have no opportunities at all. If you have a home to live in and eat regular meals every day, you are among the upper class and richer than everybody on Earth except the 1 percent of the wealthiest.

Earlier, I said there were two ways to catch an opportunity, and there are. The Movers are fast, and they can chase them down and grab them. The Mopers, on the other hand, can block their path and bring them to a dead stop. Once an opportunity is stopped it can be examined for what it truly is. So what's the moral of this story?

Well, like my Mover wife, Therese, the other Movers need to be aware that not everything is worthy of your attention, and that Movers and Mopers together are a powerful combination. My wife has been rushing around me for over 30 years and we are tied together by a love that is 10 times more powerful than any opportunity that might be thrown in our faces. That gives us our own source of power, for she can chase it down and I can block just about anything that comes our way.

You see, there is always something called Justice, which is something we have seen very little of lately. Justice originates in the heart and spirit of those who resist power. Sooner or later, the masses will call for the redistribution of wealth and there will be no stopping them. I know this is true, for it has been repeated over and over throughout the history of mankind, usually after the seating of a corrupt government, exactly like the one that lies before us with the next election.

So, enjoy yourself while you can for "the times, they are a changing!" (Bobby Dylan)

Homeless veterans by the numbers
11/5/2016

Well, another Veterans Day is here, and I think it is important to take note of it because a lot of guys gave up everything they had to serve this nation. I don't think veterans need a whole bunch of personal attention but it is nice to honor them as a group. One veteran is pretty much like all the rest. They, as a group, have many striking similarities.

The last thing I read about veterans said there we over 23 million veterans in the United States. Over 2.5 million of them are women. California has more U.S. military veterans than any other state. The median income for veterans in 2009 was approximately $35,000 a year. Some have trouble holding down a job but I won't get into that.

I'll give you a little information about veterans in general. They can be a funny group at times and dead serious at other times. They don't care much for being asked if they killed anyone, that's not a nice thing to bring up. Having someone say, "Thank you for your service" gets on their nerves as well. We don't need to be thanked.

When you're in the military, the focus isn't on you. Servicemen and servicewomen don't own a lot of material goods or fancy clothes. Staying out of the material goods and image trap is crucial to staying happy as a recently discharged veteran. It can be tough to adjust to. A lot of veterans end up being viewed as "withdrawn" or "reserved," just because they're not in the habit of making their private business public and expecting everyone else to find it interesting.

A soldier's word is his bond. They say what they mean and do what they say. The concept of a "layoff" doesn't really exist in the military. They never think they have too much beer. They know there is no such thing as a fair fight or Marquis of Queensbury rules. Rules of engagement are: bring a gun, if possible bring two guns, and bring all your friends that have guns.

They know that no combat-ready unit has ever passed inspection. They play with bombs, artillery, gunships, tanks, and infantry. To them, everything is a pillow. If they want to talk about your military experience, that's fine. But keep it relevant to the topic at hand, and keep it brief and simple. They will skim over things that won't make immediate sense to civilians. If it takes more than a few words to explain an idea in the story, they're probably better off cutting it.

There are 39,471 homeless veterans on any given night.

Demographics of homeless veterans
• 11% of the homeless adult population are veterans
• 20% of the male homeless population are veterans
• 68% reside in principal cities
• 32% reside in suburban/rural areas
• 51% of individual homeless veterans have disabilities
• 50% have serious mental illness
• 70% have substance abuse problems
• 57% are white males, compared to 38% of non-veterans
• 50% are age 51 or older, compared to 19% non-veterans

State prisons hold over 127,500 veterans, and federal prisons hold 12,500. Veterans reported longer average sentences than non-veterans, regardless of offense type.

In the United States, 22 veterans kill themselves every day

I've been noticing lately that the internet hurts my brain. Last week, the internet was inundated with Trump badmouthing Clinton and vice-versa, so at first thought, I blamed the bad politics of the current election. With the constant bickering and bitching, I can think of no other sub-group that is so dysfunctional.

Now I can see that the "hurting brain" problem is not only mine but everybody's. Well, anyone that uses the internet anyway. A simple analogy for what I'm talking about is: "Too much food makes you fat and immobile; too much information makes you numb and dumb." My hurting brain has a common case of "information overload."

We have access to too much information — information about everything. I don't know how accurate this number is, but the web says internet users overall consume 9,570,000,000,000,000,000,000 bytes of information each year. That's a lot of bytes. They say that if this information were in the form of a stack of books, it would reach all the way to Neptune. Information comes to us at a faster rate than reading books but we spend much more time gathering info on the net than turning pages.

If you partake in the gathering of information on the net, you should know that any privacy you once enjoyed is gone, gone and gone. Your internet provider has every email you have ever sent. It has every search you've ever made, and the contents of any chat rooms you may have provided. It knows your alerts, your calendar entries, your contact list, and all the information about you and all of your friends. It has every picture you shared with anybody.

Nice huh?

Once you make that little click, they have it and you can never unclick it. It stays there forever. There are 100 +/- options for everything you wish to know. Information overload is also known as option fatigue. Like I said, "It makes my brain hurt!" We have so many options for information that our brain can't process it fast enough and thus we forget what we wanted to know almost as fast as we read it. It's not like reading the local newspaper but the best analogy I can find comes from a journalist.

A 1986 book, "The Uncensored War" by press scholar Daniel C. Hallin, may help clarify where the best information comes from. Take a sheet of paper and make a big circle in the middle. In the center of that circle draw a smaller one to create a doughnut shape. Label the doughnut hole "sphere of consensus." Call the middle region "sphere of legitimate debate," and the outer region "sphere of deviance."

The "sphere of legitimate debate" is the one journalists recognize as real, normal, everyday terrain. They think of their work as taking place almost exclusively within this space. The "sphere of consensus" is the "motherhood and apple pie" of politics — the things on which everyone is thought to agree. Propositions that are seen as uncontroversial to the point of boring, true to the point of self-evident or so widely-held that they're almost universal lie within this sphere.

In the "sphere of deviance" we find "political actors and views which journalists and the political mainstream of society reject as unworthy of being heard." As in the sphere of consensus, neutrality isn't the watchword here; journalists maintain order by either keeping the deviant out of the news entirely or identifying it within the news frame as unacceptable, radical, or just plain impossible.

The authority of the press (mass media) to assume consensus, define deviance and set the terms for legitimate debate is weaker when people can connect horizontally around and about the news through the internet. Many users believe that what is on the internet is closer to "real public opinion" than what is in the mainstream media. The problem is that all this information goes in and then it is lost forever.

So what is the answer? I can only say it is "moderation." Use of your gut feelings are the tools for an uncertain world. Too much data creates only an illusion of certainty. Pick and choose places where you gather your information. Trust is everything.

Moderation, moderation, moderation!

Where is the wisdom we have lost in knowledge? Where is the knowledge we have lost in information? — TS Eliott

Super fish guy
11/26/2016

I'm a Putah Creek Council man. In case you don't know who they are, here is a statement from their web page: "The Putah Creek Council (PCC), a nonprofit organization, helps protect Putah Creek through restoration projects, tree planting, biomonitoring, workshops, and other events." Soooo, for about a hundred years, I've been a part of the volunteer labor force that helps with the restoration work in cooperation with the Solano County Water Agency (SCWA), an organization once sued by the PCC. Different story.

Okay, while doing volunteer work in the name of PCC, I often find myself under the supervision of SCWA employees Rick Fowler or Duc Jones. I cannot say enough about these two working fools. (I mean that in a good way!) Between these two guys, they're about to work me to death. In my younger days I might have been able to keep up with them, but now I just tag along and do what I can.

Duc Jones supervises a majority of SCWA's work with volunteers. By disposition, this work he is well suited for. Volunteers like his friendly, easy going nature and his professional attitude toward creek restoration work. Rick Fowler, on the other hand is a loner by nature who would just as soon have someone poke a stick in his eye as to work with a volunteer. He always tells me, "If you get in my way I'll run over you!"

Anyway, I'll get on with my story:

About a month ago, I hurt my back, pinching the sciatic nerve, which causes a constant terrible pain from my ass to my toes. I've been around the block a few times, but I have never experienced pain of this magnitude. Every move I make sends a burning pain down my leg. I can't even put on my shoes by myself — but this story is not about me, it's about old, sour Rick Fowler.

As much as it pains him, he will call me when he needs a little help. He calls me because all the other volunteers are afraid to work with him. They think he's a wild man, which in truth is a good description of him. So, the Wild Man in cahoots with Putah Creek Biologist and photographer, Ken Davis, aka "Creekman," have been concerned about the late arrival of spawning Salmon. Fowler wants to go look for them, which can be a dangerous task with the high flow of water in the creek right now.

I know he hated doing it, but for safety reasons, he had to call me to go along. (This tickles me to no end!) I get the call. I really don't want to go on a canoe trip right now because I can barely put my pants on for the sciatic pain shooting down my leg — it was awful. I agreed to go anyway because I know that if I don't go, he will go by himself. I began having flash visions of him, all alone, trapped underwater by the creek currents. Oh well!

Next morning he calls and says, "Hurry up! You're late!" So an hour later, without breakfast or coffee, I find I can barely get into the canoe before Fowler shoves off the bank into the swift current. My pain is so intense that Fowler is paddling twice as fast as I am causing the canoe to shift from port to starboard into the blackberry bushes that line both sides of the creek. I can see that by the end of the day, those berry vines are going to make Fowler a bloody mess. He knew it too, that's why he was mumbling vulgarities under his breath.

For a couple of hours we paddled like hell to control the canoe in the high currents. Suddenly, just like Jack Nicholson in "The Shining" he turns to me and with a scratched up bloody face he says, ""There they are!" There must have been ten thousand salmon trapped behind a beaver dam, all swimming in a circle waiting for Fowler as if they knew he would come for them. Now Fowler was standing in the canoe with his arms outstretched saying, "I'm here babies! It's Fowler to the rescue!"

I was breathless at the sight of all those huge fish swimming in a circle around Fowler.

Anyway, single-handedly, the Wild Man gets out into the water, tears a hole in the Beaver Dam and the fish are swimming between his legs while going upstream. Fowler was talking to each fish as it passed him by, one after the other. As I watched in amazement, there was a shining light behind Fowler's head and I knew that this guy was something special to the fish world.

I'm willing to swear on a stack of Bibles that those fish knew exactly who he was and why he was there. Unbelievable! You had to have been there...

Afterthought: That night I hobbled home, wrote this column, posted a video online and emailed it to everybody I knew who was involved in the creek works. Everyone has worked so hard to see the salmon spawning in a healthy creek, I thought they deserved to see the good results of their labors. I wanted to share the news with them!

So there it is. Hope everybody enjoys the salmon, but please keep your distance and let them spawn in peace. We don't want to disturb them right now. Oh, if I should turn up dead and lying on a muddy road somewhere, Rick Fowler probably ran over me.

Abusers are not leaders

12/9/2016

I always wanted to be special. I wanted to stand out, above and beyond the rest of my peers. I wanted to be the cool guy that everyone looked up to, like the go-to guy who fixes everything and makes everything right. My ideal vision of myself would be Superman without the Clark Kent crap. Think of how special a person like that would be.

Well, I've come to the realization that, at this late date, it's just not gonna happen. I can see now that I don't have what it takes to be someone special. Hell, I don't even think I'm average. When I think back, if I'm honest, I've never been the leader of the pack. Sure, others have followed me but at the same time, I was following someone else.

In a line of leaders, I'm so far back that I can't even see who the leader really is. I don't think I've even seen a real leader? I have to ask myself if I would even recognize a real leader. What is a leader? What makes a leader a leader? I'm going to have to think about that and get back to you later.

I think there might be a reason for this too. Like I said, "I always wanted to be special" but for some reason, I always went out of my way to blend in. It is just easier to blend in. If you aren't noticed, nobody know you're there, right? When the crap flies, it'll hit the guys in the front and the guys in the back, but the front guys and the back guys block the crap from hitting the guy in the middle.

I started thinking like this when I was very young. This philosophy came to me kinda sudden — like when my mother dropped me off at a Catholic orphanage. It was an abusive situation to which I was quick to adapt for self-preservation, which is something that comes natural to all of God's creatures. I found that there are people who do the abusing, people who are abused and finally, there are people who are skipped over because no one knows which group they belong to.

Think about it. People who abuse others only abuse those they consider to be weaker or helpless. Common sense tells you it has always been like that. The same train of thought tells you that those who are abused consider their abusers to be more dominant in nature. That's what I have observed anyway.

Abusers will abuse the same people over and over because they're afraid. They're afraid that if they attempt to abuse someone new, there's always the outside chance that this new person might be tougher than they thought and they just might get abused themselves. That tells us… what?

Abusers are not leaders. As a matter of fact, they are the farthest thing from it. They're stuck in a never-ending cycle of being broken themselves and trying to fix themselves by breaking others. It just can't be done that way. Like the old adage says, "We rise by lifting up others." You cannot lift yourself up.

True leaders know no group and they don't seek to stand out, but they stand out just the same. When I think about, it I realize I have seen and in fact know people I consider to be leaders. There are many such people in my little town of Winters, California. We all know who they are, and if we get the opportunity I think we should let them know they are appreciated. People like John Pickerel, John W. Donlevy, Jr., Craig McNamara, Woody Fridae, Rich Marovich, Carol Scianna, Jesse Loren, and many, many others.

It's people like this who make life a little easier for us all and we should celebrate them being among us.

So, in the end, I guess the way I have lived my life isn't so bad after all. I'm in a pretty good spot because it's easier for me to support a leader than to be a leader myself. I am among the many, many unseen people that our leaders can go to for assistance. The leaders know who we are just as we know who the leaders are. To those who love me, I am someone special. That's about as special as I want to be.

Our society takes all kinds of people doing all kinds of things in all kinds of ways. That's what makes the world go around. That in itself is special

Friends I've known, lost, and taken away
12/13/2016

I want to be as good a friend as I can be. This is important to me. In the whole span of my long lifetime, nothing else has ever been so important. I have my reasons for feeling this way. If I put these reasons into words within the confines of this column, I'll experience actual acute physical pain. The pain will not pass quickly, and my stomach is already beginning to tighten.

In the past, I haven't always felt the same. It's not that being a friend wasn't important to me, I just didn't think about it because I was too wrapped up within myself to worry about others. Before I continue, I think we had best take a look at what exactly a friend is. As defined in the dictionary, a friend is a person whom one knows and with whom one has a bond of mutual affection, typically exclusive of sexual or family relations.

If we look at that definition, it appears to be split into two different parts or ideas. I think we'll will agree on the first part of the definition of a friend. The second part deserves a little thought for clarification. I think the point is that sexual partners and families are much more than "friends." I guess I agree with this in principal, but I always say that my wife is my best friend.

Anyway, back to my story.

The one constant in my life was my brother Michael. He was my brother so that makes him more than a friend. There's nothing I have ever said in my life that is truer than this: He was more than a friend. Except for our time in Vietnam and some few years we were separated in St. Joseph's Orphanage, he was always with me. He died a few years ago but he is with me still.

The first night in the orphanage, the nuns took him away and it was years before I saw him again even though we existed within the walls of the same old military hospital turned into a children's home. After that I kept everyone at arm's length except for Fat Phil, who the State of Arkansas rescued from a molesting father, and he found himself in the bunk next to mine at St. Joseph's. Fat Phil became my brother.

I vividly remember the last day I saw him. When his father regained custody of him, I asked him why he would want to go back because his father made him do nasty things. He said, "It's better than staying here." Then he was gone.

The next friend I had as a boy, Butch King, died when the cave we were digging in a large sand pile caved in on him. His was the first dead body I touched, so I knew that he too was gone. Neither he nor Fat Phil ever came back.

Years later, my brother Michael found himself in Vietnam with the US Marines. He wrote that he was not having fun. I don't know what I was thinking, but I joined the Army and went to go get him. The same week I arrived in Vietnam, he was shipped out because you cannot have two brothers in a combat zone at the same time unless, like me, you sign a waiver giving up that right.

Now we get to the gist of my story. I won't go into the details — they're too horrible — but it has to do with the killing of innocent civilians. (Here comes the pain!) When these people were killed, I took away any friend they may have had or any friend they were ever going to have. They will never know what I have with my friends.

That's what I know, and when I think about my friends, I do the friendship thing for those that I left lying on the ground in Vietnam.

Coming home: Don't thank me for my service
12/28/2016

This afternoon I stopped at a red light on Mason Street in Vacaville where I witnessed a small group of people greeting a young soldier. With all the hugs and kisses, this type of heartwarming scene is pretty common for those soldiers coming home these days. Soldiers returning home from wars are as old as history, maybe older. She looked so smart in her camouflage uniform, her hair tied in a bun below a red beret. I could see she was crying as I drove away.

I couldn't get it out of my mind all day and I'm still feeling a little emotional for the sight of it. Her homecoming was so different from what I experienced when I came home after two years, one month and seven days in the Republic of Vietnam. Leaving Vietnam was one of the hardest things I have ever done. After all, I walked away leaving my brothers at arms in harm's way.

Veterans of the Vietnam War did not enjoy the experience of going home. I know I didn't. Upon release from the Army I went into the first bathroom I could find and took off my uniform and threw it into the trash. No one knew I was a soldier because like Arlo Guthrie sang in his song we were all "baby killers and mother rapers!" We all heard horror stories of people spitting on soldiers of that era.

Coming home was a very sad time for me. It was nothing like I had imagined it would be. I was Regular Army, 100 percent volunteer, eager to serve my country. I felt I did not deserve to be treated like that. It still hurts me to think about it. I guess I will never get over it. I hate the words, "Thank you for your service." Who the hell asked to be thanked for something like that? It was not something that was enjoyed and it was not a game.

Every single time I hear the song "Alice's Restaurant" I want to scream! To make it worse, everybody has to sing along with the words in a very loud manner. You might as well slap a veteran in the face with a handful of feces. If I ever see Arlo Guthrie, I would poke him right in the nose and ask him what the hell we ever did to him to write words that are so very cruel and heart wrenching for veterans of Vietnam.

Coming home is hard enough without all that crap. The old adage, "You can never go home" is so very, very true for many of us. One day we were in a combat zone and the next day we were walking on the block. Nothing changes for those that stay home and everything changes for those that serve all those horrible days and nights in a combat situation. Nobody wants to hear war stories. The government has to pay people to listen to them. War is so much harder when you have to keep it inside, locked away, where you live it over and over, every day of your life.

I can't stand to be around other Vietnam vets because I can see the pain in their eyes, smell the booze on their breath, and the anger in their hearts. I know that inside their chest, they have the same pain that I have. I am always, always on the verge of tears and much of the time just living is so very, very hard for me. Years of therapy and taking pills did absolutely nothing for me in this respect. Booze, drugs and God have no effect whatsoever and the only relief I can find is the feeling of my wife's warm breath on the back of my neck as she sleeps the deep, peaceful slumber only the innocent of heart can enjoy.

There's only room for one towel boy

1/12/2017

One day last week, my sidekick Terry Vender and I spent some time thinking about how we could live longer. We came up with some pretty good ideas on how to do it but it's ultimately up to me to decide on which direction we should go with this. Terry is a Government man so he has access to all kinds of privileged, classified information that they store in the main frame computer at the City of Winters maintenance yard.

Terry says that there's an entire underground complex under the maintenance yard that may go down more than six stories deep. He says he is not authorized to go to the lower floors because that's where the mayor and city manager have all the wild parties with the elite citizens of the City of Winters. I probably shouldn't say anything, but Terry says there have been secret meetings by all the big wheels discussing how to control all the people from Davis that flock to Winters every weekend.

I was glad to hear this, because those people from Davis keep peeing on my hedges because they drink so much beer when they drive the 100 miles or so from Davis to here. For some reason those Davis guys don't like us, so recently those Davis guys came up with a plan to dump all their sewage into Putah Creek thinking that it would all wash down here and make Winters stink. Well they never thought about the fact that for most of the year the creek flows the other way and goes to Nebraska or someplace like that.

Anyway, Terry told me that he knows this place in Davis where they have a program that will freeze you and then thaw you out in the future. He says it is called USCryotherapy, so we decided to check this place out the other night. When we entered the establishment there were two really, really fine babes that greeted us. They were both checking me out and were being really, really nice to me. Terry was getting kinda jealous.

I was figuring I might invite them to party with us but just then, the whole damn UC Davis basketball team came in, and those girls didn't want anything to do with me, or Terry either. I tried to talk to them but I guess they got annoyed because they took us into this one room they said had a temperature of about 300 below zero. To make matters worse, they made me put on some shorts and then they hid my pants. Next, they closed a big steel door that had windows so they could see us suffer. They didn't let us out until an hour or so later. I think they must have thought the window was one of those one-way vision thingies because I could see those girls having a good old time talking to those basketball players.

Man. I tell you. UC Davis must have the best looking team in the world, because these guys looked like those models that wear all those fancy clothes in the Sears catalog. Me and Terry never looked this good in our whole lives, however, I do look pretty good now, as you can see in this picture.

While Terry was in the corner crying, I got to know these guys and we became best friends. To my left is 6' 4" Brynton Lemar, the team's top scorer, and on the right is 6' 6" Chima Moneke. These guys love me and they are going to get me a pass to get into the locker room to help their coach figure stuff out. Lemar, like me, has a big brain, so he has a GPA of 3.5. When I was in school I had a 7.3, so my brain is just a little bigger.

I just have to figure out a way to dump Terry because those guys didn't want him around. They said they only have room for one towel boy and that was me. Anyway, when we walked out of that place, for some reason, my sciatica pain went away and I could jump and play and run around like a teenager. Terry was still crying and told me to shut up about the whole night.

I told Terry about the picture of me with the ball players and Terry says, "Did you take the picture with your phone?"

So I replies, "How the hell would I have the picture if I used someone else's phone — wouldn't someone else have the picture?"

Terry says, "Oh."

"Jealous," I say!

Fan mail
1/12/2017

Sometimes my fans send in little comments to my email when they like my column. Some of the comments aren't too positive but at least they are comments. My wife thinks all of these comments were written by the devil because he would be the most likely to criticize a great writer like me. While reading these comments, if you see something you have sent in, well I hope you feel guilty about making me cry.

Of course, some of these don't really mean what is written. They might be joking, right?

- "Stop babbling like an idiot. It must suck to be you."
- "Thank God someone took the time to put this crap together."
- "You write like a monkey."
- "You are too stupid to own a computer."
- "You had better watch what you write about, they are watching!"
- "You are a moron!"
- "When you run on the short bus do you hit your face on the back window?"
- From the Pulitzer Prize Committee: "Stop sending in nominations, you cannot nominate yourself, especially if you don't send in the nomination fee."
- "Dear Mr. Sanders, fresh ideas are rare in today's newspapers. Unfortunately, you wouldn't know a fresh idea if you ran into it on your short bus going wherever you go to write this crap!"
- "Donald, I think you need a six month vacation, twice a year."
- "There are three rules for good writing. Unfortunately, you don't know what they are."
- "Someone has to be an awesome writer, too bad it's not you."
- "Donald, you are quite accomplished at writing sad stories. The more I read your column, the sadder I get."
- "Donald, I'm sorry to inform you that the light at the end of the tunnel is just you being shoved out of another vagina. It is not ethical to attempt to charge a dying person a fee for helping them get into heaven. You are a very crooked man."
- "Grandpa, are you retarded? Grandma says you are."
- "Donald Sanders, this is mental abuse!"
- "Mr. Sanders, one day you will be a great writer; but not today!"
- "My goodness Mr. Sanders, this was close. This column was almost readable."
- "Ugh… Do you really have to write? Why don't you stick to pulling weeds down at the creek?"
- "Donald, I think your train of thought left the station without you."
- "Nothing screws up my Thursday like reading your column."
- "Honey, I love you but if you ever write about my side of the family again, I will kill you!"
- "Just because you can write a column doesn't mean you should."
- "Donald, I sure hope this newspaper doesn't pay you for this crap."
- "After reading this I will never read the newspaper again."
- "Really, who are you trying to bullshit?"

Well, it could be worse.

We love our neighbors — don't we?
1/26/2017

Have you ever done something so wrong that it troubled you every day since you did it? I think most of us probably have. Into us all a little guilt must creep.

I'm getting older now and when I think back through the years, I can remember every misdeed I've ever done. Misdeeds gnaw at you from the inside out and will not let you have the peaceful rest that the innocent enjoy.

Misdeeds come in many forms and sizes. They range from something as bad as murder all the way down to something as simple as an insult that you know was uncalled for. Most people, like me, know in advance that what you are about to do is a misdeed because something inside tells you, "Don't do this" or "I'm going to regret this" or "This is going to come back to me a hundred-fold!" Then comes the, "Why did I do that — it was so stupid."

Well I'm getting that familiar feeling again and I know that something I (or we) am going to do will be regretted for as long as I live. The feeling is unmistakable. You can see it and feel it long before it actually gets done. It's sad but usually there is no stopping a misdeed once it is conceived, planned, and taken into its motions.

I'll explain: One definition of happiness is — a good neighbor. Aren't neighbors great? If I could go through life just dealing with my neighbors, and no one else, I would be so happy all the time. I absolutely love my neighbors, and for that I am so grateful. My wife Therese feels the same way. Good neighbors are at the root of what makes a house a home.

Now that I've said that, I don't want to leave you hanging so I have to tell you about them. Jose and Lucia live in the little house just over the fence. Every time I see them, they make me smile. It's easy for me to see that together they are happy in their affection for each other and everybody around them. Friendliness comes natural for them.

Jose is a little older than I am, but he's in better shape physically. He's a good-looking guy and that explains his beautiful wife. Beauty seems to gather with beauty. He is a man's man, very polite and soft-spoken. He is retired now, but I know he has worked hard all of his life and now he doesn't know how to slow down. I worry about him sometimes because he works so hard at everything he does but is never so busy that he doesn't have time to lend a helping hand or a simple greeting of friendship to anyone he might meet.

Everywhere he goes in our little town, he can find a friend that is genuinely happy to see him. I see him around town, always socializing with a group of men he's probably known for years. I see that he likes them and in return, they like him. Their relationship always seems natural and easygoing. Sometimes they sit on one of the benches around town and discuss everything under the sun. They sit with the look of comfort on their faces. I like that.

Jose's wife, Lucia, has to be the best cook in town. Her tamales are to die for! No one that I know could ever deny the fact that a great amount of affection for each other is shared by the cute little Mexican American couple. I still can't believe how lucky I am that they live next door. They are so cute together. Lucia is a lovely woman, a real Latin beauty, so full of grace.

Their house is always in perfect order, all trimmed and proper. Their lawn is always perfect and I know they have to be concerned that my weeds will spill over into their side of the yard. I wouldn't be surprised if they wanted to put up a wall between my place and theirs. Yes, when it comes to neighbors, ours are the best.

When I speak of walls, it's in jest. I would never build a wall to keep my dear neighbors out, but that's exactly what is being done. It's so hard for me to understand how our government wants to build a wall along the Mexican border. Mexico is our neighbor — a very dear neighbor. We only have two, and now we want to wall one of them out?

Recently, President Donald Trump showed the entire world exactly what an ass he really is. He slings insults at our neighbors like he is the almighty God above. I am appalled and I have to wonder where this comes from.

Everything Trump says about our neighbors to the south is an insult. I don't want to repeat them, but words like these do not come from God. Donald Trump is a very scary man and I worry about the fact that he's not alone in his evil ways.

Thus comes the feeling that we are about to commit a misdeed. The way he describes our southern neighbors is not borne in reality at all. Doesn't Mr. Trump realize that we are all one people upon this Earth and none are better or worse than the other? It's obvious that the underlying reason for this wall is, with the slowing down of our foreign wars, lucrative government contracts will arise out of a 1,000-mile long wall that costs an estimated $25 billion when all is said and done.

That's a lot of zeros for a misdeed that we could all regret for the rest of our lives.

The American dream is not dead — it has just changed

2/6/2017

I believe the American dream is not dead — it has just changed, just as it has changed before. Originally, it was the pursuit of happiness, but with the industrial revolution, the definition of happiness changed and it became more of a material thing like houses, cars and bank accounts. Thus happiness was driven by greed, so there was always some other guy who had more than we had. With the stock market crash in 1929 followed by other more recent similar crashes, it's clear that this kind of happiness is unobtainable.

Now with the passing of the industrial age into the information age, the definition of happiness has again become unclear. Our government, I'll call it a democracy, when all is said and done, has done less harm and more good than any other form of government. Made up of humans, it has developed human characteristics. It travels through time trying to find its way by trial and error. It will make mistakes just as we do.

We forgot to make ourselves intelligent when we made ourselves sovereign and unfortunately, democracy feeds off of the intelligent input of its citizens. In our desire for simple and easy, we have opened ourselves to manipulation by the forces that can mold public opinion. Again we find ourselves in the process of redefining exactly what happiness should be. We are in need of some new rules and disciplines.

For me, happiness is creating a meaningful life, contributing to community and society, valuing nature, and spending time with family and friends. In the last 200 years, the government has provided the majority of us with unprecedented abundance and comfort. The rights we enjoy outnumber the wrongs. Correcting the wrongs is an ongoing process and in the end, we will certainly find the time to address what must be changed.

The rights we enjoy are not the given rights to office and power. Our rights are equal entry into every avenue that may nourish and test a man's fitness for office and power. Our rights are not a gift from God or nature but a privilege where what is good for the group is what the individual should have. Every person has their own idea of how the government should proceed, but we have yet to reach any agreement, so like its human counterparts, the government seeks its own path.

Our government has clearly dedicated itself to the spread and lengthening of education and the maintenance of public health. The form of government we enjoy can only be real and justified if equality of educational opportunity can be established. Access to education opens the doors to opportunity and in opportunity lies happiness.

We are on a grand adventure and no one knows where it will lead us. History tells us that the excessive increase in anything creates a reaction in the opposite direction. Thus a dictator rises out of democracy and the most extreme form of tyranny and slavery rise from the most extreme type of liberty.

Using the same logic, equal access to education will lead us all to a more equal access to happiness

This is a bad time of year for me. It was 46 years ago (almost to the day) that things turned sour for me.

I was a kid soldier in Vietnam like so many other American boys at the time. Unlike the Vietnamese boys, the war was an adventure for us, like something on TV or in the comic books. It was almost a game for the GIs. As a matter of fact, I had practically enjoyed my time in the war for the first 18 months and I had no reason to believe my last six months would be any different.

We all had "short-timer" calendars that would hang on the wall of our hooches. Every day we would color in another day so we knew pretty much the exact day we would get to go home. With only six months left on my calendar when, like I said, things went sour, and when things go sour, you get a bad taste in your mouth and things become not so much fun anymore. Your adventure turns into something else.

I won't go into the details of how things went sour. It's not about that. I don't want to write about that anymore, but I do want to say something about the tremendous amount of guilt and self-loathing I felt for myself when it finally dawned on me what was really going on. It's a real shock to the system when you feel you are doing God's patriotic work one day and the Devil's the next. I suffered a total failure of my belief system. I went from a good American soldier to a worthless piece of crap in the short span of 24 hours. That's just one day colored in on my short-timer's calendar.

After things went sour, I became a worthless S.O.B. I think soldiers like me were called "Sad Sack" in the WWII era. I guess you could say, "I lost my gung-ho!" I wallowed in misery and mental anguish, and I just couldn't seem to get it together, much like Humpty Dumpty. Thoughts of suicide entered my mind for the first time in many years. I closed up like a crab under the sea. I lost all communication skills. I knew I could never go home, not like this.

We all had "hooch maids" that would clean up and wash our laundry. They were good girls and they demanded respect, and when they didn't get it they would all get together and raise hell like a gaggle of geese. I treated my hooch maid like she was my mother so we got along just fine. We became close friends, so I overlooked it when I caught her stealing ammo for a rifle. I simply took the ammo and she gave me an invitation to her wedding in return. Of course, the commanding officer wouldn't let me go for my own safety.

Her invitation started me thinking along a different line. It never dawned on me that I might socialize with the Vietnamese or that they would want to socialize with me. After all, we American soldiers pretty much had a free discrimination card to do anything we wanted because they were not human, they were the enemy. So a little Vietnamese woman named Kim Truck showed me the evil in my ways. After that, I began to see discrimination and racism everywhere.

It seems like every so often our military picks a country and sends our soldiers over to show them how superior we Americans are. I thought about what in the world would give us the right to go into their countryside, into their homes to push them around, insult them, and then shoot them or spray them with Agent Orange so that 46 years later, the genetic structure of their children is still screwed up.

What gave us the right to go in there and kill millions and millions of mothers, fathers, brothers and sisters?

So, all these years later, I'm an old man that used to treat others with disrespect and ill manners. What would make me think I could do that and get away with it? After some thought I figured it all out. Treating others like that is not natural behavior. Behavior like that has to be pounded into your head by something the military calls "dehumanization."

In basic training, a soldier is broken all the way down to nothing and then they are rebuilt the way they want you to be. Soldiers are programmed over and over until they don't even know why they do what they do. All they want to do is get into that combat zone and kill some gooks!

Sooner or later our soldiers realize what they have done and find that they need some help with their mental health but the authorities don't care about this and ignore the problem. As a result, veterans live in a swill of depression and regret. They find themselves unable to cope with civilian life when they have to interact with others. For many, the guilt is too much to bear. Maybe this explains why up to 25 veterans kill themselves every day. Maybe this explains why I have all this shame coming out when I think about my military service.

In my case, everything certainly came around full circle. My actions in the Vietnam War had a devastating effect on the way I lived my life. Karma is a funny thing until it grabs you by the ass and shakes the crap out of you. It is relentless in its efforts to establish justice and equality. I have found that the amount of discrimination I give is equal to the amount of self loathing I enjoy for the rest of my life.

It does not make me happy to know that the youth of today will enjoy the same Karma that I enjoy.

A love for which there are no words
2/22/2017

For years now, I have wanted to put into words how much I love my wife Therese. Over and over, time after time, I have tried to pen the words that might let her know exactly how I feel. I have found that it is not an easy task and I think maybe it is impossible.

Even with my computer, with all its speed and information within its databanks, I cannot find what I need to tell her how I feel. I wish I was a great linguist with all the skills I would need at my fingertips, but even this might not be enough.

Therese came into my life some 35 years ago. The day I first laid eyes on her, I could tell she was something special, very special. Everything I thought about her within the first few minutes we stood face to face turned out to be spot on. I thought she was pure of soul and beautiful all the way to her toes. She says what she means and means what she says. There is nothing superficial about her and the only time she has spoken something that might not be true and straightforward was to protect me.

Through the years, I have done and said many, many things that would cause a lesser person to give up on me. When I say she has gone through hell, you can believe I was the source of everything bad that she had to fight her way through. Every time I broke her heart came back on me and to this day, it is my heart that breaks every time it comes to mind. I remember everything I did. I know I cannot go back and exchange one act for another. All I can do is see it for what it is.

Sometimes I find myself wondering what in the hell was she thinking? What did she ever see in me to think that I might deserve to have her as my wife? I think she may be a little retarded, because I can think of no legitimate reason why she would not have dumped me onto the curb many years ago. By now, you've figured out that I'm without a clue and I'll never be able to say exactly what I mean to say. Maybe I'm confused about life itself. That would explain some of the things I did to break her heart so many times.

When I look at her, I'm not alone and it's not me but we. She is everything you might think. She's my best friend, my lover, my partner, my other half, whatever, you know what I mean. When I think of what we have, I find myself looking down at everyone else because they could not possibly have as much love as I have for her. However, maybe it's just that I fail to see your love and you cannot see mine. That could be it.

She has always made love easy for me. She doesn't demand a lot from me and I demand everything from her, or so it seems. With her, I'm so much more of a man because I'm so eager to please her and to give her everything she wants that I'm capable of giving. I yearn to please her, and everything I do at this point in life is for her. I could write about this forever and would still be searching for another expression, another term, for these words of love are not enough.

For the moment, I'm content with the mere thought that maybe words aren't that important when it comes to expressing love. Maybe your actions, your everyday actions, are enough. Maybe it's enough for her to see that everything you do, you do for her.

Ooops! I could carry this on for a long, long time but I just found her to-do-list, so I'd better get busy and do some more things only for her. Truly, it is a labor of love.

The human brain is a strange yet beautiful thing. Some think it is the source of all that we say, feel, think, and do. For them, the brain is the origin of all. If we think about this idea for a few moments, it becomes something else — something so large and so diverse that it becomes impossible to understand. If we want to study and understand the human brain where would we start?

Think of yourself as a blob of brain all alone in a place devoid of light. I am assuming that the brain has told me that there is no light and everything is dark or all light and everything is light. Either way, we are unable to see or sense anything else until our brain tells us to see it. Now you're sensing something else and the brain tells you it's your hand. You don't know if the hand is the object with five fingers or everything else that surrounds the object with five fingers. The brain must tell you.

The simple task of sensing a hand becomes something so much more than a single thought because a flash of thoughts at the speed of light is what it takes for you to understand exactly what the hand is, where it came from, what it is for, and why is it there. To your surprise, while you were considering your hand your brain has expanded the dark room into something we call the universe and you are just becoming aware of it.

Think of the internet. How large is it? Where does it begin and where does it end? It has to be immense beyond proportion yet it is exactly what your brain tells you it is. Compared to the human brain, the internet is infinitely small. It is something you could put into your pocket or simply keep it in a little electronic device. The internet is simply a thought that stores other thoughts for your brain, a memory tool.

Now consider a group of brains. How will one brain connect with the other brains? How will one brain perceive the appearance of other brains? What form will they take? Will one brain have the same perception as the other brains? Will the perception be common? Will all of the brains see something similar to what the others are seeing? With infinite thoughts, I think not.

What happens now? Will the brain solve this problem? I think it probably could if it wanted but maybe the interaction between one brain and another is controlled by something else. Can the brain think of things like trust, love, hate, or the longing for something that is not there? Sure the brain can analyze love and hate, but think of the infinite number of thoughts it would take to originate love or hate. How would the brain interpret love or explain the feeling when love is lost. When love is lost what does it become? Is it no longer love?

The brain is incapable of resolving the issues of love. The brain becomes confused when confronted with the thought of love. It finds love complicated and too complex to explain. All the brain can do is associate the term of love with other terms it considers to be similar in nature but in the end there is nothing to be found that is similar in nature. Most of the time, the brain tries to associate love and hate as similar ideas but it cannot associate the two, for they have nothing in common.

I don't think the brain is capable of dealing with love and hate, for both ideas are all-consuming in nature. Love certainly consumes all, including hate. On the other hand, hate cannot consume love, and with enough thought, love could wipe hate from the face of the universe, and with it fear, lust, violence, and envy. I am a true believer when it comes to love. Love is the one thought that can bring one brain to understand another without fear, for fear is part of hate and is found nowhere in love.

One brain cannot control another brain; many have tried. All a brain can do is control its own thoughts. You can fill your brain with hate and lust and envy, but be prepared to spend eternity in the darkness of the beginning of the very first thought while trying to figure out if the hand is the thing with five fingers or everything else.

One brain can only connect with another brain if it is filled with love, trust, and caring. You can only control your own brain and it will become what you fill it with. A brain filled with thoughts of love is open and visible in the light, where other brains connect to become groups seeking connection with other groups. Only brains filled with love are capable of bringing a brain filled with hate out of the dark and into the light.

Fill your brain with love and we will conquer the universe by connecting all brains, one at a time. This is our only hope

I think my wife is going crazy. Have you ever seen a chicken with its head cut off, I mean clear off? Well that's exactly how she is acting! She's running here and there and then back again, mumbling as she goes. I suppose all the excitement is related to the upcoming wedding of one of our offspring. I've never seen her like this so I can only assume this is so.

Yesterday she was running around the house with a pen and a piece of paper making a list of what she should pick up when she goes to the store. She asked me three times what, if anything, I would like to add to her shopping list and three times I told her ice cream, Pepsi, frozen fish sticks, frozen French fries, and (oh ya) some ketchup. She writes it down and off she goes out the door. She is gone 40 minutes. All of a sudden the door pops open and she says, "I forgot my keys!"

I don't know for sure, but I think her sisters may have been infected with this craziness as well. My wife wants to buy a new dress for the wedding because she is like the hostess with the mostest. When I heard this, it was like the first clue she was going crazy on me. New dress huh? Then it dawned on me that she hasn't bought a new dress since like 1947.

What is happening!?

So off she goes with her sisters to buy a new dress. She is gone for like, two days. Every once in a while I get a text message (with a picture of her in different dresses) asking if I like this one or that one. Now I'm no dummy! I've been married to her for like 100, so I know better than to criticize how she looks in a dress, or anything for that matter. So, it's, "Oh I like that one!" or "Wow, that's nice one too!"

Yeah! I like them all!

When she gets like this, when she has that look in her eye like she's getting an idea, I try to stay out of it by staying out of her way. The other day just out of the blue she wakes me up a 4:30 a.m. I opened my eyes and there she stood above me like a vampire getting ready to suck my blood! I'm looking up at her and she is looking down at me when out of her mouth comes the words, "I need you to try on your suits to see if they still fit."

Now, I have two suits. One, my mother bought me when I was about 13 years old on the day she picked me up from the orphanage and the other I bought so I would look good at my dad's funeral, just after World War II if I remember correctly. OK, one of the coats seemed to fit and one pair of pants fit pretty well too. The only problem was that the coat was plaid and the pants were striped. It made me look like Bob Barker on "To Tell the Truth." You know, I thought, "I don't give a shit, I'm gonna wear it anyway." How long can a wedding last anyway? It's not like someone is going to take my picture anyway, right?

While all this is going on, she gives me little chores designed to get the house in order because some of the wedding guest will be coming to our house. Chores like getting little spots of glue off the base of the toilet and the floor of the shower. Now, our toilet and shower floor are always so clean you could eat off of them, so I looked and looked and I never found a single spot of glue anywhere near the toilet and shower floor. When she asked if I got the spots off I told her "Yeah, I got them." And that was the end of it.

Thennnn, she wanted me to fix the kitchen faucet. She wanted me to switch the cold water over to where the hot water is and the hot water over to where the cold water is. I tried to tell her that all this would do is move the hot water over to where the cold water is and vice versa, so what difference did it make where it was hot and where it was cold? A tear came to her eye and she said, "It makes a difference to me!" Well, that was all it took to melt me like butter and I set to work on the sink.

You know how when you work on the plumbing on an older house you fix one thing and 10 other things break and leak? Well that's the can of worms I was forced to open. One connection dripped and everything I did to fix it made it worse. I tightened that damn thing until the pipe looks like a big drill bit spiraling from top to bottom. It got so bad that I had to secretly hire a crew of plumbers at $44 dollars an hour to fix it and I still don't know why they had to dig a big hole in the back yard. There is not one single piece of plumbing anywhere in my back yard. WTH! It never ends, does it?

There was a list of chores — all rush jobs — to be done. I was feeling overwhelmed and I tried to tell her so. She says, "Just do one little chore a day! Just one!" That said, I did two of the chores on the first day and tried to take a day off. Naturally, she caught me!

"What chore did you do today?" she says.

"Well, I did two chores yesterday so I thought I would relax a little bit today."

"Oh, no, no, no!" she says. "You'd better get your act together because if I can't relax, you're not going to relax either!" says she.

Soooo, that's where I am right now! It doesn't matter that just over a year ago I had a heart attack and a quadruple bypass and I could die at any moment! I asked her, "What if I die? Who would do the stinking chores then?" Then she said it, and I knew it was true! She says, "I could go buy a drunken monkey to finish the chores you started and never finished!" She had her hands on her hips so I knew she was ready to go all the way with this one.

Well, there it is! Now I'm on my knees on the back porch looking for spots of glue on the day I was going to relax. I will never do two chores on the same day again, even if they are imaginary and I just said I did them.

I hate those damn monkeys

Shhhh… it's the turkeys…
4/22/2017

Yesterday I went over to my friend, Terry Vender's, house because I had an inkling that something was not right here in our little town of Winters, California. After I read the local newspaper, I got this uneasy feeling from my head to my knees that I just couldn't shake. Whenever I get like that, I get on my wife's nerves, so she tells me, "Why don't you go over and bother Terry?"

So I say, "Okay, maybe I will!"

Terry's a pretty smart guy. He's a government man who works for the City of Winters. He travels all around town all day long, so he knows everybody and their brother. He says he sees everything that goes on in town, so when something is not right, well, he's the guy who fixes it. He and I make a pretty good team because he is the government fixer guy and I am the big important newspaper whatever guy. Terry is my secret source of information.

Anyway, back to my story. When something bothers me, I go to Terry's house for information. He's real smart and knows exactly what is what. So, I hear power tools, so I know he's in his garage. There he is grinding his toenails with a sanding disc on a dremmel. He has like a 5th sense so he knows I'm there before he sees me.

"Sup?" he says.

Being the news guy that I am, I got right to the point in the first 10 minutes or so.

"Did you see the article on page one of the Winters Express today?" I says.

Terry says, "The one about the gang of turkeys?"

"Yep." I replied.

Terry says, "If I were you, I'd drop this one. It's a hot potato!" Terry speaks in riddles sometimes, not unlike the Zodiac killer, forcing me to interpret what I think he means. He knows everything he says will end up in the newspaper, so he chooses his words like picking melons in a corn field.

So now I'm thinking, "COVERUP!"

Terry tells me this story:

"The government and the mass media lies to the public all the time? I'm not talking about once in a while. It happens all the time. If they don't lie, they stretch the truth or twist it to suit whatever agenda they are on. It's ridiculous. Not only do they lie, they get away with it, too. No one ever gets arrested and no one goes to jail.

"Take the Kennedy assassination. The government has classified files that were frozen for 50 years. That is just long enough for anyone involved to be already dead before the file is opened. For your info, those files were just frozen again for another 10 years. I'm sick of it, but I don't know what to do about it. Sick, I say!"

He was beginning to rant now.

Yes, right there on the front page of the April 20 edition was a full-fledged cover up. Information was withheld from us and deliberately down-played so as to hide what amounts to imminent danger to the public. It's criminal and I'm going to tell!

(Note to self: Look up "imminent.")

It doesn't surprise me that this was written by Editor Debra DeAngelo. Entitled "Turkeys cut power!" the article reports that on the morning of April 18, a group of turkeys cut the power to the Golden Bear area that lies just about 100 miles outside of town. Debra quotes Brandi Merlo, PG&E spokesperson, stating that 101 customers had suffered power outages.

I suppose we're to believe that's why the lights wouldn't work in that area.

I have a friend who lives up there and according to him, they had to watch TV in the dark or by candle light. Why didn't Debra Darn DeAngelo tell us about the lights not working? Oh, and why didn't Debra "Omit the Information" DeAngelo report the rest of the information about this gang of turkeys? The night before the morning the power went out (I can't remember the date), the very same gang of turkeys were terrorizing certain residents of this very town.

Terry says an old lady with gray hair was forced off the road by this gang of turkeys just two nights ago. What's so bad about this incident is the fact that the old lady had four babies in the car and one of them bumped his head causing him to poop his diaper. It was a mess! To make matters worse, Terry says that the cops didn't respond.

"Wow," I say, "This is big news!"

So there you have it! This gang of turkeys is big trouble for Winters, California. If they can put out the power in the Golden Bear area, they can put out the power downtown. If that happens, all the money I've collected for my new charity, the "Feed the Poor Kids of Winters, California Foundation" might just come up missing. Money from this foundation has come up missing before. Terry thinks whoever took it went to the casino with him.

There you have it! I guess this gang of turkeys will be around for a while. Should you be attacked by this gang, that's just too bad. They're protected by forces we are unaware of. I don't think I'm going to write anything about this, because if those turkeys will run a car off the road with a little old lady and five babies in it, what would they do to me?

I'm just going to drop this whole thing and let Terry and the other government guys handle this one

I'm a newspaper guy
5/9/2017

I'm a "newspaper guy." I didn't say I was a good "newspaper guy," just a "newspaper guy." There is a guy like me in every newspaper office in the world. I think you know why this is true but I'll go ahead and explain anyway.

OK, say there is a guy out there in "publicland" who wants to sue the paper for like $10 million for damages, either real or imagined. This is where the "newspaper guy" comes in. "Newspaper guy" is just slang for "defendant."

Attorneys that represent newspapers, by precedent, will always name the local "newspaper guy" as the defendant in any civil action against any newspaper. Neither the newspaper nor the editor will ever be named as a defendant in a lawsuit, nor have they ever been. Newspaper editors are above the law; it's as simple as that. Of course when the "newspaper guy" finds out about this, it is too late, his name is already on the court documents.

There's a lot of things I didn't know when I took this "newspaper guy" job. Well it's not really a job since I don't get paid. There's a saying somewhere that says, "With great responsibility comes no money!" I wasn't told that, as a "newspaper guy," my sole purpose in life is to be named defendant of any suit filed against my newspaper. As a matter of fact, there are a number of things I can or can't do as a "newspaper guy."

• I can never write anything that is meaningful or logical.

• I can lie as often as I want to in everything I write because my name is always on court documents anyway and everybody already knows I'm a liar. I'm lying right now.

• Nothing I have ever written has ever made any sense at all but when I send it to the editor, it magically becomes newspaper worthy and readable, capable of winning some big award from somebody noteworthy like the NBA or some other organization that I must have forgotten.

• I can't think of anything else right now, but the three things above are enough because only a dummy would read my column anyway, right?

There are some instances of abuse, both physical and mental that "newspaper guys" suffer at the hands of their editors. At first I wasn't afraid of my editor and I thought I could take her if it came down to fisticuffs. How was I to know that such a little woman could be so brutally proficient at the pugilistic art? The pain would have been unbearable if it weren't for the coma I slipped into. If I hadn't played dead she would have gutted me like a fish. Oh, I felt like a little girl getting a spanking. It was awful.

So, what am I gonna do now? I can't run because she will catch me. I can't hide because she will find me. She will corner me and say, "Why are you shaking Don, are you cold?" I'll shake my head and tell her that I have cerebral palsy. But, like I say, she knows I'm a liar. She will laugh with a menacing grin!

"Ha ha ha ha ha ha ha ha ha ha ha!"

I have to do what I have always done. I'll wear two socks that are different colors and play like I'm deaf with a learning disability. Oh, and I can always fake the coma thingy again.

Veterans can struggle with self-worth
5/22/2017

I have a keen appreciation for women who live with disabled veterans who are suffering within themselves. I'm talking about veterans who want to live in the present but just can't seem to get out of their past. Veterans who suffer within themselves find it hard to smile when they feel like crying all the time. They're always on the verge of tears; even at their happiest moments the tears are just below the surface. They are always just below the surface.

It is the same with me. I find that as I get older, I'm beginning to think more about my wartime experiences. I become more emotional. As you age, it's normal to look back over your life and try to make sense of your experiences. For veterans, this process can trigger Late-Onset Stress Symptomatology (LOSS).

I think that's what is happening here and I don't know what to do about it. In the past, I would go to the VA and ask for help but I've decided against that because they are dealing with a younger generation of veterans now and I don't want to interfere with that.

I don't want to ask the VA to spend any more time and money on my case. They have already spent a fortune trying to "get me right," so to say. I have found that years of therapy and pills have done little to solve my mental problems; it's a hill that is just too high for me to climb.

Unfortunately, when I get on the emotional rollercoaster, so must my wife.

Imagine, if you will for a moment, how hard it must be to live with someone who is on the verge of tears all the time. I think it would drive most people insane to live with someone unable to live in the brightness of the present because living in the present, one is required to interact with others living in the now. If you're in the now, you're not alone because others are here with you at this precise moment. However, if you live in the past, there's no room for anyone else — you are alone. The present and the past are two different things, and the two cannot mix.

Average people cannot understand those who are stuck in the past and, in fact, see them as useless or near useless at the least. Some veterans are classified as "unemployable" because of that very fact. They cannot interact with others in the now, so that makes it difficult for them to hold a job. The resulting failure to feel that you are useful to society accounts for the very high rate of veteran suicide, drug abuse, and incarceration. In the past, I've had bouts with all three and in time, I found myself in dire straits.

So, the moral of my story can be summed up in one short sentence: "If you want to live, keep busy!"

Now, Memorial Day is swiftly approaching again and I have just a few things to say about that.

• Take a moment to remember the veterans that didn't come home.

• If there are any veterans out there who need help with self worth, do yourself a favor and find the office of the Putah Creek Council in downtown Winters, California, for they have a plan to make each and every one of us useful to society. It's a good plan and it works.

• Last but not least, be grateful for the help of your family and friends.

I'd like to see the real criminals in jail
7/10/2017

Americans sure are funny. The funniest thing about us is the way we think about and handle crime. We seem to jump on the most insignificant crimes, like our sons and daughters often go to jail for trying pot or some other stupid drug. At any given moment, our county jail is full to the brim with idiots that commit stupid crimes. I know I'm one of them. That's OK, we know that if we break the law and get caught that is what happens — you go to jail.

That's all well and nice but what's so funny about that, you may ask? OK, here it is. I think it would be really, really nice if one of our City of Winters cops would go out and arrest one of the real criminals of our society that do pretty much what they want, when they want and never have to worry about getting arrested. Imagine what would happen if a City of Winters cops went after and arrested one of the untouchable corporate big wheels.

The sad truth is that they wouldn't be a cop very long if they went after a real criminal. I would be wrong in assuming that if a citizen of Winters, California was a victim of fraud, at least one good cop would take note of it and in the end, someone would be arrested. Like I said, I would be wrong.

What the heck am I talking about, you may ask? Going back as far as 2011, two million sham accounts were opened, complete with forged signatures, phony email addresses, and fake PIN numbers. The criminals I'm talking about were signing up customers for checking accounts and credit cards without their knowledge. This crime affected over two million families, some of which live in Winters.

To top it off, then these criminals charged customers at least $1.5 million in fees for the bogus accounts. Many of the victims took "significant hits" to their credit scores for not staying current on accounts they didn't even know about. They'll likely have difficulty securing home and car loans at any reasonable rate for years to come, simply because their bank decided to defraud them. You would think that for a crime of this magnitude, at least one person would go to jail with the pot smokers.

Of course I'm talking about Wells Fargo Bank and the 5,300 employees that got fired for committing fraud upon the unsuspecting public. Well, it's business as usual for Wells Fargo, and no one was arrested and no one went to jail. They were fined $185 million but they profited up to $5.6 billion in just the second quarter of this year.

If you or I went out and did the same thing, the cops would grab us by the scruff of the neck and there we would sit, in a cell with the pot smokers. What the hell? What is really sad is the fact that this is not the first time something like this has happened. Do a little research and you'll see what I mean. If you want to read about something really scary, look up the BCCI Bank. They were involved in similar activities but at a larger world-wide scale. They committed fraud, murder, corporate corruption and political espionage, and nearly got away with it.

Well I take that back. They did get away with it because not one single person went to jail. They were guilty of murder for hire, fraud and blackmail, and they bought half of the senate and congress. Their activities were broadcast out into publicland and not one person went to jail. I think I'm gonna barf!

I would love to see Officer Ramirez or Officer Ramos jerk one of these big crime criminals by the scruff of the neck, but it's not gonna happen. They are too busy throwing your sons and daughters in jail for smoking pot or some other kind of crap because that is what they are forced to do.

Don't get me wrong — both of these guys are excellent cops and they do their duty very well as I know from experience. It's just that I would like to see them go to new heights. Just once, I would like to see one of the real criminals go to jail.

More thinking, less mouthing off
July 21, 2017

Every week, I read in our local newspaper, the Winters Express, about how unhappy some people are with the restoration work on Putah Creek. It's always the same group of people that do everything they can to prevent the completion of the Putah Creek Restoration Project. Today's paper reports how a newly formed environmental group, Friends of Putah Creek, has filed a petition in the courts of Solano County that will essentially halt the restoration project.

With friends like that, who needs enemies? These people don't have a clue! From what I gather, their major complaint concerns the use of equipment in the removal of invasive plants, trash removal, and channel alignment. I'm not the smartest guy in the world, but I'll be damned if I can see a way to do the project without equipment. Geeze, give me a break!

Every year, the Putah Creek Council participates with the California Coastal Commission's waterway cleanup day. Just like clockwork, every year, there is an average of 3,300 pounds of trash cleaned up just in an eight-mile stretch of Putah Creek. Take my word for it — that is a lot of trash. The bad part about this is the fact that Putah Creek has been the dumping ground for trash for over 150 years.

All along Putah Creek, there are old cars, car batteries, barrels of oil, chemicals, and I don't know what else just under the surface of the topsoil. I personally have seen things unearthed in the Nature Park that I don't know what it was, but I think it may be responsible for my sudden increase in age. In the last few years, I' turned gray, my skin is clammy, and my brain is half the size it was when the restoration project started.

Maybe the Friends of Putah Creek can find a way to remove all that toxic trash and align the channel without the use of equipment. I think not, because all they can do is complain and bitch to each other about those who are really making an effort to fix the creek. For some ungodly reason, the FOPC wants to leave the creek exactly as it is. As dumb as I am, even I can tell that we have screwed up the creek royally through the years and now the time has come to fix it before it is too far gone to fix.

Today's paper also has a letter to the editor from a guy named Jeff TenPas. He seems like a nice enough guy, but I think he may be dumber than I am. He seems to have the loudest mouth of those who are against the restoration project. He is always shooting off his mouth but what comes out doesn't make sense to me. I can't figure out what the hell is on his mind, and maybe it's better that I don't know because it just might make me angry. I don't like it when I get angry; it makes me uglier than I am already.

The Friends of Putah Creek think that if you can't fix the creek outright then you should do nothing at all. Well, like the joke says, "That's a special kind of stupid!" Do you think that maybe I'm wrong in thinking that the only way to remove old cars, batteries, and other toxic crap is to dig it out and haul it away? Maybe I'm not so dumb after all. Sometimes I amaze myself with my brilliance!

One thing I do know for sure, and that is the fact that this restoration project is a good thing. It is exactly what this creek needs. Another thing we need is for Mr. TenPas to use that brain of his in a more positive manner. He should do more thinking and less mouthing off.

What can we do to change the world?
August 10, 2017

You can't please everybody. People have tried. It doesn't matter what you do or what you say, somebody is not going to like it. That's just the way it is. That's the way it will always be because that's the way it has always been. Some say it is evil against good, the eternal struggle set into motion by God himself so that he can sit in judgment of the free will of man. If God wants us to fuss and fight all the time, then he is not the God that I have in my mind.

Today I read that a little boy named Gabriel Taye of Cincinnati, Ohio hanged himself with his necktie. It angers me and saddens me at the same time to think that an eight year old child has to see suicide as his only way out. Is this what the world has become? If this is the direction we're moving in, what will the future be like? Even if life in the future is only as good as life is today, it will still be horrible.

There is a saying that some adhere to that says, "If we don't learn from history then we are doomed to repeat it." The fact of the matter is all of recorded history is a joke — nonsense. Our knowledge of the past has always been incomplete and inaccurate. It's clouded by ambivalent evidence and biased historians. How can anyone accurately describe 10,000 years in 200 pages? Only a fool would try and only another fool would believe what he has written.

More than $14 trillion dollars was spent on international conflicts just in the last year. As it stands today, $30 billion dollars would feed the entire world. Every day there are 870 million people who are undernourished and we have the potential to end their hunger. For $39 billion dollars we could educate every child in the world at a cost of $1.17 per child per day. If my math is correct, we could feed and educate the world and still have $13.030 trillion dollars left for our conflicts.

Maybe the historians can explain to us when and where we lost the power to decide where and for what we can spend our own money. Who has the power to take all of our money and spend it on violence and conflict? If you do the numbers, 14 trillion dollars divided into 7 billion people would give each person on earth about $11,600 dollars per year, give or take a few dollars here and there.

Who decides where this money is spent? Who has that kind of power? A better question is, "How do we stop them from taking our money?" These questions have been asked at times throughout history and the answer is always the same, revolution and the redistribution of wealth. These endeavors have always failed in the span of time and today would be no different.

So, what do we do? How can we change things in the world to stop hunger and war? I don't know about you, but I'm going to keep doing what I do, like watering trees, playing with my grandchildren and loving my wife. I'm going to do what I can for my community and those I care for and I'm going to keep this dumb look on my face.

If anyone should ask me a question, I'm going to play like I am blind and deaf.

Happy birthday, Melanie!

8/19/2017

Today is Melanie Bajakian's birthday. I absolutely love this woman. She and her husband John are the owners of the Buckhorn Steakhouse and the Putah Creek Café. That isn't what I want to talk about right now, but I will bring this up later. This column is about my good friend Melanie and what a wonderful woman she is. I suppose that if this were the Middle Ages, she would be the Queen that everybody loves and adores.

She is stunningly beautiful inside and out and is the mother of two daughters so lovely that when you gaze upon them it's like butterfly's wings have brushed your eyes. I've said many times that this little town of Winters, California has the most beautiful women in the world. Beauty begets beauty, thus the entire town is beautiful. I think this every day.

Melanie is of Armenian ancestry which explains the pain you glimpse when you look into her eyes. There has to be a deep fear of violence and genocide in there, but like I said, only a glimpse. She is stern of will and steadfast in her faith — her church is right down the block from her home and it's a big part of her life. Her faith is the kind that makes devils cry.

She knows we rarely get to choose what we have to learn. It can be a cruel world and we have so much to lose. Kindness is always in her eyes. They offer comfort when there is no hope in sight and you know she would give her last breath to save your soul. She knows what love is and when others are around her, they know they have been loved — the kind of love that makes flowers bloom and often leaves people whistling as they walk and talk to everyone we meet in this little town.

There are many others living here of the same caliber. When I think of this, Woody and Rebecca Fridae first come to mind along with the Marini, Ramos, Neal, and Rominger families. I could go on naming families but I only have about 700 words in total to get my point across. There is no one living in this small town that is not important to these wonderful people, for they among anybody know that we are all in this together. Whatever affects the one affects the whole of society.

Love comes harder to these people because there are so many other people who depend on them keeping it together. They don't think about it, but they all know that everything is so fragile. If the Melanies and the Marinis should drop the ball for just one moment, this society we enjoy so much would stop and hold its breath to see if and when that ball will be picked up again. Literally thousands of people depend upon the actions of these families and their industries.

You know and I know that a business cannot survive without love. It must be nurtured just as you would one of your children. It is all too important that the nurturing come from both employer and employee. Melanie and her husband, John, know this to be true for I see it every day in the way they behave with others. There is no one I have ever known who works harder for the welfare of others than these two. Believe me; I know that should you spend a little time with these people, exhaustion will find you in the end.

These people and others like them have work that never ends. They don't work 8 hours a day like you and I do. To them, there's always something that absolutely has to be done or it all starts to unravel. Certainly they are deserving of a little love from us. It may not be readily apparent to us, but there's a constant flow of love coming down the line from those who own and operate the businesses here in Winters, California. They are the fabric of our society. Love is at the center of this and it's time to show your love as well. So, happy birthday, Melanie! Know that you are loved.

Police officers feel the fear too
10/3/2017

Yesterday was a normal day here in Winters, California. I went out in the morning to pick up trash that people toss out their windows as they drive along Putah Creek. I was surprised at the amount of trash I found, because only about a week ago there were hundreds of people picking up trash for our annual creek cleanup day. I don't know how much trash was cleaned up at that time, but I know that two large dumpsters were rented for its removal.

One of the dumpsters is still sitting near the community garden next to our water treatment plant, so I threw yesterday's trash in with the trash collected last week. I guess trash collecting will never end. That's just the way it is. There will always be a certain type of person that will throw their garbage out along the creek and there will always be a person like me to pick it up.

OK, keep reading because I'm close to coming to the point of this column.

While I was throwing my trash into the dumpster I looked up to see one of Winters Police Department's finest standing there talking to a lady that spends her time working in the community garden. Out of respect, I waved at the police officer like I always do when I see them; she smiled and waved back at me.

How sharp she looked in her police uniform. I'm sorry I don't know her name because I think a good citizen should go out of their way to know each and every police officer that serves their community. If a citizen doesn't know the police officer and the officer doesn't know the citizen, it complicates things. At the very least, it makes the officer's job a little bit harder to perform. A simple wave of respect is not enough.

I'm sorry to say that I have been a problem for the police in the past but those days are long gone; I'm an old man now. I don't know if every police officer in town knows me or my past but I don't think that really matters to them. If I cause them problems they will handle it like they always have and always will. Keeping the peace and enforcing the law is what they do. It's as simple as that.

OK, I'm getting to the point now so here it is!

Like I said earlier, yesterday was a normal day here in Winters, California, but today is different with the shootings in Las Vegas. That makes it a special day; a day to remember. Take a look at the news videos taken in the midst of the shooting and there in the horrorific chain of events displayed in the video — people are running is all directions with terror on their faces. The fear must have been immense.

Now look at the videos again. There in the middle of all the fear and terror with people running everywhere to get away from the sound of gunfire, you will see people in police uniforms running the opposite way, toward the gunfire. The fear and terror within the police officer is no less than the fear and terror in everyone else, yet they are driven to address the problem. They are either going to stop the violence or die trying.

That police officer I waved to at the community garden, the one that looked so sharp and I didn't know her name, would place herself in harm's way to protect me. I have no doubt at all that this is true. It doesn't matter that she didn't know my name; the end result would be the same. She will not run away from trouble, ever. Even the worst of society's criminals have a healthy respect for abilities of the average police officer and rightly so.

So, in the end, my point is this, "On a normal day in Winters California, a simple wave of respect is not enough."

I need a red cape and a Viking ship
10/13/2017

I'm getting older now and I'm running out of time to make the changes I want to make before I die. I know now that time is speeding up because just yesterday I was still 20 years old and a senior in high school. I was afraid I'd have to spend another year in school but the Dean told me they had to graduate me because they couldn't have a 21-year-old kid in school dating 16-year-old students. So there I was, a high school graduate, and I didn't even have to do anything.

After that came the U.S. Army and I didn't have to do anything there either. Except for a few days, it was the most boring time of my life. It was a time of venereal disease and crouch critters, but it was nothing a can of Raid couldn't handle. I really enjoyed the helicopter rides; well, all but one anyway. I liked the days I got to play with machine guns too; well, all but a couple of times anyway. The rest of my Army experience was just passing time.

All of a sudden, the war was gone for me and I was back on the block and then it was *on* — the party I mean. From 1971 until well into the '90s, I was in a fog, so don't ask me about that because your guess is as good as mine. I do remember sniffing Amyl Nitrate in the theater while watching the first Star Wars though. My brother Michael lost the cap to the bottle, so eventually the whole theater reeked of the mind-altering chemical.

That was just yesterday!

I never noticed how fast time was going because I was so messed up. Somewhere in there, I had a couple of wives, but I don't remember much about them either except the way I broke their hearts and eventually made them hate me. The first of which wanted to kill me, I think. Like I said before, the whole thing is a blur that isn't worth remembering even if I wanted too.

I wrote a book one time and I tried to be as accurate as possible, but when you're dealing with foggy memories, things get jumbled up a bit. Foggy people sometimes get credit for something someone else did or sometimes they did something before or after it really happened. One mistake that I know of in the book was the fact that my great uncle was just an uncle. You know, stuff like that.

It's a wonder that I ever got it published because fearing lawsuits, several publishers told me to go elsewhere. It took 10 years to get it printed. I'm working on a second book now, based on my grandfather's handwritten diary about his experiences in World War I. His lungs were burned by mustard gas in 1918, causing him to suffer the remainder of his life. For his trouble, he was awarded a disability pension from the Veterans Administration that amounted to one dollar a month.

That was all just yesterday too!

Like I said, I want to make some changes before I die. The first of which is I'm going to go out and buy a cape; a red one. I'm going to wear it around town here in good old Winters, California. Everybody thinks I'm a prince anyway, right? With time speeding up so fast, before you know, it I'll be laying on my deathbed and the whole town will be wondering where the old guy in the red cape went to.

Speed up a little more and I'll be dead.

Not to worry, though — I have the whole funeral thingy figured out. Tomorrow, I'm going to start building a Viking boat. I hope to have it ready by the time I die so we can put it in the Putah Creek that still won't be polluted by then. You guys can put me on the boat and push it off to float towards Davis.

Everybody can stand along the creek and shoot arrows at my body like in a real Viking funeral. Well let's make that *flaming* arrows, OK? Hopefully the damn boat will catch on fire so that by the time it gets to Davis they won't be able to identify the body and make the people of Winters take it back.

With time speeding up like it is, I think that I should smell pretty ripe by then and that's what those people in Davis deserve, because they are always coming to Winters on the weekends and I think they all stop to pee on my hedges.

If I have enough time left after building my funeral Viking boat I'm going to run an electric wire into my hedges. Maybe I should try to make time for that, but now that I think about it, I'd probably electrocute myself.

Right or wrong — can you look at yourself in the mirror?
10/30/2017

If I should do some wrong to someone, either by accident or on purpose, it becomes increasingly hard to raise my head to look upon myself in the mirror. I have memories of this as far back as 60 years ago when I was only a child at the age of 9 or 10 years old. During my long life I have committed many such wrongs that I, by nature, have always seen fit to regret. Would that I could have a chance at a time machine to make just one of these wrongs right, I would take all that I am to see it through.

But alas, I cannot.

In the consideration of humanity, I see myself as an average man. By nature, my behavior is not much different than that of my neighbors, be they white, black, yellow, or brown. As such, the rights must outweigh the wrongs and this one fact enables an average man with the ability to rise out of his bed to face another day without knowledge of how it will turn out. The ability to carry on with task after task, some of which are not in the least enjoyable stems directly from the heart as we act in the interest of those loved ones held so close by every person I am discussing.

Average men and women exist in every corner around the globe in much the same manner as you and I. The safety of a home where those we love can live in relative peace is first and foremost in our everyday thoughts and actions. Farther out, we strive to live in harmony with those with whom, by chance, we interact as neighbors and friends. It is generally the "Golden Rule" that we live by in our travels throughout the world. We give it and we expect it.

It is in our nature to care for each other in the best manner we know how, thus we go out of our way to group with others who have a heartfelt desire to create more rights than wrongs. Actions that are right are easy and natural — they make us feel good about ourselves. They make life flow like a stream through a forest, easily traversing jagged rocks, hills, corners or anything else you might imagine.

Acts that are wrong are something much more complicated but easily recognizable. We all know right from wrong. I don't know exactly where it comes from, but each and every one of us has the power to understand wrong — not only within ourselves but we can see it in others almost as instantly as they see it themselves. A wrong must be taken into consideration to commit. Deep within our hearts, souls, or whatever you want to call it, something tells us what is wrong or right. It's like we have a switch that alarms us when we are about to commit a wrong.

This is true of much of humanity, but not all of it.

There are those who are unable or unwilling to distinguish right from wrong. They have no interest in the ideas of right, wrong, love, family, children, peace, war, or anything other than the idea of the self. These things exist only as tools to be used at will whenever they please for whatever purpose they choose. They care little for behavior or laws and they do as they please.

This type of person can be very convincing and charming when it comes to persuading others to join in on their schemes to commit wrong and there is nothing they will not do to corrupt others if it aids their desired goals. Wrongs at every level must involve good people or they remain small in nature.

It must be true that wrongs committed by large corporations such as the Wells Fargo Bank originated from one bad individual. It must also be true that in order for this bank to open thousands of unlawful accounts in the name of unaware patrons, this bad person had to enlist the aid of hundreds of good people. In this one unlawful act, Wells Fargo Bank made billions of dollars in profit until they were caught red-handed with their hands in their clients' pockets.

Thousands and thousands of good people got screwed, some lost all their money, their homes and retirement, and for them there is no justice. If you or I were to commit fraud, we would go straight to jail without a doubt. As it stands, Wells Fargo was fined a couple of hundred million dollars by the Justice Department which is a drop in the bucket considering Wells Fargo made a profit of billions of dollars on these evil acts. There are many similar crimes committed daily and it is common in large corporate crime cases that deals are made so not one person is charged with a crime as long as the corporation pays the fine of whatever dollars.

This is how wrongs are committed and now the Justice Department, simply by their inaction and negligence in failing to correctly prosecute and enforce the law of the land, is complicit in the commission of this act. In the end, their pockets may be full but they still must look at themselves in the mirror and that must be hard to do. Crimes of this magnitude are committed against humanity. Wrongs like this will make your soul ugly and hard to gaze upon.

I tell you the truth when I say we cannot and will not enjoy a world of rights when we continue to ignore wrongs committed by our corporations and elected officials on such a grand scale.

Oh yeah, Trump is just a diversion tactic designed to draw your attention away from what you should be thinking about. Wake up!

If I fall asleep, it's not you, it's me
11/13/2017

There are a great many things that contribute to aging other than the passage of years, many of which I do not want to confer upon you. For instance, it's a good practice to start a column with the subject so that you can always refer back if you forget what you're writing about. There is something new that I have to contend with and I'd like to tell you about it before it happens, should I be talking with you face to face.

I find myself falling asleep at odd times during the day. It is neither out of boredom nor from exhaustion. In just a split second, BAM, I'm asleep! It doesn't matter where I am or what I'm doing, when it happens, it happens, so don't take offense; it's not you it's me.

I'll tell it in the form of a story to make it a little more entertaining for you to read.

My falling asleep problem has been going on for some time now, and with the assistance of my dear wife Therese, I have seemingly been able to keep it under control. Therese uses her elbow to combat my problem whenever it raises its ugly head. Should I feel a sharp sudden pain in my ribs, I know I've fallen asleep.

When Therese is not with me, things become a bit more complicated. At this point, it becomes an embarrassment for me, one that I try to take with a bit of humor. That's all I can do, so I'll explain.

Take the Putah Creek Council's last CreekSpeak presentation of this year entitled, "Ecology, Evolution and Conservation on Serpentine Soils." The speaker was UC Davis Professor Susan Harrison; a lovely woman, very pleasing to the eye. I didn't even know what a Serpentine was, so naturally I had to go.

Sooo, right off the bat, I contact my friend Karin Young of the Putah Creek Council and tell her I want to attend, so I would see her at the Davis Library on the designated evening. Okeedookee.

The big night arises and I don't know what I expected, but all they wanted to talk about was some kind of rock and how it affects the soil and plants where it is found. It goes to reason that if it is not found it would have no effect on anything, so if it is bad, all we have to do is not to find it, right?

Well I'll tell you right now I could not stay awake! I nodded off several times, the last of which was one of those head back, awaken with a loud snort type of naps. The room was very small and tight so I know everybody in the room had to hear my rude awakening. To make matters worse, I jumped and protected my ribs expecting an elbow, and then I ducked expecting Karin to slap me on the back of the head. Everybody there thought I was a total spaz!

I escaped out of that one alive, but yesterday I had another challenge. I had a doctor's appointment in Vallejo, some 50 minutes from where I live. I didn't know how the hell I was going to stay awake for that boring drive but as it turned out, the traffic was terrible and the stress of it kept me awake. At the doctor's I found a lovely young woman that was going to rub my neck while performing an ultrasound.

Naturally, I fell asleep and naturally, I woke myself with a loud snort! I don't know what came out but I meant to say "Sorry." She was gracious and said there was no need for an apology. So here I am looking up at this lovely girl and I have slobber dripping from my beard.

Life is so unfair!

So as I walk out of the office, I'm starting to get mad! All I could think of was why the heck my wife let me out by myself. What is wrong with her?

Then I thought about how the heck I'm going to stay awake on the way home. Coffee!

All I want for Christmas is…
12/4/2017

Now that Thanksgiving is over and done, it's time to get serious about deciding what I'm gonna get for Christmas. I started thinking about it almost eight months ago on the morning of the Fourth of July at precisely 8 a.m.

When I'm about to start thinking, I usually have a little ceremony to kick things off, kinda proper like. This time it was no different, so I looked around the kitchen for some refreshments for a toast to "thinkin' time!" All I could find was an open bottle of Turkovich wine. It would have to do.

I was almost thinkin', so I hurried up, got a glass and poured the sweet nectar into said glass, only to find that what came out would barely fill a thimble. I was sipping that wine and trying to stick my tongue in to lick the last few drops from the bottom of the aforementioned glass when all of a sudden — "POP" — I had my first thought: "Dangit, why didn't I use a short glass!"

Within just a few minutes, I finally got all the wine out of the glass and it dawned on me what I want for Christmas! The more thoughts I had about it, the more I wanted it, the more I had to have it! I was surprised that it only took a few quick thoughts because it usually takes 30 or so before I can make any kind of decision. One minute I was thinking, "What do I want for Christmas more than anything in the world?" A couple of minutes later, I knew just exactly what I wanted, and thinkin' time was over.

I want the Turkovich Winery! I really, really, really want it. I'll bet it would be so easy to buy the whole place, grapes and all. They probably don't even want it anymore. I've never met Old Man Turkovich but it says on the bottle that he has been at it for three generations. So what is that, 70 or 80 years? He's probably so tired and worried that he might have to work another generation before he can retire. Soooo, I'm gonna make them an offer and then wait and see how that goes.

I never wanted to buy a winery before but I gotta have this one. I wouldn't change a thing except I'd change the name to Sanders & Turkovich Wine. Of course I'd have to have my picture on every bottle. I'm thinking that even if I don't get to buy it, they'll want to put my picture in the label anyway. That's called wise packaging.

If Old Man Turkovich will sell me the winery, I'd drink a bottle of wine for breakfast, then I would count all my money and then drink another bottle. Then I would go back to bed at about 10 a.m. and then I'd get back up at 6 p.m. and have another bottle with dinner. Yeah, I'd have a wine dinner! I don't need no stinkin' food!

First thing I would do is let the old guy know that he could still help around the place because I really like the way he makes wine. As a matter of fact, my wife Therese is a Turkovich Wine groupie! She went so far as to join a club that drinks wine and I've never seen her do that before. There must be a thousand people in that wine club because Therese comes home with only three or four bottles.

The sad thing about that is I'm lucky to get a thimble full after Therese gets done with it. That Turkovich guy is pretty smart to make his own club. I'll bet he is the CEO or president of his wine club so he can pay himself another salary. Yeah, I better buy the wine club too.

I'll bet they are constantly running out of wine with so many people in the club plus all the people that just walk in off the street. When I own the winery, I'm gonna make all those people that aren't in the club take a number from one of those little number thingies that sit on the counter. Then I can say, "Number 32!" Then I'll skip a number to see how they react, "Number 35!" "Number 35!"

So now all I have to do is find out where the old man lives and walk up his driveway with a bucket full of crisp $20 bills! I'll wear some fancy clothes and a big white hat. I've never seen the old guy but I heard he is eight feet tall and shoots fire out of his eyes. That's kinda scary but I just gotta have that winery!

Restoration is an investment in the future
12/6/2017

Once an ecological creek restoration project has begun, practices on private land or human resistance on public land in the form of lawsuits should not impair it. When a project such as the Putah Creek Restoration reaches the starting point there has already been years of preparation, planning, proposals, arguments, submittal for permits, court actions, changes to plans, headaches and even a little crying. Beginning an environmental altering project is no easy task.

Scientific study after other scientific studies have all concluded that "hands on" management is needed to restore "hands off" wilderness character. Just reaching the starting point of a creek restoration requires the approval of a myriad of local, state and federal government agencies. These agencies examine such a project and either approve or demand changes at every level; every step of the job to be done is looked at. Like I said, "No easy task."

Creek restoration work is still in its learning stage, so if something doesn't work, other avenues will be explored until the problem is resolved. Every step of the way, everything done is considered, examined and resolved by the greatest of our minds and then approved by goverenment officials. There is little room for error but there will always be those that will think differently. There will always be human resistance.

Hardin's paper, "The Tragedy of the Commons" (1968), describes how property owners sometimes feel that they have the right to do what they want on their property. This often causes damage to adjacent or even distant ecosystems. These problems have continued for some 4,000 years, as evidenced by the inclusion of several laws in the famous Code of Hammurabi that dealt with the use of irrigation water. Individual and public behavior will always be modified for the betterment of others.

If this were not so, projects involving the environment would be next to impossible to fund in that those who provide the money ask, " Why should they fund a project to restore a damaged ecosystem if misuse of common or private land can, in a very short time, erase the labor of years or decades?"

Ecological restoration cannot be impaired by practices on private land, or on public land via lawsuit.

Anything private environmental protection groups such as "Friends of Putah Creek" can point to is already being examined and monitored by publicly funded government organizations such as Fish and Game, Department of the Interior, and county and federal government. Lawsuits that are designed to stop a creek restoration project are detrimental to the public domain and can cause a huge increase in project cost.

Phase III of the Winters Putah Creek Nature Park Restoration Project has been held up for some time now because of a lawsuit filed which apparently wants to keep a good portion of the project that lies smack in the middle of the park, untouched by restoration personnel or machines.

This restoration project is an investment in our future. It deserves a high level of stewardship, but halting the work is not acceptable, for eventually the funds we don't use will end up somewhere else down the creek. That's just the way it works. I don't care what anyone says, I have found this to be true. Funding usually goes where it is wanted and used.

Some of this information was gathered from: "The Handbook of Ecological Restoration: Volume 1, Principles of Restoration," edited by Martin R. Perrow and Anthony J. Davy

A guide to pain
12/20/2017

Pain is a beautiful thing. Think about how life would be without pain. When we don't have it, we don't think much about it. But when we do have it, it's all we think about. Pain is a personal thing. I don't know how, but I suppose there are ways to share your pain with someone else. There are times when everyone you love has pain at the same time but they can't feel yours and you can't feel theirs.

At times I have found myself wanting to take pain from others. For instance, there aren't a whole lot of things I would want to take from my son or grandson, but I would surely take their pain if I could. As a matter of fact, the mere thought of wishing to take pain from a child will give you pain, especially when you find that it cannot be done no matter how hard you try.

Seeing your children in pain is probably the hardest thing about parenting. In the right circumstance, it can kill you. I'll tell you a short story that happens to be true. The subject of the story is how even children can take pain under different situations.

My wife and I happened to be window shopping in some town around Jackson, California. I'm not sure what town it was, but that's not important anyway. As we walked, there was a loud crash of two cars slamming into each other right behind us. Instantly I ran to see if I could help. In one car there was a small boy and an elderly couple. I assumed they were his grandparents. The boy was screaming at the top of his lungs, a gash in his right hand spewing blood.

I checked the grandfather first. He didn't look good but the grandmother looked even worse. They were both in a panic and worried about the screaming boy. I thought maybe they were close to heart attacks, so I went to the passenger seat and looked at the boy's injuries. I wrapped the boy's hand with a piece of cloth from the seat next to him. It didn't stop him from screaming.

Worried about the grandparents, I made the boy look at me and then I said, "I need you to man up and stop screaming."

I told him he was scaring his grandparents so much I thought they might be having heart attacks. His screaming subsided and became more of a low crying wail. The boy understood the nature of pain almost instantly and didn't want to share it with his grandparents.

I have been around pain all of my life and I have found that there are two types — physical and mental. Physical pain is temporary, for the most part, but mental pain often never goes away. We all have pain. It comes into everyone's life at one time or another. It can affect the way we behave and others often misunderstand our behavior in different ways. For instance, they might think we are rude or that we just don't like them. It happens all the time, so don't be so quick to judge others, for they might just be in a lot of pain.

I once was a soldier, so that puts me in a group of people who have a lot of mental anguish. And I still feel pain from things that happened to me as a small child in a Catholic orphanage. Couple that pain with pain I endured while in the Republic of Vietnam as a young adult, and pow, you see one screwed up guy who seems lost in space every time you see me. A soldier's pain will never go away, so we handle it as well as we can. I still have a wallet I made from a kit given to me to occupy my time while in a military suicide ward. I'll show it to you if you like.

I wish I could tell you more about pain. But all I know is what it is and how you can spot it in others. A general rule to remember about pain is the fact that when someone strikes out at you, it's usually because they are in pain. So have a little heart and think before you strike back. A few kind words can work miracles in those situations.

I'll end this with a few words of wisdom that I thought up myself.

Never mind, I forgot already

It's my opportunity to take over
1/4/2018

I figure it's the perfect time for me to take over the Winters Express! Perfect! I picked up the paper this morning, well it was actually this afternoon because I slept until 12:45 p.m. Anyway, right there on the front page was the headline, "Charley calls it quits."

I have to have those little marks around those words or people will think I stole them! Well, for me that means a lot of extra work! Ain't that some kinda s—?

When I take over the paper, that's the first thing I'm gonna do — get rid of all those little marks. We don't need them, never did, never will! Everybody thinks we need them because if those little marks are around a sentence then everybody thinks the sentence is true. Take for instance the statement, "Donald Sanders is not the most beautiful man in town!"

With those marks, everyone would think the sentence is true when it is so obviously false.

Anyhow, old Charley Wallace is leaving his post after being at it for a hundred years or so. When he first started at the paper, he had to walk to work because cars weren't invented yet. Charlie did however have a driver's license because he was a newspaper man, so that entitled him to all the inside information from the government that cars would be a normal thing in the next five years or so.

A hundred years ago, in the "middle ages," people having that privilege were called Nobles. The rest of us were called "Pee-ons." I used to be a Pee-on but since I've been writing a column for 10 or 15 years, that is no longer the case. Believe me, now that I'm a Noble it won't be long until I'm "Citizen of the Year!" Once that happens, those people over at Turkovich Wine will have an attitude adjustment when I walk in the door!

Maybe if I put a spotlight behind me so when I open the door at Turkovich's, the light of my soul or being, whatever you want to call it, will shine in their eyes and they will think, "This guy is surely worthy of Citizen of the Year!" When they see that I'm now a Noble, I'll probably get all the free wine I could ever want.

So, if anyone would like to nominate me for Citizen of the Year, just truck over to the Chamber of Commerce, wherever that is, and simply put my name on the form they have. It's pretty simple. Not only that, the Chamber of Commerce is where all the babes hang out! Check out the picture of the two babes on page A6. If I was 30 years younger, those babes would be chasing me all over town!

"Va-Va-Voom! Va-Va-Voom!"

That's an expression (term) the Nobles use when they see a fine looking specimen of a female. Like I always say, "Winters, California has the most beautiful women in the world!" Not only that, but we have the best restaurants, the best hardware store, and we can't forget the best filling station over at Pisani's!

Oh, and music too! Winters has the best music and the best little theater over at the Palms. As a matter of fact, on the evening of January 13 a group of musicians called "Moody Slough" will play at the Palms. They are all locally born and bred genetically for the specific purpose of delightful musical pleasure to your ears. It's on a Friday night, so you can go to dinner at one of our great restaurants, then check out all the babes, and finally you can undo your belt, let your belly hang out, and listen to Moody Slough.

What a perfect night!

I expect to see you all there if you don't want to get on my list! Oh, you don't want to get on my list. Well, I would love to write some more essential information for you but I'm going to walk around town and check out the babes.

Charley, you can clean out my desk

Building bridges
2/1/2018

I think I could have done better. I'm pushin' seventy years old now and I'm a little concerned that I didn't do as much as I could have for our society. Ya know, nothin' happens in this world without a little effort from somebody — sometimes it takes a lot of effort. I'll never know for sure because I was always too concerned with my own welfare to do anything for anyone else.

To tell the truth, I've been so self-centered that it never even dawned on me that I should be concerned about the welfare of my fellow man. Oh, but I was always the first one to criticize the other guy for what he was doin' and how he was doin' it. When I think back on it, I don't think I was ever happy with the performance of any politician, ever. I always had plenty of ideas about this and that and was quick to voice my opinion about what was wrong in the good old U.S. Government. Real quick!

For example, remember that Linda Ronstadt guy who was governor of California? I told all my friends what a super nut case this guy was because he was building freeway bridges to nowhere. At that time I was workin' as a union pile driver out of Local 34 building bridges and high-rise foundations all around the Bay Area, mostly in San Francisco. So I'm thinkin', "What the hell is this guy doin'?"

Remember drivin' around and seein' a bridge that just stopped in mid-air? If a car ever drove on it, they would fly right off the end, crash, boom bang! I'd look at them and think, "If I was in charge, I would build the other side and put a road on it." I thought he was probably spending too much time with Linda's band and smoking too much pot because it drove the price up to $30 a lid. You know, supply and demand, right?

Well as it turned out, years later when all these new freeways are being built at ten times the cost they used to be, guess what? All the bridges are already built at ten times less than they would cost today! So, what the hay! I feel kinda bad about badmouthing this Brown guy. If he was still around today I would probably go up and slap him on the back and say, "Good job Gov, good lookin' out!" He's probably retired in Florida by now, him and Linda.

Well, all this got me thinkin' that maybe those politician guys aren't that bad after all. Even those guys that I blamed all these years for starting the Vietnam War and the Iraqi War by lying and makin' shit up must have had a reason for thinkin' it was the right thing to do. These were some of the greatest men of this century. It is not always popular to do what is needed for the betterment of mankind. I'm not sayin' that their actions were right or wrong. All I'm tryin' to say is that the decisions were probably not easy to make and who the hell am I to think that I would have done anything different or that I would have had a better idea?

I went into the Army in 1968 and when that didn't work out too good, I blamed them. Now that I think back on it, I just used that as an excuse to whine and get high. So while I was doing every drug I could get my hands on and braggin' about how I could do better and just wastin' my life in general, those guys in the government were doin' things that needed to be done — right or wrong they were just doin' their best.

So now I'm thinkin' I'm not so smart after all and maybe I should have been a little more helpful and a lot less critical. I have to say that I'm sorry for wastin' my time. However, if I had married my wife Therese 20 or 30 years earlier, I know I would have done a lot better. A lot better!

Yeah, I can blame it on her!

Happy Boob…er…Valentine's Day!
3/1/2018

Valentine's Day; the love day. It's a day to celebrate all the love you have for others, so we all go out and buy those little cards or a box of chocolate and pass them out to those we love or to those we feel deserve them. It's one of those days that I want to remember, but I always forget until it's too late and my wife has already thought of it first.. That's okay — she is my Valentine lover anyway.

I always send little text messages to those women who are important in my life and there are many, many women who have played a part in making me the man that I am today. Just to list a few — there is Therese of course, Jan, Jen, Tanya, Jody, Kim, Eileen, Nancy, Nancy, Chris, Patty, Patty, Anna, Libby, Amy, Melanie, Penny P, Beth F, Leslie B, Debra, Madge, Gigi, Ella, Tammy W, Josie, Sarah, Chris N, Judy H, Connie, Diane, Katie, Kellie, and of course, my Mom. Then there are women who are pleasing to the eye like Silvan, Beth, Yvonne, Raena, Morgan, Jessica, Menetta, Nicole and Vicki.

Oh, we don't want to forget Sister Conchadda, my first love. She gave me my first private room. It was a closet and kind of small but there was a lot of light that came in under the locked door. I could see feet every time someone walked down the hall. She taught me that women are smarter than men because when she found spinach in the pocket of some trousers in a mountain of laundry she knew it was mine and made me come and eat it.

There ya go, and none of you have the right to complain because all of you have played a part in making me into what I am today, right? You have all pushed and prodded me to modify my behavior like a molded bowl of Jell-O. Now I'm just like a computer program that takes out the garbage and mows the grass. Yes Ma'am, no Ma'am! You tell me when to take off my boots so I don't track mud into the house and when I stink like a man, I am told to wash it off.

You don't want me to eat doughnuts, frozen pizza, and potato chips but you make me eat a hand full of pills every morning and every evening. What the Hell? Why do women always want me to do the right thing when all I want to do is the wrong thing? I want to step in the mud and drag it in the house. I want to clutter up the yard with tools and leave the lawn mower where I can easily find it. If it's in the way, walk around it like I do.

When we go somewhere, I want to leave when I'm ready, not when you're ready. I like my hair messed up! I don't want to use "quotation marks." Women are so suspicious! When my friends John, Terry and I are out playing, we're not doing anything wrong, we just are throwing rocks into the creek, so quit worrying about us. We know that you all love us but geeze, not all the time! We don't need that much love, do we?

Valentine's Day can be dreadful for men sometimes. We don't need all that lovie-dovie stuff. Don't you know by now that if we don't throw rocks at you then we love you? That's pretty simple. Imagine how simple life would be without Valentine's Day. That would mean no guilt because we forgot about it. Without women molding us men we would still be able to hunt and gather and women could lay around in bear skins and there would be no bras! Okay, so if we should look at your boobs, no foul, no bad, no harm done. It's just a quick glance. That's all.

As a matter of fact, most men wish that Valentine's Day could be Bare Boob Day! Wouldn't that be grand? Just think of the cool text messages you would get! It would be like, "Hey Sally, nice set of cha chas!" Anyway, that was just a thought.

So now I guess you know that a lot of you are not going to get a text message from me because I forgot about Valentine's Day again and now it's too late to send them without my appearing to be a fool.

So, Happy Valentine's Day next year.

Just as beauty cannot be measured, neither can heartache
3/23/2018

Confucius says, "Everything has beauty but not everyone sees it." I believe this to be true but it isn't because beauty isn't there, it's because they have chosen not to see it. Fortunately for us, beauty never dies. It will always be there, so if we miss it now, we can always enjoy it later. It may not be the same beauty it was before, but it is still beauty.

Another thing I believe to be true is the fact that just as beauty can escape us for the moment, the mere thought of it will bring it back. This is especially true when I think about those loved ones who have passed away. They are gone but their beauty remains with me always and that is beauty in itself.

Every time I look at a rock, my friend Steve Shafer pops into my mind, or at least his spirit does. The same thing happens when I look at the stars, or any type of machine or animal, for there is Joe Tomlinson, studying them with either telescope or microscope. When they were alive, I don't know if I would have described them with the word beauty, but that's what they were — pure beauty.

Beauty never dies, thus they are always with me.

Just as beauty cannot be measured, neither can heartache and there is beauty even in that. Even the most horrible of things has beauty. "What?" you may ask, "is so beautiful about bullying, rape, murder, and child molestation?" These are all sights that cannot be un-seen but we instantly recognize these acts for the evil that they are, thus there is beauty in the way that we become the hand of God and it naturally becomes a duty to wipe evil from the face of the Earth.

From the moment I awake until I fall asleep at night, I find myself surrounded by pure beauty. There are things I cannot change, but there is beauty in the way I can understand and learn so I'm not falling into a fog of regret and guilt but living in wisdom and love instead. The soul that remains sensitive to the power of beauty can never grow old or tired.

Beauty is an essential part of our lives even though we don't always realize it. It is that special thing that makes us wonder and fall in love with people or things. Beauty gives color, love, depth, and a certain radiance to everything — that's why we seek it by all means. I will spend the rest of my life trying to make things more beautiful for others, just as we all should do.

A loving character cannot be developed in ease and quiet. The soul is strengthened, inspired, and success is achieved only through the experience of trial and suffering. Seeking the beauty in everything is the first step in purifying your mind and sharing it will illuminate your soul, opening it to love of every sort which leads you back to developing character, my friend.

Ain't life beautiful?

I've had the weirdest experiences with doctors lately. This isn't the first time, neither. Sometimes I think that doctors are a just regular person who is in a position to do pretty much whatever they like to anyone who happens to walk through their door, into their office. Up until the past few years, I've always tried to avoid contact with doctors and while I was at it, I gave lawyers and priest the same treatment.

I was raised a Catholic, so when I was on my way to Vietnam as a young man, I figured I'd better go to confession in case I got my head blown off. So here I am, sitting in this dark little box, when a voice comes from the other side of the dark little box and starts to pray. I told the voice that it had been so long since I had gone to confession that I forgot the words to the prayer. The voice replied, "Have you ever had an affair with another man?"

Well I don't have to tell you, I got the hell out of there and never went back! Some years later, I heard the exact same question from a lawyer. I was flabbergasted, so I told the lawyer to give my first ex-wife whatever the hell she wanted and I got the heck out of there too! Okay, that explains my avoidance of lawyers and priests, so let's go back to doctors.

Doctors have the strangest behavior for people that are supposed to be educated above the rest of us. I think it may be a natural fact that people with higher education are just naturally hornier that us normal folks. With me being aware of this fact, I naturally avoid going to doctors unless I needed to be sewn up to keep from bleeding to death. This worked for many years, but lately I've been getting dizzy and have been experiencing shortness of breath.

So, a couple of years ago I broke down and went to the doctor and told him I was dizzy. As soon as I said those words I could see the glint in his eye. He was thinking, "This dizzy SOB is perfect so I'll send him around from room to room, doctor to doctor, and we can all cop a feel." Next thing I know he is pulling off my shoes and socks and he wants to play with my feet! Well that felt pretty good, so when he got done playing with my feet, he told me he was going to schedule me for more test.

This guy tells me that I can't eat or drink coffee for 12 hours before my test. So I'm thinking they didn't want me to barf on them so I washed my feet, ate a sandwich with a cup of coffee that I had stashed the night before in my truck, and went in for test. Only about half of the doctors wanted to play with my feet but almost all of them wanted a small bottle of blood to take home.

One doctor wanted me to take off my shirt and to hop on a treadmill! Well, anyone who knows me will testify that I never take my shirt off in front of others because I have manboobs that jiggle when I walk. They finally talked me into it and then three of them watched as I marched on the treadmill, jiggling all the way. I think they wanted me to have a heart attack so they could have their way with me. They put these little sticky things on my chest and hooked up some wires to them and I still don't know what for!

In a very short time, I found myself in San Francisco and was told they were going to fix my heart with a quadruple bypass. So now, several years later, I'm still getting dizzy, so I'm thinking they never got near my heart but simply put some cuts on my chest to make everybody think they did! It didn't take me long to recover from that ordeal, but that's when the weird stuff really began.

Now a doctor tells me that he needs to check my colon. I don't even know what a colon is, so I went in there thinking they were going to play with my feet again. Well, as it turned out, this guy wanted to stick some weird jerry-rig up my butt! I don't want to tell you what I said to that guy so I got the hell out of there too! Then, if that wasn't enough, this guy sends me a little package and he wants me to send him a piece of poop!

Okay, I never did send it to him because I didn't know if he wanted a little piece or a whole poop! I thought to myself, "Well, old Donald ain't playin' this game!" If they want my poop, they are going to have to come up with some money because it ain't free for weirdos. So here I am again, stashing some boiled Easter eggs in my truck to eat on the way to more tests tomorrow, and I'm still dizzy. I'm going to refuse to march around half naked while doing a jiggle dance on a treadmill for the entertainment of everybody in the hospital. I think maybe they're using a hidden camera so the nurses can enjoy a fat old guy with man-boobs doing the jiggle-dance.

I'm not gonna do that but I did wash my feet, because it kinda feels good when they play with my feet.

Stand by for my next report!

The Changes of Time
4/11/2018

Things you remember about your life are not of the true events. What you are remembering is the last time you remembered the same event. The memories never get clearer, they only get fuzzier and a little less clear. Thus we leave everything behind, because every memory develops into something that is never fixed in facts of the original events of our lives.

When we are older and near the end of our time on this Earth, some of us complicate the experience with pains and trauma we have developed within our own minds. So moving forward is like driving with one foot on the brakes. In order to be free, we must leave all the hurt and pain behind. We must learn how to let go. The energy it takes to hold on to the past keeps us from moving on, so we must release the pain and the fear, for they have no base in reality.

I try to let go of something every day and that becomes easier for me as I get older. The largest of the things I have released (and the hardest), was something that I lived with for many, many years and that is the idea of enemies. From a very young age, only my enemy could show me my weaknesses. "Only my enemy could tell me who and where they were and they told me when they would strike. I found it was true that my enemy was also my teacher and it only teaches destruction." The Art of War, Sun Tzu.

The idea of the future is another biggie for me. The idea and planning for the future is nice to think about — when the future arrives, it's nothing like you had thought it would be. The truth is is that life is a constant series of unplanned events that force you to adjust and readjust to your surroundings. According to Charles Darwin, survival has absolutely nothing to do with strength and intelligence and everything to do with your ability to adjust to and manage change.

A successful life experience depends on so many things. Your actions, the actions of others, tactics, adaptability, experience, sportsmanship, friendship, and good old plain luck are all needed if you are ever to win. Associate with adaptable people — help them adapt and they will help you. It is important to remember that people only change when they have to, or when they want to. Remember that no one can truly hurt you except those you love. Everything else you can shake off as unimportant.

In days past, I would complain about opportunity. I would say all the good opportunities have been taken and they were now far and few between. There is nothing I found that was farther from the truth than this idea, for the world is changing at such a rapid pace, faster and faster every moment. New opportunities spring forth at the speed of light, but it's up to you to recognize what they are and how to catch them.

You can try to alter or correct conditions so they are more favorable to you, but it's very important to learn how to adjust yourself to conditions if you desire success. Old proverbs tell us that a wise man must adapt to circumstances and if you fall seven times, you must get back up eight times. It's true that we can't fail if we don't try.

Just as there are things you must release, there are things you must keep until the very end. It may sound old fashioned, but truth, honor and service to others will all make you happy in the end. It was all too late in my life that I found this to be true. It's important that you see this as truth. It matters not when or where you realize this, but it does matter that before you leave this world you know that all of these things, along with love freely given, will put that final smile on your face as you fade into darkness.

Today is Memorial Day

Today is Memorial Day. Well, at least it was when I wrote this column. When it comes around Memorial Day always awakens something within me that is unique and difficult to explain. It is a warm holiday. When I say "warm" I do not mean warmth that comes from the heat of a warm spring day, nor do I mean the heat of any particular war. Warm Spring days and the heat of any particular war have very little to do with the warmth I feel on Memorial Day.

For some reason, Memorial Day has become a day politicians use to advance and promote their own private agendas be it defense spending on a grand scale or revenge for stopping the "free" flow of oil. Oil and spending should have nothing to do with Memorial Day for it is a day of remembrance and love.

Memorial Day is a simple holiday. It's a day to remember those loved ones who died while in service to our country. That's pretty simple. We need to keep it simple – or do we?

Memorial Day is a private day. We tend to remember those we knew or are familiar with whom we loved in the past, thus it's kept small and close to the chest. Some say it's designed to be a day of remembrance of all who have died in service of our country. If this is so, do we limit the number of people we can remember?

Can immigrants of the first generation remember only those that served in our military or can they remember older generations that may have been in foreign armies but are still loved ones? Should we have a cutoff date for each family, dividing our veterans from theirs? If so where does it stop, where does it end?

Consider the American Civil War. Is Memorial Day only for the Yankees or is it OK to include a few Confederates? This seems to complicate things and now things are not so simple. Many families such as mine had loved ones on both sides of that conflict so I cannot help but remember both sides.

We are a nation made up of immigrants. All of us, including those of the Great American Indian Nations, have a history of immigration. This fact is the single most important building block, the cornerstone of our nation. Above anything else I love the fact that I could look at anyone from anywhere else in the world and say to them, "Yes, you and your loved ones can be Americans." "Yes, you can live here in peace, free from persecution." And "Yes, on Memorial Day you can remember those loved ones who may have fought opposite the United States."

As it stands, Memorial Day is a day of remembrance of those that served in the U. S. military. Like I say, that's pretty simple – at least for most Americans. How many German American, Japanese American, or Mexican American (and many others) have men who served in Iraq or Afghanistan whose fathers fought against the US in WWII or any other conflict throughout history? I dare say there are thousands and thousands.

I am so proud to be an American on this Memorial Day, but for me it is not that simple

Back in the old days, a guy named Diogenes spent all his time looking for an honest man, an admirable man. I don't know if he ever found one or not, but I think I can tell you why he had so much trouble. He was obviously looking in the wrong places. From what I hear this Diogenes guy liked the wine a little too much. Oh, and another thing. He was considered a genius because he was smarter than everybody else. You know as well as I do that all the really smart guys get taken advantage of by the dumber guys. That's just the way it is and it has always been that way.

In the days of the Roman Empire, there was a guy named Nero that would go out and ask all the really smart guys if they were Christians or not and they would say, "Oh yeah, I'm a Jesus guy!" Then this Nero guy would call everybody together in a stadium and feed them to a lion.

When I was in high school, I was really good at taking advantage of the smarter guys. Those smart guys always did their homework and they always had pocket liners with a bunch of pens sticking out so I would run past really quick and grab them. I did this for a long time until they started peeing in my locker.

The smart guys came and went because they graduated early, got drafted, and went to Vietnam. On the other hand, I was in high school so long because I didn't do anything. I thought I was going to miss the war entirely until the dean told me they had to graduate me because they couldn't have a 21-year-old senior dating a 15-year-old freshman girl.

So, in the end, I had to go to the war anyway, but I didn't do anything there, either. When I got home, I went into a grocery store and ran into an old friend from high school who had just gotten home from the war like I did. In high school, this guy was so good looking that the girls would swoon every time they saw him.

Anyway, back to the grocery store part of this story. His name was Dean and I ran into him near the milk spot where they stack all the milk. I looked at him and he had a flat nose with big black hairs sticking out of it like it needed a haircut. I asked, "Hey Dean what happened to your nose?" He snickered and said that a VC had shot it off and the doctors took some skin off his butt and put it on his nose hole.

He asked if I'd come over to his house and party some time so I said, "Sure." I never went over to his house and about a year later he killed himself. I think it may have been because I never went over to party with him. I never went into that store again, either. The last thing he said to me was that the girls didn't like his hairy nose. I almost said, "Yeah I can see why," but I decided against it.

I never went to party with Dean but I did party and before I knew it 30 years had passed. I met and married a wonderful girl named Therese and she took me to the Veteran's hospital because I had been crying a lot and cutting myself. They put me in the suicide ward at David Grant Hospital on Travis Air Force Base and believe it or not that's where all the smart guys are. The military had toughened them up so I didn't feel right about taking advantage of them anymore.

So now you are asking what all this has to do with Diogenes? Now pay attention, because this is what happened. In the suicide ward, the psychiatrist told me to find some volunteer work to keep me out of all this mental trouble I was finding myself in. That's when I found the Putah Creek Council and they let me help out at the creek because they didn't have to pay me.

So now, like a miracle, I found the guy that Diogenes was looking for. His name is Rich Marovich. He is the Streamkeeper of Putah Creek. I believe this guy is as close to a saint as anyone I've ever met. Not only is he honest and admirable, he is really smart. In a very short period of time, he turned me into a tree hugger with a yearning to start taking care of the environment around me.

College kids flock to him like he was passing out happiness popsicles. They want to learn everything he knows because they know that when it comes to creek restoration, he is the go-to guy. His work will be studied and his techniques will be taught around the globe because he knows what to do when it comes to cleaning up and repairing nature that man has spent years and years destroying.

If I was Diogenes, and I think I'm pretty close, I'd tell you all to look up the Putah Creek Council. If, like me, you are tired of so much darkness in your life, try doing some volunteer work down at Putah Creek. If you are lucky, you will meet The Streamkeeper and he will show you the way. Try it and judge for yourself. Rich Marovich is everything Diogenes was looking for.

These "friends" are not on the side of Putah Creek
7/22/2018

Here we go again! The so-called "Friends of Putah Creek" have taken legal action through the Solano County Superior Court, naming the Central Valley Flood Protection Board (CVFPB), the Solano County Water Agency, The City of Winters, and (correct me if I'm wrong) up to 100 as yet unnamed individuals yet to be identified. The action claims that the permit issued by CVFPB failed to satisfy the requirements of the California Environmental Quality Act (CEQA). The verification was signed by a Charlie Manson type guy named Jeff TenPas.

From what I gather, and correct me if I'm wrong, the so-called Friends of Putah Creek are seeking to stop the restoration of Putah Creek in its tracks. Personally, I think the whole idea is crazy and I fail to see what could be gained by stopping a project that has been decades in the planning at a cost of millions of dollars. Countless studies and research projects have been carried out by the top names in the environmental restoration field. The Putah Creek restoration work has undergone years and years of planning and has been studied by the top names in the field that have written countless numbers of scientific papers on the subject.

"The construction of the Monticello Dam in 1957 caused a decrease in sediment load and flow levels in Putah Creek. Putah Creek is very different today than it was a century ago. Changes include decreased flows, decreased sediment load from upstream, fish barriers in the forms of dams, and the influx of invasive Arundo. Rivers with large dams can experience an effect known as "hungry water," in which water below a dam is low in sediment content and therefore has extra energy which is spent on bank erosion (Kondolf 1997)." Putah Creek experienced this effect, and incised "over 20 feet below historic elevations" in some areas." Gina Blackledge and Gabrielle Boisramé

In 2005, the Lower Putah Creek Coordinating Committee implemented a project to move the channel of Putah Creek northward to its approximate historical course. Even before that the top names in the field have been looking, planning, studying, researching, and working with government officials to get this project up and running. Imagine the work involved after years and years of effort.

I can only rely on a paper written by Sharon Laine Fiala entitled "An Assessment of the Regulatory Process for Restoration Projects" to illustrate the process of getting government permission to carry out a project of this nature. Shannon Fiala is from the University of California at Berkeley, College of Environmental Design, and is a Master of Environmental Planning Candidate 2011 (https://escholarship.org/uc/item/29h3t2kw)

Here are a few of the regulatory agencies that have to approve this project:

• Clean Water Act: CWA Section 404 permit granted by the United States Army Corps of Engineers (USACE) for projects that involve dredging or filling 'waters of the United States,' which includes wetlands, and CWA Section 401

• Water Quality Certifications granted by the State Water Resources Control Board's (SWRCB) Regional Water Quality Control Boards (RWQCB).

• Endangered Species Act: project sponsors must begin a Section 7 consultation with the USFWS under the ESA. Project proponents will submit a Biological Assessment' to the USFWS, in order to obtain a 'Biological Opinion' that will provide explicit instructions as to how the project should avoid and/or mitigate for impacts to threatened and endangered species.

• National Environmental Policy Act: environmental impact statements (EIS) be prepared for major federal actions that have potentially significant effects on the environment.

• California Environmental Quality Act (CEQA) in1970 and the California Endangered Species Act (CESA): process typically begins with an 'Initial Study'.

• Depending on the complexity and the level of impact, habitat restoration projects must either submit 'Negative Declarations (ND),' 'Mitigated Negative Declarations (MND),' or if the impacts to these resources are too significant or too complex, proponents must prepare an 'Environmental Impact Report (EIR),'California Department of Fish and Game Code 1600 permit, 'Streambed Alteration Agreement,'

As restoration projects become increasingly complex, particularly with the rise of adaptive management and process-based restoration, agreement among scientists and regulatory staff will be critical to the implementation of these projects. There are smaller projects, also requiring permits within the greater project like vegetation removal projects, constructing Environmental Impact Reports (PEIR), revisions to existing processes, unforeseen impacts, effect and expense of the regulatory process, working with federal agencies and Environmental Consulting Firms, United States Army Corps of Engineers (USACE), National Marine Fisheries Service (NMFS), California Department of Fish and Game (CDFG) and so on. As one regulatory agency staff member stated, project sponsors are "paying more for permitting than they are for the structure."

Then there is the CWA Section 401 Water Quality Certification, CWA Section 404, Department of the Army, CDFG Notification of Streambed Alteration, CDFG SAA Fee Schedule, the Governor's Office of Planning and Research, National Marine Fisheries Service (NMFS), and the Regional Water Quality Control Board (RWQCB).

If you want to know the facts involved in this case go to "Project Evaluation of Channel Morphology, Invasive Plant Species, and Native Fish Habitat in Putah Creek in Winters, CA.

Six Years After Channel Relocation" by Gina Blackledge and Gabrielle Boisramé (https://escholarship.org/uc/item/063566w8)

So, Friends of Putah Creek, who in their right mind would seek to stop a project like this? With friends like you, who needs enemies?

"I want to find a airplane to charter and have the pilot take you and me way up high enough to see the curvature of the Earth." That was one of the last things my friend, Joe Tomlinson, wanted to do before he got so sick he wouldn't be able to do it. He made me drive him around to several of the small airports around the area so he could go in and ask if there was someone that could provide this service.

As urgent as it was, we never found a pilot to take us up. He was a little disappointed but he was not the sort of guy to cry about it. He had a whole list of things that he wanted to do, one of which was to go up to Oregon to see his kids. He asked if I would be willing to drive him up there and drop him off for a while and then fly back home to Winters, California. He wanted to stay for a couple of weeks and then I would fly back up and drive him back to California when he was ready.

We took a couple of days for the drive because he would suffer from car sickness after 5 or 6 hours on the road. Joe was a talker and a storyteller of the highest order. I imagine he could win the trophy for being able to remember the smallest details of his life experiences. We seemed to be driving around all the time and as forgetful as he was, I would hear the same stories over and over with more detail with every telling.

When I say we were in cars a lot, I do not jest. With trips to the hospital several times a week for treatment or just driving him around wherever he needed to go, it was story after story, over and over. It was like a dance, because he would tell the stories and I would act like I hadn't heard them before. Don't get me wrong, he was an interesting guy and I liked his stories, but he talked so much I couldn't get a word in edgewise to tell my own stories.

If I did get a chance to tell one of my stories, he would interrupt me and tell one of his before I could even get done. So I knew everything about him but he didn't know anything about me except maybe my name. I had a plan to tell him one of his own stories just to see what he would do, but he got too sick and I never got the chance.

Anyway, back to the story of the trip to Oregon. I got him up there and then hopped on a jet for the trip home. I don't like flying much, so I can't say as I liked the flight. I'll bet it wasn't 10 minutes after I landed in Sacramento he was on the phone wanting me to fly back up and get him. The next day I was on a flight back to Oregon.

After that, he wanted to go to Yosemite National Park, so we took a couple of days and went over there. It was a nice trip with the same old stories and the same old sickness every day, over and over. Most of the time, taking him to the doctor for treatment was as hard on me as it was on him. Every day he would get a little sicker, a little weaker until finally he just wasted away.

Joe is gone now and he has been gone for several years. He didn't want to go and I have to say that I didn't want him to go either, but it was really hard to watch him get weaker and weaker. The end of it was absolutely terrible, but I wouldn't have missed being with him for anything in the world because he was as good a friend as I have ever had.

It bothers me a little bit that I never found a pilot to take him way up high so he could see the curvature of the Earth, but I think he had seen it before, because one of my favorite stories of his was about the misty, blue sky and the green, green Earth he had seen in his youth before he ever got sick and long before he ever met me.

If Joe was here right now, I'd tell him the story of how I spent the last three years of his life with him and how that affected me. I'd tell him what a good friend he was to me and thank him for all of the stories about his life, because now it's almost like I lived it with him and I think that's pretty cool.

Sometimes I think he is still here.

Heal the world — heal ourselves

9/15/2018

I lived my entire life alone. It was always me and them. I found a woman and "I" became "we," and thus it was us and them. It was much the same when we had children. There was us and there was everything else. We were separate entities, us and nature, and we lived our lives apart, at least in our minds.

We often saw ourselves as all-important, above everything else. We consumed all that we wanted, much more than what we needed. Everything we didn't want, we threw into the trash or out the windows of our automobiles that we purchased because they could take us places faster than other automobiles.

My ancestors were among the first to arrive in this place when it was covered with forest and grasslands abundant with wildlife on the ground, in the air, and in the watershed. We took what we wanted, at first by force and later by commerce, thinking that there was an endless quantity of everything. We saw the endless forest as useless and proceeded to clear the land of every living thing. What we found was excess, so forest after forest was cut, piled, and burned to make way for roads of asphalt and cement.

Wildlife was pushed out of existence for sport and fashion. The rest we used for slave labor until worn out; then they went to the soap factory or became grease for our wheels. Any animals we don't use for sport are caged — forced fed, killed, cleaned, and eaten along with vegetables that are poison and genetically enhanced. We consume twice as much as we need, therefore half of the world's population does not get enough to eat.

Man has killed man at an ever increasing rate since early man first took molten iron from a volcano and shaped swords instead of shovels. Weapons are never great enough or can kill enough, so ever and ever more power is required until we can destroy in one day what has taken thousands of years to build. Destroy, destroy, and destroy everything in a vicious manner with great armies and war machines that now threaten total annihilation.

We worship those who are capable of the most destruction and we freely give our children to travel to foreign lands to slaughter or be slaughtered. We go to war at the slightest whim, raining death from above for reasons we neither know nor care about. Recorded history of over some 8000 years or so would be lucky to list more than 500 years free of armed conflict. Enough!

Now I'm old and wish to repair the damage I've done before I die. The problem is that I could plant and water trees on Putah Creek for a hundred years and still not make up for the damage I've done through the years. I've spewed gas into the air with my automobiles and poisoned the ground with my pesticides and herbicides.

I've held myself above the natural world and only now find myself asking nature's forgiveness for my indifference. I now find myself pushing others towards a greater relationship with nature and the environment and those striving to repair hundreds of years harm and neglect we are all guilty of committing. If we want to change our environment, we must change ourselves.

"A human being is part of the whole called by us the universe, a part limited in time and space. We experience ourselves, our thoughts and feelings as something separate from the rest, a kind of optical delusion of consciousness. Our task must be to free ourselves from this delusion by widening our circle of compassion to embrace all living creatures and the whole of nature in its

beauty. We shall require a substantially new manner of thinking if humanity is to survive."
Albert Einstein

Made in the USA
Middletown, DE
24 October 2023

41271505R00275